Peasants, Politics, and the Formation of Mexico's National State

GUERRERO, 1800-1857

p. 1-146

PETER F. GUARDINO

Peasants, Politics, and the Formation of Mexico's National State

GUERRERO, 1800-1857

STANFORD UNIVERSITY PRESS

STANFORD, CALIFORNIA

Stanford University Press
Stanford, California
© 1996 by the Board of Trustees of the
Leland Stanford Junior University
Printed in the United States of America

CIP data are at the back of the book

To Estelle Guardino,

Francis Guardino,

and Jane Walter

Acknowledgments

Many people and institutions were instrumental in the research and writing of this book. The staffs at the many archives listed in the bibliography consistently provided cheerful professional service. Many other individuals in Mexico provided valuable insights and helped orient me in my search for materials. Among those who did so in Mexico City were Jonathan Amith, Dori Burnham, Alicia Hernández, David Marley, and Mina del Valle. I benefited from the advice of Roberto Velez Pliego and Reina Cruz in Puebla and María Teresa Jarquín, Irma Cárdenas Barrazo, and Rosaura Hernández in Toluca. In Chilpancingo I profited from the insights and support of Camilio Valchi, Jesús Alvarez Hernández, and especially Jaime Salazar Adame. Also in Chilpancingo, Blanca Heredia, Arturo Solís Heredia, and Blanca Salinas Heredia aided my unsuccessful efforts to locate the papers of their famous ancestor Juan Alvarez, and Hernando Anzaldua allowed me to use the materials collected by his late father. I am also forever in debt to Efraín Bermudez and his entire family for the hospitality, friendship, and moral support they provided during my stays in Chilpancingo.

This book first took shape as a doctoral dissertation at the University of Chicago. The work is so rooted in my many years there that it is impossible for me to identify any given moment as the one in which I started the project. The research owes much to the intellectual and moral support provided by numerous fellow graduate students. These friends and colleagues include Kate Bjork, Luís Cerda, Deborah Cohen, Dawn Fogle Deaton, Robin Derby, Michael Ducey, Carlos Espinoza, Patricia Fernández, Javier Garciadiego, Robert Holden, Aldo Lauria, Laura Lewis, Paul Liffman, Lucía Melgar, Zoila Mendoza, Daniel Nugent, Andy Oorta, Friedrich Schuler, Charles Walker, Jane Walter, and Richard Warren. I also enjoyed the valuable insights of visiting faculty including Manuel Burga, Alicia Hernández, Nils Jacobsen, Scarlett O'Phelan, and Enrique Semo. Friedrich Katz provided incomparable advice on Mexican history in general and Mexican peasants in particular. More than any other single individual, John Coatsworth helped make this book what it is. He helped in so many ways that it is impossible even to begin to list them.

Financial support from a variety of sources made this work possible. Mellon and Tinker Summer Travel Grants administered by the Center for Latin American Studies at the University of Chicago supported my preliminary dissertation research in 1986 and 1987. The bulk of my research in 1988–89 was funded by a U.S. Department of Education Fulbright-Hays Dissertation Research Abroad Fellowship and a Social Science Research Council Fellowship. I completed the writing of the dissertation during a year in San Diego at the Center for U.S.-Mexican Studies of the University of California, supported by a Visiting Research Fellowship provided by the Center.

Many historians graciously read drafts of all or part of this book. These colleagues, who include many individuals mentioned above as well as Marjorie Becker, Margaret Chowning, Jeff Gould, Jaime Rodríguez, John Tutino, and Eric Van Young, strengthened the work immeasurably. I am especially grateful to Florencia Mallon for her insightful comments on several drafts and moral support at difficult moments.

I believe that all academic endeavors are collective products. I hope that I have given some idea of the variety of individuals and institutions that have helped produce whatever of value is contained in this work. However, none bear responsibility for any errors it contains. Someone's name has to go on the title page, after all.

P.G.

Contents

Abbreviations

ACDEM	Archivo de la Cámara de Diputados del Estado de México, Toluca
ACEG	Archivo del Congreso del Estado de Guerrero, Chilpancingo
AGEG	Archivo del Gobierno del Estado de Guerrero, Chilpancingo
AGN	Archivo General de la Nación, Mexico City
AGNDF	Archivo General de Notarias del Distrito Federal, Mexico City
AHEM	Archivo Histórico del Estado de México, Toluca
ANEG	Archivo de Notarias del Estado de Guerrero, Chilpancingo
ASRA	Archivo de la Secretaría de Reforma Agraria, Mexico City
BN	Biblioteca Nacional, Mexico City

Peasants, Politics,
and the Formation
of Mexico's
National State

GUERRERO, 1800-1857

Introduction

Was independence made for all of the classes of the state with the exception of only this one? No, the *patria* reconquered its political rights for the happiness of all its children; and this good should be enjoyed first of all by the Indians, along with the other farmhands and laborers.

—Juan Alvarez, *Manifiesto que dirige a la nación*, 1845

Dear Sirs:

All of those in this field and the rest of the villages who accompany us . . . invite you to join our ranks so that this way you do not pay the burdensome taxes that are ruining all of the settlements because the Government, what it is doing with the great quantities that it solicits as taxes is to exalt itself and annihilate the sons little by little, falling upon us with armed force to finish us, but now it seems that God wants to help us continue to acquire prestige with our brothers so that enough come to us and so that among all of us we ask that the head tax and all other taxes be removed.

—Juan Francisco Mendoza and Juan de Nava to the justices of
   the peace, Field of Honor, February 22, 1843

The formation of national states has been one of the most important processes in Latin American history. Latin America is currently divided into a number of national territories, each of which is governed by an organization that claims sovereign power over the territory's inhabitants and resources. This claim is largely honored by those inhabitants. Opposition to a given government is almost always conceived in terms of replacing state structures and personnel rather than abolishing them or radically altering the scope of their activities and claims for loyalty. This is as true of the violent warfare of Peru's radical Sendero Luminoso as it is of the electoral campaigns of Mexico's conservative Partido de Acción Nacional. Furthermore, each state governs a population of nominally equal individuals, each with identical rights and obligations in relation to the state. Not all inhabitants belong to this body of "citizens"; some are excluded on a variety of bases, especially age. Nevertheless, neither the concept of "citizenship" nor its boundaries are questioned by Latin American political groups today.

National states exercise sovereign power in given territories over bodies of juridically equal individuals. As recently as three centuries ago, they did not exist and were probably inconceivable to any inhabitant of Latin America. The formation of the Mexican national state took place over centuries rather than decades, but it is nevertheless possible to identify periods of relatively rapid change within this process, when possibilities took definitive form and were sorted out. One such period stretched from the cataclysmic end of Spanish royal sovereignty to the beginning of what later became known as La Reforma, when liberalism became dominant in Mexican political culture. This work analyzes this period, from roughly 1800 to roughly 1857.

This book is a study of how Mexico's national political system was formed through local struggles and alliances that involved groups from Mexico's impoverished rural majorities. Among the most important actors in these conflicts were peasants, especially those who took part in the many local, regional, and national rebellions that characterized early-nineteenth-century politics. The study focuses on a single region, Guerrero, which became a state in 1849. Guerrero's peasantry was crucial to the two most important broad-based revolts of the early nineteenth century. The region was a major stronghold of the insurgents during the War of Independence in 1810–21. Guerrero's population also formed the major social base of the 1853–55 Revolution of Ayutla, the rebellion that began La Reforma. An examination of these two episodes, and the continual political interaction between peasants and other groups in the intervening period, will help illuminate the ways in which Mexico's peasantry participated in the formation of the Mexican national state.

State Formation

In state formation, preexisting solidarities, organizations, and ties are delegitimated and the nation-state becomes the primary focus of individual loyalties as well as the most powerful institution in society. The process has two components. One is institutional: the state acquires resources and powers and reduces those of alternative organizations ranging from tribes to churches; in particular it seeks to monopolize the use of force within a territory. The other component is cultural: the state becomes the primary focus of loyalties and the most important frame of reference for political thought and political action; it represents itself as the embodiment of a "nation," or what Benedict Anderson calls an "imagined community."[1] Both components are essential to the process, but they have not always gone hand in hand. In many settings the growth of state power preceded its representation as "national." This introduction will briefly discuss some of the approaches scholars have taken to each of these components before addressing some of the problems with the literature.

The tendency of early modern territorial and monarchical states to expand their power at the expense of such institutions as churches, towns, guilds, and monastic orders has long interested social scientists. Perhaps the first historian to recognize this phenomenon as a key to the formation of modern political systems was Alexis de Tocqueville in his *The Old Regime and the French Revolution*, first published in 1856. The process was intimately linked to competition among European monarchies and the resulting need for revenue, a point stressed by the various works of Charles Tilly.[2] In Spanish America, this process of institutional change was begun by Bourbon monarchs in the eighteenth century but continued after independence. The institutional dimension of state formation in various Latin American cases has drawn the attention of a number of scholars.[3]

However, as Philip Corrigan and Derek Sayer note, state formation is more a cultural process than an institutional one.[4] The cultural and ideological nature of state formation has figured prominently in recent studies. Again, the increasing identification with national "imagined communities" that is the most prominent cultural aspect of modern state formation was often preceded by the transfer of loyalties to monarchs from more localized groups and symbols.[5] This process has what Corrigan and Sayer call "totalizing" and "individualizing" components: state formation is "totalizing" in that people become citizens of a "nation" to which they owe their primary loyalty; it is "individualizing" in that their citizenship is on an individual basis, rather than through membership in subordinate organizations. All citizens have the same rights. The state stands head and shoulders above a mass of juridically equal individuals.[6]

These approaches to state formation, valuable as they are, generally do not assign peasants and other subaltern groups any active role in the process. For instance, Barrington Moore and Theda Skocpol both emphasize the role of "backward-looking," defensive peasant mobilizations in destroying state structures but assert that "to the subsequent work of reconstruction they have brought nothing."[7] Skocpol sees peasants as "incorporated by circumstances beyond their control into political processes occurring independently of them, at the societal center."[8] In a series of works on state-building published between 1975 and 1990, Charles Tilly repeatedly asserts that in Western Europe peasants influenced state formation only through their opposition to the process.[9] Although Tilly points out that popular resistance forced state-builders to make concessions, he does not seem to believe that these concessions, such as "guarantees of rights, representative institutions, [and] courts of appeal," themselves changed the nature of the state.[10] Even in Corrigan and Sayer's seminal work the lower classes appear only through their opposition to state formation.[11] All of these authors see the state itself as the central actor in the process, whether it acts in the interests of some sector of society or with more autonomous motives.

State formation, however, was not a process through which the state unilaterally imposed itself on previously constituted societies. State-making was a dynamic and multilateral process in which social groups contested and thereby altered what the state was, what it did, and who had access to its resources.[12] In early-nineteenth-century Mexico, these issues were disputed by many different social actors, including the peasants who participated in the many local, regional, and national rebellions and political movements of the period. Mexico's peasants were central to both the destruction of the Spanish colonial state and the formation of the Mexican national state. The struggles in which peasants took part in nineteenth-century Mexico were not battles over whether there was to be a state: they were contests over *what* the state was to be. This distinction implies that peasants are not, as Eric Wolf asserts, "natural anarchists"; they seek to influence the form of the state and also use existing state institutions for their own ends.[13]

Politics in Nineteenth-Century Mexico

The first half of the nineteenth century has long been regarded as one of the most neglected periods in Mexican history. In recent years, however, historians have made great strides in unraveling the complexities of the period's political and social struggles. Many studies now go beyond rehashing the biased and confused accounts of contemporaries that previously served as the foundation for much of the historiography.[14] Historians have begun to produce nuanced studies of social groups, shifts in political economy, the changing compositions of political coalitions, and the formation of political ideologies. However, few of these studies look beyond Mexico City or attempt to understand the participation of Mexico's impoverished majorities in these conflicts.

Many of the new works are studies of social groups and their political attitudes that owe a great deal to advances in late colonial social history. Historians have produced excellent monographs on the
business and political practices of the financial speculators and factory owners who composed the richest and most influential social
group in the post-independence period. These books have brought
problems of political economy into sharper focus and have contributed to analyses of political coalitions.[15] Of particular interest have
been efforts to replicate the colonial dominant class's use of state
power to restrict and manipulate markets, reproducing the most salient features of the colonial political economy.[16]

Historians have also begun to develop a more precise understanding of the loose and shifting political coalitions and ideologies that
underlay national political conflict. Studies have identified two important groups. Though not all who were politically active belonged
to these groups, and though moderate positions may have been more
popular than either one, conflict between the extremes lay at the root
of much strife during the period. The loose group that eventually became identified as the conservatives originated in the reaction of the
former colonial dominant class and its allies to the radical political
challenge of the 1820s. This group included members of the ecclesiastical hierarchy, former officers of the royal army who formed the
core of the new Mexican army after 1820, and many speculators, factory owners, and former members of the colonial dominant class.
Centered around Mexico City but with many allies elsewhere, the
group was originally united around a deep fear of any repetition of
the cross-class coalitions formed during the War of Independence and
a vague proclivity toward the kind of collusion between state officials and economic elites that had characterized the colonial period.
It later evolved toward a more specific program of centralism and protectionism. In the late 1840s the group embraced a revalidation of
Mexico's Hispanic past and monarchism, becoming self-consciously
conservative.[17]

The conservatives were opposed by an even more amorphous coalition that included provincial landowners and merchants, professionals, urban artisans, and many army officers who began their careers in the insurgency rather than the royalist army. This coalition advocated protectionism, especially in the late 1820s and early
1830s, and explicitly traced its roots to the insurgency and identified
its enemies with Spanish colonialism. Its unifying principle was federalism, but many members eventually embraced liberalism after
the late 1840s. This group was united as much by its opposition to

the centralist, conservative coalition as it was by any set of cohesive interests.[18]

Our knowledge of early-nineteenth-century Mexican politics has advanced in recent years. Nevertheless, most studies continue to leave out the role of the working classes, both urban and rural, in political struggles. Sometimes this exclusion is implicit; other times, authors explicitly discount the possibility that lower-class actors participated in or had any effect on political conflict.[19] Often this omission is justified by the argument that political struggles were tempered by elite agreement on such basic issues as property rights and the boundaries of the polity.[20]

The empirical record does not justify this confidence in the ability of Mexico's elites to contain political conflict and to exclude large sectors of the population from politics. Mexico's peasantry entered the national political stage in 1810 and was not even temporarily excluded until after 1876. Many peasants participated actively in the political and ideological conflicts of the period. The "elite" political struggles of early-nineteenth-century Mexico were never substantially detached from the concrete realities of Mexican society.

Surprisingly, some scholars of nineteenth-century Mexican peasant rebellions also posit a wide gap between their dynamics and those of national "elite" politics.[21] Even more imply such a gap by simply leaving aside elite politics in their analyses of rebellions.[22] These views are consistent with a series of assumptions about peasants that pervade the social sciences. Peasants are often viewed as creatures predisposed to tradition, with political horizons limited to the boundaries of the village, who intervene in history sporadically and unsuccessfully to express economic grievances. Generally they are seen as at best indifferent to the state, an institution whose impact on them is almost always negative. In these views, peasants have little stake in most political conflicts and when they do intervene they do so for reasons that have little to do with those of elites.[23]

Peasants in Nineteenth-Century Mexico

Mexico's independence war was accompanied by a major change in the modes of social action employed by peasants. During the colonial period, Indian peasants often engaged in village riots that were almost always confined to a single village and that rarely involved non-peasants. They often occurred in response to some innovation in the collection of taxes, targeted a specific official, and displayed a very low level of violence. Peasants rarely admitted to planning such ac-

tions, instead claiming that they were spontaneous, and royal officials typically responded by negotiating, punishing a few ringleaders,
and removing the officials whose actions had caused tensions. Village riots did not challenge the colonial system and colonial officials
did not treat them as such a threat.[24]

[Rural revolts after 1810 were radically different from their colonial
predecessors.] They often involved peasants from dozens of villages
as well as nonpeasants of various kinds, including priests, military
men, ranchers, muleteers, and even estate owners. These revolts often addressed issues in national politics and sought alliances on a
nationwide scale, and they were usually accompanied by explicit
programmatic statements that addressed both specific peasant grievances and wider issues. In resource disputes peasants went on the
offensive, occupying lands that they claimed landowners had stolen
from them decades earlier. Clearly, something had changed in the
countryside.[25]

Charles Tilly uses the phrase "change in repertoires" to describe a
similar change in political behavior in France. The term "repertoire"
emphasizes the learned character of social action, along with impro-
visation and innovation.[26] In Mexico, however, this change in political behavior is associated with a conscious change in state relations
with Mexico's rural population that began with the Bourbon reforms
in the latter half of the eighteenth century and continued throughout
the nineteenth century. State formation often involves the extension
of the power of the central state at the expense of previously existing
institutions; in rural colonial Mexico, the most ubiquitous and important institutions were peasant villages. The Bourbon state and its
independent successors undermined the economic, social, and political power of these Indian communities. They also eliminated the legal basis under which Indians had enjoyed special rights not available
to others. Mexico's Indian peasants had long relied on these features
of the colonial system in their conflicts with both the state and private interests. Thus, historians writing in the last twenty years have
uniformly emphasized the negative character and consequences of
these changes; yet most consider them outside the context of the
shift in political behavior outlined above.[27]

Resolving the Contradictions

The central contention of this book is that the topics treated
above—state formation, nineteenth-century national politics, the
manner in which peasant political action changed with indepen-

dence, and the efforts of Mexico's political elite to transform the countryside—are all fundamentally linked. These issues are often treated separately, but such treatments lack explanatory power. Nineteenth-century political conflict extended beyond elite groups because these groups advanced different models of the state that had different implications for, and impacts on, the lives of Mexico's lower classes. These models allowed various elite groups to form alliances with segments of Mexico's peasantry as well as the urban poor, alliances that were in turn crucial in determining national political outcomes. The key feature of early-nineteenth-century Mexican political history was the participation of wide sectors of the population in politics in differing manners for varying reasons. The repertoires learned and the discourses elaborated through this participation had enduring impacts on Mexico's political system and political culture.

The connections between state formation, elite politics, and the rural and urban poor of nineteenth-century Latin America have increasingly interested historians. However, much of this interest has been expressed in broad interpretive essays rather than specific studies of movements, alliances, and discourses.[28] The specific studies that historians have completed concentrate heavily on the latter half of the nineteenth century.[29] Although the quality of these studies is generally impressive, they do not address the earlier period in which the violent transition from colonial to national statehood shaped many of the options, repertoires, and discourses available to actors in the second half of the century. This book hopes to contribute to this body of work through the study of a specific case in this earlier period.

Understanding the dynamic and multilateral connections between the formation of national states and political systems, national politics, and the struggles of the rural and urban poor requires the bridging of series of dichotomies often found in social science research: elites versus the poor, modernity versus tradition, the national versus the local.[30] These pairs of opposites are not themselves unrelated. Modern politics is often equated with elite and national politics. Conversely, the social science literature often ascribes a parochial, backward-looking view of politics to the poor in general and peasants in particular. Fortunately, a great deal of research and writing in anthropology, history, political science, and sociology has provided a series of analytical tools to aid in bridging these gaps.

One key to understanding how actors in early-nineteenth-century Mexico were able to continually form alliances across class lines lies in the fragmentation of classes. The very factors that impeded the formation of national class-based movements—kinship, geography, ethnicity, and so on—facilitated the formation of cross-class alliances, not between two or more classes of national scope but rather between different groups from within two or more classes. These alliances were the most salient feature of politics in early-nineteenth-century Mexico. Both the dominant classes and the peasantry were divided within their ranks, and this increased the fluidity of politics.[31]

Political alliances and movements that cut across class lines require languages that do the same. Social scientists concerned with the understanding of what may be loosely termed "hegemony" have greatly increased our knowledge of how political idioms can be shared across class lines and can themselves become a terrain for class conflict. First advanced as part of an effort to understand why increasing class polarization did not necessarily lead to increasingly overt class conflict, this line of analysis has resulted in fruitful debate over how various social actors justify their relationships.[32] Scholars of many different perspectives have reached convergent conclusions on some general features of the problem.

One such feature is that dominant classes, no matter how firmly entrenched in power, need to present their actions as "the embodiment of a moral code much of which represents the interests and sentiments of all classes."[33] However, this vision is itself a historical product of struggle and "is continually being tested and modified."[34] Members of the lower classes constantly struggle within the predominant moral code or discursive framework. Part of this struggle involves the selective reconstruction of the code using the elements most favorable to lower-class interests; another, perhaps more important, part involves the application of differential meanings to the symbols, values, heritages, and representations that make up the hegemonic ideology.[35] This latter component of the lower classes' struggle is in part made possible by the theoretically untidy fact that class (along with such other analytical abstractions as state and market) is actually experienced through the actions of individuals.[36] The predominant set of symbols, whether it is called a hegemonic ideology, a discursive framework, a predominant moral code, or dominant political culture, is itself an arena for conflict rather than evidence of false consciousness.[37]

Scholars employing this "hegemonic" line of analysis have without exception focused on the possibilities for lower-class political action against the dominant classes and the means through which such action is carried out and justified. Nevertheless, their insights can also be fruitfully applied to the problem of cross-class alliances. The same characteristics that allow class conflict to take place within hegemony also allow conflict between portions of classes. Furthermore, the constant conflict and negotiation that takes place within society as a whole also occurs within cross-class alliances. Cross-class movements advance visions of society, and within these visions there is space for the application of differential meanings to the symbols, terms, and values from which the visions are constructed. The ideologies, platforms, and discourses of such movements are historically constructed through conflict and negotiation in much the same manner as are the larger hegemonic systems from which they are born.

The elements that made cross-class movements possible have also been identified by scholars not specifically concerned with the theoretical problems of hegemony and culture. The heterodoxy of elites has been underlined again and again in the Latin American context,[38] and the ways in which symbols and terms can be differentially interpreted have been central features of a number of studies of political and social movements in Latin America and elsewhere.[39] The way key individuals mediate and interpret discourse has also become important to our understanding of cross-class movements.[40] All of these elements turn up repeatedly in social scientific and historical analyses.

The dichotomy between modernity and tradition also haunts studies of nineteenth-century political and social movements. Certainly the destruction of supranational monarchies and the formation of national states based on the principle of popular sovereignty entailed a transformation of political culture, but this transformation was fragmentary, halting, and by no means unidirectional. The new elements of "modern" political cultures matured within existing systems,[41] incorporating elements of the old, especially in Spain and Spanish America. Political cultures or hegemonic systems often contain heterogeneous discourses,[42] and the lack of a clear line between the "modern" and the "traditional" is particularly relevant to lower-class political expression: historians have often noted how peasants and the urban poor reformulate "traditional" rights to assert new claims, just as they reformulate elements from the hegemonic discursive framework to oppose the dominant classes.[43]

The third major dichotomy that impedes understanding of the multilateral connections between the struggles of the rural poor, the formation of national states, and national political history is that between the local and the national. Peasants are sometimes considered incapable of understanding the ideas and praxis of national politics, which are said to be the exclusive provinces of other classes. To the extent peasants ever become nationalist, this argument holds, they do so only under the tutelage of political elites.[44] However, several key understandings about states and the way they are legitimated provide clues to comprehending how the seemingly huge chasm between the village and the nation is bridged.

The most important of these understandings is the fact that nationalisms are often based on *community* myths, emphasizing cultural identity and emotional solidarity in ways "more appropriate (if at all) to village or small town life."[45] This identity of the local and the national in symbolic language is even more explicit in Spanish America, where the word *pueblo* means both "village" and "people" in the sense of a national people. Furthermore, in the nineteenth-century Mexican context, the word *república* could refer to both the Mexican republic and the *república de indios*, or corporate Indian village. Yet this identity between the local and national goes beyond language; in early-nineteenth-century Mexico, practical politics reinforced this identity in at least two ways.

First, the state, although national in conception, was (and is) experienced historically through the actions of individual local officials. In this way it is like those other abstractions of social science, the market and class. Second, national political alliances and the discourses they promoted included visions of how local politics would be organized. Although the identification of peasant politics with local politics in the literature is perhaps a valid generalization, it should be tempered by an appreciation of the way local politics become linked to regional and national politics.[46] Competing groups in national politics had both local allies and visions of what local politics should look like. In early-nineteenth-century Mexico these linkages worked in both directions: national outcomes influenced local ones and vice versa. The linkages were symbolic as well as practical: elections in particular tied local political legitimation to that of the national government.[47]

The Organization of the Book

This book focuses on the region that now forms the state of Guerrero. Guerrero became a state in 1849, when a new state government began administering large territories ceded by the existing states of Mexico and Puebla as well as a small section of Michoacán. The book often analyzes laws and other information from the states of Mexico,

Puebla, and Michoacán for the period before 1849, because they were applied in different parts of what later became Guerrero. The process through which Guerrero became a state is outlined at length in Chapter 5. For the sake of simplicity, the book frequently refers to the relevant area as "Guerrero" even when discussing events prior to 1849. Both before and after 1849, contemporaries sometimes referred to Guerrero and nearby regions as "the South," and the book uses this term also.

The first chapter in this book is a general overview of society and politics in late colonial Guerrero. It surveys the social, political, and economic systems in which Guerrero's peasantry lived, including the colonial state and class structure, the economic system, the political culture, and the specific economic and social geography of Guerrero. The chapter also examines colonial politics and social relations through the arguments and political tactics used in struggles over resources.

Chapter 2 consists of a detailed study of the War of Independence in Guerrero. Beginning in 1808, rebellion and violent conflict became important forums for political action in the area. The chapter discusses the causes that led to the outbreak of fighting, the social composition of the insurgency, the discourse that united various actors, and the way the justification for the insurgency changed over time. The chapter includes a section on the political organization of the areas governed by the insurgents. It also examines the royalist response to rebellion and the way royalist measures changed the colonial political system. The chapter concludes with an analysis of the final, guerrilla stage of the insurrection and the events that led to Mexico's independence compromise of 1821.

The third chapter concentrates on changes in laws and institutions in the immediate post-colonial era. State formation in this period is of particular interest for two reasons. First, many patterns of political behavior in the countryside that originated in this period have endured to the present day. Second, political and institutional changes in these twenty years formed the framework for national and regional political conflict throughout the nineteenth century. Some peasants were able to take advantage of the new order to establish a relatively favorable relationship with the post-independence state and thus control local politics. Although this outcome was neither widespread nor secure, it encouraged peasant participation in the wider political struggles of the first half of the nineteenth century. Competing visions of the shape of the state in rural society underlay peasant participation in national political conflict.

Chapter 4 surveys rural social and political conflict between 1820 and 1840 in a more chronological and narrative fashion in order to demonstrate how political alliances and discourses were constructed historically. This chapter unearths the local and lower-class social bases of the competing factions that dominated national politics, concentrating on the gradual formation of a loose political alliance and ideology that became known as "federalism." Mexico's dominant class eventually reacted to this challenge by embracing centralism and protectionist industrialization. The chapter ends with an analysis of how local politics in Guerrero changed under centralism.

The fifth chapter is a study of the peasant rebellions that rocked Guerrero in the early 1840s. It discusses the causes of the rebellions as well as the explicit political and economic grievances of the rebels. The chapter stresses the regional and national political ties developed by the rebels through the regional politician Juan Alvarez. It argues that the rebellions cannot be understood outside of their political context and that they had serious ramifications for regional and national politics. The rebellions were in part a reaction to the implementation of centralism in the countryside, and this reaction facilitated alliances between the peasant rebels and elite federalists that prepared the way for the national restoration of federalism in 1846 as well as the organization of the state of Guerrero as a separate political entity in 1849. Both contributed to the resolution of peasant grievances and the end of the rebellions.

The sixth and final chapter covers the 1852–57 period in the history of Guerrero and Mexico. The Revolution of Ayutla began in Guerrero, and this chapter argues that there it was largely a restaging of the 1840s rebellions. The Ayutla movement also put forward many of the elements of popular federalist discourse that had been formed in the area in earlier periods. The chapter discusses the aftermath of the revolution and the threat of radical reform it unleashed in Mexico, and concludes with a consideration of the limits of the popular federalist model of politics that had developed in Guerrero between 1800 and 1855.

State-building in Mexico went on long past 1855, but that year was a crucial turning point. It began the long toe-to-toe confrontation between conservatives and liberals that culminated in the definitive victory of Mexico's liberal model of authoritarianism ten years later. Before La Reforma, Mexico's conservatives and their centralist predecessors had not made systematic efforts to secure popular support for their programs. Their political initiatives had been deliberately insulated from the bulk of Mexico's population. In the mid-1850s the conservatives abandoned their dream of reaching and maintaining power without the aid of Mexico's masses. They began their long effort to appropriate the banner of the Catholic Church and use it to inspire popular support for their cause. In so doing, the conservatives implicitly accepted the presence of Mexico's impoverished majority in politics. Ironically, the mid-1850s were also the high tide for the popular federalist model of politics developed in Guerrero over the previous fifty years; this model was soon absorbed into the liberal ideology and movement. The liberal incorporation of federalism shows clearly that the actions and opinions of Mexican peasants weighed heavily in the formation of the liberal critique of Mexican society and thus helped shape the eventual form of the Mexican state.

CHAPTER I

Society and Politics
in Colonial Guerrero

All of the male and female Indians of this town approached armed with
clubs, stones, and arrows. . . . They took away their governor's staff of
office and jailed him.

—José Antonio Rivas, Tixtla, April 15, 1795

Our ancestors provided the funds and we have conserved them. . . .
We Indians are those who have done this: We Indians those who have
husbanded and increased the funds: We Indians those who have always
cared for them and there is no reason we the owners should be deprived
of the funds.

—The villagers of San Miguel Totolapán, Mexico City,
 December 4, 1795

Studies of peasant political action often emphasize the isola-
tion, backwardness, and economic marginality of life in the countryside. However, peasants and elites in late colonial Guerrero did not
exist in a vacuum. The economic, social, and political relationships
that they experienced were an integral part of systems centered
around Mexico City, Spain, and the Atlantic industrializing powers.
These systems were as important to the lives of Guerrero's peasants
as the age-old cycle of the agricultural seasons, even if they were not
always as visible. Rural life was not insulated from the economy and
class structure as a whole and certainly rural values and beliefs were
not divorced from New Spain's dominant political culture. Placing
peasants in their context is crucial to understanding their changing
relationships to each other, to the state, and to economic and social
elites.

Analysts of peasant resistance usually also stress the importance
of rapid change in the political, economic, and social lives of peasants
in setting off violence. Toward the end of this chapter I will detail the
kinds of change that prepared Guerrero's countryside for the explosion of 1810–11. These rapid alterations in people's lives and possibilities are of obvious importance in explaining peasant grievances
and objectives, but they are not sufficient to explain how grievances

were expressed and objectives pursued. In other words, economic and social change never leads inevitably to social movements. In many ways it was the more static aspects of their place in the colonial economic, social, and political systems that led many of Guerrero's peasants to participate in a social movement that would change Mexican politics and society forever, severing the ties between Spain and Mexico and forcing the construction of a new state on the still novel base of nationality.

Two related features of New Spain's political and economic life shaped the possibilities for social and political action in 1810–11. The first was the importance of individual agents of the colonial state in New Spain's economic life and class structure. The second was the way in which New Spain's dominant or hegemonic political culture made action against local officials in the name of the king the most common form of politics. In combination these two features made possible the rural social movement that convulsed New Spain in the second decade of the century and eventually led to Mexican independence. They also insured that the insurgency would initially take the paradoxical form of a movement to protect the king from his enemies even as it struck at the very foundations of the colonial order.

Class Structure and the State in Colonial Mexico

Perhaps the most important feature of the pre-independence political and economic system in Mexico was the way in which the power of the state, as exercised by its local agents, was used to benefit specific members of Mexico's colonial economic elite. Although the Crown employed diverse stratagems to maintain control over its agents, it was never willing or able to systematically outbid colonial elites for their services. Officials' ultimate loyalty to the Crown did not preclude accepting compensation from local sources in exchange for a certain flexibility in enforcing some royal policies. The implication of this fact is clear: the economic opportunities of individuals were conditioned not only by the complex thicket of corporate bodies and caste distinctions prescribed by law but also by the relationship each was able to develop with the local representatives of the Crown who enforced regulations. Economically, the local representatives of the state could be decisive in disputes over resource ownership. Perhaps more important, they were crucial in enforcing the legal and extralegal monopolistic and monopsonistic practices that characterized product and factor markets in colonial Mexico.[2] These relationships influenced the ideologies developed by Mexicans to attack the colonial state and to construct its replacement and had important implications for class structure.

The class structure of Mexico at the beginning of the nineteenth century was capped by a small group of extremely wealthy and powerful families, the colonial dominant class. Socially, these families combined Spanish immigrants with Creoles; economically, they constructed diversified portfolios that included commercial ventures, mines, urban real estate, and *haciendas* located in particularly profitable areas such as the central plateau near Mexico City and the Bajío with its nearby markets in mining towns. Some families used entailments or *mayorazgos* to maintain the unity of their far-flung interests, whereas others relied on more informal methods. Members of this class almost invariably resided in Mexico City and often used the Consulado de México to formulate and voice their common interests. They used clientalist relationships with members of the royal bureaucracy to manipulate internal markets in many commodities. Other institutions such as town councils and the militia officer corps also served as forums for representation and vehicles of class ideological and political cohesion, especially in the larger cities of the central plateau.[3] Members of these families occupied the most important and well-remunerated positions in the church hierarchy, including bishoprics, cathedral chapters, and the wealthier regular orders. They also controlled some important and wealthy confraternities that provided additional sources of credit.[4] This class achieved a high degree of ideological and social cohesion based on strategic marriages, the purchase of titles of nobility, and a consciousness among both Creoles and immigrants that they were Spanish. Cohesion was aided by the extremely small size of this class, perhaps 110 families in all. These families have been the subjects of an astonishing number of excellent studies over the last twenty years.[5]

Although the dominant class often voiced opposition to particular Crown policies, it was the main beneficiary of the colonial system. It guaranteed a steady transatlantic flow of revenues in exchange for the economic control of the viceroyalty. The Bourbon reforms are often seen as an assault on this group, a "second Conquest." Nevertheless, whatever their intent, the reforms ultimately resulted in a renegotiation of the relationship between this group and the Crown. Revenues sent to Spain increased, but the dominant class retained its privileged position in the Mexican economy. Furthermore, those provisions of the Bourbon reforms that most directly affected the interests of this class were abandoned.[6] Members of the dominant class successfully resisted other policies through widespread evasion and delay, aided by their clients in the viceregal bureaucracy. A classic example, often cited as a motive for an eventual shift against the Crown, is the Consolidación de Vales Reales. This measure required the repayment of all debts owed to the church and other corporations so that the capital involved could be lent to the Crown instead. The colonial dominant class stridently protested this move, and although the measure was implemented, members of this class used their widespread connections in the church and the viceregal bureaucracy to obtain relatively favorable conditions for payment. These connections, and the negotiating power inherent in the sheer size of the debts they owed, enabled them to sidestep the potentially devastating effects of the Consolidación. Far from initiating the move toward independence, or even seconding it, this group was the main supporter of the Crown in the 1810–21 war.[7]

Below this small and powerful class lay a larger but less cohesive group of individuals who were not impoverished but who lacked the access to capital and connections enjoyed by the dominant class. Some worked in the far-flung economic enterprises of the elite, whereas others struggled in competition with them. This group included many small merchants, parish priests, and muleteers, most *hacendados* and *rancheros*, the wealthiest members of Indian communities, hacienda administrators, some artisans, and a few professionals. This class was geographically, economically, and socially varied, and it lacked the institutions that the dominant class used to define and articulate its interests. Members of this group served in many ways as economic and political intermediaries between the dominant class based in Mexico City and the mass of Mexico's population.[8] They were vulnerable to crises, both political and economic, being hard hit, for instance, by the Consolidación de Vales Reales because they lacked both the connections needed to reach favorable settlements and the liquidity necessary to meet the Crown's demands. Many went bankrupt and lost properties. They were also vulnerable to the agricultural crises that the dominant class relied on to make agriculture more profitable.[9] This class was defined by what it was not—a lack of identity that would haunt it throughout the nineteenth century.

An even more diverse group occupied the lower tier of the colonial Mexican class structure. This poorest sector included most Indian villagers; Indian, mestizo, and mulatto sharecroppers; hacienda workers, both temporary and permanent; hacienda tenants; artisans and urban marginals; and day laborers in both rural and urban settings. This group was further removed from a unified class consciousness at a viceregal or even regional level, although there were significant possibilities for building horizontal solidarities at the local level. The various subgroups of this strata in Guerrero will be discussed in detail below.

New Spain's Economy and Guerrero's Peasants

In the late eighteenth century New Spain served the growing Atlantic economy as an exporter of silver and importer of the textiles flowing out of the increasingly productive industries of Europe. Although only a few wealthy merchants had direct contact with foreign customers or suppliers, linkages extended throughout the colonial Mexican economy. Thus, although events closer to home had more visible and immediate effects on the economic well-being of peasants in Guerrero, the fate of peasants was linked in significant ways with events far from the scenes of their labor. This linkage was particularly evident when war among the European powers disrupted trade.

Peasants took active part in this late colonial economy, and their economic participation is vital to an understanding of their more visible political participation, especially after 1810. Although some historians have suggested that peasants produced only for their own subsistence, this view does not take into account the diversity of peasant lands and products. Although many peasant families probably consumed most of their own maize production, peasants also produced a wide array of market crops that they traded in local or regional markets. In some regions even maize and other grains were marketed. The sources rarely show whether this market participation was "voluntary" or "coerced," but it would be simplistic to ascribe all market participation to coercion and all nonparticipation to some inchoate desire for autarky. It is even more simplistic to assume that market participation in late colonial Mexico was a relatively recent phenomenon imposed by the growth of world capitalism. Indian peasants had marketed production since before the Conquest.[10]

The economy of Guerrero was linked to larger systems through a network of merchants extending outward from Mexico City. In loan arrangements referred to as *habilitación*, *repartimiento*, or *avío*, these merchants advanced credit to producers in exchange for the right to buy their products. The system worked with the aid of colonial officials who excluded competing merchants from particular areas and helped enforce contracts. Although this intervention by colonial officials certainly promoted monopolies, by increasing merchants' profits and reducing risks it also allowed economic activities to take place that would not have been feasible in a strict free-market setting.[11] This system operated with a number of products in Guerrero, particularly cotton and cotton textiles, and was not strictly limited to products of high value or those in demand in major urban centers: even maize production was sometimes organized in this way.[12] Frequently, social scientists describe this economic pattern as forced sales or forced distribution, especially when the system involved Indian villagers. This may have been true in some cases, but complaints arose less about the coercive nature of sales than about the monopoly/monopsony problem. Peasants complained about being paid less than they felt their products were worth and about paying excessive prices for the goods they received in exchange.

These credit systems formed part of a much larger network of economic relations extending from poor peasants in the seemingly isolated villages of Guerrero to the richest men in the viceroyalty and even their counterparts in other parts of the world, most notably Spain and England. This economic network was a major factor shaping people's lives. Even the producers of goods that did not travel long distances because of the high cost of transport relative to their value were not outside the larger system, for they participated in local markets tied to the larger whole. The web was complex, but it was unbroken. The most important unifying element of this web was credit, extended by rich Mexico City merchants to their distributors in the provinces, and by these directly to producers.[13] This larger system was fundamental to the social processes and social movements of the period.

Economic and Social Geography

During the late colonial period, the geographical area encompassed by the present state of Guerrero was neither politically nor economically unified but rather was divided among two intendancies (Mexico and Puebla) and three dioceses (Valladolid, Mexico, and Puebla). The area, which included several interlocking economic networks, was defined by boundaries drawn in a protracted political struggle in the 1840s. These borders were important yet geographically arbitrary, based as they were on the relative strength of political alliances. The geographical scope of the present study is thus correspondingly arbitrary when applied to the late colonial period. The economic and social description that follows breaks the area down into seven smaller parts, emphasizing the ethnicity and social organization of the inhabitants, including patterns of resource ownership, as well as the volume and types of commerce. These seven subregions were Chilapa, Tlapa, the Tierra Caliente, the Costa Grande, Acapulco, the Costa Chica, and Taxco.

Chilapa was the only area where large numbers of Indian peasants in corporate villages coexisted with relatively large numbers of people from other classes. Chilapa was a large market town surrounded by a number of Indian peasant villages interspersed with relatively small non-Indian landholdings. The market town, also the seat of a *subdelegado*, was both an Indian republic and the home of many Creole and mestizo traders, artisans, and landowners. The town itself was a marketing center for cotton sent up from the Pacific coast, some of which was spun and woven into shawls there, and some of which was sent on to the highland destinations of Puebla and Mexico City.[14] The villages also were centers for spinning. Agriculturally, the villages produced maize and the relatively small haciendas and *ranchos* produced maize and cattle as well as low-grade sugar.[15] Landholders expanded by buying or renting noncontiguous properties, so that the more well-off tended to have several small properties rather than one large unit.[16] Indians continued to hold large quantities of land in the area, both as *tierras de repartimiento* and *bienes de comunidad.*[17] They also produced cattle for market, particularly through *cofradías.*[18] The nearby town of Tixtla was the center of a similar system, although it was oriented less toward textiles than toward transportation, serving as home for many muleteers involved in local and long-distance trade. The difference between Chilapa and Tixtla was relative, however: both towns contributed large numbers of muleteers to the pool necessary to unite the area's economy.[19]

Local merchants and landowners sent sugar to Puebla and acquired such products as salt and rice on the coast. The cultivation and processing of cotton, along with foreign trade and mining, formed one of the three pillars of the economy of Guerrero. An important step in this complex process took place in the Chilapa-Tixtla area. Highland merchants sent low-grade sugar and *petate* (woven straw used to package cotton) to the coast and bought cotton. Merchants distributed some of the cotton acquired on the coast to Indian women in the highland villages; the women spun it into thread, which the merchants then transferred to mestizo weavers who wove cloth for both regional and larger markets.[20] Other raw cotton was sent directly on to Mexico City or Puebla.[21]

Tlapa, centered around the mestizo market and administrative center of the same name further east, differed from Chilapa and Tixtla in two significant ways. First, commercially it was articulated with Puebla rather than with the Acapulco–Mexico City trade axis. Second, Indian villages dominated the area and even small mestizo and Creole landholdings were rare.[22] The population of the area was overwhelmingly indigenous, and non-Indians who engaged in agricultural production did so almost exclusively on lands rented from the villages.[23] White and mestizo merchants had a relatively small role, and Indian cofradías organized most commerce, using their funds to finance trading trips like those undertaken by Creole and mestizo merchants in other areas. The mule trade seems to have been the only part of the system that was directly organized by non-Indian merchants, with the help of administrative officials.[24] The importation of the mules necessary for transportation supported a web of exchanges of specialized village handicrafts (varieties of pottery, decorated gourds, textiles) and the raw materials needed to produce them.[25]

Indian villages also dominated the society and economy of Tierra Caliente, an area west and north of the Chilapa region containing a few small Reales de Minas, notably Tetela del Río. Most of the inhabitants of this hot, sterile, and sparsely populated area lived in Indian villages and on a few haciendas and ranchos. The lands of the latter were mostly rented from the Indians, and conflicts over these rentals were a major problem throughout the period. The *vecinos*, or non-Indians, raised cattle and small amounts of sugar. The Indians also raised cattle, particularly through cofradías, and some maize, as well as fruit on a few prized fertile and irrigated tracts. Cofradías were an important source of capital, and competition over their control was intense. The volume of trade in this area seems to have been relatively small, although there was some production of handicrafts, particularly shoes and chairs.[26]

The Costa Grande, the Pacific coast west of Acapulco, was nearly devoid of Indian villages. Its pre-Conquest population had suffered heavily in the demographic collapse because of the area's warm and humid climate. The area's rise in importance as a producer of cotton beginning in the mid-eighteenth century caused rapid growth in population and production, but this population was mostly non-Indian. The area's inhabitants produced little else except cattle and maize consumed locally as well as some contraband tobacco.[27]

Mulatto sharecroppers cultivated the cotton. Although cotton production was in the hands of hundreds of sharecroppers, marketing was highly concentrated because a few merchants and landholders controlled the market by advancing goods against the harvest. Their dominant position allowed them to set prices on both the cotton and the goods they advanced, usually textiles. The merchants sent most of the cotton to the Bajío through Michoacán and the remainder to the Chilapa-Tixtla area to be processed into textiles or rerouted to Mexico City and Puebla. Merchants from Chilapa-Tixtla entered the area at harvest time to sell petate (needed to package the cotton) and sugar in exchange for cotton. Their counterparts from Michoacán advanced textiles against the harvest, capturing a larger proportion of the harvest.[28]

Acapulco and its immediate area were very diverse ethnically, containing a hodgepodge of whites, mulattos, and Indians. The Indians who lived in settlements just outside the port were immigrants without community rights and obligations. They produced maize, cotton, and cattle, and they seem to have mixed freely both occupationally and socially with their mulatto neighbors. Most Creoles and Spaniards in the jurisdiction lived in the port itself. The port imported most of its food from other areas, especially in the fevered weeks surrounding the arrival of the annual China galleon.[29]

The port was more important as a trade nexus than as a population center. The only products produced nearby for other markets were rice sent to several highland destinations and salt sent to Taxco, where it was an important input for refining metals. Most products sent overland from Acapulco were imported by sea. This import trade was composed of two branches: cacao from Guayaquil, which went to many markets in New Spain as well as overland to Veracruz for export to Spain; and the goods off the China *nao* or galleon, which arrived once a year from the Philippines laden with spices and high-quality silk textiles. For several weeks after its arrival (usually in December or January) buyers from Mexico City attended a fair held in Acapulco. Merchants paid for imports from both Guayaquil and the Philippines in silver coin. The Acapulco trade supported large numbers of *arrieros* (muleteers), most of whom lived in Tixtla and Tepecoacuilco in the nearby highlands.[30]

The Costa Chica lay east of Acapulco and directly south of the Tlapa area. In many ways, it was similar to the Costa Grande, except that its trade connections led north through Tlapa to Puebla and more Indian villages survived there than in the Costa Grande. The major crop was cotton, grown by the mulatto sharecroppers who composed the majority of the population. Little else was produced beyond small amounts of maize and sugar. Cotton and gourds (collected, not cultivated) were important raw materials for Indian handicraft production in the mountains immediately to the north. White and mestizo merchants played a relatively small role here, possibly because of the mercantile success of the indigenous population of the Tlapa area.[31]

North and west lay Taxco, a famous mining center and the hub of an extensive trade area. Salt from the coast was an important input for the refining of silver. Because Taxco stood among dry and barren mountains, it imported vast amounts of grain from the Iguala area to its south, where Indian sharecroppers grew most of this grain on lands belonging to a cofradía of the parish of Taxco. The same area used part of its agricultural capacity to fatten pigs to send to Puebla's important bacon industry. This area was of greater interest to merchants than anywhere else in Guerrero because of the volume of trade generated by the mining industry.[32]

In summary, Indian communities were important in three areas: Chilapa, Tlapa, and Tierra Caliente. Only in the first of these did they share economic and social space with large numbers of non-peasants. In the other two, communities owned the bulk of the land, and in Tlapa they even controlled most trade via cofradías. In two other areas, Costa Grande and Costa Chica, mulatto peasants produced cotton. In the first of these, trade was controlled by outside merchants who advanced products against the harvest, whereas in the second it was not. Two other areas contained large non-Indian populations and were important centers of nonagricultural economic activity: the mining center of Taxco and Acapulco, a port for the importation of luxury goods.

The Political Culture of New Spain

Political culture, paraphrasing Keith Baker, can be understood as the set of practices and discourses through which groups and individuals in any society articulate, negotiate, enforce, and implement the competing claims they make upon one another. It is constantly created and recreated as new claims are articulated and old ones are transformed.[33] In this sense, the political culture of late colonial New Spain was changing even as it shaped and bounded relationships among peasants, elites, and the state. The gradual introduction of new political forms and ends arising from the Enlightenment was transforming a Thomistic Hapsburg system based on natural law and difference. Nevertheless, we need to resist the temptation to fix on ideological change that arises from our knowledge of Mexico's subsequent break from Spain and construction as a national republican state. The ideological transformation was important in determining the direction of political change after 1812, but it exerted little influence during the first months and even years of the insurgency. Many insurgent leaders had been exposed to the new forms of political legitimacy and justification, but when they first appealed for support they did so using older forms.

Spain's early modern empire had been created by a Hapsburg dynasty simultaneously engaged in consolidating an absolutist state in Europe. In both Old and New Worlds, the monarchy presided over a multiplicity of corporate bodies. All individuals were subjects of the monarchy but their relationships with it passed through a variety of institutions with different political and juridical attributes. The monarch presided over the whole as the interpreter of natural law; individual subjects were not viewed as equals but instead drew varying political identities from their membership in the estates, guilds, Indian villages, and other corporate groups that each filled a necessary role in the "body politic." The monarch's role was essentially regulatory, preserving balance and natural law by arbitrating disputes. Groups and individuals could oppose state or royal policies, but their opposition was tempered by the deep-seated assumption that the monarch himself was by nature benevolent and any royal decisions that violated natural law stemmed from the errors or malevolence of the king's advisors. The assumption of royal benevolence increased the overall stability of the system by elevating the level of dissent it could tolerate.[34]

New Spain's peasant majority had a specific place in this system, and that place is important in understanding the way peasants expressed themselves politically. New Spain belonged not to Spain but to the Crown itself: in theory at least it was considered a kingdom equal to its various sisters on the Iberian peninsula.[35] Within New Spain peasants, most of whom were members of corporate Indian villages, were obligated to pay tribute to the Crown, in exchange for which they received usufruct rights to parcels of land held in common by their villages. Land rights were linked to villagers' status as tributary vassals of the king. "Indian" was a legal category defined by membership in a village with corresponding rights and obligations. The Crown constituted these villages in the sixteenth and seventeenth centuries to facilitate the taxation of the New World's indigenous population and to limit the power of colonial elites by maintaining direct royal control over labor. After the Conquest and the subsequent population decline New Spain's population constructed new cultural forms out of a combination of pre-Hispanic elements and features of the new hegemonic system; the peasants' "Indian-ness" was never divorced from the political status and form of the village and thus from their identity as loyal vassals of the Crown.[36]

The Crown always had an ambiguous relationship with its sub-jects in the New World. In the case of Mexico's settled natives, the Crown had little desire to see them become slaves or even vassals of the conquerors, and to some degree saw them as useful counter-weights to the power of the wealthy in New Spain. This role required a degree of native autonomy that the conquerors and their heirs never fully accepted. Indians also benefited from a political system in which the population as a whole served as a check on the Crown's own agents. The long-term impact of these admittedly self-serving royal policies was enormous. Natives seized on the opportunities for self-defense provided by the colonial legal system and rapidly became adept at playing individual and even institutional Spanish interests against each other.[37] The availability of this option, and the forms of argument its effective use required, also influenced Indian peasants' extralegal political activities. In contrast to their counterparts on the northern or southern frontiers of New Spain, Indian peasants in Cen-tral New Spain (including Guerrero) rioted not to remove themselves from Spanish control but rather to get the king's attention.[38]

Beneath the harmonious surface maintained by the dominant po-litical culture disputes were common, serious, and often acrimoni-ous. The actors and stakes in these disputes were diverse but the state as constituted by the actions of its local agents was the com-mon denominator in all. The agents of the state were heavily in-volved in struggles over local resources even when neither they nor their superiors were officially interested parties. The state was a nec-essary party in conflicts between peasants and their priests, between peasants and local elites, between peasant villages, and even between factions within a single village. Within the dominant political cul-ture, injustice could only occur if the king's agents allowed an in-fringement of natural law and custom. When they did so, in the eyes of peasants they became fair targets of action to restore justice, in-cluding violence.

One tactic Indian peasants often used in conflicts was to hide in the uncultivated and trackless spaces between villages. This was a highly symbolic and practical act: symbolic because it removed the village and its inhabitants from the political and moral supervision of royal officials and priests; practical because it removed taxpayers from the effective reach of the state. To collect tribute from scattered peasants simply was not cost-effective.[39] Tribute, of course, had a further symbolic political meaning as homage to the Crown.[40]

The various elements of the repertoire peasants deployed in colonial conflicts were not by any means mutually exclusive. The same demands were pressed by illegal and legal means. Evasion or passive resistance, rioting, and lawsuits in royal courts were not qualitatively different, because they all served to bring violations of natural law to the attention of the king. Peasants often used all three tactics in the same dispute, which suggests that the divisions between "legal" and "illegal" or even possibly "individual" and "collective" forms of resistance or political behavior often posited by social scientists did not loom large in the minds of those who engaged in such practices.

Rural Politics

In late colonial Guerrero, political space was shared between a hierarchy of appointed colonial officials and a number of villages. The latter are perhaps more accurately described by their contemporary denomination, that of "repúblicas de indios," or Indian republics. These republics governed the political life of Indian peasants throughout Guerrero but not that of the mulatto sharecroppers of the coast. Although sometimes called "pueblos," a term currently translated as village, repúblicas de indios were not nucleated settlements. They usually consisted of one large settlement that served as the seat of government (the *cabecera*) surrounded by several smaller settlements or *sujetos*.

República governments had important powers and functions. First, as Manuel Flon, intendant of Puebla, noted in 1797,

> The means and faculties of the governors [the highest Indian village officials] are not so frivolous that they do not influence the happiness or misfortune of their respective societies. They divide and distribute the plots that others vacate; end or sentence in verbal judgment certain differences or quarrels that the Indians do not bring before the Spanish judge; choose and name the individuals they desire for the lesser jobs and public responsibilities [*cargas concejiles*]; and in some villages even make the wills and divisions of the small wealth that the deceased leave.[41]

Second, república governments were charged with collecting the Crown's tribute and, as Flon noted, administered the lands peasants received in return. Third, they served as the most important eyes and ears of the royal administration in the countryside.[42]

The repúblicas were always overseen by appointed colonial officials of Iberian or Creole origin. This was as true in the villages' stewardship of peasant resources as it was in tribute collection or the administration of justice. The appointed officials most relevant to peasants were the subdelegados and their lieutenants, or *tenientes*. Both had wide executive and judicial powers. Despite the Bourbon reforms, these royal servants usually had close, unofficial ties to local elites or members of the colonial dominant class in Mexico City. Members of the dominant class cultivated ties with officials where they had economic interests, such as on the cotton-producing coast or near the mining center of Taxco, where corn grown by Indian villagers fetched good prices. In less lucrative regions local elites took the dominant class's place in cultivating officials, as was the case in the Tierra Caliente, where ranchers who rented land sought ties with functionaries. Both officially and unofficially, colonial officials used the republics to gain access to peasant resources, while peasants sought to use the republics to defend those same resources.

One common type of colonial conflict suggests the importance to peasant settlements of their status as repúblicas de indios. Sujeto petitions for independent status had deep historical roots—Charles Gibson notes their importance in the pre-Hispanic period—and they continued through the sixteenth and seventeenth centuries. These efforts, which often resulted in the fragmentation of repúblicas, became very common in colonial Guerrero in the eighteenth century.[43] Perhaps the most powerful motive for independence was the fact that, by definition, sujetos owed tribute and labor service to the officers of the cabecera or head town that ruled them. Petitioners typically cited this motive, claiming that such obligations were divided unfairly between sujetos and cabeceras and that those fulfilling labor obligations in cabeceras sometimes had to walk long distances to participate in public works that did not benefit them.[44] Colonial officials had powerful motives for granting such requests. First, it was easier to achieve consensus on issues concerning peasants when Indian officials governed only one settlement. Second, creating smaller villages facilitated tribute collection, an important responsibility of Indian officials. Furthermore, increasing the number of repúblicas was, according to Flon, a classic case of divide and rule: "Even in the case of a mob or riot, it is easier to pacify one village than many. Rarely or never do they unite in such affairs unless they share a Governor and his subordinates; rather on the contrary the neighboring villages are those that usually provide help to contain the riot."[45]

As Flon implies here, disputes frequently broke out between recently separated villages and their former cabeceras, occasionally because the former cabecera continued to demand services, but more often because the division of a república forced a division in the lands to which it formerly held rights.[46] Such conflicts between villages, which accounted for the bulk of all lawsuits over land in late colonial Guerrero, predated the Conquest and could, like most other disputes, drag on for years.[47] They were, as Flon was well aware, perhaps the most effective barrier to any large scale peasant revolts in New Spain.

The elections through which república officers were chosen reveal much about political life within villages and how it was articulated with political structures, forces, and actors outside of the villages. Two difficulties arise in discussing elections and election disputes. First, most electoral disputes were connected to other kinds of disputes in complicated ways. Second, and perhaps more important, it is far easier to discover factions within villages than to identify their origins.[48] No good database exists with which to construct the collective biographies of the village Indians who turn up in election disputes in late-eighteenth- and early-nineteenth-century Guerrero.

The problem is not limited to electoral disputes. The records available for Guerrero rarely provide more than a glimpse of social life within villages because disputes between individual villagers that might have generated this kind of information were not recorded and preserved. Poverty and harsh weather have played havoc with local archives in Guerrero. Authorities have had little incentive to preserve records and few resources to spare for the task. Another reason such disputes were not recorded is that they were mostly resolved by república governments that often, as Flon points out, heard testimony and issued judgments in verbal form. The only disputes between villagers that routinely show up in records preserved in viceregal archives are those involving non-Indian officials.

The recent research of historians working on late colonial villages in better-documented regions has stressed economic stratification within villages and the importance of older and more wealthy villagers in community governments. The dominant vision of the colonial república has been changed from one of a self-regulating bastion of egalitarianism to one of a miniature oligarchy that nevertheless served to defend rights important to even the poorest villagers. There is no reason to believe that the norm was different in Guerrero, and the limited evidence that has survived suggests significant stratification among village residents.[49]

The powers and facilities of governors were basically those described by Manuel Flon above. Governors were elected in December of each year and took office in January with the transfer of the symbolic *vara* or staff of office. In most villages some *alcaldes* or *regidores* (aldermen) were also elected at this time. Elections took place in an assembly overseen by the parish priest and either the subdelegado or one of his tenientes, whose approval of the new village officers was required. This stipulation was important for two reasons. First, it enabled these representatives of the Crown to ensure that those chosen were men of standing who would collect tribute payments responsibly. Second, this approval was the lever that allowed the royal officials to manipulate elections. The decision as to who was allowed to vote in elections varied greatly between villages and over time. Late in the seventeenth century and early in the eighteenth voting rights were often restricted to an aristocracy, the *principales*. As time wore on, commoners pushed to become more involved in the political process, and their efforts were facilitated by the fact that nothing in written colonial law provided a basis for their exclusion. Nevertheless, voting rights typically remained restricted to older commoners who had served in the lesser posts of village government.[50]

Factions in some villages persisted for years and became well defined and developed. Perhaps the worst such case for which extensive documentation is available is that of Ajuchitlán, a village in the Tierra Caliente. One of the most important issues there seems to have been a struggle between the parish priest, the local civil officials, and the village groups they allied themselves with over the control of wealthy cofradías. The conflict went on from 1787 until at least 1793 with election disputes every year. At one point, a group of Indians became so upset that they rioted, imprisoned the teniente, and sent him to Mexico City for trial, all with the tacit if not the explicit approval of the parish priest.[51] During this period, various royal officials involved in the conflict described the village as divided into "parties," into "two bands, one known as the rabid ones and the other as the peaceful ones," or into the "gentles" and "rebels."[52] This dispute dragged on for so long precisely because both village factions were able to find support among opposing colonial officials—or perhaps because opposing officials were able to find support among factions in the village.

Bourbon Fiscal Policies and Peasant Resources

The structures discussed above informed peasant political action in the years immediately following 1808. However, they do not explain why an unusually large number of peasants spread over wide areas of Guerrero felt the need to take some kind of action. To understand that, we need to look at the different kinds of socioeconomic stress felt by different subgroups of Guerrero's peasantry in the late eighteenth and early nineteenth centuries. Some kinds of pressure were the direct result of state policies, whereas others resulted from demographic growth and economic change. However, as we'll see, all of these problems were experienced as the actions of particular colonial officials and other individuals, and all could be construed as violations of natural law or the king's justice.

Several Bourbon policies had a strong impact on different parts of the area's peasantry in the eighteenth century.[53] Bourbons tried to rationalize and increase tribute revenues, in many cases extending tribute obligations to previously exempt or overlooked groups. The colonial state also sought to increase revenues by forcing the deposit in royal coffers of funds from village community chests, either as loans or as "voluntary" donations to the Crown. As part of this effort royal officials sought to reclassify as communal funds or wealth many cofradías, which were considered unofficial because they lacked episcopal authorization. Significantly, many cofradías had already inspired bitter battles between village authorities and parish priests.

One group obligated to pay tribute that was definitely unenthusiastic about the idea was the mulatto sharecroppers of the Pacific coast. They resisted in the courts, citing their extreme poverty and unremunerated service to the Crown in militia companies. Sharecroppers also resisted through less civil means, avoiding tax collectors and even refusing outright to pay. Evasion was facilitated by the fact that mulattos were not organized into self-governing repúblicas with collective rights and responsibilities. In many places their ancestors or they themselves had moved to the coast because royal officials interested in profiting from cotton production through the repartimento granted de facto tribute exemptions through the simple expedient of not maintaining accurate tribute rolls.[54]

Recently, Carlos Marichal has noted that one way the Crown sought to meet the revenue demands of international conflicts in the late eighteenth and early nineteenth centuries was to seek voluntary donations and loans from its subjects, including Mexican peasants. This policy significantly increased the fiscal pressure on peasants, and it is unclear how "voluntary" such donations were when the requests were backed by the political authority of local colonial officials and the moral authority of the church. There is no evidence, however, that peasants resented these donations, possibly because begrudging the Crown aid would have been inconsistent with the central tenets of peasant ideology, in which peasants constantly portrayed themselves as good vassals of the Crown willing to step in and protect the Crown's justice against abuses.[55]

These donations were often taken from bienes de comunidad, the resources communities held collectively to cover routine expenses such as religious services, schoolmasters, and upkeep on village public works. Villages often paid their legal expenses from this fund. Bienes de comunidad also served as a reserve for tribute payment or even subsistence aid during years of poor harvests. Colonial law provided for the support of these funds through an annual payment of 1.5 *reales* by each tributary. The existence of such a fund was strong evidence that the settlement involved was a full-blown república de indios with a collective political life. In fact, Indians who no longer lived in such communities resisted paying the tax on the grounds that they lacked collective lands, another essential element in defining a village.[56]

There was little practical difference between resources held as cofradías and as bienes de comunidad. Cofradías were set up to organize and pay for particular religious rites and festivities, though their wealth was also sometimes used to feed villagers in times of hardship. Legally, cofradías were held under a charter granted by the church, but many cofradías in peasant villages never satisfied this formal requirement, either to prevent the interference of the parish priest or to avoid the cost involved. These organizations often owned land but more often in Guerrero their wealth consisted of cattle or cash. The latter was invested in Indian-organized trading ventures or lent out at interest to vecinos. Cofradías were particularly important in Tlapa and Tierra Caliente. In the Tlapa area they were the most important source of capital in regional trade, and in the Tierra Caliente they were perhaps the most important economic institution. In Tlapa, although cofradía cattle existed, most cofradías invested the bulk of their wealth in trading trips. In contrast, in the Tierra Caliente cofradías often lent their cash resources to merchants and kept the bulk of their wealth in cattle, the most productive investment in such an arid area.[57]

In the late colonial period, the Crown increasingly sought to exert control over these resources by redefining them as bienes de comunidad and requiring their wealth be deposited in the local royal treasuries, from which it could be dispensed as needed for legitimate expenses.[58] Because official approval was needed for such disbursements, the Crown could actually utilize the money as it saw fit. This drive for control brought with it a need for supervision, and royal officials collected detailed information on the funds communities held and the expenses they paid. Such surveillance was resented, and the general increase in pressure on village resources was one source of the discontent that later exploded.[59]

Cofradías were one of the most important targets for nonvillagers who wanted to tap Indians' economic potential, especially in areas like Tierra Caliente where there were few opportunities for Indians. Cofradía disputes often became extremely complicated and are not often reducible to the relatively simple model often found in the literature on peasants, a model in which Indians defended communal resources from powerful outsiders bent on expropriating them. Generally, however, villagers strove to minimize the intervention of outsiders because they felt that community resources were the product of their own labor and thus only they had the right to control their use. Indians stressed the origin of cofradía wealth and their success in managing it to ensure the payment of the expenses for which it was created,[60] and they expressed skepticism at the claim that priests were able or even willing to manage it as well.[61] Indians sometimes pointed out the importance of cofradías in maintaining community cohesiveness. In 1795 the villagers of San Miguel Totolapán argued that giving Spaniards control over their cofradía funds would end "the general tie of charity that has united us so closely that we think only of helping one another in all our afflictions."[62] Villagers resented the idea that the priests had the right to review and approve the yearly accounts and to charge for this service, and they were irritated by civil officials or priests who arbitrarily lent themselves or their friends funds at no interest. Peasants continually sought royal orders removing both civil officials and priests from the administration of cofradías.[63]

Demographic Change and Economic Fluctuations

Other changes that increased the problems of Guerrero's peasantry were not the result of conscious government policy. The first was population growth and the subsequent scarcity of resources, particularly land. In areas where communities dominated landholding, acrimonious conflicts between individual communities became more frequent. Where communities had rented out their holdings to *gente de razón*, population growth led communities to try to evict their tenants. In the few areas where communities competed with private landholdings population growth also led to increased tension. A second trend over time seemed perhaps even more arbitrary. In coastal Guerrero, where most peasants were mulatto sharecroppers of cotton, international politics in the late eighteenth and early nineteenth centuries led to wild swings in the prices they received for their production. Nevertheless, in many ways the unfavorable impact of both population growth and the volatile cotton economy were experienced as the result of actions of particular colonial officials, the "bad government," as peasants called it.

Some of the most severe conflicts involving peasants in colonial Guerrero arose over land that villages rented to outsiders. Many villages rented some parcels out to pay for communal expenses. In theory village governments made the decisions to rent out land, but in practice their control was limited by regulations that required the subdelegado's approval of rental contracts. Colonial regulators also sought to avoid favoritism by having rental contracts auctioned off to the highest bidder. In late-eighteenth-century Tierra Caliente, where a whole class of *vecinos de razón* lived in Indian villages and raised cattle on lands rented from the villages, conflicts arose as the Indian population grew and villages decided they needed to plant the lands they had previously rented out for income. Note that this phenomenon is the opposite of the most common dynamic in the literature on peasant movements, in which the value of land rises and landlords (presumably more wealthy than their tenants) try to push peasant tenants off lands needed for their social survival. By contrast, in the Tierra Caliente, the increased value of the land to its peasant owners led them to try to evict nonpeasant tenants who had no other means of remaining in the district, and who of course used all available means to remain on the land. Their greatest ally was the subdelegado, who had the power to delay the implementation of village decisions even when villagers went over his head to higher authorities.[64]

Two other aspects of these conflicts stand out. First, elite tenants tended to stop paying rent on the lands as time went on. Nonpayment of rent set the stage for a gradual transition from tenancy to de facto ownership. Rent arrears were more likely in cases where the royal officials had set up the contract and rent was paid into accounts under their control because the Indians themselves neither expected nor received the money. Second, because the tenants often lived in the village and sometimes were important employers, often these rental land disputes were intertwined with factional disputes in the village. A good way to obtain and preserve access to Indian land was an alliance with the subdelegado; a better way was an alliance with both the subdelegado and a significant faction in the village. Factional fights in villages seem to have had both generational and class dimensions: older and richer peasants, important in village politics, could promote their own interests by helping vecinos retain control of rental lands. Wealthier peasants could assure themselves of a labor supply by reducing poor peasants' access to land.[65]

One rental dispute in San Miguel Totolapán suggests the dimensions of village relations. The case is unusually well-documented because of the persistence of the Indians in pursuing the matter in Mexico City after they had been rebuffed at the local level. The dispute is also relatively simple to understand because, in contrast to those involving village factionalism, it features a village that stood in unified opposition against the power of a local vecino who was backed by the subdelegado.

Andres Ontañon began renting a pasture from the village of San Miguel Totolapán in 1792. Ontañon was a typical vecino of the Tierra Caliente, raising cattle, engaging in some commerce, and occasionally landing some minor or temporary government work, such as a brief stint as an interpreter in 1787 or a longer one in the more powerful position of Teniente de la Acordada (an officer charged with enforcing laws in the interstices between royal jurisdictions) in the late 1790s and early 1800s. These positions were useful not so much for income as for the possibilities they offered for gaining access to Indian resources. The trial for which he interpreted was a complicated dispute between Indian factions in the village of Ajuchitlán over the administration of cofradía wealth, and while serving as Teniente de la Acordada Ontañon was accused of using his office to try to intimidate Indians in a dispute with another vecino.[66]

In 1808 the Indians of San Miguel Totolapán tried to recover the land Ontañon rented from them. The villagers decided that they needed to plant the land because it was among their most fertile, and they were also concerned because Ontañon's cattle had strayed into their fields and damaged their crops. They wanted him to fence the animals in farther from the village. Ontañon and his son José Gregorio insisted that the Indians did not really need the land, and the subdelegado, Tomás Arnaldo, supported the Ontañons in this claim. Later, apparently when they realized that their chance of winning on that basis was slim, the Ontañons offered to let the Indians plant and graze cattle on the parcel so long as the Ontañons were allowed to continue renting it.[67]

Arnaldo was himself an interesting character. Subdelegado since

1805, he seems to have originated in the area. His *fiadores* (those who put up bonds to ensure his proper handling of tribute and the other revenues subdelegados collected) were all local cattlemen. Arnaldo had a history of delaying delivery of the bienes de comunidad and other royal accounts to the royal treasury. He also was involved in disputes over cofradías. Arnaldo continually insisted in his reports that the Indians in his jurisdiction had large amounts of land they did not need.[68] In this case, for the next two years Arnaldo refused to carry out a number of court decrees ordering him to turn over to the village the land rented by Ontañon.

The conflict escalated. As it turned out, Arnaldo had awarded the latest lease for the land to Ontañon in 1806 without the knowledge or consent of the village. Predictably, Arnaldo tried to derail the Indians' bid to regain the land by splitting the village. He sent his teniente to try to convince various villagers not to contribute money for the legal expenses of the case, and even imprisoned those who paid no heed. The Indians responded to his interference by seeking the help of their pastor, Br. Juan Ortiz.[69]

In March 1809 Arnaldo, struggling to argue his case for not implementing repeated superior orders, accused the Indians of the village of rebellion against both civil officials and priests. When the Indians put up a fence to keep Ontañon's cattle out of the field, Arnaldo again accused them of rebellion. In July 1809 Arnaldo still had not carried out the decrees. Instead he increased pressure on the village by demanding that the current governor turn over four Indians active in pursuing the matter, claiming they were "rebel ringleaders." Arnaldo stated that if they were turned over the governor would benefit but if they were not Arnaldo would raise 300 men and punish the village. Arnaldo was already holding a past governor on trumped-up charges. The Indians' Mexico City lawyer responded by comparing Arnaldo to Napoleon, "the tyrant of Europe."[70]

In September 1809 Arnaldo's deputy, Miguel Antonio de Quesada, accused the villagers of planning a riot to protest Quesada's destruction earlier in the month of the fence the Indians had put up to keep Ontañon's cattle out of their land. He claimed the Indians held "their meetings and clandestine town assemblies outside the village" to escape supervision. Quesada refused to go to the village to oversee elections for the next *gobernador*. Quesada's witnesses were all vecinos de razón who lived in the village. Most of their testimony detailed tensions in the village between villagers and vecinos, concentrating on the disrespect of the former toward the latter. One witness reported that in the clandestine meetings the Indians "were reading some papers which according to what he heard were a court order and they awaited only their lawyer in order to present it."[71] In other words the villagers were planning to present local colonial officials with an order from the officials' judicial superiors in Mexico City. For this, the Indians were accused of sedition.

In October 1809 Arnaldo received another order to turn the land over. He responded that the Indians did not really need the land and he would instead rent it out at public auction. He appointed three friends to assess how much time Ontañon should be allowed to move his cattle. The consensus was three months. Next, Arnaldo called a series of witnesses to determine if the Indians really needed the land or not. All, of course, said no. This entire proceeding went on over the repeated objections of the legal representative of the Indians.[72]

When viceregal officials sent Arnaldo new orders to turn over the land and release the gobernador he was holding in prison, Arnaldo responded by escalating once again. The letter he sent reveals both the crux of the conflict and the ways different parties construed it. In this November 3, 1809, letter, Arnaldo claimed that if the Indians succeeded in getting rid of Ontañon they would do the same with "all their tenants de razón, whom they stupidly hate," and furthermore the other villages in the area would do the same. The result would be the ruin of many families of various castes who contributed a great deal to royal revenues. He claimed that this village had always been rebellious in the matter of elections, refusing to follow advice and instead insisting on the election of whomever was "more inclined to encourage their ideas." The year before, they had refused each of four candidates Arnaldo proposed to them and he ended up refusing to go to the village to approve their election. Note that legally it was not the subdelegado's role to propose candidates to villages. Arnaldo claimed that the villagers were planning a riot and that on the day of their titular feast they had flogged two married women de razón. Finally Arnaldo stated that Miguel Felipe, the past year's governor whom he had been ordered to release, was a prisoner of state because after Felipe had returned from his last visit to Mexico City (where he was pursuing the Ontañon case) he had declared publicly that "The Cacique of Tlaxcala had told him that soon they would obey neither subdelegado nor priest nor Viceroy, but instead only him, and that Miguel Felipe himself would not have to wear a hat, but instead a crown."[73] This was an extremely serious charge. In 1801 northern New Spain had experienced an Indian revolt scare over rumors of a millenarian belief in a King of Tlaxcala.[74] In this case, it seems most likely that Arnaldo concocted the story to justify his illegal repression of the Indians of San Miguel.

Unfortunately, the documents provide no further references to this planned seditious activity. Arnaldo claimed that Felipe's trial was delayed by the death of the presiding judge, the teniente of Ajuchitlán.[75] The dispute with Ontañon continued into the next year. The last reference available is another court order to turn the land over to the villagers dated July 20, 1810. Later that same year, the tensions over the use of Indian rental lands and cofradías by outsiders exploded as villagers joined José María Morelos in defense of the captive king against "the bad government."[76]

Of course, rentals of village lands by outsiders did not account for all land disputes in colonial Guerrero. There were other disputes that more closely fit the pattern of village versus private landholding so prominent in the vast literature on Mexico's peasantry. Such disputes became more common in the eighteenth century; still, they constituted considerably less than one-third of the land disputes brought to the courts in Mexico City, which were dominated by disputes between villages.[77] In both types of cases villagers almost always claimed a dire lack of land to plant. Stating that the village needed a favorable decision in order to keep up tribute payments was a strong argument because the same royal officials who presided over suits were responsible for ensuring a flow of revenue to the Crown.[78] Even in disputes with nonpeasants the villagers' opponents were not always the wealthy and powerful haciendas so often the villains in the literature. Often opponents included relatively modest mulatto, mestizo, and Creole smallholders. However, clashes between villages and haciendas were often extremely violent. Villagers were willing to spend large sums on legal actions over land, and land disputes could drag on for many years. Perhaps more important, land disputes were also subject to the collusion between local colonial officials and the opponents of villagers that so embittered peasants.[79]

Local colonial officials were also prominent in the connections between peasants and the volatile economy. Repartimiento was the general term used to designate a system in which merchants and/or local colonial officials advanced credit to small producers in exchange for the right to buy their products. Credit was advanced in the form of money, consumer goods like textiles, capital goods like mules and plows, or raw materials like cotton or petates.[80] The products collected in this way in Guerrero included cotton, cotton thread, textiles, baskets, gourds, and maize.[81] Merchants frequently established formal and informal ties to local colonial officials because the legal mechanisms for enforcing debt payments were too expensive for the effective recovery of small sums. Merchants secured the cooperation of these officials by loaning them money or establishing partnerships with them. The system linked particular officials with particular merchants, and as a result local administrators "enforced trade monopolies on behalf of merchant backers (*habilitadores*) in the districts entrusted to them."[82] Competing merchants were excluded by the selective enforcement of tax laws and other forms of harassment.[83] In microeconomic terms, these officials and their merchant backers enjoyed monopolies in the credit market, driving up interest rates, and monopsonies in the product market, driving down the prices received by producers. They could set prices within limits imposed only by the potential for political action by their charges, either complaints to higher authorities or riots and other demonstrations. Although this involvement of local officials in economic life was formally prohibited with the Bourbon reforms, it did not cease by any means.[84]

The importance of repartimiento or avío to the economy of the area has already been emphasized. This phenomenon was also important in shaping ideas about the state and the economy, essentially precluding any separation of the two. Ideas about economic life and particularly the way local production and consumption were tied into the larger economic systems of New Spain and the world were inseparably linked to the way local colonial officials used state authority at the local level. Neither the state nor the market was the impersonal force or structure so often seen in theoretical works. Both acted together through particular individuals.[85]

The local operation of this repartimiento system presents a difficult problem for the researcher. After its official abolition in 1787, the repartimiento generally cropped up in complex disputes, usually about village elections or commercial contracts. Often merchants duplicated the system without the intervention of officials, which of course allowed more competition and thus better prices for local consumers and producers.[86] Many officials continued to participate in commerce to make ends meet but could no longer openly exclude other merchants from their areas. Some officials even used the Bourbon drive for more state activity promoting economic development to set up schemes that resembled previously existing repartimiento patterns.[87]

The disputes involving the repartimiento for both Indian and non-Indian peasants in Guerrero did not involve complaints about officials or merchants forcing unwanted goods on peasants. Instead they fell into two basic categories: complaints about prices, in which officials or merchants were accused of setting high prices on the goods they advanced to peasants and low prices on the products they received in return;[88] and complaints about excesses in collecting goods or money from peasants to pay debts. The debtors resented the confiscation of the items they had originally been advanced.[89]

Because the repartimiento relied heavily on the cooperation of village officials who distributed goods and collected debts,[90] it provided a motive for royal authorities to interfere in the selection of village officials, and this motive was actually strengthened after the repartimiento was declared illegal. Although officials could still legally force village officials to collaborate in tribute collection, they could no longer do so for the distribution of repartimiento credit or the collection of the ensuing debt, and Indian officials were not required to aid in the repartimiento. Thus, because royal officials could only enforce the repartimiento through willing allies, they had a direct interest in the outcome of village disputes.[91] This incentive led to articulation of the themes of debt, royal authority, and village autonomy in popular discourse.

Modern individuals have been socialized to believe that the prices paid for what they offer and the prices they pay for what they buy are both determined by "supply and demand," and not by the will of those with whom they do business. This was much less true in Guerrero 200 years ago.[92] Furthermore, the prevalence of the repartimiento made it much less likely that sudden changes in prices would be perceived as anonymous acts beyond the control of human agency. Even when the repartimiento did not involve the direct coercion of civil authorities it served to further personalize economic transactions.[93] It also allowed merchants much more leeway in setting prices, even if the range within which they could do so was ultimately determined by market conditions. Thus peasants tied into the system were not hopelessly naïve when they attributed unfavorable prices to the perfidy of merchants.

The cotton-growing coast was one of the areas in which the repartimiento was most prevalent. There the mulatto sharecroppers could become rich in good years and very poor in bad years. In good years they bought the most luxurious products available in New Spain, like Far Eastern silks and Pueblan pottery. In bad years they were often unable to buy goods made from the cotton they grew. Some fluctuations were caused by weather, but most resulted from market changes determined by Spain's alliances in international wars. Merchants were even more likely to be blamed under these circumstances.[94]

The disputes discussed above illuminate the structure of politics in colonial Guerrero. The region's inhabitants shared a set of values and assumptions about the state, justice, and the roles of various individuals and groups. These assumptions and the rhetoric through which they were expressed constituted a political idiom in which various groups could communicate with one another. Conflicts continually arose, however, over how these ideas were to be applied in specific instances. To the extent that there was a moral economy in the peasant world of late colonial Guerrero, it represented an ideal state of relations between colonial officials, other social groups, and peasant villages rather than a state of affairs that had ever existed in fact.[95]

The peasants of Guerrero experienced such abstractions as class, the state, and the market through the concrete actions of specific individuals. These analytical constructs were lived in specific places and times, in the merchant who bought peasants' products and advanced them credit, in the priest who preached on Sunday and perhaps manipulated community resources for his personal benefit, in the landowner whose cattle destroyed peasants' crops, in the rancher who lived on lands he rented from the village, and most especially in the local magistrate who collected the Crown's tribute and presided over disputes.[96]

Legal and violent means of settling disputes were often linked. Peasants evaded unpopular measures, rioted, and pressed claims in court. Sometimes they pursued two or more of these strategies to achieve the same end;[97] all constituted attempts to bring violations of tradition, the moral order, or natural law (fundamentally equivalent to peasants) to the attention of the king. None threatened the colonial order. Both lawsuits and the eighteenth-century village riots analyzed by William Taylor had to be justified in terms of violations of this order; the dominant political culture allowed no other option. Nevertheless, although justice was by definition granted by the Crown, villagers had largely converted into rights the privileges they held as the Crown's vassals.[98] This conversion would have enduring consequences.

Contrary to what the literature on the Mexican peasantry suggests, in Guerrero conflict between peasants and others was more common and more bitter in areas where peasant communities were strong and held most land and other resources. In these areas, economic opportunities for nonpeasants could only be obtained by tapping peasant resources such as lands rented to outsiders, cofradías, repartimiento, and bienes de comunidad. Here economic disputes were even more likely to become ideologically linked to the state, or rather the use of its power by its local representatives. Local colonial officials were more likely to be parties to disputes over the control of peasant resources than they were in those over ownership. Also, the fiscal demands of Spain's involvement in European conflicts led the Crown to use the paternalist foundations of its relations with Indians and the supervision of its officials over peasant resources to appropriate peasant wealth to meet fiscal exigencies.

The possibility of a qualitative difference between violent and nonviolent collective action was not realized until 1808. In the absence of the Crown, villages considered themselves entitled to riot against bad government. This fact suggests a basic and important difference between a riot and a court suit, though both can be considered reformist and neither is overtly revolutionary. In riots, peasants claimed the right to speak for the king and prosecute local colonial officials in the name of higher authority.[99] The implication is that not all who claimed to speak for the Crown were to be believed, and in fact the Crown could act through a village against local colonial officials who violated its justice. This belief set a crucial precedent for the movement for independence.

Tensions in Guerrero's countryside increased in the late eighteenth and early nineteenth centuries for a variety of reasons. Some were innovations in state policies designed to increase revenue; others put peasants at odds with private interests. Demographic growth increased conflict over land, and violent swings in the cotton economy led to periodic misery for some peasants. Significantly, however, even "private" economic conflicts were eventually blamed on local state officials who were seen as refusing to uphold the king's benevolent will and natural law. In many cases local officials had reasons to support private agriculturalists or merchants against peasants and did so even to the point of ignoring orders and policies handed down from Mexico City, such as the abolition of the repartimiento or the repeated refusal to remove renters from Indian lands. The combination of a political culture that encouraged peasants to oppose local colonial officials in the name of the king and a colonial system that practically required local colonial officials to support themselves through unofficial collaboration with wealthy private interests was potentially deadly.

The potential for widespread protest was held in check until 1808 by three factors. The first was the absence of any significant split in Mexico's dominant class or the social stratum directly below it. The second was the localized nature of most subaltern identities in rural Mexico, which were concentrated on membership in particular villages rather than ethnic, class, or even linguistic groups. The third was the availability of the king to make rulings on conflicts both within the elite and involving peasants. Napoleon inadvertently changed all of this in 1808 by removing the king from the scene. In doing so, he precipitated a major split in Mexico's elite that encouraged a portion of the elite to attempt to mobilize subaltern groups in Mexico to support their aims. Napoleon's actions also gave those groups a symbol to unite around, the symbol of the captive king. After all, the only two things peasants from different villages and areas had in common were Catholicism and allegiance to the king as the symbol of justice.

CHAPTER 2

The War of Independence in Guerrero, 1808-1821

We should take precautions so that the usurper does not catch us unready and unarmed. . . . The *patria* is based upon patriotism; only this support is firm, and patriotism consists in the virtue of each, and in the union of all . . . the present generation will decide the fate of future generations.

—The Cathedral Chapter of Michoacán, Valladolid,
   April 5, 1810

Except for the European Spanish, all other inhabitants will not be called Indians, mulattos, or other castes, but instead all Americans. No one will pay tribute, nor will there be slavery in the future. . . . There will be no community treasuries and the Indians will receive the rent from their lands as their own.

—José María Morelos, Aguacatillo, November 17, 1810

It is necessary that your graces, who are the most loyal to your Nation, defenders of the Sacred Religion and most loving of your *Patria* . . . gather all your fathers and sons and come with me, leaving as many people as are necessary to protect the village.

—José Eduardo de las Cabadas, San Marcos, January 17, 1811

The area that later became the state of Guerrero was a major arena of social and political conflict during Mexico's 1808–21 independence war. Beginning in 1808, the social and political landscape changed fundamentally. Before 1808 the primary forum for social and political disagreements was the colonial court system; after 1808 it became rebellion and the threat of rebellion. Before 1808 political action and peasant resistance were atomized in lawsuits and riots that rarely extended beyond a single village; after 1808 political actions in which peasants from more than one village cooperated became common. Moreover, many of these rebellions were joined or even led by people from other social classes. Through the nineteenth century and beyond, these movements have been the primary means through which groups of peasants have influenced the shape of the Mexican state and its relations with Mexican society. Thus the year

1808 is a watershed in the history of the Mexican state and the Mexican peasantry.

Post-1808 social movements were characterized by the involvement of more than one village and by the formation of alliances between groups of villages and "outsiders."[1] These phenomena required not only some congruence in material interests, however short-term, but also some ideology or programmatic content capable of uniting diverse parties who had never before acted in concert. These two elements are essential to the forms of political conflict and alliance that have prevailed in Mexico since 1808. Neither existed in central Mexico before 1808: both were common thereafter. In this way, too, 1808 represents a turning point.

The keys to understanding these changes are found in the movement for independence, its program, and popular consciousness. Not surprisingly, the insurgency in different regions of New Spain has drawn a great deal of interest from scholars. In Guerrero, New Spain's political crisis of 1808–10 provoked violent and unexpected responses that, although rooted in diverse social tensions, were focused by the political leadership that led the insurgent alliance in the area. The program and discourse that articulated the movement effectively appealed to distinct social groups while constructing a vision of a new Mexican society that was to address the concerns of all and harmonize their interests. This vision changed significantly during the fluid political conflicts that characterized Mexico and Spain in the second decade of the nineteenth century. The rebels effectively governed the Guerrero area for several years, and their organization provides more insight into insurgent goals and how the insurgent state in practice differed from the colonial order it sought to replace. Although the movement suffered severe setbacks in the middle of the decade, it survived through guerrilla warfare and won a place in the 1821 alliance that led to Mexican independence.

Popular Violence and Mexican Independence

In recent years, several scholars have analyzed popular participation in the movement for independence in New Spain. Most depict a sharp division between the elite's political motivations for rebellion and the social motivations that they attribute to New Spain's peasantry. These scholars postulate parallel and disarticulated movements at different levels; indeed, at first blush the activities and motivations of elites and peasants seem to have little in common apart from their timing. These scholars thus devote little attention to the programmatic statements of what they consider to be the elite movement, and they explain the lack of such statements attributable to the parallel popular movements by stressing the expression of popular discontents and grievances through unfocused acts of violence and occasional traces of millenarianism.[2]

This study will take the opposite tack by examining the concrete motivations of both local elites and the rural poor and showing how the program elaborated by the movement's leaders articulated both sets of concerns. Certainly there were tensions within the movement, and not all peasant concerns were consciously championed by elite leaders. I will argue, however, that peasants and local elites shared concrete interests as well as basic notions of politics, justice, and legitimacy from which a common program could be fashioned. The positions of elite and peasant rebels varied greatly over time and across regions; nonetheless, the idea that local elites joined the movement because they agreed with its program and peasants did so only to revenge past wrongs and restore a traditional equilibrium does not adequately describe events in Guerrero.

Interpretations of the movement for independence have cited two sets of factors that are not necessarily mutually exclusive. The first consists of the negative effects of the various Bourbon reforms on both peasants and elites, which include increased economic demands and attacks on the power and autonomy of various corporate groups in New Spain, among them peasant villages. Economic demands increased with changes aimed at more effective tax collection, the drive to secure "voluntary" donations and loans for the Crown, and the famous Consolidación de Vales Reales. Politically, the reforms reduced the autonomy of peasant groups in some areas of New Spain as well as the access to offices previously enjoyed by elite Creoles. The reforms also reduced clerical privileges, particularly in legal matters; William Taylor and Serge Gruzinski have detected a general drive to secularize peasants and reduce the role of the clergy in peasant life, desacralizing politics.[3]

The second cause often cited is agrarian change driven by economic development and population growth. This factor has been convincingly demonstrated for such important areas as the Bajío, Morelos, and the Guadalajara region, where Mexico's dominant class invested heavily in haciendas. They constructed irrigation works and granaries that allowed them to reap enormous profits in years of harvest failure and to hold their grain production off the market until prices rose late in the annual agricultural cycle even in good years. In the Bajío hacienda tenants were driven to more marginal, unirrigated lands, whereas in the Guadalajara region Indian villagers were forced out of the market as grain producers and back into it as workers. In Morelos competition over resources increased with rural population growth and the opportunity presented by the growing demand for agricultural products in Mexico City. Morelos provided some support for the insurgents, and the Bajío and Guadalajara regions contributed large contingents to the Hidalgo revolt.[4]

In Guerrero several features of the Bourbon reforms contributed to the rebellion. José María Morelos and other rural priests resented Bourbon attempts to limit church autonomy. Bourbon moves to tap cofradía resources and cajas de comunidad, increase tribute collection, and secure funds through voluntary loans and donations also contributed to the revolt. Nevertheless, the Bourbon reforms were implemented throughout Spanish America over a 50-year period, and although many contributed to increasing tensions it is difficult to sustain an argument citing them as a direct cause of the 1810 explosion.

There is no evidence to suggest that Guerrero experienced the severe agrarian changes that took place in the Bajío, Morelos, and Guadalajara regions in the late eighteenth and early nineteenth centuries. Population pressure was a factor in some parts of Guerrero but its effect was uneven: it contributed to tensions in the Tierra Caliente, where repúblicas sought to evict ranchero tenants and bring their lands into production for their own expanding populations, but it does not seem to have been important on the Costa Grande or in the Tlapa region, the other two areas of insurgent strength in Guerrero.

The response of village Indians to the independence movement has been of particular interest to historians. This type of peasantry has dominated the historical literature on rural Mexico since the 1930s. The assumption that villagers were traditional in orientation leads Brian Hamnett to suggest that they were in general indifferent to the 1810 movement, which he believes sought to abolish corporate privileges. John Tutino hypothesizes that in crucial areas of the central plateau villages were part of a stable symbiotic order in which they combined the use of their own resources with employment opportunities on nearby estates. Villages in these areas thus did not support the independence movement. William Taylor and Eric Van Young have noted that at least some communities in Jalisco supported the insurgents. Van Young suggests that although communities became increasingly split in the late colonial period tensions within them may have been displaced toward outsiders, leading to unified community action in moments of stress. In contrast, Rodolfo Pastor notes that communities in the Mixteca did not react unanimously. There wealthier Indians were insurgent but poorer ones and more traditional nobles were either apathetic or openly royalist.[5]

Some historians have suggested that communities participated in the movement in order to regain community lands lost to outsiders or to gain new lands.[6] Others are skeptical of this interpretation, noting the dubious origins of the only programmatic statement found to date referring to the redistribution of land.[7] Van Young has argued that the desire of communities to regain lost lands or expand their holdings was deflected through intervening variables; his hypothesis would still rank land hunger as a major motivation of the participants while accounting for the fact that no programmatic statements about land have come to light.[8] Christon Archer suggests that a great deal of unofficial agrarian reform took place during the fighting, as peasants and rancheros farmed hacienda lands in the absence of their owners.[9]

But the debate over the "agrarian nature" of peasant participation, with its implicit assumption that land must be the primary issue in peasant political action, may be misdirected. In this regard, the quintessential model is based on the events of Zapatista Morelos in 1910–20. This chapter, and those that follow, will show how other issues could also drive peasant collective action. This shift in emphasis should not be surprising, as Taylor has noted that land was not an issue in the majority of the village riots he studied for the colonial period.[10] In Guerrero, the areas where peasant support for the movement was strongest and most tenacious were not places in which haciendas had expanded at the expense of communities or even controlled a significant amount of land. The salience of issues other than land is important because many problems that concerned peasants also concerned at least some nonvillagers. Even when they did not share peasant concerns, local elites often acquiesced to changes desired by villagers.

The Outbreak of the Insurgency in Guerrero

In 1808 French troops crossed the frontier into Spain and both Fernando VII and Carlos IV resigned their rights to the Spanish throne, precipitating an uprising against the French in Spain. In New Spain these events resulted in a crisis of legitimacy. Whose authority should be recognized? Neither the new French government of Spain nor those who organized resistance to it had a clear claim. In Mexico

City urban Creoles attempted to persuade the viceroy to set up a junta to rule the viceroyalty in the name of the captive king until the situation was resolved.[11]

A group of peninsular merchants led by Gabriel de Yermo deposed the viceroy and imprisoned many of the Creole leaders involved in the autonomy attempt. Yermo's coup was conservative, designed to maintain the status quo, yet it was a direct antecedent to the Hidalgo revolt and did more than anything else to hasten the coming social explosion. In the highly charged atmosphere of 1808 the coup only exacerbated the confusion and tensions, shattering the constitutional continuity already shaken by events in Spain. In particular it replaced the reigning representative of the king in Mexico. To paraphrase Luís Villoro, the government of New Spain left the sphere of what "was" and entered that of what was "made": government had become the result of concrete and quite unsacred human will.[12] This event allowed future conspirators to view their efforts as plans to restore constitutional order.[13]

The events in Mexico City and Spain had ramifications throughout the viceroyalty. The terms of the debate were grafted onto many older disputes.[14] In Guerrero, various repúblicas de indios met to send expressions of loyalty to the king. Anti-French sentiment grew: in Tixtla that August local officials embargoed the goods of a Frenchman without superior orders. But the French were not the only targets of unauthorized actions. In Acapulco, a minor colonial official named Mariano Tabares organized an unsuccessful conspiracy that foreshadowed events to come. The conspiracy, which involved mulatto garrison soldiers and sharecroppers in the nearby district, sought "to crown a new king in America since there no longer was any in Spain and to kill the *europeos* because they were tyrants."[15] Tabares fled after he suspected that the plot had been discovered.

Responses to this crisis varied greatly, even within single villages.[16] Although a few areas can be identified as having insurgent or royalist tendencies, the inhabitants of most places oscillated from one side to the other throughout the 1810–20 period in response to opportunities, risks, and the actions of both insurgent and royalist governments.[17] This maneuvering was facilitated by the policies of both royalist and insurgent armies, which continually offered pardons to villages and individuals who wished to switch sides. There are even cases of revolts against the insurgent government when it attempted to impose unpopular measures.[18]

The prevalence of coercion further complicates attempts to explain the positions of various social groups on the basis of their interests and ideologies. Coercion was a factor in every rebellion in Guerrero throughout the early nineteenth century. Both the organizers of movements and authorities seeking to repress them used coercion to enforce loyalty. The literature on social movements often assumes the kind of unanimity that their organizers dream of but rarely encounter.

The first area of Guerrero to be affected by the independence movement was the Costa Grande. José María Morelos, a parish priest from Michoacán, arrived in the area in early November 1810 with only twenty men but by late November had recruited 3,000. This number may seem small in the light of the huge numbers Hidalgo recruited in the Bajío in the same period, but the coast was sparsely populated. By November 19 Acapulco's merchants and garrison were the only nearby groups still opposing the movement; under siege by Morelos, the city was the westernmost point of royalist control in the area. The response of the residents of the Costa Grande to Morelos was overwhelming.[19]

On October 18, 1810, the subdelegado of Tecpan, the largest population center on the Costa Grande, reported to the viceroy that he had seen no signs of disloyalty but considered his position weak because of the extreme poverty of the area's mulatto residents. The subdelegado noted that he had already exempted mulattos and Indians from the tribute because both groups resented its payment. When he reported again on November 8 the situation had changed drastically, for by then he had word of a priest from Michoacán advancing through the area, recruiting from the same villages that only a few days earlier had presented themselves voluntarily to the subdelegado to defend the king. The few Indians who answered the subdelegado's call to arms quickly deserted, leaving him with only the militia company of mulattos, who accompanied him on the first few miles of his retreat to Acapulco but soon asked for permission to leave him and return to their families. They, too, joined the insurgents.[20]

Actually, the wavering of the mulatto militia of Tecpan was rare on the Costa Grande: the other militia units in the area went over to Morelos even more quickly. These units consisted of mulatto sharecroppers who grew cotton commercially, and some officials and landowners also joined, although notably no coastal merchants became insurgents. The wealthier insurgents became leaders, often organizing their own sharecroppers. Several Indian villages also supported the movement.[21]

Although individuals and groups vacillated somewhat during the course of the war, there seems to have been a consistent base of support for the insurgents on the Costa Grande throughout the decade.[22] Even in November 1810 the area was a hotbed of anti-*gachupín* resentment. No group in Guerrero directed more hate at the European Spanish than the mulatto sharecroppers and Indian villagers who grew cotton on the Costa Grande.[23]

After securing the coast Morelos delayed several months before pushing on into the Montaña and other more northern areas. In the meantime the royalist authorities of the Montaña area began to organize for defense. Their most immediate concern was pressure from the northwest, where many villages in the Tierra Caliente and the Taxco region had risen. The nucleus of insurgent activity in the Tierra Caliente and Taxco regions began to spread south and east to the extent that royalist authorities in Chilapa and Tixtla did not feel that they could send reinforcements to Acapulco to help with the defense of that strategic position.[24]

These royalists were less concerned about insurgency closer to home. In the first few months of the war the entire elite of the Montaña remained loyal to the Mexico City government, led by the subdelegado Joaquín de Guevara (also a local landowner), the priest Manuel Mallol, and the powerful merchant and landowning Leyva family. The group also began organizing the Indians of the surrounding villages to aid in counterinsurgency efforts to the immediate north.[25] However, already there were some disturbing signs of what was to come. In early November the village Indians of Chilapa imprisoned ten europeos who had fled the insurgency in nearby Tepecoacuilco, mistaking them for insurgents. This incident suggests that the villagers were somewhat biased as to who they thought their enemies really were. Also, the authorities suspected the loyalty of the villages of Atenango del Río, Xochipala, and others who showed signs that they were "very uppity."[26]

The authorities' biggest worry, however, was the fragility of the local elite's own consensus. Accusations and counteraccusations begin to dominate their correspondence. When Chilpancingo and Zumpango del Río were attacked by the insurgents in December not only the Indians but some of the Creoles and mestizos welcomed them. They later apologized when royalist forces forced a retreat. Furthermore, officials suspected the loyalty of the key elite family of the Chilpancingo area, the Bravos, because they dragged their feet when asked for money and men for the defense effort. Troops were sent to arrest the Bravos but the family fled into the *monte*.[27] This well-connected family eventually went over to Morelos.

The royalist effort to maintain control of the Montaña collapsed in the summer of 1811. In early May the Bravo family left hiding to join the insurgency, and later that month Morelos's forces took the strategic town of Tixtla. Until August an uneasy balance of power persisted in the area: the insurgents held Tixtla but the royalists continued to control Chilapa, less than 25 kilometers away. The stalemate ended in mid-August when the insurgents crushed a royalist force sent to recapture Tixtla, and royalist authority subsequently collapsed in the entire area from Chilpancingo east to Huajuapan in present-day Oaxaca.[28]

Although Morelos clearly received some support in the Chilpancingo area, particularly from the village of Xochipala and the Bravo family, the situation in the Tixtla-Chilapa area was not as clear-cut. No spontaneous rising took place there, even when the insurgents approached. This ambivalence is particularly interesting because Chilapa was the area of Guerrero with the most frequent and acrimonious land disputes between villages and haciendas or ranchos. Even the village of Atenango del Río, which royalist authorities had suspected previously of insurgent sympathies, did not present itself to the insurgents after they had established military control of the area.[29] Farther east in Tlapa, where villages controlled virtually all of the land, the situation was different; there a relatively small force of insurgents quickly recruited large numbers of villagers and insurgent control was quickly organized with few outside forces.[30]

This pattern continued throughout the 1811–20 period. For instance, in 1812 when Morelos took the bulk of his troops to Cuautla a very small royalist force was able to spark a counterrevolution in the Chilapa area. Then and later, support for the insurgents seems to have been lukewarm and fragmented if not lacking entirely.[31] In contrast, in the Tlapa area at the lowest moments of insurgent military strength very small insurgent forces were able to catalyze large guerrilla movements.[32] This pattern implies that land conflict was not the primary motor driving social movements in Guerrero.

Farther north in the area of Tepecoacuilco, Iguala, and Taxco the story was different. A conspiracy that began in 1810 before the Hidalgo revolt linked many arrieros with the Indian gobernadores of Tepecoacuilco, Iguala, Huitzuco, and other towns. The situation was exacerbated by food scarcities and high prices near Taxco. In late 1810 the insurrection was centered in these same places and quickly spread to other villages near Taxco, often under the leadership of elected Indian officials, many of whom soon began ignoring orders sent by the subdelegado of Taxco. They were supported by forces from the Tierra Caliente. Taxco was essentially under guerrilla siege until it was finally captured by the insurgents on December 25, 1811. It was retaken by the royalists in May 1812 but the surrounding villages continued a guerrilla war against the royalists.[33] In this region the insurgency split villages: several villages joined the insurgency through "internal revolutions" in which one peasant faction deposed and exiled another, usually alleging that the exiled group was closely identified with colonial authorities and merchants. Those exiled were sometimes referred to as *agachupinado*.[34]

In the Tierra Caliente, where Indian villages owned most of the land, the insurrection began immediately without outside military support. The composition of the local insurgency was relatively complex: it was led by parish priests, landowners, and village governments, but other landowners and priests opposed it. Furthermore, the allegiances of local elites do not explain those of the rest of the local populace. For example, the owner of the Hacienda del Cubo was royalist, but many of its residents were insurgents, and the royalist pastor of Teloloapan had to be rescued from his parishioners.[35] Generally people in the Tierra Caliente seem to have been inclined to support the insurgents and continued to do so despite repeated royalist counterinsurgency campaigns from 1811 to 1820. Royalist commanders attributed this tendency to the willingness of the inhabitants to question colonial authority even before 1810.[36] Like colonial disputes, peasant support for the insurgency stemmed from tensions over such village resources as rental lands, cofradías, and cajas de comunidad.

The one area of Guerrero whose loyalty to the royalists rivaled that of the Tierra Caliente to the insurgents was the Costa Chica. This fact is puzzling, as the Costa Chica was socially and economically similar to the Costa Grande, which ignited so quickly and thoroughly upon the arrival of Morelos. Until 1813 the Costa Chica royalists held out against the insurgents who controlled the rest of Guerrero without aid from the viceregal government. They provisioned the garrison of Acapulco by sea, allowing the port to withstand the insurgent siege until the Costa Chica was subjugated by Morelos's main army in 1813. Even then the royalist forces on the Costa Chica did not surrender but instead dispersed and fought as guerrillas until the decline of Morelos's fortunes allowed them to reconquer the area. Even when the Plan of Iguala united insurgents and royalists in 1821, the residents of the Costa Chica were reluctant to accept the compromise.[37]

The Costa Chica's population of mulatto sharecroppers lived dispersed along the banks of the rivers used to irrigate their cotton crops. Their fierce loyalty to the royalists can be explained by four factors that stand out in contrast to their counterparts on the Costa Grande. First, they had been organized in militia companies since the late seventeenth century, a factor that seems to have figured prominently in their construction of their identity. Second, as militiamen they had continually and successfully sought exemption from tribute payments and thus had escaped much of the impact of increasing state demands in the Bourbon period.[38] Third, the role of European Spanish merchants in financing cotton production and thus controlling cotton trade seems to have been much smaller there, perhaps because of the success enjoyed by the Indians of the Tlapa area to the north, who employed cofradía capital in the trade.[39] The fourth factor is less abstract: Francisco Paris, who commanded royalist forces in the area and who had been subdelegado since the early 1790s, had continually supported the efforts of the militiamen to obtain exemption from tribute, and although he may have either participated in or allowed some repartimiento or habilitación in the area, he seems to have kept such activity at a level below that found on the Costa Grande, at least judging from the lack of documented complaints. Paris seems to have been one subdelegado who avoided actions that would lead to his characterization as "bad government," and his approach won him immense loyalty from the impoverished mulatto troops he commanded.[40]

Leadership

Brian Hamnett and Christon Archer have noted the importance of networks of insurgent leaders during the War of Independence.[41] Understanding which nonpeasants supported the insurgency and why they did so is necessary to any explanation of this movement. Leaving aside village officials and wealthy villagers, three overlapping groups of nonpeasants provided most of the officers of the insurgent army and its civil administration.

The first and probably largest group of leaders were arrieros, or muleteers. Arrieros were important in the first insurgent conspiracy in the region and remained prominent throughout the insurgency.[42] The most prominent arrieros (and former arrieros) were Morelos himself, who had worked as a muleteer before becoming a priest and even afterward engaged in small-scale trading, and Vicente Guerrero, who came from a family of muleteers centered in Tixtla. Others include Valerio Trujano and Juan del Carmen.[43] In this and other areas of New Spain whole villages and towns specialized in this activity and sometimes participated collectively in the revolt.[44]

Muleteers were a diverse group both ethnically and socially. They included European Spaniards, Creoles, mestizos, mulattos, and Indians; some owned their own mules, from as few as two to as many as hundreds, and others worked for the owners, either controlling a whole train or working in lesser capacities. Muleteers who traded on their own account were the independent entrepreneurs who held together New Spain's economy.[45] They were very useful to the insurrection because of their knowledge of the physical, economic and social geography of large areas and a wide variety of contacts with whom they had developed trust through business arrangements. Some had learned Indian languages through their trading activities.[46] In addition, arrieros were traditionally one of the most important conduits through which news and rumors flowed in rural areas, a factor that gave them an additional edge in recruitment.

Muleteers' support for the insurrection seems to have been rooted in their resentment of the commercial domination of well-financed peninsular merchants centered in Mexico City, though this motivation is difficult to document directly. These merchants had often obtained the cooperation of local royal officials to limit competition. The connection between anti-gachupín sentiment and economic practices will be examined in detail below; for now it should be noted that the same exclusionary practices that kept prices paid to rural producers low also affected muleteers. Colonial officials often harassed muleteers who tried to compete with protected interests.[47]

Many insurgent leaders were parish priests. The most prominent in Guerrero was José María Morelos, but numerous others also served with the insurgent forces or aided in their civil administration.[48] Much of the discourse used to justify and motivate the movement was religious in tone and substance. Two features of clerical participation must be considered. First, why did members of this group rebel? Second, how effective was their participation on either side, especially in recruiting their own parishioners?

Two basic theses have been advanced to explain the participation of priests in the movement. The first is the great disparities in income among the clergy, whose social stratification mirrored the class structure of colonial society. The most well-remunerated and important posts were those of bishoprics and their attendant cathedral chapters; lower on the scale were a few particularly wealthy chaplaincies, and then others that allowed priests to enjoy the relative comfort and security of major cities. Below these were urban parishes and relatively wealthy rural parishes near major cities and markets. The least desirable positions were in isolated, poverty-stricken, and often unhealthy rural areas. The placement of priests was controlled by the bishoprics, cathedral chapters, and ecclesiastical courts—posts held by men of the colonial dominant class.[49]

The life of José María Morelos illustrates the lack of opportunity that could frustrate a poor parish priest. Son of a moderately prosperous mestizo artisan and his Creole wife, he entered the priesthood at a relatively late age after working for some years as an arriero and rancho administrator. Morelos was denied a chaplaincy after a lengthy lawsuit during and after which he worked in two different impoverished parishes in the Michoacán hot country. In the first his mother, whom he supported, became ill and died. The colonial church certainly had not done well by Morelos.[50]

A second motive for clerical unrest in the late colonial period was the drive to reduce the privileges of the clergy as part of the general Bourbon assault on corporations and their rights. Among the measures that most irritated the lower clergy were limitations on clerical immunity, the extension of royal authority over such sources of income as chaplaincies, and the Consolidación de Vales Reales.[51] At his trial, Morelos himself listed Spanish attacks on priests and ecclesiastical wealth as among his motives for revolt.[52]

How effective were priests as recruiters for political causes in 1810–20? Their influence was obviously great, although not as overwhelming as the literature sometimes suggests.[53] Parishioners did not invariably follow the lead of their pastors. Often captured insurgents cited the pernicious influence of their pastors as a defense at their trials, but royal officials did not always accept this defense.[54] Priests who preached for one side or another against the wishes of their parishioners were imprisoned and otherwise persecuted.[55] Perhaps the most important way that priests aided the insurgency was in giving it a vital and effective ideological content.

One of the relatively unusual features of the insurgency in Guerrero was the support it received from two important landowning families. The Bravos owned the large and fertile hacienda of Chichihualco near Chilpancingo. To the insurgency they contributed five brothers, Leonardo, Miguel, Máximo, Victor, and Casimoro, as well as Leonardo's son Nicolás. The Bravos seem to have wavered for several months in 1810–11, refusing to cooperate in organizing royalist forces in their area but also not joining Morelos. Only after this attitude led the royalists to seek their arrest did they join the insurgency. Their reasons are still not clear. In an 1828 description of his political life, Nicolás Bravo admitted that he had everything to lose by revolting but did not specify why he did. One suspects that the decision was taken as a family. Later, after Leonardo was captured, Nicolás and his uncles offered to surrender and also help pacify the area if Leonardo's life was spared. The deal fell through, however, and after Leonardo was killed the family remained important in the insurgency until late in the second decade of the century.[56]

The Galeanas were the other important landowning family that joined the insurgency. Their motivation seems clearer: they were a numerous family that possessed several cotton-producing haciendas on the Costa Grande, and several were also local militia officers.[57] They contributed several leaders to the movement, the most important of whom was Hermengildo. Like the Bravos, the Galeanas were by no means one of the families that made up Mexico's ruling class; their holdings were the largest on the Costa Grande but were dwarfed in value by those of Mexico's first families. The family's culture and educational levels were similar to those of their peasant tenants.[58] The Galeanas' sharecropping of cotton land left them in the same disadvantageous position in the cotton market as their tenants,[59] and it is thus not surprising that just before the revolt Hermengildo Galeana was involved in an acrimonious dispute with two coastal europeos, apparently merchants.[60]

The Galeana and Bravo families led not only their own tenants but also other peasants during the insurgency. Their class position as local landowners did not preclude this mingling with their subordinates; rather, both families seem to have maintained relatively paternalist attitudes toward their tenants and other nearby peasants.[61] Neither family thought that the insurgency posed a threat to their position as landholders. This lack of fear suggests that these families did not consider land hunger the most important issue motivating peasant insurgents.

Ideology and Program of the Movement

The ideology of the insurgency articulated the cross-class alliance evident in the movement, providing a program that seemed to represent the aspirations of such diverse groups as Indian peasants, mulatto sharecroppers, provincial muleteers, hacendados, and priests. The various elements of this program were closely related to the political culture prevalent before 1810. Generally peasants and the provincial elite that led them focused on European-born Spaniards as the root of New Spain's problems. However, the insurgents also expressed more direct demands, and these aspirations changed as events progressed and old formulas were adapted to maintain their relevance.

The social and political explosion that rocked New Spain in 1810–11 was unforeseen and unprecedented, though the fact that New Spain's poor were capable of expressing their discontent by defying authorities was not surprising. Resistance, both through the courts and in village riots, was a common element of New Spain's political life. The shocking features of the early years of the insurgency were two: first, large numbers of poor people over a wide area cooperated in the resistance; second, the poor were joined and in fact led by substantial numbers of wealthier and more respectable folk. Certainly the latter's cooperation with the poor did not necessarily indicate that they shared the same practical and material goals and grievances. Perhaps they were simply successful manipulators of the desperate and vengeful rabble—temporarily, at least. Even in that case, their success requires explanation.

Historians who believe that the peasants who formed the mass of the rebels and the priests, muleteers, and even landowners who led the insurgents had very different goals may very well be correct. However, these different aims were not expressed in radically different ways. Late colonial Mexico did not experience the kind of "remarkable dissociation between the polite and the plebeian culture" that E. P. Thompson detected in England at the same time.[62] New Spain's poor and elite shared a common political culture to a striking degree. They were unified, in fact, by the same basic beliefs that were the only ones shared by the poor across village boundaries, namely, that the king was the ultimate guardian of justice and the Catholic Church the only guarantee of eternal salvation. Within these limits there was enormous room for disagreement, and neither parish priests nor the king's appointees were safe from sometimes violent opposition. However, even that opposition, whether in the courts or the village plaza, stressed loyalty to the king and the church.

In 1810 the shared nature of this political culture was extremely important because it allowed alliances and cooperation across class lines. The influence of the Enlightenment, Bourbon reforms, and even the French Revolution were seeping into the cracks of this edifice, and a breakup was only a few years away. However, those with doubts certainly did not make them public or attempt to recruit mass support by voicing them. Moreover, when New Spain's hegemonic political culture fragmented it did not fracture along class lines, and thus cross-class alliances remained possible.

Eric Van Young has recently remarked on the seeming incongruity of peasants claiming that their loyalty to Fernando VII required that they kill European Spaniards or drive them from New Spain. Revolution against the established order was carried out in the name of the very embodiment of that order.[63] However, this apparent contradiction is quite understandable because one of the most important ideas in the political culture of New Spain's peasantry was that the king's subjects sometimes had to speak and act in his name against the "bad government." The common village riot studied by William Taylor relies on this basic notion that the will of the king's representatives is not always that of the king.[64] The slogan "Long live the King, Death to the Bad Government" was not coined on September 15, 1810.

Furthermore, this feature of peasant political attitudes dovetailed with ideas adopted by a significant portion of New Spain's Creoles in 1808. They argued that God did not confer sovereignty on the king directly. Instead sovereignty first passed through "el Pueblo." This idea had been enunciated by pre-absolutist theologians like Francisco Suarez whose influence was never really eliminated from theological texts during the eighteenth century. The Creoles argued that in the absence of the king the "Pueblo" of New Spain, represented by such bodies as town councils, was required to exercise sovereignty to prevent chaos.[65] In an important step they included Indian village governments among those bodies on which sovereignty fell by inviting the Indian governor of the barrio of San Juan to their 1808 deliberations.[66] First Hidalgo and then Morelos drew on this body of thought to justify their actions.[67] The Indian peasant tradition in which the village (pueblo) sometimes was required to act in the name of the king was married to the political tradition in which royal sovereignty was conferred through the people (Pueblo) and sometimes devolved to them.

Thus, invoking the name of the king while recruiting for the insurgency was not a "yawning contradiction," as Van Young would have it.[68] Originally Hidalgo and Morelos, like the Creole municipal council of Mexico City in 1808, sought not independence but status as a coequal kingdom, that is, they desired autonomy from Spain under the king. They differed from the Creole autonomists of 1808 in that, after the European Spaniards resorted to force, any who sought to oppose them must also use the same means.[69]

The strength of the association between the figure of the king and popular notions of justice was such in 1808–10 that the "royalist" hue of insurgent discourse was inevitable. However, the evidence suggests that it need not have fixed on the defense of Fernando VII. In the 1808 Acapulco conspiracy mentioned earlier, the conspirators,

led by Mariano Tabares, sought to crown a new king in Mexico because there was no longer a king in Spain.[70] Nevertheless, Fernando
VII soon became the undisputed symbol of popular hopes, and even
Tabares began to support his return. Fernando dominated the symbolic field of battle, his captivity and obvious claim to the throne
making him the perfect wild card because in his absence practically
any agenda could be attributed to him. Also, by pinning their appeal
on the existing king the insurgents avoided the thorny question of
choosing a new one. No doubt Hidalgo's decision to support the legitimacy of Fernando VII was also influenced by events in Spain,
where the resistance to the French was legitimated in this way.

If the insurgent movement retained a royalist hue, it also did not
break with the past in the religious tone of its rhetoric. As Enrique
Florescano and David Brading have noted, religion was *the* "unifying element of the ethnic, economic, cultural and political diversity
which was New Spain."[71] Religion was the linchpin of the ideological system that organized everyday life and political relations, and it
is impossible to imagine any movement mobilizing large numbers of
people with a purely secular ideology.

The religious tone of the insurgency actually had two distinct
components. The first originated in Old Testament stories of the op-
pressions and rebellions of the Hebrews, which were held up as examples of just rebellion that God rewarded with success. Documents
in which Morelos, other priests, and nonclerical insurgents made
this kind of reference are almost unlimited in number. These references remained common in political proclamations in Guerrero even
after the death of Morelos. Most also contained references to the impiety of the Spanish, an element examined in greater detail below.[72]
It should be noted that these ideas were not exclusive to New Spain:
in the Andes, Tupac Amaru also frequently used such images "comparing, for instance, the situation in Peru with the oppression of the
Hebrews in Israel."[73]

The second component is more well known. The Virgin of Guadalupe was the most pervasive symbol of the movement, used on flags
and uniforms and in proclamations and passwords.[74] This symbol has
been the subject of countless works; perhaps the most important for
our purposes is the recent work of William Taylor, who rejects the
notion that Guadalupe was already an object of devotion for large
masses of Indian villagers before 1810 but instead suggests that the
symbol became nationally important only after independence. He
does note, however, that the symbol of Guadalupe, unlike others,
was recognized in various regions and among distinct social groups
well before the insurgency and that it exerted a more general appeal

than that of other patron saints, even if it signified different ideas to different groups.[75]

Guadalupe, however, did not necessarily represent the overthrow of the established order. In fact, she was used quite frequently in royalist propaganda and religious observances.[76] As Taylor demonstrates, Guadalupe was a two-sided symbol: on the one hand, she offered a new beginning, "inviting her believers to escape the restraints of the established order"; on the other hand, she served as a mediator who fostered the "acceptance and legitimation of Spanish authority."[77] This insight suggests a parallel with ideas about the Spanish king: the king was a symbol of the ultimate legitimacy of the colonial order, yet it was in his name that peasants and others attacked aspects of that order.

A crucial element in the discourse of the insurgency was enmity toward European-born Spaniards. When the insurgency exploded on the coast in late 1810 this anti-Spanish prejudice was its major banner.[78] Anti-Spanish sentiment was obviously related to political attitudes about the legitimacy of the king and the illegitimacy of the government of New Spain as well as the religious facets just discussed. Notably, the words used to describe the European Spanish in the first years of the insurgency were "europeo" and "gachupín." More formal documents occasionally included the term "español europeo," never simply "español"; these usages consciously excluded Creoles from being identified as enemies of the movement.

The ire displayed against gachupines in Guerrero was intense. Actions against them resulted both from the official insurgent policy elaborated by Morelos and his lieutenants and from popular hatred. For instance, when twelve Spaniards were beheaded in Tecpan in early 1811, the executions were ordered by a Creole leader, but, according to a witness, "even the women demonstrated great pleasure."[79] Official policy and popular ire coincided to a remarkable degree. Both stemmed from conscious and unconscious ideas about the role the European-born Spanish played in local and viceregal society. The prevalence of anti-Spanish feelings among certain kinds of peasants makes it difficult to attribute these feelings exclusively to Creole resentment of Spanish predominance in filling civil and ecclesiastical posts. At the same time, the appearance of such sentiment in late 1810 and early 1811 implies that it could not have been solely or primarily a reaction to the ferocity of the counterinsurgency tactics employed by peninsular troops who arrived after 1812. Also, despite royalist misconceptions, this anger was not directed against all white people.[80]

The basic axis of anti-gachupín sentiment was, paradoxically, anti-

French. The connections are surprisingly clear. Most viceregal officials in 1810–11 had been appointed under the influence of the royal favorite Manuel Godoy, seen as the man who betrayed Spain to Napoleon. Furthermore, many of Godoy's allies had remained in José Napoleon Bonaparte's government in Spain, rather than joining the groups resisting France. Also, the Europeans' 1808 coup in Mexico City nipped in the bud a movement against recognizing the Bonaparte government in Spain. Although the new government of the viceroyalty also refused to recognize Bonaparte, its anti-Napoleonic credentials seemed weak. More important, in the twenty years since the beginning of the French Revolution the Spanish Crown had propagandized extensively against the French, arguing that the French were atheist and impious as well as the declared enemies of the Crown. This flood of material appeared in two waves. The first surged in the early 1790s after the execution of the French king. After Spain became an ally of revolutionary France, anti-French propaganda subsided until the events of 1808 released a new flood. Much of the literature in the new wave was nationalist in tone, using such words as *patria* and *nación*. In one of the ironies of history, during most of the war insurgents applied to the royalists such terms as *esclavos* and *tiranos*, which had been introduced into the political discourse of New Spain to stiffen the resolve of the king's subjects and extract funds for use against Napoleon.[81]

Considered in the above context, the idea that the gachupines and their government in Mexico City were secret allies of Napoleon and traitors to the king was not at all absurd or naïve. Nor was this a strange peasant millenarian belief: it was a cornerstone of the discourse elaborated by the leaders of the insurgency.[82] Its importance continued even after the viceregal government recognized the Spanish Cortes and outweighed, in Morelos's mind at least, loyalty to the Crown. At his trial Morelos insisted that he thought Fernando VII would never return to Spain and that even if he did, Morelos would not have obeyed him if he returned "*napoleónico*."[83] The anti-French hysteria encouraged by official propaganda before the revolt was transformed into anti-gachupín sentiment very quickly. Even the measures taken were the same: in August 1808 local officials in Tixtla embargoed the goods of a Frenchman; by 1811 the wealth being confiscated belonged to the European Spanish.[84] The insurgents in fact identified very closely with the resistance to the French on the Peninsula and assumed that these good or loyal Spaniards would recognize the insurgency or at least fulfill many of its goals.[85]

Two other aspects of the idea that gachupines were afrancesado are important. First, as noted above, much of the anti-French discourse in New Spain before 1808 stressed French atheism, heresy, and impiety. Insurgent propaganda also emphasized these characteristics when portraying the gachupines. The image of the Spanish heretic jibed with the notion that the insurgency was a holy war in defense of religion and clerical privilege, a justification used with frequency.[86] The idea that the europeos were heretics and the king had ordered their death had also surfaced in the earlier Tupac Amaru rebellion in the Andes.[87] Furthermore, at least occasionally the gachupines were identified as Jewish,[88] an association interesting because of two possible connotations. The first was the notion of the alien trying to blend into society contained in the history of the Spanish preoccupation with the *conversos*, Spanish Catholics who converted from Judaism under royal pressure. The second is the symbol of the greedy and usurious Jew prevalent in European anti-Semitism.[89] This image of greed resonated with the other connotations of the word "gachupín."

European Spanish merchants, often working with European Spanish officials, were able to corner the market as buyers and sellers of certain commodities in late colonial Guerrero. They did this by advancing goods against the production of cotton, textiles, and maize. The vast majority of the merchants and local colonial officials involved in these practices were born in Spain, and these business tactics were important in determining attitudes toward the gachupines. This was particularly true on the coast, where mulatto sharecroppers produced cotton for markets in the interior of New Spain. Their welfare varied widely from year to year not so much because of agricultural problems as because of variations in the cotton market driven by the vicissitudes of the Napoleonic wars.[90] When Great Britain was at war with Spain, British control of the sea prevented European textiles from reaching the colony and textiles produced there sold well, raising the price of cotton. When peace prevailed European textiles depressed the market for goods woven in New Spain and the sharecroppers saw their income decrease substantially. This fall in welfare took the concrete form of a Spanish merchant protected and aided by Spanish officials giving sharecroppers less for the fruits of their labor. This phenomenon also affected some Indian peasants who spun cotton, but its impact was less profound because they were not exclusively dependent on the textile trade. Spanish merchants had become the personification of market forces in Guerrero, especially on the coast. Thus it is not surprising that merchants were singled out for harsh treatment.[91] In Guerrero the Spanish were persecuted first and most thoroughly on the Costa Grande, where Spanish merchants most thoroughly controlled trade.

Criticizing the greed of Spanish merchants was a strand of the popular ideology of the insurgency, but it also formed part of the official discourse of the movement. In documents produced by insurgent leaders the European merchants were "monopolists" and only wanted to "fatten their purses, extracting the blood of the poor like leeches with their usurious monopolies and frauds."[92] Official insurgent policy called for imprisoning the European Spaniards and confiscating their goods in the name of the Nation. Imprisoned Spaniards were harassed by their jailers. Eventually the insurgents killed many Spaniards either to prevent their escape when royalist forces neared or in reprisal for the executions of insurgent prisoners.[93]

Although the goals of both leadership and masses of the movement coincided in the repression of the European Spanish, there was room for disagreement over exactly who could be defined as a gachupín. Confining popular ire to the Europeans and maintaining unity among the various castes and classes that composed his coalition constantly preoccupied Morelos. In the summer of 1811, for instance, two of Morelos's officers tried to take control of the movement on the coast, redefining the category "gachupín" to include all whites. Morelos quickly repressed their conspiracy. Interestingly enough, one of the two was Mariano Tabares, leader of the 1808 Acapulco conspiracy.[94] Nevertheless, Morelos seems to have been generally successful in preventing the arbitrary imprisonment or execution of Creoles who did not actively oppose the insurgency.

Anti-gachupín sentiment was tied to business practices characterized as usury and monopoly. Monopoly was criticized as an infringement of free trade, an argument used in the courts and in administrative dispositions from at least the mid-eighteenth century. The idea that usury was a sin was a tenet of Catholicism discussed, along with disapproval of defrauding the poor of their daily sustenance, in books Morelos read as a seminarian and a parish priest. The insurgents criticized Spaniards for both monopoly and usury and, not surprisingly, converted these beliefs into practical measures.[95] For instance, the confiscation of gachupín wealth made the debts owed to them property of the Nation. These debts were in turn forgiven, effectively relieving many peasants and other individuals of debts incurred for at least one year of agricultural or handicraft production. Village Indians were given official sanction to trade with whomever they preferred, another symbolic and practical blow to the repartimiento system. In some areas the insurgents explicitly abolished the repartimiento to secure the support of villagers; in others merchants' flight from the insurgents caused its de facto abolition. Later, after insurgent administration was more established, officials took further measures against "monopolists," including provision for each village's election of "a public attorney, to prevent all monopoly."[96]

The insurgent leaders also sought peasant support through more direct appeals. Conflicts over the control of village lands rented to outsiders were important in some parts of Guerrero, particularly the Tierra Caliente. An early decree of Morelos returned such lands to the villages and prohibited outsiders from renting them in the future. Aware that the colonial administration had borrowed large sums from village cajas de comunidad and cofradías in the name of the Crown without repayment, the insurgents were careful to offer interest when asking for loans, along with assurances that the loans would be repaid soon. More important, the management of such village resources underwent a de facto change: during the war, villages stopped depositing the money earned by cofradías and other communal institutions in government treasuries and submitting their accounts for approval. Later, some insurgent leaders tried to regain control over this potential source of revenue but the earlier system was not successfully reestablished.[97]

The insurgents abolished the tribute, which was particularly resented by the mulattos of the Costa Grande, and publicized the abolition to secure the loyalty of Indian villagers. The royalists likewise considered tribute an important issue for Indians, and an early response to the Hidalgo rebellion was a viceregal order ending tribute payments in New Spain. The Spanish Constitution of 1812 again abolished tribute, but Fernando VII reinstated it in 1815. Later the insurgents legislated a graduated head tax that taxed the poor, including Indians and mulattos, at about half the rate previously charged for tribute, but this tax may not have been actually implemented. After the insurgents abolished tribute, Indians became liable for the alcabala, but this excise tax was lowered from 8 to 4 percent.[98]

One of Morelos's first acts on arrival in coastal Guerrero in 1810 was to decree that "with the exception of the Europeans, all other inhabitants will not be called Indians, mulattos, or other castes, but instead all generally *americanos*" (his emphasis).[99] This measure was an obvious attempt to construct an alliance of all groups against the European Spanish. Moreover, Morelos was trying to recruit the mulatto sharecroppers of the coast, who resented the payment of tribute associated with their caste identification. Mulattos were the only group in New Spain that gained absolutely nothing from the caste system: they did not receive the guaranteed access to resources and legal protection enjoyed by Indians, yet they were expected to pay tribute as well as the alcabala, which Indians were not required to pay. Mulattos were thus most likely to favor the abolition of the caste system and applaud the related idea that all men should enjoy equal rights and obligations. The insurgents also abolished slavery. There were few slaves in New Spain but the abolition of slavery removed a further stigma from mulattos, the only group in the region that could be enslaved under colonial law.[100]

There is no evidence that peasant villages in Guerrero attempted to recover land from neighboring haciendas during the insurgency; nor were such attempts condoned by the insurgent leadership.[101] To my knowledge, there exists only one documented case in which the insurgent leadership was asked to resolve a land dispute between a village and a hacienda. Although this case did not take place in Guerrero, it illustrates the attitude of the leadership. In 1812 the village of Tlastitaca in Xanteleico tried to recover lands and water it had lost to two haciendas forty years before. Morelos wrote to the villagers that because "the actual circumstances of the War do not permit us to verify lands or waters, you should stay in the same state you are in, and petition when we are in Mexico, when we will take care of you in Justice."[102] Notably, although several haciendas were confiscated from Spaniards, these were not distributed among peasants or others but instead were cultivated to provide revenue for the movement.[103]

The ideology of the insurgency evolved substantially over time. The "legitimist" orientation of 1810–11 had become by 1813–14 a drive for an independent Mexico governed by a republican constitution. The transition was rapid but not without roots in colonial political culture: in the eighteenth century the Enlightenment and the reinvigorated Bourbon monarchy had begun to change the political culture of New Spain. Competition with other European powers had led the Bourbons to enthusiastically embrace the new intellectual trends sweeping Europe while simultaneously striving to control innovations that might limit royal power. The monarchy proved to be the most active and important promoter of the Enlightenment and a new official orthodoxy soon coexisted uneasily with its Hapsburg predecessors.

These changes affected New Spain's political culture in three ways. First, the Crown itself weakened some of the corporate bodies and estates that formed the Old Regime by reducing their privileges and autonomy.[104] Second, the new ideas introduced a new role for the monarch as a promoter of public well-being rather than a relatively simple upholder of natural law.[105] Third, the monarchy's enthusiasm for economic development led it to support new forums for the exchange and production of information, including newspapers and organizations where educated individuals could meet to discuss the issues of the day. According to François Furet, similar developments in France led directly to the growth of what he calls a "new political sociability" in which individuals met outside their previous roles in traditional corporations to develop and express consensual opinions.[106]

However, the impact of these changes should not be exaggerated. In New Spain the strength of the new political sociability or public sphere was limited by the relatively small size of the social strata that was able to participate. The new Bourbon Enlightenment ethic did not replace its predecessors but instead joined them in a system that allowed multiple and contradictory discourses to coexist. Thus, although Hidalgo and Morelos had some previous familiarity with Enlightenment political thought, they did not rely on this repertoire in 1810. Hidalgo was not even accused of owning or using such forbidden works when he was tried by the Inquisition after his capture.[107]

As was mentioned earlier, in its first years the insurgent leadership generally justified its actions in the name of the king. The leaders defined their movement in opposition to the Napoleonic invaders of Spain and the gachupín government of New Spain that was planning to betray the king and turn New Spain over to Napoleon. The leadership justified its right to govern New Spain in the king's name using an amalgam of pre-absolutist political doctrine under which God conferred sovereignty on the king though the "people" and common notions of the right of the aggrieved to oppose "bad government" while continuing to recognize the authority of the king. The insurgents identified with the peninsular resistance to Napoleon and expected the juntas and later the Cortes to recognize them as the true patriots of New Spain.

This legitimist orientation was gradually transformed between 1810 and 1814. Two elements acted in succession to drive this transformation: the first was the increasing sense that Fernando VII himself had betrayed Spain, becoming "Napoleonic"; the second was the refusal of the Spanish Cortes to recognize the insurgency and the independence of New Spain under the sovereign. Obviously neither the king nor the Spanish patriots could be relied on, and "America" would have to go it alone. By the 1814 writing of the Constitution of Apatzingán the insurgents had embraced the basic tenets of liberal nationalism and popular sovereignty so conspicuous in their absence from the Grito de Dolores.[108]

By 1814 insurgent views of the constitution of the polity were substantially different from those prevalent in 1810. The Kingdom became the Nation, the subject became the citizen. A new repertoire had been embraced, most elements of which had been introduced under the direction of the Crown itself in the late eighteenth century. Other elements became prominent in royal appeals for funds to support the Crown in the years immediately prior to the insurgency. These appeals, usually addressed through parish priests and local officials, often stressed patriotic themes, using words like nación and patria, and emphasized how vital the contributions of all subjects were to the defense of the king and his kingdom.[109] The influence of the rapidly evolving situation in Spain on the insurgent leadership was crucial; the Cortes's own transition from legitimation on the basis of pre-absolutist doctrine to liberalism and constitutionalism pulled the leadership of the insurgency in the same direction. Newspapers brought Spanish news and political discussions to the insurgents.[110]

The efforts first of Bourbon monarchs and then of the liberal Cortes to forge a Spanish nation provided the repertoire the insurgents drew on in forging their own. Both the liberal Cortes and the insurgent leadership justified their entrance onto the historical stage by invoking seventeenth-century theologians but then rapidly embraced new idols. Nevertheless, what occurred in both Mexico and Spain was less a sudden change in hegemonic political ideas than a melding of "modern Enlightenment principles with the Spanish political and legal tradition."[111] It was thus not unthinkable for the insurgents to accept a constitutional monarchy in 1821. The actual functioning both of the insurgent Constitution of Apatzingán and the Spanish Constitution of 1812 in New Spain clearly demonstrates the syncretic nature of political culture in the early nineteenth century.

The Insurgent State

Until 1815 the insurgents controlled most of what is now the state of Guerrero. There they set up an organized, functioning government; in this way Guerrero's experience with the insurgency differed from the relatively short-lived reign of the Hidalgo movement in the Bajío and the Guadalajara region as well as the effective military control insurgent guerrillas enjoyed at various times in other areas of the viceroyalty. Moreover, the insurgent government produced large numbers of documents, some of which were confiscated by royalist forces and survive in the Archivo General de la Nación in Mexico City, affording a more complete view of insurgent government organization than that offered by propaganda and constitutions. Although the demands of the war itself obviously modified insurgent practice, these documents provide key information on the state and society the insurgents sought to construct. In Guerrero the rebels were consciously *constructing*, and not just destroying, as is shown by the extensive use of such phrases as "our new system" and "our national system."[112]

Village-based organization was the one constant of the insurgent state during the war. Though organizational structures over the villages varied from complex administrative and fiscal bureaucracies appointed and overseen by congresses to more minimalist military command systems, the insurgents relied on the village as the basic cell of their government for many of the same reasons the colonial state did, and kept in place many of the colonial regulations governing village elections. First, collecting resources to support higher government and the army would have been impossible without making individuals acquainted with local society responsible for quotas. Also, village governments enjoyed a legitimacy that more innovative arrangements would have lacked.[113] Unlike Hidalgo, Morelos organized a relatively traditional army, but he also provided for a militia system based on the villages that became ever more important as the insurgents were increasingly forced to adopt guerrilla tactics.

In other ways the insurgent system did not imitate its predecessor. The 1814 Constitution of Apatzingán called for the indirect election of both a congress and a three-person executive but did not discuss the election of officials of lower rank. Although the constitution in theory called for universal male suffrage, there was considerable variation in the actual elections for this and other congresses.[114] In practice, Indians and other local residents elected local officials and replaced functionaries who they felt had abused their offices,[115] thus facilitating the practical desire of insurgent leaders to ensure maximum support for their movement through the consensual choice of officials.

Much insurgent correspondence suggests that first Morelos and later the Congress took over many of the functions carried out in the colonial period by the viceroy and the Audiencia. Disputes that were not resolved at the local level were sent further up the chain of authority. This procedure was not spelled out in early rebel decrees and may have begun simply because it was the most logical thing for ag-grieved parties to do. However, later both Morelos and Congress ex-plicitly upheld the right to appeal decisions taken by insurgent of-ficials.[116] The disputes documented varied considerably, including, for instance, several disputes between villages over resources, fac-tional disputes within villages, and disagreements between priests and their parishioners over parochial fees or the control of cofradías.[117] Some cases were carried over from the late colonial period, and ar-guments were generally similar to those used in colonial days, but claimants' loyalty or disloyalty to the movement became a further issue. Groups sometimes complained of the excesses of insurgent military commanders in collecting rations and money for the war.[118]

Both on paper and in practice, the rudimentary state constructed by the insurgents resembled the viceregal government it sought to replace, but with important differences. The insurgents' need for the active support of the populace in the areas they controlled, combined with the loss of legitimacy that the Crown had suffered before 1808, eventually forced the insurgents to adopt a representative form of government justified by the sovereignty of "the people." Besides the practical power conceded by the insurgent government, localities were also organized for defense, and if power truly grows out of the barrel of a gun, it was shared widely. At times the insurgent drive for an armed populace went to ridiculous extremes: when Viceroy Felix Calleja published a counterinsurgency plan that restricted the carry-ing of arms in New Spain, Morelos countered with a "Contra Plan de Calleja" that *required* all males over the age of twelve to carry arms.[119]

The Guerrilla War

Between 1810 and 1814 the insurgents sought to destroy the gov-ernment of New Spain by forming large armies, steadily conquering the viceroyalty, and setting up civil administrations in the territories they came to control. In areas left without large troop formations the insurgents relied on guerrilla militias to frustrate royalist counterof-fensives. This strategy almost worked, but the royalist army continu-ally prevailed in large-scale battles because of its advantage in train-ing and armament. The failure of the insurgent approach became definitive when Morelos's last large army was defeated near Vallado-lid in December 1813. From that moment, Morelos concentrated on defending previously gained territory, reinforcing the guerrilla sys-tem, and protecting the Congress that headed his civilian government.[120] Morelos was performing this last task when he was captured in November 1815.

Once the strategy based on large armies had failed, the ground rules of the contest changed. From 1814 to 1820 the insurgents' ability to organize local support for their cause vied with the royalists' efforts to pacify areas. As Christon Archer points out, the war was not over. From 1814 to 1820 bands of insurgents exercised effective political control over large areas of New Spain, disrupting commerce, preventing the collection of revenue, and winning many relatively small military actions. Although arguably the insurgents no longer had much hope of a military and political victory, they were not losing, especially in the area covered by this study, where Vicente Guerrero and other leaders were able to consistently revitalize their support despite unfavorable military odds.[121]

The insurgents' strength in the South ebbed and flowed. In 1814 the royalists advanced on three regions that had been under insurgent control since 1811 and in all three met fierce guerrilla resistance. In the Tierra Caliente and Tlapa this resistance was organized around village governments whereas on the Costa Grande it was led by the hacendado Hermengildo Galeana until his death that June.[122] The defeat of Morelos's armies outside the South had little impact on local support for the movement: from 1814 to 1817, the insurgents under Vicente Guerrero controlled the Tlapa area and guerrillas held out in large numbers both on the Costa Grande and in the Tierra Caliente. After his military defeat in Tlapa, Guerrero simply shifted his efforts to the other two areas and rapidly regained strength.

Insurgent strength in Tlapa was concentrated in the villages. There were no haciendas in Tlapa, and the villages controlled almost all land. Guerrero received broad support, and only eight to ten families of the market town of Tlapa itself consistently aided the royalists. In October 1815 the local royalist commander Juan Mota recommended abandoning the whole area. In November 1815 his superior, José Gabriel de Armijo, reported that over 100 villages in the area were actively aiding the insurgents. However, by May 1817 the royalists' ability to bring large detachments to bear on rebel strong points and carry out severe repression had taken its toll. After losing several pitched battles Vicente Guerrero left Tlapa.[123]

On the Costa Grande west of Acapulco, the mulatto sharecroppers had joined Morelos in large numbers early in the movement and the insurgents governed there until royalist detachments began to operate in the area in 1814. Royalist counterinsurgency measures initially seemed to be effective and quickly led to the death of Hermengildo Galeana in 1814. But the inhabitants of the coast continued to resist because, according to royalist commanders, they wished to continue "the independent and abandoned life that the flags of the insurrection provided them."[124] Continuing under Isidro Montes de Oca and Juan Alvarez against superior royalist forces, the insurgency there reached a low point in mid-1817, then rebounded quickly, so that by April 1819 even the royalists admitted that the rebels could concentrate groups of 400 to 500 men for attacks. Insurgent forces diminished again later that year, then began to recover strength in 1820.[125]

Guerrillas also resisted the royalists in the Tierra Caliente. Royalist commanders repeatedly complained of the peasants' willingness to provide the rebels with information and food while refusing to give intelligence to the counterinsurgency forces.[126] However, the preponderance of resources enjoyed by the government again took its toll and by June 1818 many rebels had accepted royalist pardons.[127] Soon thereafter Vicente Guerrero resumed ambushing patrols, and by the autumn of 1818 insurgents had overrun the area. Guerrero began issuing his own pardons to individuals who had accepted those of the government. This revival raged unchecked until the royalists inflicted some military reverses on Guerrero's troops in late 1819, but in 1820 the insurgents began yet another resurgence.[128]

Royalist Tactics

José Gabriel de Armijo, commander of the royalist military in the South during the guerrilla war, fully understood that the real issue was control of the population.[129] The guerrillas sought to bring their forces in concentrated numbers against small detachments of royalist troops and to avoid larger ones, only actually fighting when victory was certain. They relied heavily on the rural population to conceal their movements and provide information and food. The royalists responded with tactics designed to cut off the insurgents from the rural population in various ways.[130]

The royalists relied heavily on the timeworn strategy of making a few individuals responsible for the conduct of larger groups.[131] Royalist troops executed the governors of Indian villages that provided food to the rebels or failed to report insurgent troop movements. This method was of such obvious utility to royalist commanders that at least one settlement that did not have a village government before the war was given one.[132] Royalists also copied the colonial practice of making villages collectively responsible for the actions of their members by threatening that villages that aided the insurgents would be *diezmados* (tithed). Every tenth villager, apparently selected randomly, was killed.[133]

The royalists also organized village defense forces called "patriot companies." This tactic was another way of making villages collectively responsible for their attitudes toward the insurgency. Previously, villages could justify giving rebel bands whatever they wanted by claiming that armed insurgents had coerced them. Once the village's men had been organized into groups and given arms, no matter how useless, they were faced with a choice between resisting the insurgents and being shot for cowardice upon the arrival of royalist regulars.[134] This policy varied in effectiveness. At its best it provided the royalists with enthusiastic and knowledgeable local auxiliaries; at its worst the inhabitants pressed into service simply deserted at the earliest opportunity.[135]

Royalist officers often issued pardons to former insurgents. This practice became so ubiquitous that the numbers of rural people who accepted pardons came into use as an indicator of the effectiveness of royalist policies and officers, and long lists of pardoned individuals were sent to Mexico City.[136] However, like the body counts military officers have used to demonstrate their prowess in other times and places, pardon lists were often misleading. Individuals and villages that accepted pardons often were just waiting for more favorable conditions before resuming the struggle. As noted above, the insurgents sometimes offered their own pardons to those who had accepted royalist offers.[137]

Royalist officers worked to concentrate the rural population in the centers of villages, where it was easier to control and isolate from the guerrillas. This policy was difficult because pueblos were not the nucleated settlements prescribed by colonial law and often agricultural lands were far-flung and inaccessible. The montes, or areas beyond the boundaries of village and hacienda settlements, had always been areas outside of the practical and symbolic supervision of colonial officials. Whole villages literally deserted from colonial society when royalist troops arrived. Convincing such a village to return and accept royal authority was considered an important accomplishment.[138] Other royalist measures required that people taking up residence in a village report to the royal judge; in areas that were particularly isolated and supportive of the rebels this policy was enforced to the extent of moving whole villages and destroying all crops.[139]

After the army had reestablished military control over a particular area, or had claimed to do so, the next challenge was to reestablish colonial administration. This task proved difficult, as the insurgents had often destroyed archives, making the collection of alcabalas and tribute almost impossible. Furthermore, the destruction and insecurity of the war diminished economic activity to the point where the taxes and lawsuits that officials relied on for their salaries were not sufficient. The hostility of the residents was sometimes aroused by attempts to collect back taxes for the years they lived under insurgent government. These problems were compounded by the extra burden placed on the population by militia service and extra levies to supply royalist garrisons.[140]

The problems of defeating tenacious guerrilla resistance and then reestablishing civil authority were simply insurmountable in Guerrero. As Armijo understood, every time he was forced to reduce troop strength in an area the insurgency reappeared. It was clear to him that he was facing a mobile and resilient enemy that had the sympathies of the bulk of the population.[141] The colonial government would never regain the legitimacy that had allowed it to rule New Spain with minimal force for hundreds of years.

The Plan of Iguala and Mexican Independence

One of the most durable misconceptions in Mexican history is that of "conservative independence." According to this formula, the insurgents were defeated and both the Plan of Iguala and Mexico's subsequent independence stemmed from a conservative reaction to the reinstatement of the liberal Constitution of 1812 in Spain: Mexico's dominant class chose independence to preserve the traditional power structure of the viceroyalty from pressures for reform originating in Spain.[142] This interpretation is based on a series of assertions, the first being that the insurgents had been virtually eliminated from the political scene by 1820,[143] the second that the settlement reached in 1821 abrogated the Constitution of 1812 recently reimplemented in New Spain,[144] and the third that the insurgents were forced by their own weakness to accept independence "under principles very different from their own."[145] The "conservative independence" thesis was first advanced by Lucás Alamán in the mid-nineteenth century and has remained attractive to twentieth-century historians.[146] These historians have correctly identified the Plan of Iguala as an important moment in the political life of the new nation but have erred in most of their specific reasons for doing so and have consequently undermined their overall interpretation. This section will examine each of their three assertions in the light of the evidence available.

New Spain had not been pacified as of 1820. Furthermore, it could never have returned to the degree of consensus that had maintained the colonial system with very little recourse to force before 1808. The crisis that had touched off the war was unresolved, and this crisis, combined with the effects of the war itself, had irrevocably damaged the legitimacy of the colonial system. In the words of Jaime Rodríguez, by 1820 "New Spaniards obeyed the government principally because it possessed the monopoly of force."[147] For instance, royalist commanders in Guerrero understood that even where insurgent support was relatively weak any reduction in royalist troop strength could lead to an outbreak of violence.[148] Moreover, from the point of view of New Spain's dominant class the situation was exceedingly fragile because the provincial Creole military officers who actually exercised the monopoly of force did not differ greatly in social origins and political attitudes from those who the colonial dominant class had thwarted in 1808.[149]

The idea that the insurgents had been defeated by 1820 was an optimistic assessment that not even royalist commanders believed. The rebels were again recovering strength in Guerrero and could not be eliminated without a massive commitment of troops that rebel activity elsewhere in New Spain would not permit. Furthermore, as has been noted, insurgents who had accepted pardons often returned to the struggle when circumstances became more favorable. Although Brian Hamnett's estimate that in the autumn of 1820 the rebels could muster only about 900 men in the South is a reasonable one, it hardly indicates that the war was over.[150] Modern counterinsurgency doctrine, in an age in which technology allows regular forces to move hundreds of miles per day and restricts guerrillas to the same 20 or 30 they could make in 1820, suggests that even a stalemate against 900 guerrillas would require about 9,000 troops. The royalist army, which could move no faster than the guerrillas themselves, never was able to commit more than 4,000 men to the South after 1814. In other words, despite royalist propaganda, there was no end in sight in 1820. Royalist commanders knew this and insisted that they needed more troops to have a chance of defeating the insurgents.[151]

The problems of Mexico's dominant class were compounded when Spanish liberals forced Fernando VII to republish the Constitution of 1812.[152] It seems doubtful that the dominant class feared reform from Spain. In the preceding 50 years, the Mexican dominant class had

succeeded in blunting or turning to its advantage most Bourbon reform efforts.[153] In 1820, however, the liberal constitution, with its
implied radical reordering of Mexican society, already had several potential political bases in Mexico. These included the insurgents, the
royalist military officers mentioned above, and a diverse array of provincial Creole and mestizo rancheros, hacendados, merchants, minor
officials, muleteers, and Indian townspeople. Some had overtly or
covertly supported the insurgency at various moments and others
had not, but many found the Spanish constitution attractive.

The viceregal government's impotence against the insurgency put
the insurgents and the royalist military in touch immediately. Royalist commanders approached the insurgents throughout the viceroyalty to suggest that the revived Constitution of 1812 offered
the insurgents everything they sought. Both José Gabriel de Armijo
and Carlos Moya wrote Vicente Guerrero to convince him that the
constitution's representative system of government and abolition of
caste distinctions would end the domination of New Spain by the
European Spanish. Other rebels received similar offers. The royalists
supplemented these private overtures with proclamations aimed at
rank-and-file insurgents.[154] Pamphlets published in Mexico City under the new press freedom also stressed this theme. Other pamphlets, aimed at royalists, emphasized the need to negotiate with the
insurgents.[155]

The newly operative constitution had other supporters in Guerrero. One of its most revolutionary provisions allowed locations
with more than 1,000 inhabitants to become municipalities, elect-
ing officials with political autonomy to counterbalance officials appointed from above. Many such municipalities were erected in New
Spain in 1820 and 1821.[156] Between July 1820 and January 1821 no
less than 71 municipalities were set up in Guerrero, including many
organized around Indian villages.[157] Both municipalities and the constitution's abolition of caste distinctions and tribute were popular.
Furthermore, as Christon Archer points out, the first acts of many
municipalities ended extraordinary war taxes and disbanded the militias that towns were required to support.[158] Meanwhile, Mexico
City pamphleteers tried to sell New Spain's poor on the benefits of
the constitution; distrusting the colonial dominant class, these writ-
ers suggested that a new revolution might be needed to preserve the
new freedoms.[159]

José Gabriel de Armijo resigned as commander of royalist forces
in the South in November 1820, claiming that his poor health prevented him from effectively dealing with the latest insurgent of-

fensive. Agustín de Iturbide replaced him. Iturbide had a relatively simple plan: he sought to quickly defeat the rebels and then unilaterally declare Mexico's independence from Spain, offering the Bourbon family a chance to continue their dynasty in the New World. This "Brazilian solution" to the problem faced by Mexico's dominant class would secure continued political legitimacy *and* guarantee proprietorship of the Mexican state. The problem with this plan was that the insurgents refused to fade away[160] but instead continued their recent successes, defeating Iturbide's forces repeatedly and convincing him that he could not end the war quickly.[161] Iturbide was forced to enter into negotiations with Guerrero.

The insurgents had not accepted pardons under the Spanish constitution for three reasons. First, accepting pardons would have constituted an admission that their cause was illegitimate. Second, the insurgents were not confident that future political events in Spain would not at some date undo what the Spanish liberals had accomplished. Third, the constitution denied the rights of citizenship to mulattos.[162] All these issues were discussed when Iturbide and Guerrero began negotiating via written correspondence in December 1820. Iturbide first suggested that Guerrero accept a pardon, in exchange for which Iturbide would allow Guerrero to continue in command of his troops and the Mexican representatives to the new Spanish Cortes would propose that the constitution be amended to provide citizenship for mulattos. Iturbide further suggested that Fernando VII or another member of the Bourbon family might be persuaded to transfer his throne to Mexico. Iturbide ended this letter by remarking that he was not worried by the battles he had just lost because the government would send as many troops as he needed to defeat the insurgents.[163] Guerrero responded that if the Spanish liberals did not accept the Mexican deputies' proposals in 1812 at the height of the war with France they were not likely to when they faced no such threat. He reiterated his rejection of racial limitations on citizenship but offered to put his forces under Iturbide's command if Iturbide accepted the principle of independence.[164] Thus Guerrero's position was laid out: independence under the Spanish constitution with the condition that citizenship be extended to all men. Iturbide accepted this model and it became the basis for the Plan of Iguala. Notably, Guerrero had proposed essentially the same compromise to another royalist officer in August 1820, soon after the constitution was promulgated in New Spain.[165]

The Plan of Iguala did not bring a "conservative independence" in reaction to the liberal Spanish constitution; it specifically left that constitution in effect in New Spain, but it varied from the constitution in preserving the clerical legal privileges and extending to all suffrage and eligibility for public office.[166] The settlement also offered the insurgents other important concessions: it reaffirmed the legitimacy of their cause and their ability to participate in the politics of the new Mexico, and it effectively ceded to them control of the areas in which they were strongest. The man who succeeded Iturbide as military commandant of the South was none other than Vicente Guerrero.

Between March and September 1821 resistance to Iturbide and Guerrero collapsed. Guerrero's adherence quickly assured that of other insurgents. Relatively little fighting took place as both leaders concentrated on convincing the officers of the former royalist army to embrace their proposal.[167] José Gabriel de Armijo was sent back to the South to contain the rapidly spreading movement but soon despaired, informing his superior that the entire region was lost because the troops and militias there would not oppose the new alliance. Former insurgents who had previously accepted pardons also joined the movement. The collapse was swift and sudden, but it left many issues unresolved, as we will see in subsequent chapters.[168]

The study of the social movement that mobilized large numbers of rural Mexicans between 1810 and 1821 has been impeded by its characterization as an "independence" movement. The idea that it resulted in independence with relatively few social changes has obscured the initial motivations of both poor and relatively wealthy participants. The insurgency and its program must be viewed in the context of the political culture of colonial New Spain. The initial justifications of both peasants and nonpeasants were conservative and legitimist in nature, and although the program later became more republican it continued to reconcile this "progressivism" with its preoccupation with ancient rights. Significantly, both peasants and the rural priests, landowners, and muleteers who led the movement subscribed to this relatively cohesive set of ideas, sharing enough common assumptions about politics, legitimacy, and justice to fashion a discourse based on reconciling their interests in conscious contradiction to the group they considered their common enemy, the European Spanish who made up the colonial dominant class centered in Mexico City. Socially the movement in Guerrero sought to end the abuses of state power endemic to the colonial system by making local officials accountable to the populace.

The timing of the insurgency in New Spain is critical to understanding its nature. Guerrero did not experience the agrarian changes that primed the Bajío and the Guadalajara region for revolt. The Bourbon reforms placed more fiscal pressure on various social groups in rural Guerrero and reduced the autonomy of peasant villages, but these changes do not seem sufficient to explain the cataclysmic collapse of order that took place. Moreover, the insurgency was not triggered by the breakdown of the state's repressive capacity, a factor so crucial to Theda Skocpol's theory of revolutions. New Spain's government had never relied heavily on force to preserve order.[169] The proximate cause of the explosion was instead the colonial government's loss of legitimacy due to the confused events in Spain and the attendant split in New Spain's upper classes. The trigger was more a legitimacy vacuum than a power vacuum, and it was this legitimacy vacuum that allowed the articulation of the cross-class alliances that turned New Spain into a battlefield. Nothing inherent in Mexico's class structure made the explosion inevitable. As Steven Topik suggested recently, Mexican independence might have been more like Brazil's truly conservative independence if the Spanish royal family had joined their Portuguese peers in fleeing to the New World.[170]

The poor rural people who fought and bore the brunt of the war were not motivated by the agrarian demands so often attributed to Mexican peasants. A review of the areas that supported the insurgents most constantly and thoroughly clearly suggests that Indian peasants were more likely to participate in areas where village communities dominated both demographically and in resource ownership. In these areas villages controlled almost all the land and other resources. As a consequence non-Indians who wished to prosper economically had to do so by manipulating resources that the peasants claimed as their own, including village lands rented to outsiders as well as cattle and money held by cofradías and cajas de comunidad. Mulatto peasants who sharecropped on coastal lands also were stalwart insurgents, but significantly they did not revolt against the owners of the land but instead targeted the merchants that connected them to the wider economy.

The independence war clearly defied the dichotomies between national and local, elite and poor, and modern and traditional that permeate much social scientific research on rural resistance and state formation. The 1808 political crisis was viceregal or "national" in scope but it provided the opportunity for diverse groups to express local grievances. The crisis first split Mexico's elite but that division encouraged impoverished people to press claims outside the courts. Both elites and the poor first justified their actions through calls for a restoration of traditional justice, but the backward-looking movement forced major changes in Mexican politics. Nationalism in Guerrero, as elsewhere, may have been a "modern" ideology but its force originated in a vision of the past. Moreover, the political vision of the rebels changed dramatically during the decade of fighting, as shown by the leadership's embrace of republican representative government. Although evidence of changing popular attitudes is more difficult to find it is noteworthy that by 1821 Guerrero stressed the need to extend citizenship rights to his mulatto followers.

The New Spain that became Mexico in 1821 was profoundly different from that which existed in 1808, particularly in rural areas. Politics in the countryside changed forever with the collapse of the legitimacy that had channeled most conflict into the colonial courts. From then on village peasants most commonly sought social and political goals through alliances with other villages and nonpeasants. The insurgent coalition was the first of these movements, and it suggests several necessary aspects of such phenomena: the need for a common set of enemies; the need for congruent if not common goals, at least locally; and finally the need for a program capable of uniting it and articulating the desires of its members in a way understandable to all. Such a program only became possible in 1808, but the collapse of colonial assumptions about politics, justice, and legitimacy made such programs easier to fashion in subsequent years. Movements of many peasant villages in alliance with other actors became the most important tools with which Mexico's peasantry exerted pressure on the shape of the state in the nineteenth and early twentieth centuries.

CHAPTER 3

State Formation in Republican Guerrero, 1820-1840

It would be difficult, when Spanish villages obtain certain liberty and privileges, to deny Cocula the satisfaction of the installation of its own town council, as it should have and as the Sacred Code desires. . . . The town council should be installed to improve and quicken the administration of justice, and the other benefits that the spirit of the Constitution brings us.

—The military commander, justice, governor of natives, and other residents of the village of Cocula, July 29, 1820

[Many town councils] are no more than the tyrants of the villages, especially in Indian villages, where the town councils practice more arbitrariness and tricks than did their former Republics.

—José María Bermudez, Acapulco, February 1, 1830

We ask that the town council be restored with all the requirements the law calls for, because when the current town council was elected, the entire village was fugitive in the hills.

—Nicolás Tolentino, Lucas Martin, Nicolás Melchor, Nicolás Antonio, Francisco Martin, Juan Manuel Reyes, all past aldermen of the Municipality of Zitlala, in union with the native commons; Chilapa, April 29, 1833

Between 1820 and 1840 legislative change and its local interpretation transformed political life in the Mexican countryside and helped determine the local social bases of the political struggles that rocked Mexico until 1880. State formation in this period also had a lasting impact on the shape of the Mexican state in the countryside; some of the patterns of interaction between local power and the central government developed then are still visible today. During this process, peasants affected state formation in two important ways: they supported regional and national political alliances, and they shaped laws as they were implemented.

This chapter will concentrate on legislation and how it was interpreted in practice. Laws were made real only when they came into contact with local conditions and structures of power and their content was modified accordingly. The crucial step in this process was that of assigning local definitions to the terms found in state legislation.

State formation generally is seen as a process in which old solidarities, organizations, and ties are delegitimated and the nation-state becomes the primary focus of loyalties.[1] States or the elites who dominate them seek to remake the political and social world to approach a model in which no intervening organizations, corporations, or solidarities stand between the state and the individual.[2] The ideal end result is the citizen, an individual beholden to the state, his employer, and no one else. Nevertheless, in practice a state often extends its power by reinforcing and reconstructing old solidarities and even constructing new ones when its own weakness gives rise to a need for allies. This pattern was particularly evident early in the global era of state formation when previous organizations and solidarities were relatively strong, but it recurs even today when a state is weak.

When national political elites and the state seek allies through reinforcing old solidarities and constructing new ones, they recast those organizations or loci of identity as agencies of the state. State-builders are certainly not in the business of creating or reinforcing autonomous organizations that people might use later to oppose state policies. However, the careful crafting of laws and regulations that subordinate these bodies to central power often founders because of the ability of the subordinated to manipulate and transform them into the bearers of their own demands and their own interpretation of the hegemonic political culture. Paradoxically, subordinate groups even use organizations created to facilitate state control to set limits on state demands and construct movements aimed at overthrowing or reshaping the state. Privileges are often recast and reasserted as rights.[3]

In nineteenth-century rural Mexico, the most important old solidarity was that of the village, or more accurately, the "república de indios." The second term is more apt because "pueblo," so often translated as "village," usually referred to a relatively large territorial unit including one head town and several subject settlements. Often these repúblicas were not nucleated clusters of dwellings but rather the centers of dispersed groups of habitations that had been created by the colonial state to facilitate the administration of justice and the collection of tribute. To create them the state reformulated an eclectic mix of pre-Hispanic practices, Spanish law and tradition, and the utopian ideals of missionary clergymen. In theory the república was both a corporation with rights of its own and an appendage of royal administration; in practice it became a powerful locus for resisting some uses of colonial authority while reaffirming loyalty to the king and hence the system as a whole. Thus the república serves as an excellent example of how hegemonic institutions and ideology work in practice.

After independence, the municipality became the key institution of local political life. The new municipalities differed from the repúblicas in two important respects: first, although their size varied over time, they were always larger than the old repúblicas and usually included several former repúblicas; second, they were not restricted to individuals of Indian ancestry. By the end of the colonial period "Indian" survived more as a political category than as an ethnic one, denoting anyone who resided in a república and had the rights and obligations associated with membership. Municipalities opened local political power to people who had not previously been members of Indian republics; this change carried the danger that resources belonging to the republics might now be diverted from their traditional uses.

Andrés Lira González and Rodolfo Pastor, the two authors who have most concerned themselves with the local effects of Mexican state formation in the early nineteenth century, have both emphasized its negative impact on Mexico's Indian peasantry. They argue that the new municipalities were less autonomous than the repúblicas and outsiders gained control of peasant resources through the new institutions.[4] In contrast, this study will demonstrate that peasants used diverse strategies to counteract these threats and were often successful. Peasants struggled fiercely to defend established rights and to assert new ones, both through manipulating new institutions and influencing political outcomes at the center. The outcomes outlined by Pastor and Lira González were not inevitable but varied over time as the result of both local and national political conflict. The twenty years following independence set the stage for a local political struggle that would continue for the rest of the nineteenth century.

The Elaboration of Projects at the Center

Processes in the center partially underpinned this local struggle. When Mexico became independent in 1821, the principles that had governed the colonial state, including the unification of corporate groups through the king, were no longer viable. The basic relationship between the polity and civil society had to be reformulated. Beginning in the 1820s lawmakers enacted constitutions and laws that specified the patterns of government at the national, state, and local levels, many of which are still visible in the structure of the Mexican state today. These new constitutional and administrative measures were not produced by a political elite detached from the realities of Mexican social life but were based on practical experiences. Lawmakers were reordering their social and political world, and they often did so by renovating and strengthening key elements of the political order carried over from the colonial period.

Laws and constitutions often consciously deferred to the past, striving explicitly to recover aspects of the colonial state's legendary legitimacy to cement the new order. The first constitution applied in Mexico was the Spanish Constitution of 1812, product of a movement that saw itself as a "traditional revolution," codifying already existing precepts rather than creating new ones. The preamble of the constitution invoked "God, All-powerful, Father, Son, and Holy Spirit, Author and Supreme Legislator of Society," and subsequent early state and federal constitutions used similar forms. This formula defined "the divine origin of society and power, an origin not only compatible with the attribution of sovereignty to the community, but also very much in keeping with the Spanish tradition which denied the doctrine of the immediate divine origin of monarchic power."[5] In the new order most political acts were still legitimated through religious ceremonies and the participation of the clergy.

Furthermore, many colonial laws remained in force for at least the first half of the century, and colonial legal precedents were used to decide cases whenever independent governments had not specifically dealt with the relevant issues.[6] Lira González notes that the Mexico City legal arena was a veritable "Tower of Babel" as late as the 1840s, with lawyers drawing on an eclectic legal education and both old and new legislation to argue cases. A truly radical shift did not occur until there was a generational shift in the legal profession around midcentury.[7] This confused arena improved the leverage of peasants in their struggle to retain old rights and acquire new ones.

Press restrictions were lifted in New Spain as a result of the 1820 liberal revolution in Spain, and immediately a lively political debate ensued in both newspapers and pamphlets. The problem of order was linked to the problem of reform. The new system would have to prevent Mexico's majority peasant population from engaging in acts of disorder either by sealing the peasantry off from the elite allies who had facilitated the 1810 explosion or by instituting reforms to defuse social tensions.[8] Those who favored isolating the peasantry from potential allies endeavored to reconstruct elite consensus, emphasizing the horrors of class war manifest in the 1810s, the threat to property rights posed by class tensions, and the unsuitability of Mexico's Indian peasantry for modern politics.[9] This movement was a classic attempt by a small elite group to convince those directly below it that their interests also lay in the protection of order against a potential threat from farther below.

A second group of pundits sought to incorporate Mexico's peasantry into politics as potential allies against the remnants of the colonial elite. Its members also cherished order but thought it could be best achieved through reform. They emphasized the value of Mexico's Indian peasants, who they believed could become ideal citizens if they were extended the benefits of education,[10] and insisted that both peasants and the urban poor were legitimate political actors in the new order and thus among those who could be appealed to in forming alliances. This group also favored defusing social tensions through reform, even agrarian reform that would require a reinterpretation of property rights based on the illegitimacy of the Conquest and rights obtained thereby.[11]

The Origins and Importance of the Municipal System

Mexico's first formal constitution, the Spanish Constitution of 1812, has had a profound impact on Mexican political culture.[12] The viceregal government promulgated the constitution but soon suspended some features in the Mexico City area, particularly those dealing with freedom of the press and municipal elections; in 1812–13 the constitution was implemented only in urban areas and provinces not affected by the insurgency, especially in its provisions regarding local power.[13] The 1812 constitution was a very liberal document that heavily influenced the insurgent Constitution of Apatzingán, written almost two years later. Not surprisingly, New Spain's Mexico City–based dominant class applauded Fernando VII's 1814 revocation of this constitution.[14] The Liberal Revolution of 1820 in Spain restored the 1812 constitution in Mexico, the Plan of Iguala left it in effect, and it remained the general law of the land until the promulgation of Mexico's 1824 constitution.[15]

One of the most revolutionary provisions of the Spanish constitution allowed the establishment of municipalities in "villages . . . where it is convenient" and required their establishment "in those which by themselves or with their territory arrive at one thousand souls."[16] Significantly, the same viceregal government that had restricted this provision to urban centers in 1812 allowed its implementation in rural areas in 1820. In 1820–21 municipalities were erected all over New Spain, with no less than 71 appearing in Guerrero between July 1820 and January 1821. This process continued at a slower pace until the mid-1820s when new state laws began to take effect.[17]

The importance of municipalities to both state formation and the local social roots of national political struggles in the early nineteenth century cannot be overemphasized. Most people came into contact with state power at the municipal level of government, and the state built new means of collective and individual identification at this level. The possibilities for the distribution of local power were what most changed with the coming of independence, and the way in which they changed is the most important factor in explaining both state formation and the insertion of some of Mexico's impoverished rural majority into nineteenth-century political processes.

Andrés Lira González and Rodolfo Pastor have emphasized the negative aspects of this change, correctly pointing out that the new local political institutions were agencies of the central government designed to reduce opportunities for local autonomy.[18] But the central government had no effective means of enforcing its aims and directives at the local level. New Spain's colonial administration had experienced the same problem, but it appointed its officials and the substantial bond required of colonial officeholders ensured that state authority on the periphery remained at the disposal of wealthy local interests or members of the Mexico City elite. In contrast, from 1820 to 1835 municipal office was the object of local struggle in which relatively powerless people, including peasants, competed through both bullet and ballot.[19] Municipalities, like other institutions that state-builders designed to suit their own aims, were not always understood by local groups as simple agencies of the state but were defined in part by local traditions and objectives.[20]

Lira González and Pastor also point out that the republican innovations had a negative impact on peasants by allowing local elites access to Indian village resources.[21] It is true that local mestizo and Creole landowners, merchants, and politicians often inserted themselves into communities and subverted the management and eventual ownership of community resources, but this scenario was only one of several possible outcomes contingent on the local balance of power. Lira González himself notes that peasants sometimes successfully used the new institutions to protect their resources.[22] Furthermore, even during the colonial period local elites had been able to tap república resources through the subdelegados. When the nominal control of peasant resources shifted from the repúblicas and subdelegados to the municipalities, a struggle began in which the elected character of municipal institutions, the reduced legitimacy of the new central state, and its lack of an effective monopoly over the use of force often favored peasants, allowing them to either control or ignore the new institutions.

The new municipality thus had a dual role as agency of the nation-state and the strategic high ground in struggles over local resources. It affected the life of Mexico's rural poor in very direct ways and served as their primary link to the idea and praxis of the nation-state. Because the municipality's intermediate role between the national state and the rural majority was both practical and symbolic, it emerged as the most important institution of the new order.

From its inception under the Spanish constitution, the municipality became the symbolic center of rural political life, taking precedence over other local institutions in ceremonies. Furthermore, the principal role in ceremonies legitimating new municipalities belonged to the officers of other recently constituted ones.[23] Leaders of local political movements aimed at overthrowing the central government or extracting concessions from it typically appealed to municipalities for support; such endorsements, whether voluntary or coerced, bestowed legitimacy on their causes by virtue of the municipalities' symbolic position as "the organs of their villages and their united will."[24] Municipalities also took on symbolic importance in the eyes of the central state, first as the arbiters of primary elections in a new era of popular sovereignty, and second as a key to transforming Mexico's poor into suitable citizens for a modern state. Municipalities would fund education and provide practical experience in politics.[25]

In the 1820s and early 1830s most state and central government laws were actually executed by municipal officers. Municipal governments had judicial functions, especially for minor offenses, as well as important police powers and oversight of local public markets. Laws typically gave municipalities responsibility for pursuing both state and local objectives.[26]

Municipalities were also the central government's chief source of political intelligence in the countryside. A complex network of information conduits extended downward from the president through the minister of the interior, state governors, their secretaries, and prefects or *jefes políticos* to the lowest tier composed of municipal officers and their deputies in outlying settlements.[27] The military command structure and the church hierarchy paralleled this system, but though the three systems overlapped and often exchanged information, the most important was undoubtedly that of civilian administration.

One of the primary reasons states create or reinforce organizations at the local level is to collect taxes, as was the case with the colonial repúblicas de indios. After independence municipalities also filled this role and were particularly active in collecting extraordinary taxes to support troops.[28]

Long ago, Max Weber noted that one of the dimensions of "stateness" is monopoly over the use of force in conflict.[29] The new Mexican state farmed out part of this attribute to local forces, which were often organized and controlled by municipalities,[30] because it simply did not have the resources needed to maintain regular troops throughout the country. State-builders did not rely on militias light-heartedly: many members of Mexico's dominant class expressed discomfort with the local power inherent in the militia. In contrast, many radical and moderate federalists sought to reinforce the militia as a counterweight to both the regular army and the power of Mexico City in general. The fierce debate concentrated on the control of militia units, for even the most conservative politicians recognized the impossibility of dispensing entirely with militias.[31] Militia units organized support for and legitimated political movements, but service was not always seen as an opportunity to promote social goals: units often had a hard time enlisting members. Militias in Guerrero had no such problem, however, because of the perceived need to defend the region's coastline and its high degree of mobilization in the War of Independence.[32]

Municipalities and State Formation Under Federalism, 1820–1835

Before the widespread application of the Spanish liberal constitution in 1820, local political power was grudgingly shared between Crown officials appointed from Mexico City and semiautonomous repúblicas de indios whose officials were elected annually. In practice the royal officials were the more powerful because they combined judicial and executive functions and were given substantial authority to oversee the political and economic life of the repúblicas. After independence—or after 1820, to be more accurate—the balance of power shifted decisively. Although the central and state governments appointed a tier of administrative officials in place of the royal offi-

cers, these administrators had less formal power, were fewer in number, and, perhaps most important, represented an order that did not
enjoy the legitimacy of the colonial system.[33] Much of their formal
and practical power passed to the new municipalities.

The new municipalities, however, were not the former repúblicas.
The end of caste distinctions meant that they represented not only
the former constituents of the repúblicas but also local Creole and
mestizo groups of varying socioeconomic origins. Often these groups
had a history of severe conflict and the new institutions only shifted
the locus of the conflict and increased its intensity. Even where these
groups had cooperated before independence the new laws invalidated
old arrangements. Before independence the aid of royal officials was
the most crucial weapon in any local conflict; after independence
control of town councils played this role, especially in areas where
local Creoles and mestizos depended on access to lands that formerly
had been rented to them by the repúblicas.[34] Whereas repúblicas had
helped Indians who sought to assert their authority over Creoles and
mestizos who lived in their towns and used their resources, now
Creoles and mestizos were sometimes able to take legal control of
these same resources through the new institutions. However, where
Indians were able to control the new town councils, they could assert
their authority over the Creoles and mestizos, much to the distress
of those groups.

One of the keys to local political conflict was the provision for
remarkably wide suffrage. The Constitution of 1812, which regulated municipal as well as national elections, mandated universal
male suffrage and an end to caste distinctions. These provisions
were put into practice in some parts of New Spain in 1812–14 and
were instituted more widely beginning in 1820. This Spanish constitution and its Mexican successors of the 1820s at both state and
national levels often did deny the right to vote to several categories
of males, namely, the unemployed, illiterates, vagrants, and servants.
However, notwithstanding Brian Hamnett's suggestion that such restrictions excluded a significant percentage of the Latin American
population, several mitigating factors should be considered. First,
the regulations governing elections stated specifically that the category of servants did not include most wage earners and hacienda
residents but instead applied only to the personal servants of the
wealthy. Second, although several state constitutions also required
literacy, they usually delayed the implementation of this provision
for a period of years. The phrase usually used to exclude the unemployed specified that voters must possess an "oficio o industria

honesta" (honest occupation or industry);[35] this definition was debatable, as will be seen in subsequent chapters. Finally, any evaluation of these provisions should take notice of the fact that between 1820 and 1835 suffrage was wider in Mexico than it was in the United States, Great Britain, and most Western European countries.[36] It was the formal provision for wide suffrage that allowed Indian peasants to compete, sometimes successfully, for control of the new town councils.

Another factor that worked to the advantage of Indian peasants was the similarity between the new bodies and the traditional repúblicas. For instance, the new municipalities obtained their funding from the same sources as the former repúblicas, including land rentals, taxes collected from vendors on local market days, fines levied on minor offenders, and a small tax on all residents,[37] and used that funding for the same purposes, among them administrative expenses, local public works, and schools. Municipalities also underwrote religious expenses, especially those entailed in celebrating titular patron feasts.[38] This expenditure of public funds on religion is not as strange as it sounds, for the post-independence governments relied extensively on religious authority to legitimate the new state and even to spread the new civic virtues.[39] Sums spent on religious titular feasts and the new national holidays were often grouped together in accounts, and national holidays also involved religious celebrations.[40] The new state seems to have been trying to associate itself with ceremonies that reaffirmed local solidarities in order to build its newly imagined national community.[41]

The ability to tax is a key attribute of states.[42] For Guerrero's peasantry, one achievement of the 1810–20 war was a 62.5 percent decline in the level of taxation from the colonial tribute rate of 2 pesos annually to the equivalent of one day's income each trimester, or approximately 2 reales.[43] Some peasants paid 1.5 reales; richer ones paid more.[44] In Guerrero taxation remained low through the early 1830s and, as we shall see later, resurfaced as a crucial issue in the peasant movements of the 1840s.

One of the primary duties of the former repúblicas de indios had been collecting Indian tribute, and tax collection became an important function of the new municipalities. The new personal tax was charged to all, including non-Indians. It was legislated at the state level, which meant that in present-day Guerrero it was administered by two different states, Puebla and Mexico. The state of Mexico experienced difficulty collecting the tax in Guerrero until 1827, when the state government ceded the tax to the municipalities, who used it specifically to finance schools. The state of Puebla also conceded this tax to municipalities frequently on a case-by-case basis.[45] Within municipalities, controversy arose when the funds received were deposited in the head town and used for works there; subject settlements continually requested that they be allowed to spend the funds collected from their own inhabitants. Government rulings on this divisive subject varied.[46]

This tax was not perceived as a continuation of colonial tribute but was associated with the colonial "real y medio," a tax paid by república members for the bienes de comunidad.[47] Only those who considered themselves members of a particular república and derived the benefits of república membership, including access to community lands, paid the real y medio.[48] In other words, payment of this colonial tax was an expression of membership in one of the "old solidarities" that it is often assumed state formation worked against.

The state benefited from its association with this older locus of identity. For instance, the governor of Puebla noted in 1826 that the personal tax was difficult to collect and the only groups who paid it regularly were government employees, some clerics, and, significantly, the members of Indian villages.[49] Furthermore, in practice the payment of this tax was sometimes associated with the notion of citizenship; in some municipalities, all those who paid were referred to in official documents as "citizens," a title connoting membership in the community and voting rights in municipal elections.[50]

Rodolfo Pastor suggests that in the early republican period Indian peasants in Oaxaca did not consider themselves citizens but continued to identify themselves primarily as members of a particular village.[51] Similarly, François Xavier Guerra suggests that most country people, especially Indians, felt more attraction to notions of community cohesion than they did to the new individualism implied by the concept of citizenship.[52] But the notion of citizenship prevalent in at least some villages of Guerrero was not at all associated with a new individualism but rather represented a new manifestation of community membership. This vision of the imagined national community as an extension of the local one was expressed in such documents as Vicente Guerrero's 1815 exhortation of the Indian peasants of the Tlapa area that those "that want to demarcate themselves with the glorious surname of citizens should form their assemblies and frankly apply the procedures which seem to them most convenient not for my liberty nor for that of their own persons nor that of private interests but instead for that of general Liberty . . . and of the common benefit to the honor of this very noble *Pueblo*."[53] Guerrero explicitly disassociates citizenship from individualism here. The fact that the Spanish word "pueblo" denotes both "village" and "people," as in a national people, further facilitated this conflation of local and national community. Tristan Platt notes that Bolivian Indian peasants held similar ideas of citizenship in the same period.[54] It cannot be assumed that the concept of citizenship always carried the individualizing meaning usually associated with it, as "unifying representations from the perspective of the 'State' may well be differentially understood from 'below.'"[55] The case at hand implies that the differential understandings of unifying representations held by those below do not always serve as barriers to projects the state advocates from above. Instead, the state may benefit from strengthening these representations, building the imagined national community.

Another feature that worked to the advantage of Indian peasants was their familiarity with elections. Recently, Guerra has asserted that suffrage in nineteenth-century Mexico was always fictitious and that elections were only significant to the extent that they legitimated power gained earlier by other means.[56] The evidence does not support this statement. Although electoral fraud of various kinds abounded, many elections were hotly contested and were important arenas of political conflict, especially at the local level. There is evidence of widespread participation in elections, particularly in the 1820s. Electoral politics took on even more importance in former Indian communities, where citizenship as identified by tax rolls became identified with the right to vote for the municipal officials who controlled resources.[57] Yet electoral participation was only one strategy used by actors in local political conflict, and its popularity and effectiveness varied considerably.

Electoral conflicts in repúblicas were common before independence. Non-Indians did not participate in elections in rural Mexico before 1812 and thus after independence they lacked experience in this particular kind of politics. Furthermore, factionalism in villages often had introduced Indian peasants to elections as divisive struggles between groups. In contrast, it seems that it took non-Indians most of the 1820s to become accustomed to electoral politics as struggles between groups with different interests rather than as exercises in selecting the most qualified candidates for office. The ceremonies surrounding elections as legislated in the 1820s were very similar to those used in colonial repúblicas, probably because of their common origins in Spanish municipal practice.[58] However, the new elections differed from república elections in that all men over

25 years of age were allowed to vote; in colonial repúblicas voting rights had been determined according to local traditions and were typically extended only to the *pasados,* a small group of older men, former officials, and other members of the village elite.[59]

Post-independence elections were indirect. In municipal elections voters chose electors who in turn chose municipal officers; in state and federal elections several such steps intervened between voters and candidates for office.[60] In the initial elections each voter cast his ballot for various electors by presenting a list that he had either elaborated himself or acquired in printed form from a candidate or party. He was then required to sign this list in the presence of election officials, or if illiterate, to assent to the list as read aloud by an official, who would sign it on his behalf. Voters who had not previously elaborated or acquired such a list could usually state their preferences orally to election officials, who would then write out a list. Obviously, there was no secret ballot, although in some states secondary electors voted secretly at the next level.[61]

Local elections were also relevant to national and state politics. Loose factions of politicians strove to influence elections at the initial level, and elections were often hotly contested despite the influence of local political bosses of various types. Although official records of elections are not uncommon, most of the evidence on electoral organizing exists in the private correspondence of politicians who had little reason to keep up pretenses.[62] In elections for state and federal office, most attempts to influence outcomes took place at the secondary levels, with local political bosses typically directing electors to consult with their allies at the state level to coordinate their efforts.[63]

The new town councils in former Indian villages continued many political traditions from the days of the repúblicas, to the extent that state and federal administrative officials complained that the councils were functioning as if they were still repúblicas.[64] For instance, the council frequently used expressions carried over from the repúblicas such as claiming to act in the name of the *común.* Often they included the names of past as well as present officials in documents, a common practice of colonial repúblicas that had no legal weight in the new order.[65] Even the agents municipal councils appointed to govern subject towns took on attributes of the repúblicas; for instance, in 1829 the "auxiliary aldermen" of Santiago Sacango awarded a power of attorney to a Mexico City lawyer in the name of the "Indian commons of said *pueblo.*" In the document they consciously or unconsciously presented themselves as the successors of the repúblicas by using this common colonial legal formula.[66]

The new municipalities were less numerous than the repúblicas they replaced. The Constitution of 1812, implemented in 1820, allowed the establishment of municipalities wherever authorities decided it was convenient and required their establishment in any settlement which with its surrounding area reached a population of 1,000. The Mexican constitution that succeeded it in 1824 allowed each state to regulate local government, and though some states preserved the large number of municipalities then in practice, others, concerned about decentralization and practices they considered irregular, reduced the number of municipalities.[67] The states that governed most of Guerrero severely reduced the number of municipalities. Puebla required the establishment of town councils in district capitals, the head towns of parishes, and villages with a permanent vicar and allowed the state governor to establish municipalities in villages with 3,000 or more inhabitants. The state of Mexico also reduced the number of municipalities, requiring them only in district capitals and settlements of more than 4,000 inhabitants. Mexico also allowed town councils in areas where several settlements together reached that sum, though only on approval of local administrative officials. These provisions required many municipalities formed between 1820 and 1824 to give up their status; nevertheless, the number of municipalities in the state of Mexico far exceeded the minimum number required by law, and their number in Guerrero crept upward between 1825 and 1835.[68] The state of Mexico's legislature later ended the veto of administrative officials and gave itself the discretionary power—which it used frequently—to erect municipalities wherever necessary.[69]

Many municipal officers elected in the early 1820s under the Spanish constitution were illiterate.[70] Most states tried to prevent this problem by requiring of their municipal officers both literacy and enough income to allow them to devote sufficient time to their functions. The typical phrasing of this second requirement, "some farm, capital, or branch of industry that suffices to provide a regular subsistence," suggests that it was not an attempt to exclude the poor from political power. After all, these same states did not impose property qualifications on state legislators and prefects who received salaries.[71] Indeed, in the early independence period the enforcement of these requirements was loose enough to allow most peasants to take part. Moreover, even in the colonial period the more powerful república offices had usually been filled by relatively wealthy individuals.[72]

Local Political Conflict, *1820–1835*

The interlocking features described above suggest an early post-independence political order that was relatively favorable to peasants and that addressed some of the demands expressed during the second decade of the eighteenth century. Achieving favorable political outcomes in this order required a particular set of interpretations of the laws defining the form and content of local government; because these interpretations were not applied universally, the fate of peasants in the early post-independence political order varied both geographically and chronologically. This section will briefly discuss the geographical variations in outcomes, and the next section will discuss the chronological ones.

Laws were interpreted and disputes worked out in the context of differing local balances of power and actual practices varied greatly. In the interest of simplicity this section will describe two situations at opposite extremes in which different local political situations led to the elaboration and application of two distinct visions of what the local government should be like. These visions informed the local social bases of Mexico's early-nineteenth-century political conflict between federalists and centralists. For this reason, the two kinds of areas in which these visions were applied will be designated federalist and centralist, despite the fact that very few Mexicans described themselves as centralists before the mid-1830s.

In federalist areas the number of municipalities closely approached the number of pre-independence repúblicas. Some municipalities were direct descendants of repúblicas, whereas others united several former repúblicas in which few mestizos or Creoles resided. Some regions in which Indian repúblicas did not exist before independence also fell into this pattern. In federalist areas suffrage was wide in practice as well as law. Often peasants were less averse to personal taxes collected for municipal purposes because the expenditure of revenues was less centralized. In these places citizenship was more likely to be given the connotation of membership in the local and national communities. Here the term federalism came to signify the diffusion of power at the local level that eliminated or reduced the ability of officials appointed in Mexico City or state capitals to interfere in local affairs.[73]

The areas that followed the federalist pattern correspond to those in which insurgent mobilization was strong and sustained in the 1810–20 period. Peasants often had taken part in the war to oppose the activities of local colonial officials on behalf of such "outsiders" as Spanish merchants, local mestizo and Creole rancheros, and the officials themselves. These struggles predisposed peasants toward making maximum use of postwar legislation to reduce or eliminate the power of such outsiders. In such areas the fighting and economic dislocation of the rebellion years had driven out local elites who might otherwise have sought to control the new institutions. Moreover, peasants in these areas acquired greater exposure to the possibilities the new politics held for achieving both individual and collective goals. In Guerrero federalist areas included the Costa Grande and the Tierra Caliente.

Centralist areas present a very different picture. There the number of municipalities was much smaller than that of former Indian repúblicas. Local mestizo and Creole elites often controlled municipalities, and they used this control to effectively disenfranchise peasants and obtain access to the lands Indian communities had rented out for revenue. Cabeceras governed by mestizo and Creole elites used their status as municipal capitals to dominate surrounding Indian villages and to siphon off resources from Indian communities through taxation.[74] This outcome is the one suggested by François Xavier Guerra and described as having occurred in the Mixteca Alta by Rodolfo Pastor.[75] In centralist areas reigned the negative consequences of early republican state formation later postulated by Pastor and Andrés Lira González. Centralist areas of Guerrero included Chilapa and Tixtla. There insurgent mobilization had been low in 1810–20, and this fact helped determine post-independence outcomes. Grievances against outsiders had not been strong before the war, local elites survived with their fortunes largely intact, and peasants saw politics with some suspicion and even fear of the potential costs of political involvement.

This geographical distinction describes outcomes more accurately than it does peasant attitudes toward politics. In federalist areas the peasants fought attempts by the local elite to manipulate the new institutions and usually succeeded; in centralist areas they tried to shake off the stifling control of local elites but usually failed. These attempts reveal much about how various groups perceived the new institutions and also suggest the determinants of various outcomes. Both perceptions and determinants will be relevant in explaining rebellions and alliances in the 1820–55 period.

Struggles over the form and content of the state at the local level are revealed in two distinct yet related kinds of disputes. The first took place over the drawing of municipal boundaries and the selection of towns as municipal capitals. This kind of dispute has been common throughout Latin America and is a direct descendant of the colonial disputes over república boundaries and capitals described in Chapter 1. One example is that of Cocula, an Indian república near Iguala. In 1820 the new town council of Iguala claimed jurisdiction over Cocula and prevented its residents from forming their own town council. The former república immediately appealed to higher officials, noting that it filled the prerequisites for municipalities established by the constitution and claiming that to deny it the "privileges and liberty" attained by "Pueblos Españoles" would be unjust. Authorities granted this request. Colonial officials often resisted similar bids for independence fiercely; for instance, the local subdelegado sent armed men to arrest the new Indian town council of Mochitlán in 1821.[76]

In the mid-1820s laws reduced the number of municipalities, and Cocula was among the localities that lost its status. Towns often resented this change, but the reduction occurred at a moment of little elite political strife and thus most towns chose to acquiesce rather than rebel.[77] The new laws did allow some leeway for those seeking municipal status. In the state of Mexico, for example, the state legislature could form new municipalities in areas where several settlements together made up the minimum population required or in other places where a new municipality was considered necessary. It also could redraw municipal boundaries, moving settlements from one municipality to another,[78] often at the request of the villages themselves. Surprisingly, villages sometimes sought to move from a municipality formed out of several Indian villages to one centered on a mestizo town. The motive for this type of petition seems to have been to avoid competing with other Indian towns for the use of pastures and wild products gathered in uncultivated areas. The law authorized municipalities to regulate such lands, and Indian cabeceras were more likely to exercise this control than mestizo towns. Still, Indian villages more often sought the right to elect their own officers, or to move the municipal capital to their town.[79]

The second type of clash is perhaps more familiar. Elections were important sources of local power and election results were often disputed, as they had been in colonial repúblicas. Allegations of fraud and electoral irregularities were common.[80] Those who controlled electoral machinery often closed the polls in the cabecera early in the day, not allowing the residents of outlying villages enough time to arrive and cast ballots.[81] Others held elections without announcing them in the public manner prescribed by law, again to prevent voters who did not belong to the ruling clique from participating.[82] Another popular tactic, common in cases where violent political strife coincided with scheduled elections, was to frighten people away from the polls. In the early 1830s, for instance, the officer in charge of the local militia force regularly intimidated the inhabitants of Chilapa and Zitlala into not voting.[83]

The Centralist Counterrevolution in Government

To date, the rural social bases of political movements in early-nineteenth-century Mexico have been largely obscure, mainly because historians have been predisposed to see the contest as one between anticlerical liberals and conservative supporters of the church. Prior to 1855–56, however, the church issue was considered relatively minor by many of the most important participants in politics. The 1833 and 1847 efforts to limit the economic and temporal power of the church led by Valentín Gómez Farías were repudiated by many men who considered themselves progressives, including some who had helped put Gómez Farías in power. This situation changed dramatically in the 1850s after the war with the United States; by then various church leaders had accentuated the church/state problem with their resistance to using church funds to fight the U.S. invasion and their later support for the conservatives in Puebla's 1856 insurrection and the War of the Reform.

In the 1820–50 period Mexican politics divided not so much along a liberal/conservative axis as along a centralist/federalist one. This statement is potentially confusing. In the 1820s no politician openly claimed to be a centralist and by the 1840s many centralists were toying with monarchism; nonetheless, there was a clear distinction between those who sought to centralize power and those who sought to further disperse it. By the late 1820s and early 1830s those who sought to disperse power began to identify themselves as federalists and their opponents as centralists. This formulation, which the centralists labeled demagoguery, proved correct in 1835 when the centralists showed their true colors.

Chapter 4 will further examine the coalitions suggested above. This section will instead discuss the centralism of the 1830s as it affected rural Mexico. The key point is that centralism was not, as François Xavier Guerra would have it, a mere substitution of the "name of State for that of department"[84] but an attempt to restrict political power to a smaller group of men higher up in Mexico's class structure. Centralism eliminated states and state legislatures, instituted strict property qualifications for suffrage and stricter ones for officeholding, and severely reduced the number of municipalities.[85] These provisions and other legislation limited the ability of Mexico's peasantry to legally protect land from usurpers. Centralists also made determined efforts to extract more revenue from these same peasants. These practical changes in political institutions and power were paralleled by centralist attempts to elaborate and impose new ideological patterns of deference and hierarchy, and the combination was explosive, as will be seen in Chapter 5.

Centralism was not formally instituted until 1835, but even earlier the term had acquired a popular definition in Guerrero and was common in political discourse. Popular political culture in Guerrero defined "centralism" as the reduction of the power of humble people to govern their own affairs. Peasants and others associated it with the interests of a restricted group of families in Mexico City, often referred to as the "pretended aristocracy." Centralism was criticized because it would lead to a concentration of power in the hands of a small group of authorities who neither knew nor cared about the world outside Mexico City.[86] It was also associated with fears of domination by the Spanish-born, the possibility of a Spanish reconquest, and even the reinstitution of monarchy under a transplanted Spanish king. These ideas were not generally distinguished from each other and their prevalence in Guerrero frustrated centralist officials who decried them as ignorant, demagogic rhetoric.[87] However, the Spanish desire for reconquest posed a real threat in the late 1820s, and more than a few centralists embraced monarchism between the 1840s and the 1860s. The identification of a group loosely described as an aristocracy and their association with both Spanish colonialism and the dominance of the Spanish-born over Mexico's political and economic life constituted a reasonable reading of the class structure of late colonial Mexico described in Chapter 1. In other words, Guerrero's federalist politicians and their poor rural constituents did not elaborate their critique in ignorance.

Generally speaking, centralism was foreshadowed by the uneasiness of both local elites and their state and national counterparts about the way Mexico's rural poor interpreted the new laws of the early 1820s. This uneasiness led to attempts to reduce the number of municipalities in the mid-1820s, ostensibly because of the ignorance of the officials elected in rural municipalities and their inability to follow correct procedures. This reconcentration of power was deeply resented and gave Guerrero's poor a clear sense of what was at stake.[88]

Centralism, as articulated and implemented in the late 1830s, is often depicted as an attempt to control restless provincial elites, but

it was also an effort of the Mexico City–based dominant class to restrict peasant power in the Meseta Central areas where its members
owned haciendas. The latter motive underlay the severe reduction in
the number of municipalities,[89] upon which local elites in some pe-
ripheral areas eagerly seized as the answer to their own social control
problems. The overtly centralist Orizaba proclamation of 1835 was
seconded by town councils in the centralist area two months before
it was in the federalist area.[90]

The centralist system constructed beginning in 1835 represented
a radical counterrevolution that reversed the dispersion of power
that had occurred under federalism. Governors appointed by the national government replaced elected state governors. Small departmental councils with only advisory and administrative powers replaced state legislatures, greatly weakening the capacity of state
governments to formulate positions opposing the national government. The number of municipalities was severely reduced: they
would now exist only in departmental (state) capitals, places where
they had existed before 1808, ports with populations over 4,000, and
other towns with at least 8,000 inhabitants. These municipal regulations, which eliminated almost every municipality in Guerrero,
led to sweeping changes throughout Mexico.[91] Provisions regarding
municipalities became less strict again beginning in the mid-1840s
but municipalities never again were as widespread as they had been
in the early 1820s.[92]

Centralist regimes also severely restricted suffrage. Under the
Siete Leyes of 1836 only those with annual incomes of more than 100
pesos could vote,[93] and the 1843 Bases Orgánicas further limited suffrage to those with annual incomes of more than 200 pesos.[94] Both
standards eliminated Mexico's peasantry.[95] The peasantry was also
not included in the complicated requirements under which members
of various occupational groups were to select a new constitutional
congress in early 1846. Under these rules Mexico's polity was divided
into property holders, merchants, mine owners, manufacturers, professionals, magistrates, bureaucrats, clerics, and army officers. Peasants did not own enough land to qualify as property holders; the
number of eligible property holders in the Department of Mexico,
including Mexico City, was so reduced that their names could be
published in a 32-page document. Only 17 of these 890 people resided in Guerrero.[96] Universal male suffrage was not restored until
the elections of 1848 and even then its implementation would be
brief.[97] Property qualifications for office also increased under central-

ism; for instance, as of 1837 town council members had to possess a "physical or moral" capital that produced at least 500 pesos per year.[98]

Centralism also drastically changed the level and nature of taxation in the countryside. In the 1820s and 1830s peasants in Guerrero paid approximately 0.75 peso per year as *contribución personal*, which municipalities collected to support local schools. Beginning in the early 1840s national governments became much more interested in the peasantry as a source of revenue: an 1841 law provided for a personal tax graduated according to income and individuals with annual incomes under 500 pesos paid 1.5 pesos per year. A year later this tax was replaced with the *capitación*, which called for 1.5 pesos per year from every inhabitant of the country. This new tax supplemented a graduated income tax on those who made more than 300 pesos annually. The new personal taxes encountered widespread peasant opposition, expressed through both evasion and rebellions (see Chapter 5), which forced the government to establish an exception for "*jornaleros* [wage earners] and domestic servants" in July 1843. Only those who worked for others and were paid on a daily basis were excepted as jornaleros.[99]

In 1845 Ygnacio Piquero, a functionary of the national Secretaría de Hacienda, published a lengthy pamphlet entitled "Brief Instruction about the Direct Taxes Established in the Nation since 1836."[100] Piquero was the author of the 1842 capitación law and was also influential in drafting other revenue legislation of the period. This work thus provides a window into the reasoning that drove efforts to increase the revenue extracted from individuals as well as the connection between these measures and the larger project of state formation. Some of the motivation was purely fiscal. Piquero and other politicians expected that personal taxes would be easy to collect and would produce 2.5 million pesos annually.[101]

These taxes were also associated with some classic ideas about state formation. In his "Brief Instruction" Piquero reproduced an 1841 report in which he justified his proposed capitación with the ideal of a state that served a community of civic equals. A tax demanding equal payments from all regardless of station was just because "the poor man can demand the protection of the authorities the same way the rich man can; equally he can demand that justice be administered to him. . . . In the same way . . . the poor and the rich should contribute with a little for the expenses that society incurs to maintain the troops who defend the territory, to pay the authorities and other agents of public power." The capitación was proposed as a supplement to more progressive taxes.[102] Later, when certain congressmen objected to the capitación because of the poor's insolvency, Piquero responded with an even more elaborate justification, stating that if the poor were not required to contribute they would be isolated from the "social body." Without a stake in the government they would not be inclined to care about "the survival or ruin of the government or . . . the stability of institutions." Piquero argued that it was easy for the poor to acquire subsistence-level income and that any surplus they retained was spent on religious feasts and drunkenness. Thus it was necessary to tax them to force them to work. Finally, Piquero noted that his opponents' comparison of the new tax to the colonial tribute was not entirely off base; the only problem with the tribute, he said, which received little resistance from Indians, was that it had been collected solely from Indians.[103]

Contrary to Piquero's expectation, peasants resented the capitación, which was added to the earlier tax used for education at the local level to effect an increase in personal taxes of 200 percent. A peasant who in 1834 paid 0.75 peso per year now paid 2.25 pesos. This rate exceeded the usual colonial tribute rate of 2 pesos per year.[104] The new tax, which unlike the earlier tax funded distant national and later departmental governments,[105] was imposed just as new restrictions on citizenship and new laws reducing the number of municipalities disenfranchised the rural peasant majority.

The centralist regime dramatically reduced the number of municipalities to limit local power, but it needed nevertheless to reconcile this project to the basic realities of life in the countryside. The government simply could not afford to leave the vast number of small peasant villages without supervision, so it placed this task in the hands of unsalaried justices of the peace. Prefects usually appointed these functionaries from among local residents, replacing earlier practice in which similar officials were either elected popularly or appointed by town councils to govern outlying settlements.[106]

The centralist justice of the peace was an apparent step forward in a state project designed to eliminate or reduce old solidarities that stood between the state and individual citizens. The change from elected representatives of localities to executive agents of centralized power was particularly pronounced where municipalities based on former repúblicas lost their status. In practice, however, the centralizing effect of this innovation was tempered by the need to "keep the peace" in the countryside without spending much money, for which reason justices of the peace were often informally chosen, or at least approved, by local residents. The government also removed justices who aroused the ire of their communities in order to preserve social peace.[107]

In practice justices filled many of the functions formerly assigned to town councils and, before that, repúblicas. The most obvious of these was tax collection, particularly the new personal taxes, but justices also organized labor for public works and communal expenses, a technically illegal prerogative sometimes tolerated by the central government.[108] Prefects had no choice but to let justices represent communities in land disputes, as in 1840 when the justice of San Juan Tetelzingo called together "los alcaldes pasados y viejos" (the former aldermen and old men) to consult on a boundary dispute.[109] In some cases authorities even demanded that justices assume this role, as in 1840 when a prefect ordered the justice of Mochitlán to gather "los pasados y biejos" of his community to recognize a boundary.[110] Justices nominally appointed by the central state actually organized some of the peasant invasions of neighboring landholdings so common throughout Mexico in the post-independence years.[111]

Clearly even the centralists, hostile to any dispersion of power, had to make some concessions to social realities in the countryside. The organizations and officials that Indian peasants had used earlier to administer their lands and communal expenses had been under attack since before independence, yet peasants consistently either maintained such institutions without the recognition of higher authorities or, more commonly, appropriated the new institutions the central government designed to govern the countryside. Communities survived not only because of the defiance of their constituents but also because the central government needed a presence in the countryside. The central government could not create a corps of officials sufficiently numerous, educated, and motivated to enforce its wishes in the countryside without making major concessions to the will of the rural population. Nor could it finance such a bureaucracy and the military force that would be needed to enforce its dictates. Thus, in practice, communities continued to exist.[112]

State Formation and Agrarian History

The post-independence fate of the lands held in common by Indian villages has dominated the historiography of the Mexican countryside. The land issue has generally been overemphasized in studies of rural conflict in this period. However, because this issue is one in which the dispositions of centralized power were modified by the activities of various local groups, it seems worthwhile to analyze how state formation intersected with the more traditional, economic basis of the land problem in rural conflict.

In 1825 the state of Mexico enacted its basic law governing municipal administration, assigning to municipalities "the lands which the *pueblos* have possessed in common along with the other rights and shares which belong to them." This rule seems to have been designed to finance town councils by allowing them to rent out lands villages had formerly rented for the same purpose. In the text of the law, this provision is grouped with other forms of municipal revenue and lacks association with the liberal, privatizing bent often associated with this period.[113] Still, the provision aroused controversy in the countryside. The problem was simple: even in the heyday of federalism in the mid-1820s municipalities were much fewer than the former *repúblicas* and thus, applied literally, the 1825 law would have taken lands from subject towns and put them under the control of cabeceras. Furthermore, the law was vague; the phrase "the lands which the *pueblos* have possessed in common" seems designed to exclude the tierras de repartimiento that Indians typically possessed as individuals while holding legal title in common, but this interpretation was debatable.[114] The state government further confused the situation in 1833 when it tried to further improve municipal revenues by assigning municipalities the "unappropriated or idle land which exists in the territory of their municipalities."[115] This provision could be interpreted as applying only to unclaimed and unused lands or as including any lands not held according to legitimate titles.[116]

The drive to divide tierras de repartimiento among their possessors further compounded the confusion. This effort was not an attempt to move from a rural economy based on collective agriculture to one in which individuals farmed independently but rather an attempt to change a system in which individual peasant plots could not be sold outside the community to one in which peasants held individual legal title and thus were free to sell to anyone. The state of Mexico confined its efforts in this regard to a constitutional provision allowing prefects to carry out such distribution. Puebla, which also governed part of present-day Guerrero, decreed a division in 1828, but the governor never published the law because the legislature failed to send him the information necessary to form relevant regulations. A new law followed in 1836.[117]

The vague and sometimes conflicting dispositions of these laws were confusing, and they provoked a variety of responses from the many groups and individuals they touched. For instance, in 1830 the town council of Tixtla attempted to collect rent from the Indian possessors of tierras de repartimiento, basing its claim on the 1825 law under which "the lands which the *pueblos* have possessed in common" became municipal property. A councilman representing the Indians protested the proposed annual rent of 2 reales per individual, arguing that the land in question was "property" of the Indians. The Indians also noted that the Spanish government had never charged rent. The position of the council majority was weak. Fearing that any attempt to collect the new rents would provoke a riot yet realizing that its authority would be ridiculed if no such attempt were made,[118] the council remained adamant. Prefect José María Bermudez argued that "the Indians are gaining ground little by little . . . and if this is not corrected in time the ill will be incurable." He also suggested that what the Indians in question really wanted was to return to the time when they were "slaves" of their repúblicas. The state cabinet recommended that the state insist on the collection of rents.[119]

Up to this point the Tixtla incident seems a typically callous attempt to appropriate the resources formerly held by Indian communities. But events took a new course. The state governor asked the prefect to verify whether the lands in question were actually tierras de repartimiento, noting that the law applied only to bienes de comunidad, land that colonial repúblicas had possessed in common and rented out for revenue. The cabinet had not considered this interpretation. In a rambling letter that completely avoided the question posed by the governor, Bermudez insisted that all Indian lands were "commons" and thus all should pass to the town councils under the law. He again attributed the problem to both the supposed aggressiveness of the Indians and an imputed rejection of the equality provided by the post-independence legislation.[120] When asked again for the information, local authorities reported that the Indians had never paid rent, which suggested that the lands were tierras de repartimiento.[121] However, by the time this information reached the state government its personnel had changed and the new authorities supported the interpretation originally proffered by the town council under which all lands formerly held by repúblicas passed to the municipalities.[122] There is no evidence that the town council ever successfully collected the rent.

This case demonstrates how complicated the interpretation and implementation of the new laws could be. Because the case surfaced in a cabecera, the seat of a town council interested in gaining revenue, the council was able to collect information on the lands and attempt to implement an interpretation that favored it. More often state governments were simply unable to enforce laws for lack of effective agents; local officials rarely risked collecting accurate information in the face of Indian reticence.[123] For instance, in 1835 the governor of the state of Mexico criticized the continued administration of peasant lands by the legally nonexistent "commons," which spent money supporting useless and wasteful festivals and "harassing the neighboring landowners with suits,"[124] but reports forwarded by the government's local agents suggest the government's powerlessness in the matter.

In 1839 the prefect of Taxco reported that village lands were administered by "what is called the commons of the *Pueblo* which is an assemblage of the most notable Indians made by the free election of the residents, which distributes the land among the same residents for cultivation and dedicates part for the sustainment of the divine cult, often making the most costly sacrifices in its defense when some landowner tries (as happens frequently) to appropriate some part."[125] His counterpart in Teloloapan reported that the resistance of the "commons" had prevented the agents of the state from administering village lands.[126] The justices of the peace in Cocula noted that they could not administer the land because the Indians claimed it as their property, and the justices saw some validity in this claim.[127] Some reports stated that Indians continued to use the former village lands without paying rent because they owned them;[128] others emphasized the interpretation that gave the Indians rights as property holders by virtue of the fact that the village lands were farmed by individuals and transmitted from fathers to sons.[129] In still other localities officials said that residents did not pay rent because they instead provided labor for public works; by 1842 this arrangement had been reached in Tixtla, site of the dispute discussed above.[130] Even when town councils pressed for the right to charge rents they were not always backed by the state government.[131]

Three factors conspired against the implementation of state laws that legislated the abolition of repúblicas and the transfer of their lands to the new town councils. First, as suggested by the case of Tixtla, the laws themselves were contradictory or vague and the application of uniform criteria in even single cases was sometimes prevented by turnover in government personnel. Second, often officials agreed with Indian claims that the land was their property. Third, the Indians resisted. Peasants sometimes resisted violently, other times pressed claims through judicial or administrative channels, and yet other times passively refused to provide the information needed to implement laws. The last tactic was often more than sufficient in an era of chronic government shortfalls in revenue; in fact, it had been effective even when the wealthier colonial state tried to inventory peasant resources.[132]

Before independence Indian peasants continually used the court system to defend or press claims to resources, particularly land and water. Such claims were almost always made in the name of the república, which also served as an organizational vehicle to raise the money needed to finance legal action. After independence repúblicas no longer legally existed, yet villages without municipal councils continued to grant powers of attorney and press claims. Some states set up procedures for these actions, but even in states lacking such legal mechanisms villages asserted their legal existence and were often recognized by the courts.[133]

This situation irked many government officials even under federalism, and the centralists moved quickly to end it upon reaching power. An 1838 law assigned the right to grant powers of attorney to the justices of the peace, but its provisions gave rise to numerous complications. To begin with, the law required that all the justices of a former municipality agree on a single representative. Very often land disputes took place between villages of the same municipality, and in this new system the same lawyer might represent both parties to a dispute.[134] Perhaps the most obstructive of the new law's provisions was its stipulation that villages obtain the approval of prefects before pressing lawsuits. Prefects often had friends and clients who were interested parties in the suit (and sometimes had a conflict of interest themselves), and they were able to block legal action simply by claiming that it was too costly for the peasants.[135] The new law made it much more difficult for villages to press legal claims.

This chapter has surveyed state formation in rural Mexico in the 1820–40 period with two goals in mind. First, it sought to demonstrate how state formation involved actors outside of capital cities and elites. State formation was a multifaceted process that involved not only the writing of laws but also their interpretation, a process whose outcomes were determined by both the aspirations of state-builders in the center and the varying balances of political power on the periphery. Second, the chapter sought to introduce the issues that state formation raised in the countryside. Later we will see how these issues made state formation fundamental to both the construction of national political alliances and the origins and demands of nineteenth-century peasant revolts.

Perhaps the most striking feature of state formation in early republican Mexico was the tendency of state-makers to defer to the power of local agencies and institutions. The most prominent of these was the municipality, which paradoxically became both the most important executive agent of the central state and the most important bearer of the demands that peasants and other rural people made on the state. National politicians sought to impose a model under which individuals related directly to the national state with little recourse to intermediate solidarities or organizations. To exert power, however, they were forced to use and even reinforce these same organizations and solidarities.

Understanding state formation and rural society in early independent Mexico requires the bridging of three "common-sense" dichotomies that pervade much research on both subjects: local versus national, modern versus traditional, and elite versus poor. In early-nineteenth-century Mexico laws were written in the national or state capitals, but they were interpreted locally in quite varied and shifting ways. The first few years after Mexico became independent were years of great institutional and legal innovation, but many innovations drew their force from association with existing features of the political and social landscape. Moreover, although laws were invariably written by people of wealth and power, circumstances often gave relatively poor people in rural Mexico leverage with which to shape laws as they were implemented.

For a brief time in the 1820s and early 1830s, some peasants and other local groups were able to implement very favorable interpretations of the new legislation. They used wide suffrage to control municipalities and defend their resources and limited the power of the appointed officials whose colonial counterparts had exploited peasant resources. These peasants also paid substantially less in taxes than they had before independence. But their success was largely contingent on the local balance of power, and in other areas peasants lost control over local politics to mestizo and Creole elites.

This geographical distinction was the basis on which the local meanings of federalism and centralism were elaborated. Notably, the local federalist interpretation was not always shared by national federalists, who often had no more use for the Indian peasantry than did their centralist counterparts. Some federalist politicians were horrified by the diffusion of power with which their alliance became associated.[136] Nevertheless, these vernacular interpretations underlay local participation in the national political struggles of the early independence period. Peasants interpreted and experienced the national move to centralism in the late 1830s as an extension of the unfavorable outcome reached in some areas to all. The triumph of centralism was coupled with a sharp rise in taxation and legal changes that reduced the ability of peasants to press claims to resources through the courts. Centralist legislation of the late 1830s sparked the grievances over taxes, land, and local autonomy underpinning the peasant upheavals of the 1840s that will be examined in Chapter 5.

CHAPTER 4

National Politics and Local Social Movements in Guerrero, 1820-1840

The bastard application of economic principles and the unconsidered latitude that was given to foreign commerce aggravated our economic necessities, and the cry against this system, so ruinous in its bases and results, is uniform throughout the Republic.

—Vicente Guerrero, Mexico City, 1829

This is not a war of principles, nor one to sustain political opinions. It is a desolating war whose objective is to ruin all property; to entirely subvert property; to cause a desolation a hundred times more terrible than that of 1810 and the following years.

—Lucás Alamán, Mexico City, March 12, 1830

[Our objective is] to sustain the sovereignty of the States, force the reinstatement of the deputies, and prevent the federal system from being changed for the central, which is how the agents of the European tyrant desire to subjugate us.

—Juan Alvarez, Dos Arroyos, November 9, 1830

The previous chapter discussed laws, state formation, and political conflict in early republican Guerrero. The present chapter examines the same 1820–40 period in a different way, concentrating on the constitution of alliances and the formation of ideologies in national and local politics. Although its structure is basically narrative and chronological, the simultaneous examination of local and national politics requires the interweaving of these two levels of analysis. Thus the narrative alternates between the local and the national while exploring their myriad ties.

Most attempts to understand national politics in this important period have overlooked the local dimensions and bases of politics. Analyses of national politics have generally been confined to descriptions of two loose groups of relatively high income and status centered in Mexico City. Michael Costeloe, in the most complete synthesis of the period, asserts that politics were totally confined to these elite groups.[1] Only recently have scholars moved to analyze the impact of regional elites on national politics.[2] This chapter proceeds a step further in the same direction, arguing that the vagaries of elite political allegiances cannot be understood without reference to their varying bases of support, which included, although perhaps intermittently, some of the poorest people in Mexico.

The cataclysmic struggle between liberals and conservatives dominates the political historiography of nineteenth-century Mexico. This conflict came to a head after the Mexican-American War and sent armies marching over much of Mexico almost continually for the next twenty years. Several recent works have probed the social and ideological bases of this conflict in the 1850–70 period,[3] but with few exceptions historians have uncritically accepted the triumphant liberals' assertions that they were the historical heirs of the 1810–21 independence war and that the political history of the 1820–60 period can thus be understood in terms of the later struggles. This analysis implied that liberals and conservatives or at least their precursors could be identified even immediately after the 1821 Treaty of Cordoba.[4] In this analysis the liberals agreed with Lucás Alamán's thesis of a conservative independence achieved almost without reference to the social aspirations of the insurgents.[5] However, accepting the radicals of the 1820s as both the heirs of the insurgents and the direct ancestors of the liberals of midcentury fails to explain the relative political quiet of 1821–28.

The view set forth in this chapter differs from the traditional view in two important ways. First, it asserts that the political polarization of Mexico in the late 1820s did not flow directly from dissatisfaction with the terms under which independence had been achieved. As explained in Chapter 2, the Plan of Iguala did not represent a conservative reaction—the only conservative provision in the Plan, that guaranteeing clerical privileges, was certainly compatible with the insurgent program elaborated by Morelos—but incorporated many of the aims of the insurgents. The increasing fragmentation of political consensus after 1826 resulted from two related causes: the first was the generalized perception of a counteroffensive organized by Mexico's dominant class against the gains achieved in the early 1820s; the second was the popular discontent caused by Mexico's insertion into the world economy as a market for textiles from the newly industrializing North Atlantic nations. These two factors pushed both provincial elites and some lower-class sectors to define their interests in opposition to those of a Mexico City–based dominant class that they identified with the continuation of Spanish colonialism. This polarization resulted in the 1828 Revolution of La Acordada, which crystallized the alignments whose opposition and relative balance of power underlay successive changes of government in the 1828–35 period.

The second way in which this chapter differs from traditional interpretations of the period is its assertion that the contending forces of the 1820–40 period were not liberal and conservative but are better described as federalist and centralist. The position of the church and other corporations in Mexican society was not central to either of these latter ideologies; both focused instead on the distribution of power in society and the economy. Federalists were no more likely to attack corporations than their centralist adversaries, and vice versa. Clerics as a group did not actively support any particular political faction or position in this period.[6] Certainly a small group of men centered around Valentín Gómez Farías and José Luís Mora could be considered liberals by later standards, but these men were a tiny part of a much larger federalist alliance. When these "liberals" tried to implement anticlerical reforms they were repudiated by most of their allies. In the end the tenets of federalism and centralism that will be analyzed here were absorbed into liberalism and conservatism, but into the 1850s the latter ideologies continued to rely on the former to mobilize support.

The previous chapter detailed how the varying interpretations of laws in the 1820–40 period underlay the local definitions of the two main political currents of the time, federalism and centralism, as well as the constitution of local political alliances. In the early 1820s peasants in some areas of Guerrero were able to interpret post-independence laws and constitutions in relatively favorable ways. They used provisions for wide suffrage to control municipalities and defend resources from outsiders who had earlier manipulated them with the help of intrusive colonial officials. Peasants also enjoyed substantially lower personal taxes than those levied before independence. Increased autonomy and lower taxes eventually came to constitute the definition of "federalism" at the local level. However, these favorable interpretations were not implemented uniformly. In some places local elites controlled the new institutions and were thus able to access the resources associated with them. This situation became known as "centralism," even when it took place under the federalist constitution in force from 1824 to 1835.

Guerrero was successfully pacified in the early 1820s, and most former insurgents were satisfied with the results of their struggle. However, the precipitous decline of the textile industry under the impact of the flood of imports eventually destroyed this fragile peace. The local response came in the form of anti-Spanish agitation and support for the radical *yorkino* movement that culminated in the Vicente Guerrero presidency of 1829. This alliance was overthrown after a few dizzying months in office, and the more conservative government that followed eventually suppressed the ensuing guerrilla war. The federalist coalition reached power again in 1833 but its disintegration precipitated the centralist counterrevolution institutionalized in 1835. Centralism cut off the increasingly dissatisfied peasants of Guerrero from their allies in national politics, though not for long; the 1840s were dominated by an increasingly bitter struggle between resurgent federalist alliances and their centralist opponents.

Guerrero to 1829: Peace, Economic Decline, and Nationalism

From 1821 to 1827 Guerrero was remarkably quiet, especially in comparison to both earlier and later periods. Most insurgents in Guerrero accepted Iturbide's and subsequent governments because they had achieved many of their goals. The 1821 appointment of Vicente Guerrero to the military and civil command of the area aided its initial pacification.[7] For several years former insurgents received pensions, and some were also promised public lands, although such land grants are difficult to confirm for the Guerrero area.[8]

More general factors also contributed to the pacification. Independence seems to have eliminated or moderated the impact of repartimiento monopolies,[9] a tendency undoubtedly reinforced by the diffusion of power that occurred under the liberal Spanish constitution in effect from 1820 to 1824. As detailed in Chapter 3, this constitution and the constitution of 1824 were interpreted in ways favorable to the peasantry in precisely those areas where peasants had been most active in the insurgency. Furthermore, both local and national leaders attempted to heal the divisions established during the war and create a new national identity. Iturbide, for instance, arranged for Indian women to dress as Spaniards and Spanish women to dress as Indians in public festivals.[10]

Such symbolic efforts were not enough to save Iturbide or solve the fiscal problems Mexico faced as a newly independent nation. When Iturbide was overthrown in 1823, former insurgents in Guerrero were generally unenthusiastic about the movement against him. The little mobilization that took place seems to have relied far more extensively than previous and subsequent movements on the personal prestige of such leaders as Vicente Guerrero, Juan Alvarez, and Isidro Montes de Oca.[11] The larger and more popular movements that would later characterize the area required two preconditions: a counteroffensive by Mexico's declining dominant class, and the local economic dislocation caused by Mexico's precipitous and uneven post-independence depression.

Mexico's post-independence economic troubles began before the outbreak of the independence movement. Stagnation resulted from the decline in mining productivity caused by falling silver prices, the disruption of commercial and credit networks begun with the Bourbon reforms and accelerated by international and domestic conflicts, and the withdrawal of capital from Mexico's economy, first to finance Spain's wars and later the independence war. Moreover, the market for native manufactures was damaged by imports from Europe and the United States both before and after independence.[12] In Guerrero trade through Acapulco was disrupted by the War of Independence yet briefly returned to old patterns in the mid-1820s. In place of the Spanish galleon popularly called the "China galleon," English and Italian ships brought Asian textiles from Calcutta and Canton rather than the Philippines. They also brought cacao from Guayaquil, as did Mexican and Colombian coasters.[13] The available evidence is not sufficient to compare the volume of trade in the mid-1820s to that before independence. What is clear is that the new trade declined drastically after the mid-1820s, probably because the general decline of the Mexican economy reduced demand for luxury goods.[14] Traffic continued at low levels until the late 1840s, when ships bound for a California flushed with gold-rush fever began to call for provisions and water. This activity resulted in a short and shallow boom in the area immediately around Acapulco which soon thereafter settled into a sustained but modest business.[15]

In the colonial period coastal Guerrero produced large amounts of raw cotton, some of which was spun and woven into coarse textiles in the Chilapa area, but most of which was sent to the textile centers of Puebla, Mexico City, and the Bajío. This cotton trade declined severely during the independence war and afterward continued to decline in the face of competition from European and U.S. imports.[16] The trade made a partial revival with the implementation of the protectionist project of the 1830s, but transportation costs continued to impede competition with cotton grown on the Gulf coast. Several attempts to alleviate this difficulty by ginning the cotton before transport failed. Furthermore, by the early 1840s the protectionist policies that had allowed the coastal cotton production to survive were being surreptitiously undermined by mill owners eager to buy cheap cotton from the United States.[17]

The third pillar of the area's economy before independence was mining centered around Taxco. The mines' physical plant survived the war intact, as the insurgents only occupied Taxco once and did little damage.[18] Lack of capital stalled the industry until the late 1820s, at which point a minor boom took hold, but by the late 1830s production slowed and few seemed willing to invest under uncertain conditions.[19]

The expulsion of the Spanish in the 1820s was one of the most important moments in the development of Mexican nationalism. The expulsion movement defined the boundaries of Mexican nationality by excluding a portion of those who were legally Mexicans. The remainder of this section discusses the development and content of anti-Spanish ideology in Mexico as a whole and Guerrero in particular; my argument stresses how nationalist ideology was inseparable from internal class conflict and political struggle because anti-Spanish ideology and action were both products of and important factors in these internal processes. Nationalism is difficult to separate out from other issues in a meaningful way.

The most important factor contributing to the expulsion movement was the predominance of Spanish merchants in the economy, which made them the most likely scapegoats for Mexico's depression. Various groups elaborated a specific historical interpretation of Spanish dominance, attributing the supremacy of Spanish merchants to their ability to manipulate state power to restrict credit and product markets during the colonial period. Although by the 1820s the continuance of Spanish dominance probably owed more to their connections with English firms than it did to privileged access to the state, the image of Spanish merchants continued to be based on their earlier practices.[20] This image was particularly strong in coastal Guerrero.

Sentiment against the Spanish was also nourished by other factors, including the role Spanish troops had played in the savage counterinsurgency war of the 1810–20 period.[21] The Spanish in Mexico were also associated with Spain's futile attempt to reconquer its former colony, a threat that had seemed very real to the bankrupt country and that was undoubtedly aided through intelligence provided by Spanish Mexicans.[22] Perhaps the most important factor was the political activity of the Spanish in Mexico;[23] many provoked the ire of the pro-federalist majority by their involvement with the centralist coalition. The campaign against the Spanish was part of an effort to

demonize and denationalize that entire group and cannot be separated from other aspects of political conflict and ideology.

This connection between anti-Spanish campaigns and politics in
general can be seen in the first anti-Spanish efforts taken by Iturbide
in the waning months of his rule. Iturbide seized the Mexican property of Spaniards residing in Spain, prohibited Spaniards from leaving the country with money, and drew "loans" from them by force.
In this case, the Spanish were targeted because many were supporting the ultimately successful anti-Iturbide movement led by Santa
Anna; Iturbide recognized the propaganda value of associating his
enemies with a potential Spanish reconquest. Although many Spaniards supported the winning side in this clash, their efforts proved of
little value because the new Constituent Congress was controlled by
provincial elites who were the natural competitors of the Spanish.[24]

Anti-Spanish agitation began again in 1824 when state legislatures, supported by sometimes violent public demonstrations, dismissed Spaniards from military and civil posts.[25] To defuse increasing anti-Spanish agitation, the national legislature passed a May
1827 law that excluded the Spanish from public office but allowed
them to continue drawing their salaries; when demonstrations
against the Spanish continued, various state legislatures expelled
the Spaniards from their territories. The national legislature passed
an expulsion law in December 1827, and in February 1828 the government provided amnesty to those who had participated in anti-
Spanish movements. Still the anti-Spanish forces raged, decrying the
number of Spaniards granted exceptions from expulsion, and agitation continued until a more severe law was passed in 1829.[26]

Guerrero was the site of anti-Spanish movements on the Costa
Grande, in the area around Taxco, and in the Tierra Caliente. Different groups supported the anti-Spanish movements in each area: on
the coast the mulatto sharecroppers who had been the backbone of
the independence movement drove the new agitation; in Taxco the
municipal councils, basically composed of small merchants and artisans, opposed the Spaniards; and in the Tierra Caliente Indian villagers, also former insurgents, joined the anti-Spanish crusade. These
three groups expressed different grievances and even different definitions of who the Spanish were.

The most prominent of these groups in state and national politics
was that of the mulatto sharecroppers who formed the coastal militia. These militia units pronounced against the Spanish in 1827 and
again in 1828. In September 1827 Lieutenant José María Gallardo and
his men killed one Spaniard and wounded two others; he then or-

dered the municipal authorities to expel the remaining Spanish from their jurisdictions. Gallardo also issued a call for the expulsion of all the Spanish remaining in the republic, insisting that all Spanish were loyal supporters of Fernando VII, by then a powerful symbol of absolutism in Mexican political discourse. Gallardo and his men dispersed when he received assurances that the Spanish would be expelled and his supporters would not be punished,[27] and that December the Congress passed the first national expulsion law.

Several aspects of this incident illustrate how the different threads of national alliances, political discourse, and local politics were woven together. Gallardo, like most of his contemporaries, was a former insurgent. The three Spaniards singled out for physical attack were, in Gallardo's word's, "observed enemies of the fatherland";[28] at least two of them, Francisco Gargamala and José Cuenca, were merchants, and the men who assaulted them were almost certainly among their customers. Most of the Spanish in the coastal area in 1827 were merchants involved in the cotton trade, which seems to have still operated through the lending of goods and money against the harvest. Gargamala had arrived in the area in 1821, probably after the Plan of Iguala ended the War of Independence and provided explicit guarantees that the Spanish would be allowed to play a role in Mexican society. José Cuenca, the only one killed, had arrived on the coast in 1814 with the returning royalist armies. Cuenca was also involved in local politics and had recently been accused of cheating in municipal elections. Cuenca used the power gained in this way in an effort to exclude a powerful competitor in buying the coastal cotton harvest.[29]

The second expulsion movement of the coast had an even more explicit link to national politics: in December 1827 Nicolás Bravo led a rebellion against the Victoria government. The movement did not receive the support expected and an army led by Vicente Guerrero quickly defeated Bravo's troops near Otumba in the state of Mexico. Rumors linked Bravo's rebellion to a recently exposed conspiracy to return Mexico to Spanish rule. The rumors were false, but appearances proved enough to convince two important militia leaders of the Costa Grande that the moment had arrived to make their weight felt. In January 1828 Isidro Montes de Oca and Juan Alvarez called for the expulsion of the Spanish, emphasizing the danger of a Spanish invasion and the need to preserve "liberty." They vowed to march to Mexico City and use their arms against the "Bourbonists and centralists," a phrase that shows that by early 1828 the opponents of popular power were already being accused of centralism, although they themselves would not embrace the term until the mid-1830s.

Again the physical removal of Spaniards was to occur immediately, before the passage of an expulsion law. The militia was to bring them as prisoners on its march to Mexico City.[30] Like other movements, this one declared its explicit support for the government in power, and the militia went home after receiving assurances that action would be taken against the Spanish.

Both the 1827 and 1828 movements were led by militia officers, but this is not to say that the sharecroppers of the coast were blindly manipulated by provincial elites who only sought the economic, political, and social space that would be vacated by the departing Spanish. The leaders themselves were men not very socially distinct from the sharecroppers. Isidro Montes de Oca had only become a prominent insurgent in the latter stages of the War of Independence, when most of the wealthier leaders had been killed or captured; before the war he was a mulatto sharecropper who could not read or write.[31] Juan Alvarez was the mestizo son of a coastal landowner, and the Spanish official who was executor of his father's will forced Alvarez to work as a cattle herd. He had joined the insurgents during the war and lost most of his wealth to marauding Spanish troops. Like Montes de Oca, Alvarez did not reach even moderate prominence until 1818–20.[32] Montes de Oca and Alvarez had reached relatively high militia ranks by 1828, but their cultural and social milieu was that of the majority of the coastal inhabitants, whom observers repeatedly characterized as hating the Spanish.[33] For instance, a few months after the 1828 movement the government refused to permit the return of the Spaniards expelled from the area, arguing that the inhabitants so hated the Spaniards that the government would not be able to protect them or even identify any who might attack them.[34] The tide of anti-Spanish resentment did not ebb, and after Vicente Guerrero became president the coast was instrumental in pressing for a new expulsion law in 1829.[35]

Taxco was the second location in Guerrero in which anti-Spanish agitation was strong. There most Spaniards were mine owners and merchants. The leaders of the anti-Spanish movement in this mining town were the local artisans and merchants who served on the town council; they conspired to support the 1827 coastal rebellion and assassinate local Spaniards. Simultaneously the state government asked the town council to determine which local Spanish residents were exempt from a state of Mexico law that decreed expulsion for every Spaniard who had continued to support the Spanish government after the Treaty of Cordoba officially ended the war. Not surprisingly, the town council reported that all Spaniards resident in the town should be expelled because all had continued to oppose Mexico's independence. Later this area also contributed large sums to the defense of Mexico against the Spanish invasion.[36]

Anti-Spanish agitation in the Tierra Caliente illustrates how peasants could define the political and social categories sanctioned by higher authorities in surprising ways to address their own concerns. In the late colonial period the Indian villagers had struggled both inside and outside the courts to evict Creoles and mestizos (vecinos de razón) who rented village lands with the aid of colonial officials. This conflict underlay the villagers' tenacious support for the insurgents in the 1810–20 period.[37] After 1825 the large size of the area's municipalities suggests that town councils were controlled by the vecinos de razón, who in turn may have used their offices to continue renting the república lands that passed to the councils.[38] At any rate, conflict intensified.

In 1827 an anonymous group issued a call to expel all Spaniards and Englishmen and crown an Indian as king.[39] This movement dropped from sight but two years later a civil war broke out as villages interpreted the 1829 expulsion law as they saw fit. Beginning in San Miguel Totolapan, one of the most conflictive villages in the late colonial period, the movement quickly extended to practically every village of the Tierra Caliente. The villagers refused to obey local authorities and affirmed that the vecinos de razón who used their lands were foreigners and in fact Spaniards subject to the expulsion law. The villagers referred to the vecinos as *chaquetas*, a term used to denote the Spanish troops who had opposed the insurgency there in the 1810–20 period, and fought to drive out their mestizo and Creole neighbors.[40] This movement quickly merged with the forces supporting Vicente Guerrero after he was forced out of the presidency in 1829. Thereafter, every time radical federalists revolted in the South during the 1830s they received the support of Tierra Caliente peasants, who always referred to their opponents as "chaquetas."[41]

This case illustrates many of the elements that shaped the process of state formation and the connection between peasant movements and national politics in the 1810–55 period. These peasants clearly conflated the national community with their local one. The vecinos' long years of residence on village lands did not erase their identity as outsiders to the villages and to the nation who were thus subject to the expulsion decree. Nor was this sense of "community" confined to the village in a practical sense. The villages constructed an alliance among themselves, a step they had been incapable of or uninterested in taking before 1810, and allied themselves with federalist outsiders, specifically the movement that sought to return Guerrero to the national presidency after his ouster in 1829. Notably the villages involved in these activities in the 1820s had all cooperated during the 1810–21 insurgency. Elite observers did not believe that this movement had a legitimate political program and allies, and they certainly saw it as a less-than-positive indication of the progress made in nation-state formation after 1810.[42] Government officials believed that these peasants had misinterpreted the drive to make Mexico into a modern, republican nation-state, but the fact that such a misunderstanding was possible proves that the message was reaching peasants and being interpreted.

National Politics to 1828

From 1823 to 1828 Mexico experienced a political calm that would not be replicated until the Porfiriato. Furthermore, this peace, unlike the Pax Porfiriana, was not obtained at the price of preventing political competition. Political institutions functioned surprisingly well for several years. Nevertheless, the hope that the violence and instability of the 1810s was over collapsed in 1828 when a political group refused to accept electoral results and took power by force of arms. The fragile basis of the 1823–28 political peace and its breakdown is crucial to explaining the instability that would plague Mexico for the next half century.

Political calm was the result of revenue and compromise. The revenue came from British loans, which temporarily stemmed the unending tide of fiscal crises.[43] The compromise was of a dual nature. Its first aspect was Mexico's 1824 constitution, which recognized the de facto power of regional interests yet also provided the Mexico City–based dominant class with enough checks and balances to suggest that sharing power was not disastrous to its interests. Its second aspect was embodied in the person of Mexico's first president, Guadalupe Victoria, who had been an insurgent and whose election suggested to his former comrades and other radicals that they would be able to fulfill some of their goals. Victoria also was acceptable to the dominant class, particularly because his ministerial choices implied that he would not advocate radical policies.[44]

The political peace soon began to unravel as the government ran out of money,[45] as radicals began to experiment with electoral organizing and its implied mass mobilization, and as Mexico's economy was battered by shortages of capital and the dislocation caused by the massive flood of imports under its liberal tariff policy.[46] This last factor provided the radicals with a cause. The radicals also benefited because some peasants who had won local political power believed that the national government was supporting its reconquest by elites. The result was the increasing polarization that culminated in the 1828 Revolution of La Acordada.

Some modern historians have emphasized Mexico's Masonic lodges as the cause of this polarization rather than its result.[47] Some contemporary observers saw the lodges as the underlying cause of political strife because they believed that the goal of politics ought to be choosing the most qualified officeholders rather than the correct programs. Yet too strong a focus on the lodges can be misleading. The lodges became prominent because loosely defined groups with different ideas about what government should do needed organizational vehicles. They were particularly important when national politics largely involved contesting elections, and they faded from view after 1829 because various groups made elections less important by subverting or ignoring their results. Masonic lodges were not effective tools in organizing conspiracies and revolts because they could not come to clandestine decisions and, more important, they were largely an urban phenomenon that was ultimately less powerful than regular army and militia units and peasant villages.

The two Masonic organizations represented different groups. The *escoseses* or Scottish-rite masons, identified with the former colonial dominant class, were basically wealthy merchants with additional investments in mining and agriculture.[48] They were joined by some army officers, particularly former members of the royalist army and insurgents who had accepted pardons before 1820.[49] The *escosés* group also included the so-called Bourbonists, who had pushed for a centralist constitution in the post-Iturbide period but had been defeated by the states.[50] The *yorkino* or York-rite lodges had a broader membership centered around former insurgents and radical intellectuals but including substantial contingents of provincial merchants and artisans.[51] Both factions were very conscious of these sociological distinctions, although they described them in different ways. For instance, the yorkino José María Alpuche described the escoseses as "the civil, military, and clerical aristocracy of the Federal District," whereas to escosés Lucás Alamán they were everyone "respectable for their fortune, education, and knowledge."[52]

The yorkino program contained many of the elements that would concern Mexican radicals for the rest of the century. They represented an alliance between the ideological heirs of the insurgents and intellectuals heavily influenced by European and North American ideas, the most prominent of whom was Lorenzo de Zavala. David Brading and Eugene Harrell both describe these two wings as "populists" and "radicals" respectively,[53] but the differences are not really captured by this terminology. The insurgents were arguably as "radical" as Zavala in that they directly opposed Mexico's dominant class by supporting the expulsion of the Spanish. They also pushed harder for the diffusion of power in Mexican society through their extreme federalism. Similarly, in some ways Zavala was as "populist" as his counterparts, repeatedly advocating agrarian reform in an open manner uncharacteristic of the former insurgents. Still, there were real differences. The "populists" focused on the expulsion of the Spanish and protectionism in rhetoric stressing Mexico's class structure and the need to preserve Mexico's independence. They saw themselves as the heirs of the insurgents.[54] Zavala and his group opposed both protectionism and the expulsion, advocating instead the expansion of agriculture and agrarian reform aimed at making uncultivated land and church property available for development, ideas that became dogma for the liberals who emerged later in the century.[55]

Zavala and his cohorts were a minority in the yorkinos of the late 1820s and their ideas were generally pushed aside in favor of more emotional appeals. The most prominent features of yorkino ideology decried the continuing domination of Mexican society by those who had controlled it before independence, the continuing presence of the Spanish in prominent positions, and the threat this posed to independence itself. These issues were linked to the economic dislocation caused by imports. The resulting complex of ideas and symbols was persuasive, consistent, and extremely frightening to Mexico's ruling class, perhaps more so than any threat they faced between the dark days of 1813–14 and the Mexican Revolution.

Radical rhetoric continually linked the escoseses and their successors with Spain's domination of Mexico, the possibility of a reconquest, and the negation of the social gains of independence. Radicals rejected the notion that Spain's control of Mexico had ever been paternalistic or benevolent, emphasizing its colonial and rapacious nature. They accused their opponents of being feudal lords whose continued domination would hold down Mexico's nascent middle class and continue the poverty and ignorance of its peasants and workers. The radicals also rejected the conciliation of interests that had been central to the Plan of Iguala and Treaty of Cordoba as well as the corporatist ideology that these documents inherited. They divided Mexico into haves and have-nots and insisted that the latter would have to forcibly take what was due them from the former.[56]

As many authors have noted, the anti-Spanish element of all this ideology was clearly connected to protectionism.[57] The flood of imports that spread hunger among Mexican artisans and cotton growers was mostly brokered by Spanish merchants operating out of Mexico City, the former members of the Consulado. These merchants and their agents in the provinces became symbols for adverse market conditions and thus the targets of popular ire. The insistence of those versed in the new liberal economic orthodoxy, which held that lower textile prices ultimately benefited everyone, was counterintuitive to people who were seeing their standard of living fall steeply.

The central tenet of the "populists" was their belief in a species of radical, grassroots democracy[58] that included wide suffrage and rejection of the idea that politics were only a matter of choosing the most qualified candidate for every office. Instead the yorkinos asserted the right to form parties and promote programs and explicitly championed the rise to political power of Mexico's middle classes. This brand of democracy could be extremely raucous, as mobs drove legislatures from their chambers and governors from their offices.[59] It also resonated with the local meaning of federalism in Guerrero explained in the previous chapter.

Political competition increased in the late 1820s, but it was mostly manifested in elections. One of the key moments came when the yorkinos won the elections for the state legislature of Mexico in October 1827. The escosés-dominated outgoing legislature claimed the yorkinos had committed fraud and annulled the election and reelected the escosés Melchor Muzquiz as governor, but the national legislature, by then dominated by yorkinos, overturned the nullification. Muzquiz was unable to govern with an opposition legislature and resigned in March 1828, to be replaced by Lorenzo de Zavala.[60]

Two of Zavala's initiatives as governor were extremely threatening to the Mexico City–based dominant class: first, he strengthened the state militia to establish a counterweight to the professional army;[61] second, he openly speculated about the necessity and justice of an agrarian reform. Though acknowledging the need to respect property rights, Zavala deplored the large disparities of wealth in the countryside and proposed a tax on the state's absentee landlords,[62] most of whom were members of the dominant class who resided in the Federal District. Zavala backed up this rhetoric with a determined attack on the land rights of the Duke of Monteleone, the Italian aristocrat who had inherited the lands granted to Hernán Cortés. The brief against Monteleone expressed the idea that rights gained by conquest had no validity and stressed the feudal nature of the rights, which had until independence included feudal dues. Monteleone's defense, skillfully constructed and publicized by Lucás Alamán, was based on the dual assertions that the properties were no longer feudal, as the Spanish Cortes had abolished the feudal dues, and that Monteleone's rights were no different from those of other land-owners because all were based on the Conquest. An attack on Monteleone was an attack on all private property in Mexico.[63] This latter argument was particularly powerful because some members of the state legislature were promoting agrarian reform using an argument similar to Zavala's.[64] Furthermore, Zavala was rumored to be providing support for villages in their disputes with hacendados.[65]

The escoseses lost ground steadily in local elections throughout 1827. By December they felt that dramatic measures were their only hope. On December 23 a hacienda administrator named Manuel Montaño revolted near Otumba in central Mexico. His program called for the abolition of secret societies, the resignation of the cabinet, the return of the American diplomat Joel Poinsett to the United States, and the strict enforcement of the Constitution and other laws. Nicolás Bravo, the escosés vice-president, left Mexico City and joined the rebels[66] and President Victoria sent Vicente Guerrero with a military force to subdue them. Rumors tied Bravo and the Montaño rebels to a previous conspiracy to aid Spain's reconquest of Mexico, and Guerrero, organizing support for the government, declared that Bravo's true object was to return Mexico to Spanish domination.[67] Guerrero's troops subdued the rebels after a brief skirmish.

Bravo was exiled and the escosés party lost most of its remaining popularity,[68] but its demise did not end political strife. The more audacious yorkinos intensified their critique of the results of independence and they quickly split into radical and moderate factions.[69] This split became a rift in the presidential election of 1828.

The presidential election of 1828 was pivotal in Mexico's post-independence political history. The Mexican political system proved unequal to the task of transferring power from one constitutionally chosen chief executive to another. One of the two factions disputing power was both unwilling to accept defeat and powerful enough to overthrow the government, and its example paved the way for the next forty years of Mexican political history.

Class quickly became the dominant issue in this election, as it had not in the earlier election of Guadalupe Victoria. Two factions of the yorkino lodge disputed the election: the moderates supported Manuel Gómez Pedraza, a former royalist military officer who as minister of war under Victoria had generally stayed out of the yorkino-escosés struggle; the radicals supported Vicente Guerrero, a former insurgent general of moderate wealth and mixed race.[70] The moderate program was unclear but generally seemed to involve slowing the expulsion of the Spanish and promising more security for Mexico's upper classes.[71] Most of Guerrero's propaganda emphasized his background as the most important surviving insurgent leader and portrayed the remaining Spanish nationals as a threat to Mexico's independence. The radical yorkinos constantly stressed Gómez Pedraza's links to the Spanish: the expulsion had become an increasingly powerful symbol of social radicalism dreaded by many members of Mexico's upper classes. Some of the propaganda favoring Guerrero also suggested that Mexico's struggling artisans would receive protection under a Guerrero government.[72]

The choice of the president lay with the state legislatures, each of which had one vote. The state legislatures themselves had been elected indirectly over the previous few years, some before the anti-escosés reaction that followed the Montaño movement.[73] The outcome depended most on the balance of political power in each state during the most recent election of its state legislature. State governors could also bring some pressure to bear on legislatures.[74] The opinion of the military forces in each state, particularly in the state capitals, was an unforeseen factor: the military had no constitutional role, yet afterward many claimed that the military had brought pressure to bear through threats.[75] When all the votes were counted Guerrero was defeated by a vote of eleven to nine. Chiapas, Guanajuato, Jalisco, Nuevo León, Oaxaca, Puebla, Querétaro, Veracruz, and Zacatecas voted for Gómez Pedraza; Chihuahua, Coahuila, Mexico, Michoacán, Sonora, San Luís, Tamaulipas, and the Yucatán voted for Guerrero. Tabasco's deadlock was counted as one vote for each candidate.[76]

In September 1828 Antonio López de Santa Anna revolted in Veracruz. His manifesto condemned a pro-Spanish, escosés, aristocratic conspiracy to place Gómez Pedraza in the presidency by threatening and suborning the state legislatures.[77] This movement was seconded by several militia forces on the Costa Grande but initially received little support elsewhere. The rebels continued in a species of limbo in which neither side acted decisively until December when Lorenzo de Zavala organized another conspiracy in Mexico City, which Guerrero joined. The government folded after a mob sacked the Parián, center for the activities of Mexico's importers, and Vicente Guerrero became president.[78]

The mulatto militia of the Costa Grande led by Juan Alvarez and

Isidro Montes de Oca was among the first military forces to second Santa Anna's move.[79] Militia units further inland initially opposed the move but soon joined the rebels,[80] and groups in the Tierra Caliente and the Montaña also took part.[81] In support of the rebellion Alvarez led militiamen all the way to Cuernavaca, just south of Mexico City.[82] Despite this extravagant show of support, municipal forces from areas outside the immediate vicinity of Mexico City were hardly decisive on this occasion; most of the fighting took place in Mexico City and was over too soon for troops from so far away to make themselves felt. Even so, the relatively quick action by these groups, which began in October, increased the insecurity of the government and helped pave the way for the later events in Mexico City.

Several aspects of these events illustrate general phenomena. Most of the *pronuncamientos* that resulted in changes of government in Mexico from 1820–55 originated in areas other than Mexico City and the "coups" they launched occurred over substantial periods of time. In this case three months elapsed between Santa Anna's initial revolt and the fall of the government. The typical strategy was for a group to pronounce in some provincial area and then set up defensive positions to await the reaction of the government, holding out until groups in other areas began to second its program. Many groups waited until the fall of the government was all but assured before they made their moves. Usually the garrison of Mexico City was the last to join a successful movement. Fighting in Mexico City was rare, although the Revolution of La Acordada was an obvious exception.

Another aspect of the events of late 1828 is also worth noting: both Juan Alvarez and Lorenzo de Zavala sought the support of members of Mexico's rural masses in a national political conflict. Alvarez took militiamen from southern Guerrero all the way to central Mexico, organized support in the Indian areas of the Montaña,[83] and sent agents to agitate in the Taxco region and in the area now known as Morelos.[84] Zavala, as governor of the state of Mexico, distributed weapons to militiamen throughout the state in anticipation of a revolt and possible clash with the regular army.[85] What did these men have to offer their allies? What ideological or pragmatic content did their movement have?

The movement drew on the local disputes over the distribution of power described in the previous chapter. Its primary rallying point was the threat the Spanish posed to independence:[86] the Spaniards were associated with "absolutism" and "tyranny," two terms that had been prominent in insurgent rhetoric during the latter part of the independence war. In the words of one supporter, action was needed because the nation was "plunging into an absolutism which will make the great undertakings of liberty, independence and sovereignty illusory."[87] On a practical level the issue of the expulsion was tied to protection from the flood of foreign imports that put urban artisans out of work and depressed cotton prices for the mulatto sharecroppers of coastal Guerrero. This flood was a major grievance in the sack of the Parián.[88] The symbol of the Spaniards also contained an element of class, as both Gómez Pedraza and the Mexico City–based dominant class were tied to Spanish colonialism,[89] and this connection was reinforced by Gómez Pedraza's background as a royalist military officer during the War of Independence.[90] Not surprisingly, many proclamations explicitly called on old insurgents to aid in the effort[91] and opponents of the movement were called "chaquetas" and "royalists."[92] The major motifs of proclamations in support of the movement were independence, the total expulsion of the Spanish, and the plot of the aristocracy.

The Guerrero Government

The government of Vicente Guerrero and Lorenzo de Zavala held power in Mexico for slightly less than one year. It became an important reference point in the political struggles of the 1830s, thanks to its reputation of radicalism and the way it came to power on the shoulders of the ragged mulattos of coastal Guerrero and Veracruz and the urban mob of Mexico City. This government was the most frightening experience of Mexico's ruling class since those months in 1813–14 when it had seemed that Morelos might overthrow the royal government. Nevertheless, despite rumors to the contrary, the Guerrero government did not implement a land reform or other redistributive measures. What, then, was its program and to what extent did it carry out its goals?

Guerrero's options were limited by the near bankruptcy of the government, the very strong possibility of a Spanish attempt to recover its most important colony, and a powerful internal opposition;[93] this combination ultimately destroyed his government. A fourth problem of lesser moment was the deterioration of Guerrero's relationship with Zavala during their year in office because Zavala did not support several elements of Guerrero's program that were designed to gratify his impoverished supporters. Zavala objected to the populist tone of the administration and was less than enthusiastic about the expulsion of the Spanish. He also disagreed with Guerrero's protectionism.[94]

Many authors have remarked on the populist and egalitarian tone of the Guerrero administration, and indeed some of Guerrero's gestures foreshadowed those of twentieth-century Latin American populists. Guerrero, for instance, invited the poor of Mexico to his birthday party,[95] and he understood the symbolic value that abolishing slavery had for his mulatto supporters, even if there were few or no slaves in Mexico.[96] Pamphleteers used Guerrero's mestizo origins to imply links to Mexico's Indian majority and suggested that a land reform was impending though the government made no official mention of the possibility.[97] The abolition of the tobacco monopoly was also undoubtedly popular with some of his supporters.[98]

The administration also stressed measures against foreigners and protectionism. These efforts were most directly manifested in the second expulsion law, but more extreme measures were also proposed by some of Guerrero's supporters, including bills that would have made it illegal for foreigners to trade or lend money for mortgages and a proposal that any merchandise imported by foreigners be dispensed in "public stores." Although these measures did not become law, they suggest the tone of the period.[99]

Anti-Spanish sentiment was linked to the most concrete measure Guerrero's government took to aid its impoverished supporters, prohibiting the importation of textiles and other goods that competed with the products of Mexican artisans. Guerrero made his position on this issue clear in his inaugural address when he criticized the "bastard application of economic principles" that had allowed foreign merchandise to displace Mexican workers.[100] The government signed protective measures in May 1829 but enforcement was delayed, first by Zavala's obstructionism as minister of finance and then by the need for customs revenues to finance the defense against impending Spanish invasion.[101] Guerrero's supporters justified protectionism with arguments that would be echoed in both the protectionist scheme of the 1830s and twentieth-century policies. Its proponents argued that if Mexican workers were protected their income would generate demand for other Mexican products, and that foreigners prohibited from selling imported goods would import the manufacturing technology that Mexico needed to compete with other nations.[102] Thus, the most radical government to take power in Mexico before 1855 did not champion economic liberalism.

This government also differed from its liberal successors in that it did not take measures against church wealth. Guerrero pledged to protect religion in his inaugural address, noting that Catholicism was one of the bases of the 1824 Constitution, and his government sought and received the help of the clerical hierarchy in preparing resistance to the impending Spanish invasion. The Archdiocese of Mexico published a pamphlet criticizing Spanish claims that religion would return when the Spanish did; this pro-independence stand was particularly important because the Mexican government and the papacy continued to dispute the right to appoint clerical officials.[103]

In what ways, then, did the Guerrero government foreshadow the liberal movement that later emerged? The most important was the manner in which it explicitly embraced federalism and accused its detractors of centralism. In his inaugural address Guerrero championed egalitarianism and the general diffusion of power at the local level, insisting that "the interest of the localities is the most adequate to guarantee the interest of individuals. As authorities multiply, needs are examined and known more: everywhere there is a nearby power to do good and avoid evil. The authorities are found in all classes of the people, and the true titles of superiority, the only ones that cause distinction and preference, are discovered wherever talent and virtue appear."[104] A caveat is in order here: Harrell correctly notes that even as the yorkinos advertised their federalism they expanded the power of the federal government vis-à-vis the states, claiming the authority of the former to annul acts of the latter.[105] They undoubtedly rationalized this contradiction by linking their opponents to the threatened Spanish invasion.

The invasion dominated 1829. The government, forced to raise funds quickly, resorted to large tax increases, including a graduated income tax. In July the Spanish finally landed near Tampico, and to raise even more funds the government imposed forced loans and confiscated half the income from the properties of Spaniards living outside of Mexico. Antonio López de Santa Anna led an energetic defense and the Spanish did not receive the support they expected from inside Mexico. The Spanish invasion force quickly capitulated and was repatriated.[106]

Guerrero's government did not long outlast the Spanish invasion force. From August 1829 until his ouster in late December Guerrero ruled by decree under emergency powers, exacerbating the fears of Mexico's upper classes[107] and alienating important federalists in the states with several of his emergency revenue measures.[108] A more decisive factor in Guerrero's fall was the mobilization of Mexico's reserves, which were retained even after the invading force surrendered. A section of the reserves in Jalapa, calling for the reduction of extraordinary executive power and the strict observance of the constitution,[109] asked Vice-president Anastasio Bustamante and Santa

Anna to lead them, and Bustamante accepted. Guerrero set forth to meet them with a force from Mexico City, but rebel supporters soon took over the capital and the despairing president retired to his farm near Tixtla, where he refused the offers of nearby Indian villages to defend him.[110]

Guerrero was undone by the generalized fear of a president who reached power with the aid of some segments of Mexico's impoverished majority. This fear only increased when Guerrero was given near dictatorial powers to respond to the Spanish invasion and refused to give them up after the immediate crisis had passed. The rich feared mob rule, the treasury was practically bankrupt, and even some of Guerrero's supporters welcomed the coup because of their perception that the president had undermined the autonomy of the states. Under these circumstances it is perhaps surprising that the government lasted as long as it did.

Mexico's Senate declared it "morally impossible" for Guerrero to govern in a 22 to 3 vote, and the Chamber of Deputies declared it simply "impossible" by a 23 to 17 margin. Guerrero's enemies launched a massive press campaign to discredit the former president and his intellectual capacity, and the Ministry of War ordered all military commanders to second the Plan de Jalapa. Juan Alvarez did so on January 4, 1830, in Acapulco, apparently at the urging of Guerrero himself. Guerrero's supporters were removed from office in Mexico and other states,[111] and for a short time it seemed that the plotters had succeeded in eliminating Guerrero from the political scene with a minimum of bloodshed.

The War of the South

The Bustamante administration's policy of removing state officials who had supported Guerrero backfired. Wholesale turnover of local officials to suit a new administration in Mexico City was exactly what the states had sought to prevent by imposing federalism on Mexico City in 1824. Moreover, this policy eliminated any motive state officials had for acquiescing to the coup. Soon the unrenovated state legislatures began issuing calls for resistance, and though most of these vocalizations were largely symbolic, in Michoacán Governor José Salgado and military commander Juan José Codallos gathered troops. This turn of events convinced the key actors in Guerrero that it was possible to fight the regime, and they did so with a vengeance.

Vicente Guerrero, Juan Alvarez, and Isidro Montes de Oca sent emissaries out to the states to organize support. Alvarez and Montes de

Oca concentrated on the coast, where they could call on reserves of anti-Spanish resentment fueled by the continuing depression of the market for coastal cotton. Guerrero moved first in the Montaña near his hometown of Tixtla, where Indian peasants had been skirmishing with their mestizo neighbors over control of several town councils and cotton spinners had suffered from the importation of foreign textiles, then moved on to the Tierra Caliente, an area he had organized during the darkest hours of the 1810–20 insurgency. There Indian peasants had interpreted the anti-Spanish legislation as authorization to expel non-Indian tenants from their lands, continuing a long struggle.

The movement to restore Guerrero was not based on a one-sided relationship in which a politician exploited hapless peasants to advance his personal cause. Many peasants had already sent emissaries to Guerrero in January and February when he was still keeping a low profile; they, too, sought allies in their disputes. In the "War of the South," as it was called, the patterns of alliance that would predominate in the area through the 1850s reached a breadth and depth not seen since 1820. This guerrilla war, which lasted from March 1830 to March 1831, repeated some patterns from the War of Independence and also forged new ones.

This type of alliance between segments of Mexico's impoverished rural majority and provincial elites was the worst nightmare of the Mexico City–based dominant class. In the past such an alliance had underlay the ruinous independence war. The dominant class feared these movements less for the demands pressed by the poorest members of the alliances than for the way in which they became articulated to those of provincial elites. The dominant class would probably have allowed peasants to control a few town councils in remote areas of Mexico, but it could not afford to allow other states to pass into radical control, particularly states like Mexico and Michoacán where its members had substantial economic interests.[112] Thus to prevent provincial elites in other parts of the country from joining the movement it was necessary to make the rebel's goals seem much more radical than they were.

The key figures of the Bustamante administration portrayed the War of the South as one of survival for Mexico's dominant class and property owners in general. Lucás Alamán, minister of the interior, described the class he represented as "religious men, of honor, of property, of education, of virtues, from whom they (the rebels) meant to take all their wealth, all influence in public life, and ultimately to exile and destroy."[113] The reference to exile here suggests the way in which the movement to expel the Spanish seemed to threaten the dominant class in general. The object of the rebels was, according to Alamán, not political; it was to "ruin all property; entirely subvert property; cause a desolation a hundred times more terrible than that of the 1810s."[114] The War of Independence surfaces here as the traumatic experience it was for Mexico's dominant class, which had been pushed to the wall in 1810–13. The war was between civilization and barbarism, according to Alamán: the southern rebellion had "the character of the invasions of the barbarous peoples of the North upon the provinces of the Roman Empire."[115] José Antonio Facio, minister of war, claimed that Guerrero convinced Indian villages to join the rebellion by promising them the properties of neighboring landowners.[116] Melchor Muzquiz, governor of the state of Mexico, painted the revolutionaries as little better than bandits.[117]

The rebels gained support in three areas of Guerrero. The first, the Costa Grande, had been the center of anti-Spanish activity in Guerrero, and though the Spanish merchants of the area had been driven out or killed before 1829, the cotton economy had not recovered and Guerrero's protectionist measures had not even been implemented because of the need for customs revenues imposed by the Spanish invasion. Thus the mulatto sharecroppers of cotton in the coastal militia were ready to follow their commanders in what was basically seen as a continuation of the anti-Spanish crusade. They were joined by the Indians of Atoyac and Tecpan, who resented the control that the cotton merchants had exercised over the town council of the latter.[118]

The Tierra Caliente, the second area where the rebels received strong support, had also been prominent in the agitation for the expulsion of the Spanish, but there it had been understood as the expulsion of the mestizo and Creole rancheros who rented or squatted on Indian lands. The conflict between the rancheros and the Indian villagers had fueled the villagers' support for the insurgents during the 1810–20 period. Vicente Guerrero had commanded the Tierra Caliente insurgents during the latter part of the war, and the same tensions now led the Indians to support Guerrero again.[119]

The two areas described above had experienced the radical interpretations of post-independence laws that underlay the local meaning of the word "federalism," and it is therefore not surprising that Guerrero received support there. However, he also gained support in some areas where the local elite led by Nicolás Bravo had retained control after the independence war. One of these was the western part of the Montaña near Tixtla and Chilapa; Indians there had generally not supported the insurgency but now at least some villages swung their weight behind Guerrero. They apparently had two motives. The first was increasing frustration with the control that local mestizo and Creole elites exercised over municipal governments by using the militia for electoral intimidation and fraud; in at least one case Guerrero promised a village control of its own government after the war. The second motive was Guerrero's protectionism, which appealed to the Indians because they had produced large quantities of cotton textiles for the markets of the Meseta Central before independence and now were devastated by the post-independence flood of imports. Surprisingly, it was these formerly inactive Indians who sent emissaries to Guerrero before he decided to oppose the new government.[120]

The political beliefs of the rebels were in most ways similar to those that had led them to push for Guerrero's presidency during and after the 1828 election. The proclamations and letters of 1830 again stressed the need to preserve Mexico's independence in the face of an aristocratic, pro-Spanish plot to subvert it, and the troops of the central government were often characterized as gachupines.[121] The external threat was linked to an internal one: the rebels claimed that the mechanism being used to subvert independence was centralism, and federalism became a major element of the rebels' political identity. This particular conceptual link was to become one of the most enduring features of local political discourse.

"Federalism" had certainly entered the Mexican political vocabulary before 1830, and local radicals had begun to call their adversaries "centralists" as early as 1828. Nevertheless, until 1830 "federalism" was a term most often invoked by state governors and legislatures to protest some action of the national government. Most politicians called themselves "federalist" at one time or another, as federalism was enshrined in the Mexican constitution and was thus a safe principle to advocate; also, most groups found themselves at odds with some action of the central government at one time or another. After 1830, however, the members of one coalition in Mexican politics began consistently to describe themselves as "federalists" and their adversaries as "centralists." This was a key change in Mexican political culture.

In Guerrero this change came about in two steps. First, when the national government annulled state elections and replaced the radicals in state offices, Guerrero and Alvarez made the relatively routine accusation of centralism.[122] This accusation had been made by state governments before, even while Guerrero himself was president.[123]

Second, Guerrero and Alvarez linked the idea of federalism with the widely accepted tenets of local yorkino radicalism in proclamations and letters they sent to organize support among the area's peasantry. Centralism was not just illegal because it violated the constitution: it was pernicious because it was part of an aristocratic plot to undermine Mexico's independence and hand Mexico back to the Spanish, negating everything achieved in the independence war.[124] Alvarez summed up this complex of ideas at the beginning of the revolt when he stated that the objective was "to sustain the sovereignty of the States, force the reinstatement of the deputies and prevent the federal system from being changed for the central, which is how the agents of the European tyrant desire to subjugate us."[125] This formulation was soon echoed in rumors circulating among parts of the peasantry suggesting that the government's troops aimed to centralize power and persecute former insurgents.[126]

The appeal was the more effective because rumors that foreigners were behind a conspiracy to centralize the government had emerged on the coast while Guerrero was still in office. An informant on the coast told the prefect of Acapulco that during the summer of 1829 he had attended a meeting during which Isidro Montes de Oca and his lieutenants planned an anti-centralist demonstration. Montes de Oca had asserted that "twelve or fourteen governors directed by damaging intentions contributed to centralization and the permanence of the Spaniards, causing other obvious evils; and that also problems came from foreign commerce which had become very generalized, and it was necessary to contain it."[127] Although this particular movement never surfaced, the report suggests the content and tone of political conversation on the Costa Grande before the overthrow of Guerrero.

Government officials interpreted the support of various Indian peasant villages for the rebels as evidence that the rebellion was a caste war and assumed that Guerrero and Alvarez obtained this support by promising the Indians the land owned by whites.[128] There is no evidence that this promise was made, or that the Indians even wanted such land; instead the two areas where substantial numbers of Indian peasants supported the rebels were dominated by other tensions. In the Chilapa-Tixtla area Indian peasants and local elites had struggled over control of town governments; in the Tierra Caliente Indians wanted to evict mestizo and Creole rancheros from village lands they rented. In both areas the Indians identified their adversaries as gachupines or supporters of gachupines.[129]

The guerrilla war in the South lasted for more than a year. There was a clear pattern to the fighting: the rebels were soundly defeated when they occasionally marched north with large forces of men, but they were successful in cutting off, harassing, and repelling the advances of government forces under even the most experienced generals. In the summer of 1830, for instance, the government sent José Gabriel de Armijo, who had commanded royalist forces in Guerrero from 1815 to 1819, to root out the rebels. Alvarez's forces retreated, then cut Armijo off from reinforcements and supplies before attacking his weakened troops. Armijo was killed as he fled.[130] However, when Alvarez went on the offensive he was in turn defeated near Tixtla. By the end of the year the war had reached a stalemate: the government could not conquer the coastal areas or put down the guerrillas further north, but the rebels could not seriously threaten the government without allies elsewhere.[131]

Guerrero himself played little or no military role in the war, but he was a vital symbol and the government arranged for his elimination. On January 14, 1831, Francisco Picaluga, captain of an Italian ship that carried supplies for the rebels, invited Guerrero aboard for dinner in Acapulco, imprisoned him, and set sail for Oaxaca, where he delivered Guerrero to the government. Guerrero was tried in Oaxaca and executed on February 14.[132] Although the rebels tried to continue the war, it became apparent that this exercise was useless and between March and May all except Juan José Codallos accepted government pardons. Codallos refused and was executed.[133]

National Politics, 1831–1835

Josefina Vázquez has recently pointed out that the Bustamante regime was not overtly centralist but instead received this label when historians uncritically accepted the views of the regime's partisan critics.[134] Although Vázquez is undoubtedly correct, she leaves aside the important question of why those critics accused the regime of centralism in the first place. The answer is complex. The regime was never able to leave behind the image it presented in early 1830 as it dissolved state governments and replaced them with its supporters. Moreover, centralism was an effective criticism for the regime's opponents to make because it was what provincial elites feared most. In some regional political cultures centralism rapidly became associated with the powerful negative images of the aristocratic plot to undermine independence and the domination of Mexico by the Spanish. The Bustamante government was soon identified with these so-called aristocrats,[135] members of the Mexico City–based dominant class who were still linked in popular memory with the former vice-regal government. This group was accused of being antinational, of obstructing the expulsion law, and even of desiring its repeal.[136] Moreover, although the Bustamante government did not abrogate the federalist constitution, it moved quickly to restrict popular political participation in the federal territories directly under its jurisdiction.[137]

The Bustamante regime's intensive campaigns against its opponents aroused the ire of many politicians who had been happy or at least relieved to see Guerrero go. Eventually they interested key military officers in opposing Bustamante, and in January 1832 Santa Anna began a movement in Veracruz against the Bustamante government, accusing it of centralism and calling for the resignation of the cabinet. The government was unable to repress the movement and on July 5 Santa Anna issued another plan that, surprisingly, called for the return of Gómez Pedraza to the presidency as the legitimate winner of the 1828 election. In December Bustamante agreed that Gómez Pedraza should retain the presidency until new legislatures were elected, and in March 1833 Santa Anna was elected president and Valentín Gómez Farías became vice-president.[138] Santa Anna took leave of his post, and Gómez Farías became acting chief executive.

The events of the next few months are often presented as precursors of later liberal/conservative struggles,[139] but the participants did not necessarily see them that way. The term "liberal" had been in use for some time in Mexico, but its meaning was much more general than the one later assigned to it, and the term "conservative" did not make its appearance before the mid-1840s.[140] The frictions between Gómez Farías and the church that characterized these months stemmed initially not from secular assaults on church property but instead from disagreement over whether the post-independence government had the right to exercise the former royal prerogative of appointing church officials.[141] When Gómez Farías later sought to tap church wealth it was basically a desperate attempt to resolve government fiscal problems.[142] Furthermore, Gómez Farías's opponents were not all "conservatives" but included many "liberal" politicians who had earlier supported him.[143] Santa Anna returned to power and abolished most of Gómez Farías's reforms, but Santa Anna seems to have been motivated more by Gómez Farías's attack on the privileges of the army than his disagreements with the Church.[144] The reactionary nature of Santa Anna's actions on his return stemmed from the same fear of popular radicalism that had destroyed Vicente Guerrero.[145]

Local Politics, 1831–1835

Juan Alvarez assumed the leadership of the radical coalition in the
South after Vicente Guerrero's death in 1831. Alvarez was born in
Atoyac on the Costa Grande in 1790 to a mestizo mother and a father
of Spanish or Creole blood who owned land on the Costa Grande and
who, like others, combined ranching with some trading. Alvarez received three or four years of primary education in Mexico City, and
although he never became an educated man he was certainly not illiterate. When Alvarez's father died in 1807, the Spanish subdelegado
of Acapulco, executor of the estate, refused to turn over to the son
his inheritance of 27,000 pesos' worth of goods and real estate and
instead made him work as a cowherd. Alvarez joined the insurgents
early in the War of Independence but was wounded several times and
spent much of the war in hiding recuperating from various wounds.
By the end of the war he was crippled from the knees down; he could
ride a horse but he needed crutches to walk. From 1818 to 1820 he
led insurgent guerrillas on the Costa Grande and reached the rank of
colonel, but he was never as famous as his contemporaries Vicente
Guerrero, Guadalupe Victoria, and Nicolás Bravo. After the triumph
of Iturbide in 1821 Alvarez became commander of the garrison at
Acapulco.[146]

Alvarez lost all or most of his inherited wealth during the insurgency. It is unclear how he recuperated his fortune, but by 1836 he
was able to buy the Hacienda La Brea near Acapulco for 20,000 pesos.
He renamed it La Providencia and by 1859 the cattle ranch had over
300 inhabitants. Alvarez was not an extremely wealthy man and
never controlled enough land to make his sharecroppers or peons an
important part of his military forces.[147]

Alvarez's political power stemmed from two sources: his popularity with the mulatto militia of the Costa Grande, which he seems
to have achieved by stressing the radical, anti-Spanish goals of the
1810 movement; and his skill at organizing larger movements after
1830, which he accomplished mostly by mail, belying the traditional
image of the *caudillo* or *cacique*. Alvarez's personal archive, reputed
to be huge by the 1850s, was lost in a struggle among his descendants
later in the century, but the volume of his correspondence can be
seen in the thousands of letters bearing his signature that survive in
public depositories.[148]

A period of relative calm ensued when the Bustamante government provided amnesty to the rebels of the area in 1831. This peace
was marred, however, by fears that the amnesty would not be re-

spected and by the general feeling that the Bustamante government was centralist in deed if not name. The villagers of Atoyac, for instance, did not turn in their arms or officially accept the amnesty because they feared repression by their local opponents. They stopped fighting but remained in hiding in the monte, the area between villages that traditionally offered sanctuary from government control. Government forces raided Atoyac and raped the daughters and wives of the men in hiding. In January 1832 the local commander, Lieutenant Colonel Cesario Ramos, began trying to round up the peasants who worked the village fields, and several skirmishes ensued. Eventually Juan Alvarez, enemy of the government and bitter rival of Ramos, was asked to mediate and succeeded in quieting the situation, but his mediation ended when he seconded Santa Anna's Plan of Veracruz in August 1832. The peasants of Atoyac and Tecpan once more joined a successful national movement and gained temporary ascendancy over their enemies.[149]

Alvarez's proclamation on this occasion accused the government of excessive taxation and allowing foreign commerce to ruin the cotton industry, and supporting proclamations from Tecpan accused Lucás Alamán and his cronies of despotism and demanded a "constitutional, popular, and federal" government.[150] Isidro Montes de Oca insisted the rebels were fighting "aristocratic centralism."[151] In the letter in which he tried unsuccessfully to convince Nicolás Bravo and his forces further inland to second the plan, Alvarez referred to Alamán as a "dependent of the Duke of Monteleone," the heir of Cortés, and to his party as "aristocrats." Alvarez claimed to be struggling against domestic tyrants much as he and Bravo both had opposed foreign tyrants. In reply, Bravo denied that he was an aristocrat and pointed out that he had left a very comfortable life to join Morelos. In the end they signed a regional peace treaty under which they agreed to suspend hostilities although Bravo continued to recognize the Bustamante government and Alvarez to oppose it. Little fighting ensued. After the fall of the Bustamante government Bravo and Alvarez signed another document that was basically a mutual nonaggression pact.[152]

The pact did not ensure peace in Guerrero. In June 1833 the mestizo market town of Chilapa pronounced against the government of Gómez Farías under its militia colonel Luís Dominguez, and Bravo joined them later that year. This conflict, in which the rancheros and other wealthy inhabitants of Chilapa and Chilpancingo supported Bravo and Dominguez while the outlying Indian villages backed Alvarez, went back to the 1820s and early 1830s, when Dominguez had several times used his troops to prevent villagers from voting in municipal elections. In March 1834 Dominguez was killed when Alvarez took Chilapa with the support of some of the surrounding Indian villages. In the national press Bravo accused Alvarez of personally killing Dominguez. This regional civil war sputtered to a close after Santa Anna dismissed Gómez Farías in Mexico City.[153]

By early 1835 the local federalists were certain that Santa Anna's reaction threatened federalism itself. They again began clandestinely organizing the villagers of the Montaña against the area's mestizo and Creole elite. In March 1835 Alvarez pronounced against Santa Anna, claiming he had betrayed federalism, and called for reinstating the state and federal authorities that Santa Anna had removed along with all others who had lost posts because of differences of political opinion. Alvarez's plan proposed a general amnesty for political crimes committed by all except Santa Anna himself. Alvarez also issued a call to arms in which he eulogized Vicente Guerrero, dubbed Guerrero's party the "popular party" and "los Populares," and claimed that Santa Anna's dictatorial actions were subverting the federation. He ended this missive with the slogan "God, Liberty, and Federation." Alvarez began this rebellion in alliance with the powerful state of Zacatecas and its militia, the largest in Mexico, but the Zacatecas militia fled after a brief skirmish and support was not forthcoming from other regions of Mexico. After a relatively brief period of fighting Alvarez negotiated yet another treaty with Bravo in which he and the other leaders of the revolt agreed to exile for themselves (with salaries intact) and amnesty for their followers. In the end Alvarez did not leave the country[154] but instead retired with the permission of the government to his new hacienda, where he remained for more than five years before participating in another revolt.

National Politics and Political Economy in Centralist Mexico, 1835–1840

The adoption of the so-called "Seven Laws" in 1836 officially enshrined centralism as Mexico's constitutional system. Centralism replaced states and their elected governors with departments run by governors appointed by the national government. It replaced state legislatures with small departmental councils with only advisory and administrative powers. It also cut back severely on the number of municipalities, authorizing them only in departmental capitals, cities that had possessed town councils before 1808, ports with at least 4,000 inhabitants, and other towns with at least 8,000. This measure eliminated most municipalities in Guerrero. Centralist measures also severely reduced suffrage: after 1836 only persons with over 100 pesos of annual income were allowed to vote. Personal taxes increased threefold.[155]

Both Josefina Vázquez and Barbara Tenenbaum have recently suggested that historians have not devoted sufficient attention to centralism. Vázquez has convincingly argued that the church was not vocal or decisive in its support of the centralist movement, although some centralists tried to stress their support for religion. Centralism's bases of support rested squarely on what remained of the colonial dominant class and army officers like Santa Anna and Bustamante who feared the growth of state militias as rivals to their power.[156] Tenenbaum has suggested the basic similarities between centralism and the colonial political system, the most important similarity being the fact that, in her words, "under centralism, the wealthy and powerful could organize their networks in Mexico City to help their interests within a department, a practice unthinkable under federalism."[157] This was the crucial feature of the centralist project.

Before independence the control that Mexico's colonial dominant class exercised over the economy depended on its members' access to the bureaucrats who selectively enforced the thousands of economic regulations produced by a mercantilist state. After independence federalism weakened this control. Centralism constituted an effort of the remnants of the colonial dominant class to reestablish its control over Mexico's political and economic system, and the dominant class had many allies in this effort, for centralism promised to end political strife after six years of almost constant insecurity. Even members of provincial elites who had previously experimented with cross-class alliances were ready to trade some political power for the promised economic benefits of peace.[158] The centralists also pursued an economic project that promised to help their staunchest opponents, namely, the cotton farmers and artisans whose livelihood had been all but wiped out after independence by imports of cotton textiles.

The drive to develop a protected textile industry began in direct response to the political militancy of Mexico's artisans in the late 1820s. Artisans had supported Guerrero and joined anti-Spanish campaigns, but although Guerrero banned textile imports, this decree was not implemented because the government needed customs revenue to face the Spanish invasion. After Guerrero's overthrow the

Bustamante administration annulled the protectionist legislation but set aside a fraction of the duties collected on imported textiles to foster industrial development. The famous Banco de Avío was founded to loan these funds to entrepreneurs so they could import modern technology. Nevertheless, both artisans and the new factories continued to face foreign competition until the formal implementation of centralism in the mid-1830s.[159]

Two factors led the centralists to embrace protectionism: first, the new factory owners enjoyed considerable influence in the new government; second, the centralists wanted to disarticulate the alliance between provincial elites and the urban artisans of central Mexico that had driven radical politics. The artisans were given the protection against foreign textiles they had clamored for, and the weavers were protected because initially there were only enough power looms in Mexico to weave half of the power-spun yarn. Cotton growers and sheep ranchers would also benefit, as imports of cotton and wool were prohibited. Thus the shift to protectionism was expected to obtain the acquiescence of many former radicals both in central Mexico and on the federalist periphery.[160]

This promising state of affairs was short-lived: the new system had severe internal and external limitations. Internally the structure of privilege that lay at the heart of the system was vulnerable to manipulation by the most politically powerful members of the coalition. Individuals obtained advantages in the factor market through their access to government power holders. This chicanery was *economically* viable but quickly tore apart the *political* coalition that supported protection. Externally factories in Great Britain and the United States could deliver textiles to Mexico at prices so low that protection rapidly foundered under a tide of contraband. Furthermore, foreign manufacturers' comparative advantage lay in their access to cotton grown in the southern United States rather than in productivity differentials in the factories themselves. Mexico's first industrialists soon sought relief by jettisoning their erstwhile allies in the protectionist coalition, the cotton growers who could not compete with plantation owners in the southern United States.

When the Banco de Avío was established to promote modern industrial development in Mexico, its board of directors was given wide discretion in choosing the recipients of loans. The board was essentially controlled by the now-reduced colonial dominant class of Mexico City–based merchants and financiers, and it is not surprising that these men loaned money to themselves and their acquaintances, with five of the first six loans they offered going to enterprises located within 60 miles of Mexico City.[161] Investment in factories rapidly came to be dominated by the *agiotistas*, whose connections enabled them to obtain exemptions from government policies.[162]

External factors determined how this power would be used. For a brief period Mexican prohibitions on textile imports were effectively enforced by France's blockade of Mexico during the so-called "Pastry War," but contraband soon began to flow in because British manufacturers could deliver a pound of yarn in Mexico for less money than their Mexican competitors paid just to buy the locally grown cotton needed to make it.[163] By 1840 various schemes began to surface that would allow the limited importation of raw cotton. Some industrialists supported these plans, which were opposed bitterly by cotton growers on both coasts. Industrialists based their arguments on the scarcity of raw cotton, whereas growers charged that industrialists were really concerned with the issue of price. Other industrialists used their personal connections with politicians, particularly Santa Anna, to obtain import licenses.[164] The protectionist coalition began to fall apart. In the end the protectionist political economy became linked to centralism, economic privilege, and undue influence just as these pillars of the colonial system came under renewed attack.[165]

Local Politics After 1835

The year 1835 marked a minor watershed in local politics. From 1810 to 1835 groups pressing local grievances had many opportunities to ally themselves with regional and national coalitions simply by seconding the pronouncement of militia officers like Alvarez, Bravo, or Montes de Oca. The availability of these regional allies also allowed villages to construct horizontal alliances with each other. Beginning in 1835 a momentary lull in national political strife precluded this kind of alliance, and popular demands were again expressed in isolated riots similar to those common in colonial Mexico.[166] Although peasants tried to attract allies with the same antiforeign, federalist language that had facilitated earlier alliances, the prospects for successful national movements were so low that regional intermediaries refused to be drawn into rebellions. However, they also refused to repress rebellions and usually endeavored to preserve their influence among peasants by brokering compromise solutions. For a brief period the consensus of national elites succeeded in uncoupling local politics from national politics.

An 1838 incident on the Costa Grande illustrates how local politics had changed. The mulatto sharecroppers of the coast had supported the insurgents during the War of Independence because of their longstanding frustration with the Spanish merchants who advanced them money and goods against the cotton they cultivated. From 1827 to 1835 they blamed the local Spanish merchants for the depressed cotton prices caused by competition from imported textiles and joined the radical anti-Spanish movements led by Guerrero and Alvarez. The sharecroppers had established a consistent pattern of blaming merchants for the economic hardships caused by the vagaries of the textile market. Because the merchants were often foreigners, sharecroppers tied themselves to national political movements.

The Spanish merchants who had earlier controlled the cotton market were driven out in the late 1820s, but their place was taken by new entrepreneurs who established cotton gins on the coast. The most prominent was Juan Ashley, an Englishman who arrived in 1825 and whose good relations with Guerrero and Alvarez overcame the initial resistance of the Spanish merchants who ran the municipal council of Tecpan in the mid-1820s. The Englishman quickly became the most important buyer of local cotton. His position in the market only improved with the expulsion of the Spanish, and soon his only competition was provided by itinerant peddlers who traded manufactured goods for small amounts of cotton.[167]

Popular beliefs about the economy and politics connected the usurious behavior of foreign buyers of cotton to foreign threats to Mexico's independence. Ashley first ran afoul of those beliefs in January 1835 when Lieutenant José María Gallardo, the militia officer who had led the 1827 persecution of the Spanish in Tecpan, issued a call for the expulsion of the English from the coast. Gallardo wanted to eliminate "the bloodsucking horrors of a portion of the globe which is bleeding the coast without providing any benefits at all";[168] he later recanted, stating that he was inebriated when he issued the call. Ashley considered emigrating from the coast, but the support and reassurances of local authorities both defused the crisis and convinced him to stay on.[169]

But Ashley's luck ran out when France engaged Mexico in the so-called "Pastry War" of 1838. News of the war spread rapidly even to this remote area, where the governor of the state requested information on the feasibility of mobilizing the local militia. The rhetorical and real similarities of the French landing in Veracruz to the 1829 Spanish invasion resonated with popular hatred of merchants and foreigners despite the promise of good fortune contained in the recent prohibition of imports of raw cotton and finished textiles.[170] The nationalist hysteria that followed soon found a clear target.

On December 24, 1838, a party of armed men from the nearby village of San Gerónimo rode into Tecpan and, claiming to have secret orders from their general, sacked Ashley's house and killed him. On January 1 they returned, burned down the building that housed Ashley's cotton gin, and killed a German employee of Ashley's. The commander of their militia unit, Luís Pinzón, was ordered to apprehend the killers and made an ineffectual search of the surrounding area. When questioned about his inaction, Pinzón stated that he could not have arrested the perpetrators without causing a mutiny because almost his entire company had taken part in the crime. Another witness added that the inhabitants of both Tecpan and San Gerónimo had openly shouted "Long live the Federation and Death to Foreigners!" and that Pinzón's militiamen wore on their hats the slogan "Death to foreigners!"[171] A defense lawyer made the plausible claim that the majority of the population "publicly approved of the conduct of the murderers."[172]

When word of the disorder reached Mexico City, the national government asked Juan Alvarez to intervene, and he arrested the killers with the help of militia troops from other parts of the region. The local militia company had to be reorganized because most of its officers had been arrested. The prisoners were sent to Acapulco under guard; their subsequent fate is unknown.[173] Isolated from potential allies, these men were arrested for actions that ten years earlier had been acceptable. Although this incident was not officially sanctioned, the language used demonstrates clearly that the negative attributes associated with the Spanish in the past had been generalized and applied to all foreigners.

Two broad national political coalitions developed between 1820 and 1840. These coalitions did not arise directly from the independence war but instead developed from the breakdown of the post-independence settlement in the mid-1820s. The coalition that later identified itself as first "centralist" and then "conservative" was centered around two groups, the more important of which was the remnant of Mexico's colonial dominant class, a series of families with large investments in commerce and agriculture in economically important zones like the Meseta Central and the Bajío. In the colonial period these families had used their ties with royal officials to protect their economic interests, reduce risks, and manipulate markets. After independence they eventually opted for centralism and protectionism to accomplish the same ends. They were joined by army officers from the former royalist army who sought to protect and take advantage of their political power, and who entered into strategic alliances with diverse groups throughout Mexico. Notably, the Church was not really a member of this coalition, at least before 1840.[174]

Their opponents, a more diverse lot, included former insurgent officers, provincial merchants, artisans, professionals, and many intellectuals. These federalists championed protectionism and nationalism and most were by no means classical liberals. This coalition also entered into alliances with assorted groups in provincial Mexico.[175]

Both coalitions seemed to begin as Masonic lodges in the late 1820s but quickly outlived their Masonic names and forms of organization. In fact, the lodges were just a convenient means to express preexisting differences in interests and political beliefs. They died out as soon as more descriptive expressions of identity became available, namely, the labels of "centralism" and "federalism." The coalitions were very loose and many groups and individuals threw their weight from one to the other based on the circumstances of the moment.

These two coalitions developed distinct political programs and ideologies. The centralists saw themselves as the preservers of order against the threat of Mexico's masses. They looked back with horror on the independence war and explicitly argued that Mexico needed a centralized, authoritarian form of government. Their opponents saw themselves as the heirs of the insurgents. They believed that political power should be divided along the broadest possible lines. To them, the realization of Mexico's independence required federalism. It also required that the enemies of independence be neutralized.

The nationalist episode known as the expulsion of the Spanish was inseparable from this internal political struggle. The Spanish became targets because of their position in the ongoing political struggle and in the economy itself. Politically many of the Spanish supported the party of order; economically Spanish merchants continued to occupy important positions in wholesale trade and moneylending. The groups that worked to expel them believed that the Spanish derived their prominent position from their privileged access to the colonial government before independence and that they were responsible for the hardships forced on the textile sector under the pressure of cheap imported goods. Furthermore, because the most prominent Spaniards were members of the dominant class, federalist politicians were able to use the expulsion issue to demonize and denationalize that entire group. This episode demonstrates how misleading it can be to separate nationalism from internal politics.

National politics were indeed inseparable from local politics and vice versa. The aforementioned national coalitions drew life from their ability to forge alliances with local groups both in Mexico City and in the provinces. In the case of Guerrero local groups, including peasants, time and time again affected national outcomes by supporting these coalitions while simultaneously advancing their own interests. Those active in national politics had to mobilize support through alliances with local groups; likewise, groups with local grievances found it expeditious to take stands in wider struggles. It was through this symbiotic process that national politics were "made," to borrow a term from Florencia Mallon.[176]

The legacies of the 1820–40 period were important. The coalitions that emerged during the period formed the bases of Mexican politics through the 1850s and beyond, and elements of the centralist and federalist ideologies developed then dominated Mexican political discourse for many years. Furthermore, patterns of alliance between national politicians and local groups, including peasants, worked out in this period became increasingly important in shaping the Mexican state over the next decades. These patterns were not neutralized successfully until Porfirio Díaz ascended to power in the late nineteenth century. Even then, they would resurface during the Mexican Revolution.

CHAPTER 5

Guerrero in the 1840s: Peasant Rebellions and Elite Politics

The village saw fit to name me.
—Miguel Francisco, justice of the peace of Jocutla, 1840

Federation or death. Long live America: and death forever to tyranny.
The whites, the blacks, and we the Indians, we are all Mexicans. Let it
be understood, iniquitous tyrants, that the domestic fight is not a caste
war, but instead because we are suffering many pains . . . from the
multitude of taxes, even because our lungs live and breathe. . . . today
the day has arrived in which we the Indians punish anyone who is
against our law.
—Anonymous, district of Tlapa, April 1846

In the 1840s many of Guerrero's peasants participated in
large-scale rebellions, both separately and in alliance with other
groups in local and national politics. The relationship between peasant mobilization and national politics was reciprocal: laws and institutional changes emanating from the national level affected peasants' economic well-being and their position in local politics, and
peasants looked beyond their localities for allies. In the 1840s events
in national political life affected both the timing and results of rebellions; at the same time, peasant political activity in Guerrero influenced outcomes in national conflicts.

This close relationship between peasant actions and national politics belies the separations between the peasantry and elites and the
local and the national that dominate much social-science literature.
Peasants in Guerrero had cooperated effectively with people from
other classes and had taken positions on national issues during the
War of Independence and the regional anti-Spanish and federalist
movements of the late 1820s and early 1830s, but the 1840s were
different in a crucial way. In the 1840s peasants themselves took the
initiative, both in beginning violent political movements and in forging alliances among different peasant groups and with nonpeasants.
Rather than responding to elite calls for action, peasants issued
their own.

A second development in Guerrero's politics was a geographic and social shift in political participation as the center of political activity shifted from the mulatto cotton farmers of the Costa Grande to the Indians of the Montaña. Some of these peasants or their parents and neighbors had participated in the War of Independence and some had participated in less violent struggles over local political power in the 1820s and 1830s. This northward and eastward expansion of lower-class political activity and the regional federalist alliance from the Costa Grande toward the mountains and valleys of Central Mexico would continue in subsequent decades, and its implications would eventually become crucial to Mexican politics.

Because no peasant rebellion has ever resulted in the formation of a political and economic system dominated by peasants, many historians stress the defeat and repression of peasant efforts to change their lives. Yet in the 1840s many of Guerrero's peasants took advantage of opportunities and achieved their goals. Success was easier when these goals were limited to changes in state policies affecting local political power and taxation, but some villages also eventually succeeded in having their interpretation of local land rights recognized by the state after years of effective occupation.

Setting the Stage

The circumstances that made possible the initial outbreak and subsequent spread of the peasant rebellions of the 1840s were formed by national political events, local political alignments, land disputes, and changes in the relationship between the peasantry and the state under centralism. Of these four elements, the first two determined the ability of peasants to find allies on both the national and local political scene and the second two determined the timing and grievances of the rebellions. The combination vastly changed the political landscape in Guerrero and contributed to a critical development at the national level.

Political calm had settled over Mexico in the late 1830s. Many of the political actors who had contributed to the strife of the 1828–35 period were willing to give the new constitutional system the benefit of the doubt; this was particularly true of cotton growers and weavers, who seemed likely to benefit from the protection of the textile industry. But the protectionist coalition began to break down when some of its members used their influence with centralist politicians to obtain exemptions from the ban on raw cotton imports. Others went further, openly lobbying to overturn the policy.[1]

Evidence of this breakdown can be seen in the 1841–42 movement that overthrew President Anastasio Bustamante. Although this movement was neither explicitly federalist nor protectionist, many of its supporters were. In Guerrero, for instance, both Bravo and Alvarez, who had been quiet since 1836, seconded the 1841 movement while almost simultaneously joining the calls of local cotton growers and weavers to preserve protectionism. Alvarez had not seconded the federalist rebellion of Gordiano Guzmán in nearby Michoacán in 1837–38, although his sympathies clearly lay with the rebels and he sheltered Guzmán after the rebellion faded away. Bravo's and Alvarez's perceptions of the central government clearly changed when its promise of a revived cotton economy began to self-destruct.[2] This breakdown of the centralist, protectionist project paved the way for the national instability of the 1840s.

The local political situation in Guerrero also laid the groundwork for the rebellions. At the end of the 1830s an uneasy peace continued between two local factions: the centralists, led by Nicolás Bravo, controlled central and eastern Guerrero, including most of the areas where the 1840s rebellions would take place, while the federalists, led by Alvarez, controlled the Costa Grande. These groups had faced off in a series of bitter conflicts and negotiated agreements in the 1830s during which it became apparent that Alvarez had allies within the area dominated by the centralists, particularly in the disenfranchised Indian villages. These allies, whom local authorities persecuted in the late 1830s and whom Alvarez gave refuge on his hacienda, would provide Alvarez with contacts in the area after 1840. Some also became prominent leaders of the peasant rebellions.[3]

The conflict between local factions was tempered by a shared interest in forming a new department or state. Bravo and Alvarez cooperated in this effort throughout the 1840s. In 1841 they convened an assembly of representatives from the towns and villages of the region, which included many individuals who would become prominent in the 1840s rebellions, to discuss the need for a new state and its possible boundaries. Later Alvarez and Bravo produced a joint manifesto for the assembly, indicating that a new state was necessary because under the current system the area never succeeded in placing representatives in the national legislature. They also argued that many laws concerning local administration written in Toluca were unsuited to local conditions and complained that distance from the centers of power prevented effective actions to aid residents.[4] This drive for administrative and political autonomy united local centralists and federalists.

These elements of national and local politics provided the explosive context in which a series of land disputes near Chilapa came to a head in the late 1830s and early 1840s. These complex land disputes had roots going back over 100 years. The way in which these land disputes were played out was inextricably tied to the dual struggle over local political power and the nature of the state, which had driven politics in the region since before independence.

In the Chilapa region of the Montaña, Indian villagers formed the vast majority of the local population. In the late eighteenth and early nineteenth centuries they had shared the area with a tightly knit, locally powerful group of small merchants, officials, and landowners, many of whom resided in the head town of Chilapa and produced sugar at small mills, some on lands rented from the villages. Land disputes, including those between villages and these vecinos, were endemic and many had been under way since long before independence.[5] Local land rights were particularly ambiguous because most of the area fell under the jurisdiction of the mayorazgo or *cacicazgo* of Guerrero or the Moctezumas, a single entity that went under various names. The mayorazgo included one of the few surviving *encomiendas,* or privately held grants of tribute rights, in New Spain. The various families that held this entailment during the colonial period gradually let many of its rights lapse, and much of the land passed into the possession of squatters, both Indian and Creole. The owners continued to run a small sugar operation of their own, however, and as late as 1775 eight villages still paid tribute to the mayorazgo. Some Indians also rented lands from the family.[6]

Developments after independence further confused the agrarian situation. The desirability of land increased when the local textile industry relied on by many villages and members of the local elite declined because of competition from cheap imported cloth. Mexico's national legislature abolished entailments. The Guerrero family, led by two brothers resident in Mexico City and Cuernavaca, could now sell what remained of the mayorazgo's operations in Chilapa. The state of Mexico also enacted several laws that affected both village and vacant lands: on paper these measures transferred both types of land to municipalities, but in practice many ambiguities continued to exist, as were described in Chapter 3.

The final steps leading up to the Chilapa confrontation took place in the late 1830s. The Indian peasants who had struggled for local power using earlier laws on municipalities and suffrage were defeated, apparently definitively, and the Indians of both the head town of Chilapa and the surrounding villages were excluded from politics under the income requirements for citizenship imposed by centralism in 1836. Also, the rights of the mayorazgo were bought by Manuel Herrera, a local notable prominent in the municipal government,[7] who promptly used his position in local politics to reassert rights the earlier owners had let lapse and reinterpret some of them in ways that can only be described as remarkable.

Herrera claimed that the tribute that the villages had paid to the mayorazgo before independence was in fact rent, and that therefore the mayorazgo owned all the land used by the villages within its jurisdiction.[8] As the new owner of the remnants of an Indian cacicazgo, he claimed to have bought entire villages. The claim was particularly outrageous from the peasant point of view because the amounts paid in tribute had been extremely small—no village had paid more than 140 pesos annually—amounts simply too minuscule to misconstrue as rent. Moreover, the tribute had been abolished with independence.

Why did Herrera stake such an incendiary claim? The obvious answer is that he had every reason to believe he could do so successfully because the Indians' federalist allies had withdrawn from both local and national politics, and because centralist provisions regarding municipalities and citizenship had put the local elite firmly in command of the judicial and administrative machinery. As mayor of Chilapa, Herrera supported his peers in conflicts, ordering the Indians to pay rent on disputed lands, and thus could count on the help of other landowners in his own battles. In addition, the laws themselves seemed to preclude litigation by the peasants. In the strictest sense of the law their villages did not exist. Land held by the peasants under colonial titles had technically passed to the municipalities, as had land to which no one held title, and the only lawyer who could adjudicate such claims under the centralist law of 1837 was the *síndico* or legal representative of the municipality.[9] In sum, the local centralist faction represented by Herrera and his peers controlled the legal, administrative, and military apparatus of the area, and all laws seemed to preclude resistance. Under these circumstances Herrera's claim does not appear so ridiculous.

The land conflict in Chilapa does not by itself account for the intensity, size, and widespread scope of the peasant rebellions that engulfed Guerrero in the 1840s. Peasants who lived far from the disputed lands also rebelled. Three other factors came into play: first, unknown to Herrera and his cronies, the relative consensus of elites at the national level was already crumbling, and these fissures would vastly widen the peasants' room to maneuver; second, centralist laws regarding local government were also unpopular in other areas of

Guerrero; third, and most important, the centralist attempt to tax Mexico's peasantry inspired deep and widespread resentment. These factors allowed unrest to spread far beyond the areas affected by conflicts over land tenure, and even to areas where peasants owned all the land.

Centralism had severely reduced the number of municipalities and restricted suffrage to those with an annual income of 100 pesos or more. Most municipal functions were taken over by officials appointed by departmental governments.[10] In practice these provisions virtually eliminated the ability of peasants to compete for local political power. Although prior laws were not always interpreted in ways favorable to peasants, they had at least offered that possibility. Now peasants were totally excluded from decision making.

The unfavorable trend of events was compounded by centralist attempts to increase the taxes paid by peasants. In the 1820s and 1830s peasants paid about 0.75 peso annually as contribución personal, which municipalities collected for local schools. In 1841 a national personal income tax was enacted under which peasants along with all others whose annual incomes did not exceed 500 pesos were to pay 1.5 pesos per year in addition to the earlier tax, and in 1842 the income tax was replaced by the capitación, a head tax of 1.5 pesos.[11] Again this was to be imposed in addition to the local school tax, leaving each peasant with an annual bill of 2.25 pesos. This burden compared unfavorably with the colonial tribute of around 2 pesos, and peasants knew it. The taxes, and their successors, were unpopular and difficult to collect throughout Mexico,[12] but nowhere did they become a bigger issue than in Guerrero. The centralist government in Mexico City, like its supporters in Chilapa, badly underestimated the power of the people it had disenfranchised.

The Movements

The developments outlined above all helped set the stage for the sustained peasant mobilization that was to characterize the 1840s in Guerrero, but alone they provide only a framework. The assault on peasant land rights in Chilapa encouraged by the skewed balance of local political power provided the spark, just as unfavorable laws regarding local government and taxes helped the movements grow far beyond their initial base. The breakdown of political agreements at the national level provided the space within which peasants could enter national politics just as the local elite movement toward regional autonomy furnished the framework within which peasants would realize many of their goals. However, the specific ways in which peasants developed alliances, elaborated programs, and affected outcomes were contingent on the rapidly shifting situation. For this reason a detailed narrative of the movements is needed to analyze the goals and tactics of both peasants and other actors.

From 1838 to 1840 the municipal council and prefect of Chilapa successfully prevented the Indians of the area from litigating with Manuel Herrera. The prefect claimed that only the síndico of the council could represent the peasants and the síndico refused to do so.[13] In July 1840 the inhabitants of Jocutla, one of the villages that Manuel Herrera claimed owed him rent, refused to pay. The village's justice of the peace was imprisoned, escaped, and took refuge with his villagers in the uncultivated monte nearby.[14]

In January 1841 the new prefect of Chilapa, José Vicente Villada, appealed to Juan Alvarez to defuse what he considered a dangerous situation. Villada asked Alvarez to send his secretary, Manuel Primo Tapia, to convince the Indians that they would be allowed to pursue their claims in court. Alvarez hesitated, afraid that he would be accused of fomenting unrest, but he eventually acquiesced, and Tapia negotiated a compromise under which the síndico of the municipality would delegate his authority to represent the peasants to two of their representatives, Miguel Salgado and Juan Prisciliano Castro. However, when Tapia left Chilapa a mysterious letter surfaced in which a fictitious Indian leader requested the aid of Chilpancingo's Indians in a revolt to recover lands. Significantly, it specifically referred to land that Chilpancingo had supposedly lost to the Bravo family. With the cooperation of the Bravos the local authorities of Chilapa imprisoned Salgado and several peasants, then sent troops to search the surrounding villages for the ringleaders of the alleged plot. Many peasants again fled to the monte, and the Indians sent emissaries to Alvarez. They were quickly followed by the elders of the villages, who took refuge on Alvarez's hacienda.

This turn of events upset Alvarez. He sent explanations of the situation to the federal and departmental authorities as well as to Bravo. Alvarez was particularly concerned that he might be accused of plotting against the authorities, but his letters also show anger that Herrera and his cronies were using their control of local government to deny the Indians access to the courts. Alvarez's efforts seem to have been successful: in April the governor of the department ordered the prefect to cease persecuting the villagers, to allow the villages to select their own legal representatives, and to report on the progress of the matter in the courts. Alvarez published a pamphlet in Mexico

City to prove that he had only intervened at the request of the authorities.[15]

Alvarez arranged for Ignacio Rayón to serve as the villagers' lawyer. Rayón was in Chilapa for only one month when violence broke out in March 1842, not, as one would expect, over the dispute with Herrera but rather over a 100-year-old conflict between the village of Quechultenango and the Hacienda de San Sebastián Buenavista. The Indians claimed that much of the hacienda's land belonged to them. The owner in the early 1840s, a Spanish doctor named Rafael Gutiérrez Martínez, exacerbated the conflict by diverting water from the stream that irrigated the remaining village lands and by refusing to allow the Indians to cut wood or gather fruit on hacienda land. Renting lands from the hacienda became the only alternative for many villagers. Worse, the town council of Chilapa appointed the administrator of the hacienda, Gabriel de la Torre, as justice of the peace for the village. In March 1842 Gutiérrez Martínez struck an Indian who owed him rent and sent his employee de la Torre, acting as justice, to collect rent from another. Unable to find the peasant he sought, the administrator burned his hut. Two nights later the peasants attacked the hacienda, killing both Gutiérrez Martínez and de la Torre as well as the latter's brother.[16]

The rebellion quickly spread to the other nearby villages involved in the land disputes and villagers fled for the monte en masse. On April 17 a militia force pursuing villagers was ambushed in the monte. Nicolás Bravo took charge of the government forces but the peasants refused his call to return to their homes, continuing instead to attack and burn the properties of their opponents. Finally, at Bravo's urging, Alvarez again tried to mediate the dispute. He traveled to the area with only Tapia to accompany him and convinced the peasants to accept an amnesty in May 1842. The only promise Alvarez made regarding land was that the peasants would be allowed to pursue their claims in court.[17]

The peace did not last. Frictions between the peasants and the residents of the head town continued. The peasants, complaining of being harassed and threatened when they went to the market in Chilapa, refused to turn in their arms,[18] while the townsmen, fearing further outbreaks, continued to pursue peasants who refused to disarm. The volatile situation again ignited when the peasants heard of the new capitación; refusing to pay and renewing demands for their land, the peasants of the Chilapa area revolted in early 1843.

The new tax dramatically changed the situation because it affected a much wider area and a much greater number of peasants than the land disputes. Unrest quickly spread east to the Montaña around Tlapa, west to the Tierra Caliente, and north to the Taxco region. The peasants of the Chilapa area found thousands of allies in villages that did not share their anxiety over land tenure but were willing to take a stand against the tax.

Peasants killed the collectors of the new tax in the Taxco area and in the Tierra Caliente,[19] the latter of which had a history of resisting taxation by post-independence governments. In the eastern Montaña peasants refused to pay and besieged the district capital of Tlapa, and in all three areas large numbers of villages united behind leaders who issued proclamations opposing the new tax. Even around Chilapa villages not affected by the land disputes now joined the rebellion, this time uniting with some rancheros.[20]

The increased scope of the unrest fostered by the new taxes convinced Nicolás Bravo, military commander of the region, that it was necessary to make concessions on the land disputes. He agreed to negotiate with several representatives of the peasants, including Alvarez's son Diego. A May 31, 1843, agreement provided for an amnesty and submitted the land disputes to a committee composed of one representative of the villages, one of the landowners, and a neutral arbitrator selected jointly by the first two. The agreement also bound the national government to provide a minimum of land to villages whose lands were still insufficient after arbitration.

For a brief time it appeared that this agreement would succeed. The two sides ratified the accord and exchanged prisoners. The peasants quickly named Ignacio Rayón as their representative, but the landowners dragged their feet and continued to harass villagers who appeared in Chilapa to trade. Soon, in a climate of distrust that boded ill for the future, the villages refused to send representatives to Chilapa for ceremonies marking the renovation of their justices of the peace. Bravo resigned as military commander, citing his inability to force the landowners to proceed with the arbitration. Beyond the immediate Chilapa area, rebelling villages who were not parties to the agreement continued to oppose the tax.[21]

Up until this point the peasant rebellions of the 1840s in the South had remained separate from elite struggles in national politics. Although some peasant proclamations attempted to reach out to potential allies on political questions, these overtures generally fell on deaf ears. Things began to change in 1844 when authorities, who had been forced to suspend tax collections in the area the previous year, again received orders from President Santa Anna to collect the tax. Some villages found pretexts under which to request exemptions and several officials resigned rather than attempt collection. Realizing that determined opposition could stymie the government, peasants rebelled again in August in the Chilapa and Tlapa areas, as well as in several villages of the nearby Oaxacan Mixteca. In September militia captain Miguel Casarrubias, a mestizo ranchero who had also participated in the movements of the previous year, took command of the rebels and attempted to moderate rebel demands to increase the likelihood of acquiring allies. His tactics proved effective: the mestizo inhabitants of the market towns also resented the capitación. Casarrubias besieged Chilapa, which fell after a few days when the town council and some of the town elite agreed to surrender in return for Casarrubias's assurances of their safety. The rebellion began to sputter after Casarrubias was killed in November; nevertheless, three of the most important peasant leaders seconded the anti–Santa Anna Plan of Jalisco on November 26.[22]

Events took a new turn when Alvarez and Bravo both decided to participate in the revolt against Santa Anna. Although Santa Anna was overthrown without their direct aid they feared a countermovement. Thus, with Bravo's agreement, Alvarez directed a proclamation to the rebellious villages in December blaming Santa Anna for the odious tax and urging villagers to join him in support of the new government. He recruited around 1,000 peasants and set off for Mexico City,[23] but the force returned when the new government later decided that its support was unnecessary. Peasant participation in national politics on this occasion was limited and peasants in the Tlapa area continued their rebellion.

In February 1845 President José Joaquín de Herrera sent Alvarez to pacify the rebellious peasants from the Oaxacan Mixteca to the Tierra Caliente. Because Joaquín Rea, the landowners' representative under the 1843 treaty, refused to participate in the arbitration, Alvarez suggested that the government buy out Chilapa's landowners. More important, Alvarez exempted the peasants from the head tax, a move vigorously opposed by the departmental governments of Puebla and Oaxaca. In his travels Alvarez addressed several meetings of village representatives, collecting the military weapons peasants had acquired during the fighting and recommending that several officials be replaced.[24]

National politics remained important to local events. Some of Alvarez's allies on the national scene invited him to take part in an upcoming federalist movement, but he refused because he suspected that many of these men were more interested in advancing their personal fortunes than the principles they professed. Furthermore, Joaquín Rea and Vicente Bernardo Cervantes, a parish priest in the Montaña, were using the proposed revolt to conspire against Alvarez: Cervantes tried to convince his parishioners that Alvarez meant to sell them into slavery on the pretext of recruiting them to defend the nation. When the conspirators revolted in Mexico City Alvarez refused to support them and the revolt failed.[25]

Throughout the summer and fall of 1845 peasant grievances and elite politics intersected in Guerrero. Joaquín Rea, an ally of Bravo and commander of the military forces on the Costa Chica southeast of Acapulco, had unsuccessfully opposed the 1844–45 rebellions in the Montaña. Alvarez now sought to settle the land question and simultaneously rid himself of a rival by insisting that Rea proceed to Chilapa to carry out his duties under the 1843 treaty as representative of Chilapa's landowners. When Alvarez used his connections with the Herrera government in Mexico City to obtain orders to that effect, Rea refused to obey, asserting that Alvarez had already awarded the disputed lands to the peasants and was using the arbitration to lure Rea into an ambush. Rea and Alvarez traded accusations: Rea said that Alvarez was behind all the rebellions, while Alvarez continued to insist that Rea and the priest Cervantes were conspiring against the government. In October 1845, when Cervantes's parishioners rioted over his interference in village elections and killed their pastor, Rea blamed Alvarez. In the end Rea did not go to Chilapa but the government allowed him to retain his command.[26]

The national political situation changed again in late 1845 when General Mariano Paredes revolted in San Luís Potosí against the Herrera regime. At first glance this was not an unusual movement and the original plan provided for little more than a change of government, but weeks before the revolt rumors indicated that Paredes had actually conspired to institute a monarchy in Mexico with the aid of the Spanish government. Not surprisingly, Alvarez opposed the movement. Rea plotted to support Paredes in the South but the effort was discovered and neutralized. On the national scene Paredes succeeded and became president, but he was too weak to replace Alvarez as commander of the South, and frictions between Alvarez and Paredes set the stage for greater involvement in national politics on the part of some of Guerrero's peasants.[27]

The villages of the Tlapa region revolted in late January 1846. They took an explicit position in national politics by claiming that their revolt was against Paredes and his friends who, in their words, sought to impose "a tyranny more detestable than that of General Santa Anna. . . . Long live the Fatherland and Death Forever to Despotism."[28] They were seconded by some villages in the Taxco region and also received covert support from villages near Chilapa. Joaquín Rea tried to repress the rebellion but when he pursued the rebels into the district of Chilapa the authorities there threatened to oppose him with armed force. By late February the government became aware that villages in the Tierra Caliente were also preparing to rebel. Worse, a section of Rea's own militia on the Costa Chica deserted and revolted against him. Alvarez seems to have encouraged all of these movements but had not yet made any overt moves.[29]

On April 15, 1846, Alvarez called for the overthrow of Paredes to forestall his monarchist ambitions. Surprisingly he proposed that Santa Anna resume the presidency. The movement quickly encompassed not only the peasants of the Tlapa region who were already in revolt but also the Costa Chica militia and peasants in Chilapa, Taxco, and the Tierra Caliente. Alvarez and these peasants of the South remained alone in their defiance of Paredes until the garrison of Guadalajara revolted in May. The final blow against Paredes came when the Mexico City garrison turned against him in August. From April until August a fierce war continued in the South between the peasants of Alvarez's forces and troops led by Rea and Angel Guzmán sent to repress them.[30]

The South was quiet for more than a year following the triumph of the 1846 movement. Most peasant demands had been met and Alvarez, Rea, and Bravo put aside their differences to prepare for the war with the United States. When it seemed that peasant unrest would resurge in late 1847, the war itself became an important argument used to calm them. In 1847 Domingo Santiago, a peasant leader since the early 1840s, began to plan a new rebellion to press the still unsettled land claims in the Chilapa area and Alvarez moved quickly to demobilize the Indians, pointing out the danger the impending U.S. invasion posed to all. The appeal succeeded and Alvarez was quickly able to recruit troops to take to the coming war in central Mexico.[31]

The invasion was not the only political development that reduced peasant unrest. Alvarez and Bravo continued to press for the new state of Guerrero. Alvarez told national politicians that a new state would reduce peasant unrest and simultaneously told peasants that a new state would more effectively attend to their interests and complaints. For instance, when an abortive rebellion broke out in 1847 on the Costa Chica among villages that had remained on the margins of earlier movements, apparently encouraged by enemies of Alvarez to discredit his promise to maintain order, he used the incident in his arguments for a new state.[32]

Two more rebellions broke out in 1849 during the final push for statehood. Domingo Santiago led a movement in Chilapa that again called for tax reduction. When Alvarez exhorted the villages to make peace so as not to impede statehood, insisting that the new state would write laws to protect peasant interests, they complied. The second rebellion near Taxco called for the return of Santa Anna and the abrogation of the Treaty of Guadalupe Hidalgo. Alvarez claimed that his enemies in Mexico City had provided the proclamation disseminated by the conspiracy's leader, Faustino Villalva, a prominent leader in earlier movements going back to the federalist rebellions of the mid-1830s. On this occasion Villalva fled when it was clear that neither the peasants of the area nor Alvarez were willing to support him.[33]

The Rebellions: Organization, Ideology, and Alliances

In the regions of Guerrero in which the 1840s rebellions occurred, language posed an important obstacle to alliances among villages. In the Montaña the inhabitants of the villages belonged to no less than four language groups: Nahuatl, Mixtec, Amuzgo, and Tlapaneco. Often villagers of varying ethnic backgrounds cooperating in rebellions communicated with each other in Spanish, which had probably been spoken at the regional markets, or *tianguis*, for many years. Spanish was also the language taught in village schools and used in litigation, arguably the colonial source of many peasant political ideas. Perhaps most important, it was the language of the written word.

Communication across distances in nineteenth-century Mexico was by default *written* communication, and anyone who wanted to reach an audience beyond the few dozen or hundred that could be scraped together at important village functions had to communicate across such distances. Thus it should not surprise that peasants who organized rebellions spanning dozens of villages and many square miles left so much written evidence of their political activity.

The evidence falls into two broad categories. The first consists of political proclamations issued by peasant leaders. Like their elite counterparts peasant leaders issued proclamations or "plans" to justify their actions and secure allies,[34] but unlike their elite allies they often issued such proclamations in the form of a circular. A single copy of a proclamation was addressed to as many as 20 or 30 villages, each of which signed the document to acknowledge receipt and passed it on to the next in the chain. In the end it was returned to the originator. The circular, a technique obviously borrowed from administrative cost-cutting procedures, reduced pressure on a leader's own capacity to produce documents. Elites typically did not go to such lengths because they had more access to trained scribes and even printing presses.

The second category is that of private correspondence between village leaders describing events, asking for aid, and offering support. Some of this correspondence contains evidence of very conscious organizing and bargaining among villages; common strategies included offering to defy an order from some authority if others would agree to follow suit, and working to forge agreements to resist authorities' attempts to employ force. Correspondence, like circulars, was almost always addressed to the justices of the peace who were the highest civil officials in each village.[35] At the beginning of the 1840s laws provided that such officials would be chosen either by prefects or the nearest municipal council, but as a practical matter these authorities usually found it more convenient to ratify whatever individual the village offered to serve in the post. After the rebellions began it became even more common for justices to be chosen by the villages themselves.

Both private correspondence and proclamations contained implicit and explicit agreements among villages and individuals. One of the most counterintuitive predictions of the rational-choice literature in political science is that such agreements need to be enforced even if goals are genuinely shared, and the evidence for the 1840s rebellions in Guerrero fully supports this contention. Peasants often threatened the use of force to enforce commitments to rebellions, and they also carried out such threats.[36] Coercion proved as necessary for peasant organization as it did for the organization of the state itself.

The peasants were able to communicate about common goals. But what goals could unite peasants from such a wide area? Many years later Emiliano Zapata was able to organize a large peasant movement around the issue of land stolen from peasants by expanding commercial estates. The Zapatista movement constitutes the unconscious model of many historians of peasant movements in Mexico and elsewhere. Two historians of the 1840s movements, Leticia Reina and John Hart, go so far as to infer estate expansion from the presence of rebellions.[37] But the Zapatista movement was an exceptional case in which rapid estate expansion affected a large number of villages almost simultaneously. Peasant political action had more diverse causes in other areas of Mexico both during the Mexican Revolution and in earlier periods. In 1840s Guerrero, the evidence indicates that although land grievances were extremely important in the immediate surroundings of Chilapa where the rebellions began, they were basically nonexistent through much of the area affected by the movements, particularly the Tierra Caliente, the Taxco region, and the eastern Montaña near Tlapa. Land was not an issue in most areas and was not a demand of most peasants. Even in Chilapa the problem lay less with expanding estates than with local officials' attempts to use their political power to reinvent the land rights of long moribund operations. There is no evidence of rapid estate expansion and peasants acknowledged that at least some of the lands they claimed had been appropriated by landowners more than 100 years previously.

What grievance, then, could unite peasants over such a large area? The short answer is taxes, particularly attempts to raise the head tax on peasants to levels approaching or surpassing that of the colonial tribute.[38] The overwhelming majority of the documents in which either the peasants themselves stated their grievances or others explained the motives for the rebellions refer to these taxes. Some also criticized the alcabala or excise tax and the tobacco monopoly.[39] A few documents specifically indicate that the low head taxes used to support village schools and municipal governments from 1820 to the late 1830s were acceptable to peasants.[40] Peasant political activity expanded far beyond the narrow area around Chilapa when taxes became an issue.

The predominance of taxation as a grievance was important for several reasons. First, it vastly increased the possibilities for alliances among peasant villages and between peasants and outsiders because tax cuts did not threaten individual or group interests: whereas disputed land had to be taken from an individual, taxes were merely withheld from an anonymous state. Second, taxes affected peasants even in areas where land ownership was not in dispute. Third, and most important, these particular taxes were associated with the centralist governments of the 1835–46 period; this association fostered peasant alliances with elite federalists, as did other factors to be examined below.

The ideology of peasant rebels is often the most difficult problem faced by modern researchers. Some documents that shed light on peasant thought were produced with the aid of nonpeasants, and even those written by villagers probably reflect the views of wealthier peasants, who were more likely to have attended village schools with their curriculum of reading, writing, catechism, and commercial arithmetic.[41] Perhaps more important, such documents were produced with conscious political goals, whether they addressed other villages or authorities and elites. Furthermore, peasants used many concepts and symbols common to the political discourses of society as a whole. For all these reasons identifying elements of autonomous peasant ideology is a doubtful undertaking. Yet despite these caveats, the documents do show how peasant leaders addressed themselves to both other peasants and nonpeasants in their efforts to influence political processes and institutions. This knowledge is itself worthwhile, regardless of the impossibility of discerning any private thoughts peasants may have had about politics,[42] and it takes on even more value when considered in the context of the concrete political actions that peasants took when they established military superiority.

Peasant expression in word and deed during the rebellions of the 1840s had five related major themes. The first was the control of local government. The second theme was citizenship and its boundaries. The third, which to a certain extent eventually subsumed the first two, was an explicit commitment to federalism as the peasants understood it. The final two were more negative, in the sense that they stressed what peasants opposed, namely, monarchy and the Spanish, as they defined these terms. Taken in conjunction, the various themes in peasant political ideology prepared the ground for explicit and implicit alliances with the federalists in national politics. Generally these five themes emanated from trends in state/peasant relations during the previous 30 years, when peasants first tried to take advantage of the provisions regarding local power enacted under Mexico's first two constitutions (1812 and 1824) and then saw their gains reversed by centralism. Peasant ideology was also informed by peasant experiences in their alliances with radical elites, first during the War of Independence and then during the radical federalist movements of the 1829–35 period.

Perhaps the best evidence that peasants were specifically concerned with the local content of the state as well as their economic conflict with local elites is found in their actions. For instance, peasant actions in the Chilapa area in 1842 show that peasants were concerned both with recovering lands from private operations and eliminating those operations as productive units. They occupied the land, destroyed machinery, burned buildings, and turned the estates' own work animals loose to eat and trample their crops. However, both at this moment and later in the 1840s peasants also consciously constituted themselves as the local embodiment of the state. In the words of an elite observer of the 1842 events, the peasants "took the name of the Government," drafting soldiers, imprisoning criminals, and forcing members of the elite to contribute their labor to public works. Likewise a description of the activities of a peasant leader organizing a rebellion in 1845 insists that he was "abrogating faculties like those of a political authority."[43]

Peasant rebels asserted their right to choose their own *jueces de paz* or justices of the peace without interference from outsiders. On paper these officials were chosen by prefects, but even before the rebellions began prefects often allowed villages to name their own candidates subject to the prefect's approval. Jueces began to fill the role played by village governments in the colonial period, representing the state to peasants and vice versa. In 1840, when the *juez* or justice of Xocutla was removed from his post and imprisoned for refusing orders to collect rent on disputed lands, he responded that he should be returned to his post because "the village saw fit to name me."[44] By the mid-1840s peasants were often unwilling to submit their choices for juez even for pro forma approval by higher authorities.[45] Outsiders infringing on village autonomy now faced considerable risk, as was the case with the parish priest Vicente Bernardo Cervantes, who was killed in 1845 by the rioting villagers of Tlacoapa as he discussed the election of village judges.[46] Moreover, peasant interest in government posts extended beyond the village level. When the rebels took Chilapa in 1844 they replaced the district judge who had favored landowners with one of their own, a former juez de paz, and imprisoned and humiliated the former prefect.[47]

This peasant concern with the state was clearly rooted in the way elites used local government power after the centralist counteroffensive of the late 1830s, a key feature of which was the implementation of income requirements for citizenship that excluded the peasantry from voting in local elections. Thus it is not surprising that citizenship emerged as a theme in rebel documents. Contrary to the suggestions of François Guerra and Rodolfo Pastor, what emerged was not peasant resistance to becoming citizens but instead a struggle over the definitions and limits of citizenship. Peasants in their drive for local power called themselves "citizens" in explicit rejection of the more restrictive definitions of citizenship contained in the constitutions of the late 1830s and early 1840s. The theme of "citizenship" emerged increasingly in proclamations until by 1846 the majority of proclamations used this word. The peasant emphasis on citizenship rejected the widespread elite notion that peasants "did not know how to be citizens"[48] and also claimed a place in Mexico's imagined political community. As an 1846 document insisted, "Whites, blacks, and we the Indians, we are all Mexicans."[49]

Federalism was also an increasingly prominent theme. Over the course of the 1840s peasant proclamations moved toward an explicit commitment to federalism along two parallel tracks. Indian peasants already associated federalism with the relatively favorable political situation of the 1820s and early 1830s, characterized by low taxes and a wide dispersion of local political power. In fact, Indian peasants seem to have linked village autonomy with the federalist constitution of 1824 even though they had actually enjoyed more autonomy under the Spanish constitution during the early 1820s. In any event, both periods presented a marked contrast with the centralist counterrevolution of the late 1830s. In the 1840s villages asserted their right to name their own authorities, particularly justices of the peace, and sometimes also reasserted rights to the municipal status they had enjoyed earlier under the federalists. For instance, an 1843 proclamation referred to three villages that did not currently have municipal status as "municipalities" and called peasant rebels under arms a "municipal corps."[50] The peasants opposed the arbitrary abuse of power that they associated with centralism. As another 1843 rebel proclamation put it, "The sovereignty of the *pueblos* asks that republican law rule, not whims."[51] This statement takes on even more force because the authors may have been referring to the law of the *república de indios* rather than that of the Mexican republic.[52]

The Indian peasants of the Montaña followed a second track toward explicit federalism by appropriating the specific version of federalism that the mulatto cotton farmers of the Costa Grande had constructed in the late 1820s and early 1830s. This federalism, which strongly identified itself with the 1810–21 insurgency, opposed a centralism allegedly promoted by aristocratic plotters to prepare Mexico for the renewed domination of the Spanish monarchy and foreign merchants. This theme was closely related to a peasant version of the independence war in which they had shaken off the tyranny of Fernando VII and the gachupines; calling themselves "americanos," some peasants continued to identify their enemies as "chaquetas" or "gachupines" and claimed that the government they opposed represented Fernando VII.[53] The monarchist conspiracy of Paredes provided a concrete threat against which to mobilize this sentiment; militia officers now condemned the government using rhetoric similar to that used earlier by peasant leaders.[54] Overall the discourse surrounding the Paredes conspiracy resonated with that of earlier anti-Spanish movements, and at least one Spanish citizen was killed in the Tierra Caliente.[55]

These two routes to federalism intersected in the Indian peasants' explicit embrace of this political movement in 1846. Centralism had not fulfilled its promises of reduced political conflict and revived prosperity, and federalism had again become an option in national politics.[56] In 1846 the desire of some members of the national political elite for a federalist restoration resonated with the peasant drive to recover local political power and to attract the coastal militia as allies in regional politics. Significantly, the first peasant proclamation to explicitly endorse federalism surfaced in February and March, weeks before Alvarez issued his own call to restore federalism.[57]

Ideology was obviously important in the relationship between peasant and elite politics in the 1840s, but while considering this relationship further we need to keep in mind the pragmatic basis of the balance of power between rural elites and peasants in early-nineteenth-century Mexico. Crudely put, the state's capacity to repress peasants in an agrarian society depends on the wealthy's ability to tax both peasants and themselves to fund armed forces. As Barbara Tenenbaum has demonstrated, this relationship broke down in nineteenth-century Mexico because few actors there were willing to pay their share of the cost of government, and the national government needed to borrow money at enormous interest rates just to pay regular expenses.[58] The government simply did not have the resources to repress rebellions, particularly when they took place far from the national or state capitals, and this lack of resources put enormous pressure on political officials to end rebellions peacefully. Sometimes they resisted that pressure with the aid of the local elites threatened by peasant action, but the government's options remained limited by its poverty.[59] The government's weakness made peasant rebels much more attractive to potential elite allies than they would have otherwise been.

The peasant rebellions of the 1840s in Guerrero became more closely tied to elite politics as they progressed. The trend was the opposite of that found in contemporary rebellions in the Yucatán, which began with strong connections to elite politics that quickly weakened.[60] In Guerrero the relationship between peasant politics and elite politics often involved Juan Alvarez. Fernando Díaz y Díaz has stressed the patron/client aspects of the relationship between Alvarez and rebellious peasants: documents often show Alvarez acting much as twentieth-century caciques have operated, interceding with higher authorities for peasants, recommending officials he considered sympathetic to peasants for posts, and complaining about those he considered abusive. Alvarez often asked officials to free peasants arrested as troublemakers. He asked state governors to legislate against *tiendas de raya* or company stores, served as a conduit for peasant complaints both inside and outside of Guerrero, and mediated disputes between peasant groups. Above all he argued insistently against head taxes on peasants.[61]

However, unlike twentieth-century Mexican caciques with access to the post-revolutionary agrarian reform machinery, Alvarez could do little to satisfy peasant demands regarding land. In the Chilapa area he set up an arbitration mechanism to resolve disputes; when that faltered he argued unsuccessfully that the government should buy out the landowners. For the most part Alvarez could do little more than arrange for lawyers to represent peasants in court.[62] Although he could and did argue the justice of peasant claims, his arguments had no effect on the legal machinery.

Alvarez's ability to help peasants achieve better treatment from officials, lower taxes, and the possession if not legal ownership of land was important, but the strength of his ties to the peasantry owed as much to fundamental congruences of ideology as to common interests. An extreme federalist, Alvarez insisted that peasants should be citizens of the new nation-state. As he insisted as early as 1841, well before the rebellions broke out: "We are all citizens and we all have rights and obligations."[63] He also saw fundamental similarities between the peasant tradition of annual elections for local office and the basic tenets of popular sovereignty so common to nineteenth-century political ideologies. In 1841, when the village of Mescala sought his help in convincing the authorities to allow them to choose a new justice of the peace, he interceded, pointing out that "it is the custom that our villages replace their judges each year, and this idea conforms very well with the system of government that rules us, which wishes the command of the people's authorities to be alternating."[64] Alvarez sustained these ideas both publicly and privately, even during the centralist period when they were out of favor, and it was these congruences between Alvarez's political beliefs and those of the peasantry that anchored their relationship. These ideas and the political idiom through which they were expressed had been historically constructed during the struggles of 1810–20, the late 1820s, and the early 1830s. Consistently identifying the Mexico City–based remnants of the colonial dominant class with the Spanish and monarchism, this popular federalism sought a return to an idealized version of the low taxes, dispersion of local power, and wide suffrage some peasants of Guerrero had experienced in the 1820s. Many nationally prominent federalists did not agree with this definition of federalism, and even the degree to which Alvarez shared this vision is perhaps debatable. Nevertheless, their application of federalist terms to their own political realities allowed Guerrero's peasants to ally themselves with Alvarez and other federalists both locally and nationally.[65]

The 1840s rebellions were widely reported and debated in Mexico City. Alvarez's sympathy for the peasants was very public: he made his views clear to his superiors in the Ministry of War, his civilian allies in the state and national governments, and the literate Mexico City audience that most historians have seen as the center of nineteenth-century political life. Events in Chilapa were the subject of particularly fierce public debate in newspapers and pamphlets. In 1841 Alvarez responded to accusations that he was fomenting peasant unrest by publishing a 47-page pamphlet in Mexico City. After being forced out of Chilapa in 1845, the landowners published a lengthy complaint in the Mexico City press and Alvarez replied with a 180-page pamphlet. That November, Carlos María de Bustamante, the most vitriolic and famous of Mexico's nineteenth-century political pamphleteers, pressed the landowners' view in Congress and when Congress refused to support the landowners published another attack on Alvarez. Throughout this debate Alvarez also insisted on the justice of the peasants' cause in private correspondence. Moreover, in public as well as private documents Alvarez argued not only the justice of peasant demands but also the just motive they provided for peasant rebellion.[66]

Some of the connections between peasant politics in Guerrero and national politics were based on Alvarez's relations with various military officers who served as presidents or war ministers in the 1840s. Not all trusted Alvarez, but eventually each accepted that attacking his power in Guerrero was useless and possibly dangerous. Alvarez had better relations with key civilian federalist politicians such as Valentín Gómez Farías, with whom he corresponded regularly, though the two men never met and Alvarez was extremely critical of some of Gómez Farías's political decisions.[67] A closer friend was Mariano Riva Palacio, son-in-law of Vicente Guerrero. Alvarez managed the land owned by Riva Palacio's wife in Guerrero, and as Riva Palacio grew in prominence throughout the 1840s, eventually becoming governor of the state of Mexico, Alvarez often contacted Riva Palacio to publicize his positions and advise him on the national situation.[68] Alvarez also became close to several young lawyers who entered politics in the 1840s and later became prominent liberals. Some of these men helped peasants pursue land claims, and others served as Alvarez's personal secretaries.[69] Notably, Alvarez was never directly associated with such liberal ideologues as José María Luís Mora, whose views have so colored our vision of the relationship between liberalism and peasants. In fact, one of Alvarez's closer political allies was Juan Rodríguez Puebla, a radical Mexico City Indian whom Mora criticized as reactionary for defending the lands and schools of Mexico City's Indian neighborhoods.[70]

The most potent tool local elites had to prevent alliances between peasants and other political actors was the charge of "caste war." The colonial dominant class borrowed this phrase from descriptions of the Haitian War of Independence to delegitimize the efforts of Hidalgo and Morelos and make any alliance between dissatisfied provincial elites and peasants unthinkable. It was also used to whip up hysteria against later peasant movements. Promoting "caste war" was the most severe charge Alvarez's enemies leveled against him in the national press. On the whole, however, the standard hysterical accusation seems to have had little effect on the development of alliances with Guerrero's peasants. Although the charge was used to justify the imprisonment of some Mexico City federalists in 1843, it was not credible enough to threaten their careers, and Alvarez himself was so entrenched in his local political position that he had little to fear and less reason to distance himself from the peasantry.[71]

Peasants and National Politics: The Restoration of Federalism and the War with the United States

The rebellions of the 1840s in Guerrero influenced both local and national politics. Nationally they contributed to two developments: first was the August 1846 restoration of the 1824 federalist constitution, which reinstituted federalism as Mexico's system of government after an eleven-year absence; second was the resistance to the United States in 1846–48. The return to federalism and the debates surrounding the conduct of the war in turn set the stage for two later episodes crucial to the construction of the Mexican nation-state, La Reforma and the nationalist resistance to the Second Empire.

The 1846 movements against Mariano Paredes called for the return of Antonio López de Santa Anna to power. In hindsight the alliance of radical federalists like Gómez Farías and Alvarez with Santa Anna often seems naive, but the federalists had not forgotten his early services, particularly his roles in the overthrow of Iturbide and the defeat of the 1829 Spanish invasion. Santa Anna had always been solidly antimonarchist, and his performance against foreign invaders in 1829 and 1838 had been exemplary. He seemed the man most likely to quickly organize an army and take decisive action against an invader.

What requires more explanation is why many of Mexico's leading politicians decided to conduct the resistance to the invasion under the Constitution of 1824, an instrument that in 1835 had been perceived as completely discredited. This question has been largely ignored by both nineteenth-century historians and their modern heirs, who typically mention the restoration only briefly before moving on to the war with the United States.[72] The federalists believed that it would be easier to organize broad support for the war if political power were dispersed. Reinstating the federalist constitution also reinstituted the various state constitutions written under it and many of the laws that had governed local political life between 1824 and 1835. In Guerrero this meant a return to an era of popular rights, with many town councils, wide suffrage, and low taxes—in other words, the rights, eroded under centralist rule, that constituted the local definition of federalism. Not surprisingly, the movement that restored federalism began in Guerrero, and the rebellious peasants of the Montaña provided its most important support for several months.[73] The peasant rebels successfully exercised a powerful influence on national events at a crucial juncture.

Juan Alvarez and the peasants of Guerrero also played a role in the war with the United States, although that role was not as large as Alvarez would have liked. Alvarez had been suspicious of U.S. intentions for several years and feared the political uses that could be made of the growing U.S. commercial presence in Mexico.[74] When the war came Alvarez was ordered to raise troops in the South, and because the government was unable to allocate funds he also collected donations of food, money, and clothing for his recruits. He raised 3,000 men and set off for the capital in May 1847. Although no direct evidence is available, it seems likely that at least part of this force was drawn from former peasant rebels. Alvarez had been preparing for their recruitment for several years, lecturing peasant rebels on the coming need to unite against the North Americans. Also, a song popular in the area a few years later associates resistance to the U.S. invaders with resistance to taxes and "tyranny," two symbols prominent in peasant discourse during the 1840s rebellions.[75]

Alvarez and several other prominent politicians advocated fighting a guerrilla war, arming as many people as possible and not facing the enemy's main army. Santa Anna opposed this strategy, convinced that if he could concentrate enough troops he could overcome the superior arms and training of the North Americans in a set-piece battle. Many wealthy Mexicans felt that the social mobilization and disruption inherent to the guerrilla strategy would be in itself disastrous. Events proved that the Mexican army was neither well organized nor well armed enough to take advantage of its numerical superiority. The achievements of the guerrillas were more mixed; although there was no shortage of offers to organize guerrillas, they never succeeded in isolating the North American army from its base in Veracruz, and the refusal of some government officials to cooperate with the guerrillas weakened their efforts.[76]

Alvarez operated independently during most of the struggle for the Central Plateau. He organized guerrillas, observed the main North American forces, and recruited local villagers to construct fortifications and obstruct roads in advance of the enemy. Alvarez took part in only one of the major battles, that of Molino del Rey, in which a carefully planned counterattack failed when a regular army officer refused to accept orders from Alvarez, his social inferior. After the evacuation of Mexico City Alvarez and his old enemy Rea organized guerrillas around Puebla.[77]

At this point, another major division became visible in the Mexican political elite: Many felt that the loss of Mexico City made pursuing the war hopeless, whereas others insisted on continuing the fight. Not surprisingly, this second group contained many politicians who had all along advocated guerrilla tactics. Alvarez remained a major figure in the months that followed, returning to Guerrero to raise new troops, this time definitely recruiting peasants from the Chilapa area who had participated in the rebellions of the 1840s. Alvarez's position placed him at odds with the governor of the state of Mexico, Francisco Olaguibel, who did not want to continue the war. When Alvarez seized tax revenues to feed his guerrillas, Olaguibel accused him of stealing government funds. Olaguibel also refused to release the state government's weapons to villages that requested them to fight the North Americans. The frustrated Alvarez overthrew the state government and imprisoned Olaguibel. Many guerrillas continued to oppose the North Americans even after the Treaty of Guadalupe Hidalgo nominally ended the war.[78]

During the North American invasion some politicians advocated arming and organizing Mexico's population to fight a guerrilla war. They were convinced that a significant portion of Mexico's population could be persuaded to oppose the invaders, that guerrilla war could be sustained without class revolution, and that the loss of Mexico City was not a fatal blow. These politicians were for the most part overruled by a Mexican elite that lacked confidence in its authority over Mexico's rural majority and feared the possibility of caste war. It is possible that a guerrilla war would have cost much more than it gained. However, less than twenty years later, in an even more fiercely divided Mexico, the guerrilla struggle that continued after the loss of every major city was largely successful in preserving Mexico's independence.

Peasants and Local Politics: The Creation of the State of Guerrero

In 1849 regions from the states of Mexico, Puebla, and Michoacán seceded to form the new state of Guerrero. The establishment of the new state had been a goal of the regional elite since 1841, but the 1841 proposal had been much more limited, including only territory from the state of Mexico. Guerrero eventually also incorporated the eastern Montaña, which had belonged to Puebla, and a single municipality of the Tierra Caliente that had belonged to Michoacán. Furthermore, whereas the 1841 movement had mostly concerned the regional elite, the 1849 push was driven by peasant mobilization in the intervening decade. It was the activity of Guerrero's peasantry on the political stage that eventually convinced the national government as well as the states of Mexico and Puebla that a new state was necessary if not desirable.

In 1841 Alvarez and Bravo, speaking for an official assembly of regional notables, offered several reasons why a new administrative division was desirable. The regional elite argued that the current system diluted their power in national politics. In elections for the national Congress, secondary electors chosen by Guerrero's population traveled to Toluca (capital of the state of Mexico), where their votes were outweighed by those of electors from other parts of the state. Alvarez and Bravo also argued that laws written in Toluca often were not suited to conditions in Guerrero.[79] By the end of the 1840s these motives were augmented by Alvarez's clashes with the state governments of Mexico and Puebla: Puebla had refused to ratify exemptions granted to peasants distressed by head taxes, and Mexico's governor had refused funds to organize guerrillas against the North Americans.

The national government also had reasons to support the formation of the new state. The Gómez Farías–Santa Anna administration and the government of José Joaquín Herrera that followed needed the support of Alvarez. Herrera was a close ally of Alvarez, who had helped place him in the presidency in 1844 and opposed several movements to overthrow him. More important, the government believed that the new state was needed to prevent further peasant unrest. Throughout 1847 and 1848 the national government tried to persuade Puebla, Mexico, and Michoacán to voluntarily cede the affected territory.[80]

The governor of Mexico, Francisco Olaguibel, opposed the movement for statehood throughout 1847 and 1848. Various challenges to his authority combined the desire to continue the war with the United States with that to form the new state. Olaguibel's successor, Mariano Arizcorreta, also opposed the creation of Guerrero, but in October 1848 the state legislature conditionally approved the secession of the Acapulco, Chilapa, and Taxco districts, pending the approval of Michoacán and Puebla. As the months progressed it became increasingly clear to Arizcorreta that the state of Mexico no longer controlled the territory involved. The state government did not receive taxes due and officials did not obey its orders. Worse, Alvarez sent agitators to nearby municipalities trying to enlarge the area affected. Arizcorreta and the state legislature gave in, and in May 1849 the state of Mexico ratified the federal decree creating the new state.[81]

The debate in the state of Puebla was more open and more interesting. In 1848 a legislative committee advised against the measure, alleging that most of the affected area was inhabited by Indians who were idolatrous, incestuous, and did not speak Spanish. The committee claimed that the attempt to form a new state was preparation for caste war and that the Indians would gather strength in the new state to attack the hated white race. A fierce debate ensued in the legislature. Two delegates who favored separation argued that it was the only way to prevent new peasant rebellions, but their opponents insisted that an area mostly populated by peasants could not exist independently as a state. On October 9, 1848, the legislature rejected separation in a nine to two vote. The governor vetoed their resolution; arguing that the secession was already a fact and that Puebla no longer controlled the region, he proposed a compromise in which the legislature would condition the separation on the consent of the inhabitants of the area. The legislature needed a unanimous vote to override the governor's veto and on October 13 the override failed, seven to five. On October 16 the legislature approved the governor's proposal. In early 1849, the government held a plebiscite in the districts of Tlapa and the Costa Chica, and though authorities annulled many pro-separation ballots prepared in the same handwriting, the separatists still collected more than two-thirds of the votes cast.[82]

Mexico and Puebla eventually agreed to cede territory to the new state, but Michoacán roundly refused to do the same, thus negating Mexico's approval, which was contingent upon the approval of the other two states. Faced with this impasse and the growing threat to order in the area, the national Congress created the new state through a constitutional reform; this measure could be ratified with the approval of two-thirds of all state legislatures and did not require the specific approval of those who lost territory. Realizing that the game was lost, all three of the affected legislatures ratified the measure in May 1849.[83]

Clearly, portions of Guerrero's peasantry supported the formation of the new state, but their motives are not easily discernible in the documents. Alvarez argued that the new state would enact laws to deal with peasant necessities but he made no documented promises more explicit than this. What did Alvarez mean? Why did peasants support the organization of a new state whose administrative center was much closer to them geographically? To understand this it is necessary to turn to the specific impact the new state had on peasant life.

The new political unit brought change in several areas that had concerned peasants throughout the 1840s, and that had already been affected to some degree by the 1846 restoration of federalism. These areas included taxation, access to the courts, the distribution of local political power through municipalities, suffrage, and citizenship. All of these concerns were quickly addressed in the laws of the new state.

The new state government removed most of the taxes that peasants had protested earlier in the decade. The head tax was set at 0.5 real per month, or 0.75 peso annually, much lower than the capitación and its successors, which had cost peasants around 2.25 pesos per year. The new tax was equivalent to the low personal taxes of the 1820s and early 1830s. Most peasants would not have received this tax reduction if Guerrero had not become a state, for though Puebla lowered its personal tax to a similar level in 1849, the tax in the state of Mexico remained 1 real per month. Significantly, the new state exempted propertyless militia members from the head tax.[84]

Guerrero's government changed both the number of municipalities and their distribution. The number had increased with the 1846 adoption of federalism, which had restored the political jurisdictions in force under federalist state constitutions. The new state of Guerrero further augmented the number of municipalities, this time more slowly and selectively, adding six in the first two years of its existence and continuing thereafter at a more leisurely pace. Furthermore, the legislature changed the administration of those settlements too small to be municipal capitals. Aldermen in subject villages and justices of the peace in settlements were still selected by municipal councils but their appointments were now annual rather than indefinite. Juan Alvarez had argued for this practice since the early 1840s on the grounds that it merged modern politics and peasant tradition.[85]

Suffrage in early-nineteenth-century Mexico and the attitudes displayed toward it varied greatly. At a time when few if any countries allowed all men to vote, some famous liberals such as José María Luís Mora distrusted universal male suffrage. Mexico had approximated universal male suffrage from 1820 to 1835 under the Spanish Constitution of 1812 and the federalist Constitution of 1824. Both denied the vote to servants, but laws specifically excluded hacienda workers from this category. Laws often required voters to have an "oficio o industria honesta" (honest occupation or industry), and before 1836 suffrage was sometimes restricted through officials' interpretation and manipulation of this provision.[86] The centralists restricted the vote more severely beginning in 1836, first to those with annual incomes over 100 pesos and then to those with double that amount. Both standards more than sufficed to eliminate peasants from the electoral rolls.[87]

The restoration of federalism laid the groundwork for a general return to universal male suffrage legislated at the state level. The new state of Guerrero quickly instituted universal male suffrage and unlike some states did not require literacy of municipal officers. Suffrage was important in local politics because municipal elections were indirect to only one degree: in other words, voters selected electors who in turn directly chose municipal officials. Suffrage was less important for higher offices because several such steps separated the voters from the final selection. Nevertheless, all elections remained important and incumbents were sometimes unpleasantly surprised by election results.[88]

Suffrage was only one component of the larger issue of citizenship or membership in the polity. During the 1820s and early 1830s peasants' right to vote had often been disputed by local elites who later benefited greatly from the centralist reaction. Citizenship was also an issue during the debate in the legislature of Puebla over the secession of Tlapa; even in that unfriendly forum those who felt the peasantry was not ready for citizenship were answered by peers less pessimistic about the progress of Mexican state formation. These representatives portrayed peasants as religiously orthodox, civilized, and willing to pay school taxes.[89] The key question surrounding citizenship differed only slightly in the Constitutional Congress of Guerrero. All of the legislators felt that a "profesión, arte o industria útil y honestia" (useful and honest profession, art, or industry) should be a prerequisite of citizenship. Did this mean that the poor could not vote or hold office? After some debate the delegates agreed that the phrase "industria útil" included "jornaleros," a term commonly used to refer not only to day laborers but also to peasants engaged in agriculture on village common lands.[90] In Guerrero, where the vast majority of the population were peasants, this decision was vital both for practical politics and as a symbolic assertion of the poor's inclusion in the economic and political body of the new Mexico.[91]

The constitution of the new state contained another noteworthy provision, namely, the right to *acción popular* against any inhabitant of the state engaged in treason against the state of Guerrero or the republic. Inhabitants were explicitly empowered to take action against any judge or functionary accepting a bribe or betraying a trust. In practical effect this article provided a legal right to rebellion, not against the state or nation but against government officials in the name of the state. It sanctioned the organized protests against the abuse of rights that had characterized colonial peasant riots.[92]

Incidents along the state border suggest the more subtle changes wrought by the establishment of the new state. In 1850 Juan Clara, a peasant leader from Chiautla just across the Puebla border, fled into Guerrero with some of his men after a failed insurrection. The local alderman informed Alvarez that he would organize an armed force to intimidate the rebels into leaving the state. When the federal government heard that Alvarez had approved the alderman's plan, it reminded Alvarez that Guerrero's authorities should capture the rebels, not just escort them to the state line. Clara moved on before this order reached the appropriate officials.[93]

A second incident was far more serious. In the early 1850s the village of Cacahuimilpa on the border with the state of Mexico clashed with an hacendado from the Mexican side over land. The hacendado was unfortunately a friend of Angel Pérez Palacios, military commander of that part of Mexico, and in late 1853 the hacendado and Pérez Palacios organized a party of armed men that crossed the border and attacked the village, killing six people. Pérez Palacios claimed that the village had been preparing to rebel. Guerrero's governor protested energetically, stating that the villagers' only crime consisted of suing the hacendado. Nevertheless, he had previously ordered authorities not to oppose incursions from across the state line because he did not want to risk an armed confrontation with the federal government.[94] This incident illustrates the limits the national balance of power placed upon the efforts of even the most dedicated champions of popular rights, limits that will be discussed at length in the following chapter.

In the 1840s Guerrero experienced some of the largest and most sustained peasant mobilizations in Mexican history. This chapter has sought to explain the specific historical context in which the rebellions took place, the forms they took, and the effects they had both on local and national politics. These three issues were intimately related. Peasant actions and their results cannot be extracted from the tumultuous elite or national politics of the period. Furthermore, our understanding of national politics must take into account the actions of peasants. Mexican elites did not achieve the degree of consensus that would have been necessary to exclude the majority of the population from politics. Mexican state formation was conditioned not only by elite struggles over political economy and the apportionment of political power but also by a continuing debate over the necessity and wisdom of incorporating Mexico's impoverished rural majority.

The peasant rebellions of the 1840s had complex roots. National agreements over Mexico's political economy were foundering under increasingly adverse market forces, and they dragged down with them the grudging consensus that upheld centralism. Local elites were also divided. In the Chilapa area self-confident landowners tried to use their political power to alter land tenure arrangements, but the same centralist government that seemed to ensure their political power undermined it by extracting more revenue from the peasantry it had just disenfranchised. The unpopular new taxes spread peasant unrest far beyond the area affected by the land disputes. This combination of factors led to peasant mobilization remarkable for its size, staying power, and effect on national politics.

Peasants in the 1840s showed a remarkable ability to overcome obstacles that had prevented rebellions of more than one village during the colonial period, and they began to do so before any direct intervention from rebellious elites. From 1810 through the 1830s, rebellious elites directed letters and proclamations to the peasantry; in the 1840s, peasants wrote letters and proclamations addressed to both other peasants and to elite factions. Using a political vocabulary acquired during the elite-led movements of earlier decades, peasants took advantage of a balance of power that made the repression of rebellions almost impossible, forging alliances with federalists both locally and nationally.

These alliances altered both national and local politics. Nationally, they contributed to the restoration of federalism in 1846 and encouraged attempts to resist the North American invasion through guerrilla war, paving the way for the adoption of guerrilla tactics in the war against the French two decades later. Locally, peasant/elite alliances formed the heart of the eventually successful movement to establish a state of Guerrero. The new state covered almost exactly the area involved in the earlier peasant movements. This development institutionalized the achievement of many peasant goals, and although it did not definitively settle peasant land claims, peasants remained in de facto possession of disputed tracts for many years. In some cases this possession was legalized by agreements that the state government facilitated in the mid-1880s.[95]

CHAPTER 6

The Revolution of Ayutla and La Reforma

We are decided against the federation, against the elected representative system we have followed until now, against elected town councils and all so-called popular elections that do not rest on other bases.

—Lucás Alamán, Mexico City, March 23, 1853

The Southerners are republicans of good faith. . . . We the inhabitants of the South want a nation represented by whatever Mexicans are honest and patriotic and refuse the pernicious influence of those classes that call themselves privileged to exploit the people, which feed on its blood. . . . [We want] one law for all, guarantees for the citizen that the classes stop sucking the substance of the fatherland [and] that all division between brothers disappear.

—Juan Alvarez, Acapulco, 1854

[Some hacendados] slowly take possession of private plots, ejidos, and communal lands, when those exist, and then, with the most unheard-of impudence, call it their property, without presenting any legal title of acquisition, more than enough reason for the pueblos to cry for justice, protection, aid; but the courts are deaf to their cries and requests, and scorn, persecution, and imprisonment are the prizes given to those who ask for what is theirs.

—Alvarez, La Providencia, 1857

Historians of widely varying perspectives have long agreed that the period between 1855 and 1867 was a crucial moment in the formation of the Mexican state and Mexican political culture. During La Reforma, as the period is known, the liberal authoritarianism that characterizes Mexico to this day definitively defeated its conservative rival. This liberal model is characterized by regular elections, universal suffrage, the inclusion of provincial elites in decision making, and the demobilization of popular challenges through the selective fulfillment of demands rather than widespread repression. The Mexican liberal model is unique among Latin American authoritarianisms, and is in large part responsible for the stability the Mexican state has enjoyed for most of the twentieth century.

Recent historical research has suggested various reasons for the triumph of the liberals and their model. John Coatsworth notes that the liberals' strength in coastal provinces gave them access to tariff revenue; Richard Sinkin suggests that the liberals increased their popularity among the urban middle classes by selling them church property; and Barbara Tenenbaum detects a shift in the attitudes of the moneylenders who financed Mexico's nineteenth-century governments. Florencia Mallon, Guy Thomson, and Paul Garner have convincingly demonstrated that peasants in at least a few key areas supported the liberals, especially in the 1850s and 1860s.[1] This peasant support was crucial to both the liberal victory over the conservatives and the later triumph of Porfirio Díaz over his liberal competitors.

La Reforma began with the Revolution of Ayutla, named for the village in Guerrero where it was officially inaugurated. Paradoxically, this rebellion is often attributed to the unremarkable and decidedly unideological opposition of a provincial cacique to a central government attempting to limit his power. Jan Bazant has recently put forward an extreme version of this interpretation, arguing that the cacique involved, Juan Alvarez, was altogether uninterested in national politics. In Bazant's words, "as long as central governments, liberal or conservative, did not meddle in his domain, his relations with them were good."[2] In this view of the origins of La Reforma, liberal elite intellectuals colonized the Ayutla movement and made it a vehicle for their ambitious reform program. Mexico's poor, who provided the great mass of cannon fodder for both the Ayutla movement and the armies that marched throughout Mexico for the next ten years, contributed little or nothing to the eventually triumphant model.

This chapter will present a very different interpretation, showing that the Ayutla movement possessed not only a social base in Guerrero but also a well-defined ideological content that, although not coterminous with the liberalism often associated with La Reforma, was congruent with it and represented a strain within it. This ideological current, which I have described earlier as popular federalism, was historically constructed during a series of movements from 1810 through the 1840s. In Guerrero these direct ancestors of the Ayutla movement all integrated peasants and members of the local elite in pursuit of regional and national goals. Many elements of the discourse and political tactics that unified liberal peasants and liberal elites throughout Mexico in the 1850s and 1860s were fashioned earlier in places like Guerrero. The Ayutla movement arose from the animosity of large parts of Guerrero's society to the specific model of the state promoted by Antonio López de Santa Anna and his allies during his last administration. Guerrero's version of popular federalist politics did not triumph in La Reforma but its victory certainly seemed possible to both its supporters and enemies, especially in the months immediately after the Ayutla rebels took power. The relationship between the popular federalist roots of the Revolution of Ayutla and the debates of the pivotal Constitutional Congress of 1856–57 represents one key to understanding the period. Between 1855 and 1857 the popular federalist project reached its height and its limit, the latter perhaps most visible in the attempt to extend federalism from Guerrero to the neighboring area now known as Morelos.

The Origins of the Revolution

After its disastrous war with the United States, Mexico enjoyed several years of relative political peace under the moderate federalist governments of José Joaquín Herrera and his successor Mariano Arista until an 1852 rebellion initiated in Guadalajara ended the Arista presidency. The movement began as a conflict over the governorship of Jalisco but quickly expanded into a national struggle in which an alliance between Santa Anna's personal following and the new conservative party sought to end federalism once and for all. Arista's resignation precipitated several months of frantic political maneuvering that culminated in Santa Anna's return from exile to govern the country once again.[3]

The conservatives, Santa Anna's most important allies, were the successors of the centralists; or, to put it more accurately, centralism was subsumed into a new political current that more self-consciously modeled its goals on the colonial order. The conservatives had honed their ideas in the debate over Mexico's failure in the war with the United States,[4] and with Santa Anna's help they now sought to put their ideas into practice. These views, similar in many ways to those they had earlier expressed as centralists, found their most intelligent and vocal spokesperson in Lucás Alamán, who had several times filled ministerial posts in centralist regimes.

The conservatives believed that a strong government would allow Mexico to grow economically. The state needed the authority and arms to impose order. As Alamán explained their "political faith" to Santa Anna, "We are decided against the federation, against the elected representative system which we have followed until now, against elected town councils and all so-called popular elections which do not rest on other bases. We believe a new territorial division is necessary to entirely confound and make forgotten the current form of the States and to facilitate good administration, as an effective method to prevent the federation from returning."[5] This was not a simple exchange of the term "state" for that of "department," as François Xavier Guerra would have it;[6] rather, the conservatives sought to reconstitute Mexican order on a new basis. The Revolution of Ayutla represented a reaction to this vision.

The conservative project advanced by Santa Anna was a direct assault on the popular federalism rooted in Guerrero. Although the conservative project encountered opposition elsewhere, it was no accident that the movement against it began in the South. Santa Anna and his allies attacked the states themselves, centralizing the collection and disbursement of revenues, removing their title of "free, sovereign, and independent," and finally abolishing them altogether. The new regime also struck at the municipal system, restricting town councils to the capitals of states and prefectures and replacing the abolished councils with appointed officials. The new regime also reinstated the capitación or head tax and many other taxes.[7]

These very concrete measures were only part of the conservative project. The conservatives also sought to change the way that political order was conceived and legitimated. They planned to return to the corporatism that had supported the pre-Bourbon colonial state by seeking to revive the idea that individuals' claims to rights emanated from their membership in corporations. They encouraged the church and strengthened its ties to the state, reinstating the civil enforcement of tithes and allowing the Jesuits to return to Mexico, and their aversion to the Enlightenment reached the extreme of organized book burnings. But this corporatism did not extend to the economic arena: the conservatives were committed to the strengthening of individual property rights in a market economy, not to the strengthening of Indian communities. Communities were allowed property rights but not political control, and peasants who lived on haciendas were prevented from organizing politically.[8]

Legitimating the new order also required symbolic changes. Santa Anna instituted a new noble order called the Order of Guadalupe, and after some debate his allies agreed that the new president should be addressed as "His Extremely Serene Highness." Changes were also made in the way Mexican history was portrayed in public ceremonies. In 1851 the public speech pronounced on Independence Day in Guerrero had not surprisingly emphasized the role of Vicente Guerrero and the strength of his movement before the Plan of Iguala; in

1854 the writer mentioned Guerrero's name only once and praised Iturbide in twelve of the nineteen pages of his speech.[9]

The administration's image in the South was further tarnished by its association with Lucás Alamán, the regime's intellectual leader until his death. Alamán was extremely unpopular in the South for two reasons. First, as minister of the interior in the centralist regimes of the early 1830s, he was considered responsible for the 1831 execution of Vicente Guerrero. Second, as longtime administrator for the Mexican holdings of the Duke of Monteleone, Cortés's heir, he had lamented the 1848 withdrawal of the North American troops who protected haciendas in what is now Morelos from their peasant neighbors. Alvarez openly opposed the inclusion of Alamán in Santa Anna's cabinet and many of his followers celebrated Alamán's 1853 death.[10]

The elements of the conservative project outlined above suggest that, like most early-nineteenth-century political conflicts, the Revolution of Ayutla was far from devoid of ideology. Santa Anna implemented a very cohesive and consistent conservative program, and the revolution was a reaction to that program. In most regions opposition resulted primarily from Santa Anna's taxes and forced loans, and Santa Anna's enemies were more unified by their opposition to his government than by any shared vision of the shape of things to come. However, in Guerrero opposition to Santa Anna's government took the very specific form of popular federalism, which had been constructed during the struggles of the previous decades. This opposition was above all an argument about who would be included in the Mexican polity and against the "privileged classes . . . which feed on their [the people's] blood," as Alvarez insisted in an 1854 proclamation.[11]

The Ayutla movement shared its participants as well as its ideology with the earlier conflicts. After Alvarez, the movement's most famous elite leader was the Pueblan Ignacio Comonfort, who beginning in 1830 had filled various military and civil posts within the part of Guerrero that then belonged to Puebla. Comonfort served in several congresses of the 1840s, had been a widely respected prefect in Tlapa before the rebellions of the 1840s, and had been asked by Alvarez himself to return to the post to negotiate with the area's peasants. An owner of land in Guerrero and an agent for several landowners on the Costa Chica, Comonfort was politically identified with the moderate federalists who were soon to be known as *moderatos*. He eventually left Guerrero, served in the municipal government of Mexico City, and in the early 1850s was named customs administrator of Acapulco.[12] Comonfort's moderate politics were unusual among the leaders of the Ayutla movement. He almost seems to have been caught up in the rebellion through his geographic and personal connections rather than his convictions.

Other moderates, both centralist and federalist, for the most part stayed clear of the movement. The best example was Nicolás Bravo, who declined the conspirators' invitation to join and in fact propagandized against the rebels, although his poor health did not allow him to take part in government counterinsurgency operations. Another moderate officer, Rómulo del Valle, joined the revolt but deserted almost immediately.[13] Ironically, the officer who initiated the original call to arms was a former royalist who had been a bitter enemy of Alvarez for most of the 1840s. Florencio Villarreal had recently reconciled with Alvarez and was fired when he protested Santa Anna's attempt to remove his Costa Chica command from Alvarez's area of responsibility.[14]

Most leaders of the Ayutla movement, including of course Juan Alvarez, had long histories of federalist activity in the South. Tomás Moreno had been among Alvarez's closest collaborators since the late 1830s and had served as commander of Acapulco and interim governor of Guerrero. Gordiano Guzmán was a former insurgent who had led several federalist revolts in southern Michoacán in the 1830s and 1840s.[15] Juan Alvarez's son, Diego, also took part in the movement. A few intellectuals arrived from exile to join Alvarez's secretarial corps, among them Eligio Romero and Benito Juárez,[16] but until the triumph of the rebels their role was limited; they left little trace even in revolutionary propaganda, which stayed true in style and content to the popular federalism of the previous decades.

The bulk of the rebel's strength consisted of the Montaña peasants who had fought in the 1840s rebellions, notably Faustino Villalva and his son Jesús, Pedro Beltrán, Juan Antonio, Juan de Nava, the Pinzon family, and Mariano Nava. The same villages were mentioned in military dispatches, the same properties were attacked, and peasants again refused to pay the capitación. In the mountains the conflict reenacted the struggle between the elites of the market towns and the surrounding villages; on the coast the movement relied on the mulatto sharecroppers who had formed the backbone of every anti-Spanish and federalist movement since 1810.[17]

A Revolution Unfolds

The movement against Santa Anna began to unfold in Guerrero almost before he became president. Alvarez opposed the Plan of Jalisco, which called for Santa Anna's return to Mexico, and threatened to punish any commanders in Guerrero who expressed support for it. The movement against President Mariano Arista began in July 1852 and ended with his resignation on January 5, 1853, yet as of March 20 Alvarez still had not accepted the Plan of Jalisco and under his direction the entire state refused to recognize the interim government in Mexico City. Although the state government was eventually forced to acknowledge the new administration, it was clearly unpopular among Guerrero's political elite even before Santa Anna took office. Alvarez in particular pointed out that he was restraining his political beliefs to preserve the public peace.[18] In the first months of his rule Santa Anna could do little about the situation, and although he replaced officials and exiled opponents elsewhere, he made no such moves in Guerrero, fearing a potential revolt. Instead he actually confirmed Alvarez and his allies in their posts and even appointed Alvarez to his new Order of Guadalupe.[19]

This uneasy state of affairs did not last. In February 1854 Santa Anna dismissed Villarreal and Comonfort from their posts and informed Alvarez that he was sending regular troops to the area to protect Acapulco from a French filibuster. Santa Anna also told Alvarez that he wanted to replace various political and military officials in Guerrero. The final straw came when Santa Anna assigned military command of Guerrero to Angel Pérez Palacios, the longtime military commander of Cuernavaca and leader of government forces against the 1840s peasant rebels in the South.[20]

The federalist response was not long in coming. Alvarez had been preparing to revolt for several months, and had already offered refuge to intellectual allies like Mariano Riva Palacio and Eligio Romero. In January 1854 Alvarez met with the peasant leaders he would rely on during the revolution. Next he arrested several of Santa Anna's local supporters. In February he sent two letters to Santa Anna vowing to resist, and at the end of the month he issued a proclamation to his supporters justifying the revolt. All this activity culminated in the proclamation of the Plan of Ayutla on March 1, 1854.[21]

This complicated dance, in which Santa Anna sought to neutralize Alvarez and the latter reacted, undoubtedly underlies the predominate view of the Ayutla movement. In this version the revolt had no particular ideological agenda and was a purely defensive reaction by a regional strongman against attempts to eliminate him. First popularized by Justo Sierra in the nineteenth century, this interpretation has been taken up by such twentieth-century social scientists as Jan Bazant, Fernando Díaz y Díaz, and Richard Sinkin.[22] It overlooks the extremely cohesive state project of Santa Anna and the conservatives as well as the historical formation of popular federalism in Guerrero in the preceding decades.

The interpretation also stems from an unfruitful search in the Plan of Ayutla itself for elements of the eventually triumphant "liberal" project epitomized by the Constitution of 1857 and the Laws of the Reform. The problems with this search are twofold. First, historians have looked for the wrong thing: the Ayutla movement was federalist, not liberal, although that federalism was later incorporated into Mexican liberalism. Second, historians have looked at the wrong document: the Plan of Ayutla was purposefully vague because it was designed as an umbrella document for all Mexicans who opposed Santa Anna. In its generality it resembled other contemporary "plans." The ideology of the Ayutla rebels is found in other documents produced to inspire support for the movement. The premises of these documents varied from region to region, but at least within the South they elucidated a cohesive social project in direct opposition to that of Santa Anna and his conservative cronies.

Even the Plan of Ayutla contained significant references to the ideals of popular federalism. For example, it noted the threat Santa Anna posed to Mexican independence, accused him of monarchist ambitions, and called for the election of a new constitutional congress that would "exclusively occupy itself with constituting the nation under the form of a popular representative republic." Republicanism and opposition to both monarchy and threats to Mexico's independence had all been important elements of popular federalism in Guerrero since the 1820s. Carmen Vázquez Mantecón has noted the plan's emphasis on the high taxes levied by Santa Anna, but the plan specifically called for the immediate cessation of only one tax, the capitación.[23] The removal of this head tax had been a key demand of the 1840s peasant movements in Guerrero.

Other documents produced for the rebellion also utilized the language of previous federalist movements, linking the rebellion to the defense of Mexican "independence" and "liberty" against "tyranny."[24] They accused Santa Anna of bringing back the symbols of Spanish rule and of serving the "oligarchic" class that had killed Vicente Guerrero and was sucking Mexico's blood, and they emphasized the idea of citizenship and the inclusion of all Mexicans in the political system.[25] In Alvarez's words, the rebels wanted "one law for all, guarantees for the citizen, that the classes stop sucking the substance from the fatherland, [and] that the division between brothers disappear."[26] Some documents even advocated protectionism.[27] In one proclamation Alvarez accused Santa Anna of conspiring to return Mexico to Spanish rule,[28] and even in his private correspondence with Santa Anna before the outbreak of hostilities he emphasized that his "political beliefs" prevented his approval of Santa Anna's embrace of the conservatives.[29] Far from nonideological, the movement against Santa Anna in Guerrero was informed by the well-known tenets of popular federalism. Again, popular federalism was not coterminous with the liberalism that would become identified with the Reform, although a few documents associated with the Ayutla movement approximate later liberalism on some issues.[30]

The Revolution of Ayutla was not a barracks revolt but a guerrilla war. Except for his mestizo and Creole elite supporters in Chilapa and Tlapa, Santa Anna relied on troops from other states, which entered Guerrero as occupying armies. The rebels did not confront these large bodies of government troops but instead harried them, capturing supplies and animals, attacking isolated groups, and facilitating desertion. Any force that ventured too far south was cut off. Between campaigns the insurgents raised crops and prevented the government forces from foraging. In the words of one observer, "Hunger devours the large armies and the *Pintos* [Alvarez's supporters] devour the little ones." The largest confrontation came when Santa Anna himself led an army all the way to Acapulco; cut off from Mexico City so absolutely that not even news reached the capital, he was forced to retreat after one inconclusive assault.[31] In many ways the fighting in the 1850s resembled the "War of the South" fought in the early 1830s after Vicente Guerrero was deposed.

Santa Anna responded to these tactics with savage counterinsurgency warfare. He ordered that all goods of known rebels be confiscated, to the extent of allowing Angel Pérez Palacios to confiscate from rebellious peasants land that did not technically belong to them as individuals. Government troops hung rebels captured bearing arms and destroyed the huts and crops of rebellious peasants. Government troops also burned Alvarez's own hacienda, La Providencia. Government officers tried to restrict traffic between towns and prevent the cultivation of lands they could not directly supervise. All of these measures were complemented by periodic offers of pardons, and all rebounded against Santa Anna when rebel commanders used the very savagery of the government to motivate their followers.[32]

The Revolution of Ayutla was portrayed in the official press as class and race warfare. This aspect of the revolt was also reminiscent of the "War of the South" of the early 1830s. The government's propaganda effort built on the controversies surrounding Alvarez's actions during the peasant rebellions of the 1840s as well as elite memories of the threat posed by Vicente Guerrero and the radical federalists in the late 1820s. One newspaper insisted that only three kinds of men could follow Alvarez: Indians, those who wanted the extermination of the white race, and federalists in bad faith. Alvarez and his troops were portrayed as a threat to private property. They were accused of promoting anarchy, caste war, the domination of the masses, and the confiscation of large properties. Alvarez was described as a stupid, animalistic, autocratic, feudal lord, the "Panther of the South."[33] Significantly, this vision of the threat posed by Alvarez was shared by some liberals. For instance, Benito Gómez Farías wrote in a letter to his famous brother Valentín that one needed to be an "imbecile or evildoer to support a revolution directed by Alvarez." In another letter Benito cheered reports of government victories.[34] This image of Alvarez and his followers was to play a vital role in shaping events after the triumph of the Ayutla movement.

The same propaganda sought to shape public perceptions of Santa Anna's regime by continually trumpeting fictitious victories over the rebels. Santa Anna traveled with a personal staff that organized demonstrations of public adulation for the president and then sent reports to Mexico City describing spontaneous displays of affection.[35] Perhaps the most cynical effort in this vein was the December 1, 1854, referendum inspired by Louis Napoleon's example in France. In each locality voters were required to sign their names in one of two columns in special notebooks, confirming Santa Anna's rule or stating that he should not continue in office. The government issued assurances that no one would be punished for voting against Santa Anna. No one believed them, and almost all those who voted did so affirmatively. In Guerrero the referendum was only held in areas still controlled by government troops. Only nine people there voted against Santa Anna. The government later decided to treat all those who had voted against the president as conspirators and to replace any government employees who had abstained. The overwhelming vote for Santa Anna was played up in the press as more evidence of his popularity.[36]

The revolution began in March 1854 and did not triumph until August 1855, nineteen months later. From the beginning the rebels' challenge was to survive the first attempts to repress them and then expand their operations. Santa Anna's challenge was to snuff out the movement before it made his government seem vulnerable and encouraged other ambitious or disaffected groups to begin activities against him. This quandary explains the refusal of the official press to acknowledge government defeats.

The eventually successful anti–Santa Anna movement displayed a distinct geography. In the first months fighting was largely confined to Guerrero and neighboring areas of Michoacán and the state of Mexico, including what is now Morelos. Gradually the movement expanded within each of these states until in August the first outbreak outside the South took place in Tamaulipas. In December a few villages rebelled in Oaxaca. By March 1855 the rebels were recruiting throughout Michoacán, Mexico, and Morelos as well as in isolated areas of Oaxaca. In May Santiago Vidaurri began a separate rebellion against Santa Anna in Nuevo León, and in June various groups in the Sierra Gorda, Oaxaca, and Jalisco pronounced for the Plan of Ayutla. Finally, in August army garrisons in San Luís Potosí, Zacatecas, and Mexico City denounced Santa Anna.

The Revolution of Ayutla was very much a product of the South. Its survival there and gradual growth finally made Santa Anna's position untenable by emboldening opponents of the regime elsewhere. Santa Anna left Mexico City for exile in August 1855.[37]

Aftermath of a Revolution: The Threats of Popular Federalism and Social Liberalism

Santa Anna's resignation sparked intense political maneuvering throughout Mexico. The professional army that had supported his rule remained largely intact, and it was not entirely clear that all the anti–Santa Anna forces would accept the Plan of Ayutla and the leadership of Alvarez. Nevertheless, over a period of weeks most armed groups accepted the Ayutla scheme under which representatives from each state would select an interim president who would in turn convoke a constitutional congress. On October 4, 1855, a group of representatives meeting in Cuernavaca elected Alvarez president of Mexico. Rather than ending the struggle, however, this act marked the beginning of a new phase.

In early November Alvarez finally entered the capital accompanied by a brigade of his troops from Guerrero, the so-called "Pintos," whose ragged clothing and swarthy complexions reinforced the fear already inspired by their leader's reputation. They were obviously peasants, and even their officers seemed to be poor men. Many did not possess shoes. The Mexico City–based elite feared and loathed the arrival of the Pintos more than they had any event since the elevation of Vicente Guerrero to the presidency 25 years before. The regular army garrison of Mexico City tried to prevent demonstrations celebrating Alvarez's election by arresting anyone found with fireworks, and some group with access to the cathedral lowered the bells to the ground so that they could not be rung to celebrate Alvarez's arrival.[38] Despite these fears the arrival of Alvarez did not lead to radical agrarian reform or generalized caste war. This section explores how these possibilities were forestalled.

As Guy Thomson notes, the victory of the Revolution of Ayutla was a victory of the periphery over the center, of militia units over the regular army, and of the countryside over the city. However, the army still survived, as did the Mexico City elite that composed the core of the conservative party.[39] Worse, the Ayutla coalition was divided from the start. The coalition included popular federalists like Alvarez, social liberals like Ponciano Arriaga, anticlerical radicals like Juárez, and moderates like Comonfort. These divisions were all displayed in Alvarez's first cabinet: as secretary of war Comonfort sought to preserve the army to counterbalance the radical reformers; as secretary of the interior, Arriaga was interested in agrarian reform; as secretary of justice and ecclesiastical affairs, Juárez sought to reduce the power of the church. Ocampo, secretary of foreign relations, agreed with both Arriaga and Juárez. Alvarez struggled to balance these competing factions but resignations began almost immediately.[40]

Comonfort eventually dominated the situation, and Ocampo resigned. Alvarez, attacked in the press for his political beliefs and embittered by the dissension in the cabinet, resigned on December 8, naming Comonfort acting president. Alvarez left Mexico City convinced that Comonfort had a better chance of reconciling the various factions than he himself did. But as Florencia Mallon suggests, Alvarez's withdrawal was as much a result of the fear generated by the social base he was known to represent as of political infighting. His resignation sparked rioting in Mexico City among National Guard troops and radicals convinced that Comonfort would lead a counterrevolution. Many moderates urged the new president to do just that but instead he bided his time.[41]

Several generations of historians have stressed the Constitutional Congress of 1856–57 as the heart of La Reforma.[42] The Congress elaborated the Constitution of 1857, which definitively enshrined universal male suffrage and remained Mexico's constitution for 60 years. The constitution included such keynotes of Mexican liberalism as the Ley Juárez, which abolished *fueros*, or exemptions from the jurisdictions of ordinary courts, and the Ley Lerdo, which decreed the sale of all real estate belonging to corporations, including the church and peasant communities. Nevertheless, the Congress rejected any redistribution of private property. It was through the actions of the Congress that La Reforma came to be associated with attacks on the army, the church, and even peasant communities rather than an effort to radically change the distribution of property.

These results were not, however, a foregone conclusion and were not so certain to the actors involved. Charles Hale has convincingly portrayed the coalescence of two opposed political parties after the war with the United States and the increasing effervescence of political debate.[43] But the increase in tensions was more than just an expression of two opposed elite visions of how to achieve stability and social peace in Mexico; it was accompanied by a sense of rising class tensions in the countryside and a very real fear on the part of many Mexican landowners of both "caste war" and radical, government-sponsored agrarian reform. These two fears were inseparable and mutually reinforcing, and although in the end the new Congress upheld the ideal of private property, it did not do so automatically. The threat posed by Alvarez, his brand of popular federalism, and his peasant supporters was paralleled by that posed by young radical reformers in the Congress. Land reform was only one of many issues that occupied the Congress, and arguably was not a concern of all peasants, but the idealistic reformers of the Congress were engaged in a determined if ultimately futile effort to make the new constitution address what they saw as the needs of Mexico's peasantry and to establish peasants as the foundation of the new political order. Their effort loomed large in the fears of Mexico's property owners.

To understand the landowners' fear, it is instructive to return to the late 1840s and early 1850s, when several alarming developments frightened Mexican property owners. The most terrible, yet most remote, was the Caste War of the Yucatán, which began in 1847 and continued for years before the horrified eyes of Mexico's elite. A second, much closer, was the peasant rebellion of the Sierra Gorda.[44] The third consisted of the 1840s peasant rebellions in Guerrero. The Sierra Gorda rebellion, and to an even greater extent the Guerrero movements, drove home to property owners the political fact that they could not count on all nonpeasants to automatically support landowners in conflicts. Even closer to home, peasants in present-day Morelos also engaged in violent conflict with hacendados in 1848–49, claiming the support of Alvarez. More important, the governor of the state of Mexico refused to back the hacendados in Morelos and elsewhere in his jurisdiction. Finally, the governor of Michoacán also criticized the abuses of hacendados during Arista's presidency. These last two incidents were particularly important in informing the fear with which certain sectors of Mexican society regarded the beginning of La Reforma and thus merit closer inspection.

In July 1849 Mariano Arizcorreta, governor of the state of Mexico, feared possible peasant revolts in his state. He was especially preoccupied by the area now known as Morelos, which had been tense since February 1848, when National Guard troops organized by Alvarez to fight the North Americans had helped peasants occupy lands claimed by hacendados. Alvarez ordered the troops to cease their activities in the name of national unity, and they complied. Next, to reduce tensions, Arizcorreta tried to pressure the landowners, members of the Mexico City–based national dominant class, to make some concessions. He stated that the peasants were resentful because the hacendados had usurped peasant lands, and also paid their laborers with script only valid for purchases from the haciendas' own stores. The hacendados responded by publishing a vitriolic attack on Arizcorreta linking his mediating efforts, as well as his failure to provide troops to execute a court judgment against a village in another part of the state, with the peasant rebellions in progress in the Yucatán and the Sierra Gorda. The hacendados resolved to arm themselves and their employees against peasant attacks, claiming that "the entire society and the very cause of civilization" was threatened by "the enemies of order, who want the villages to clash with the landowners, in order to overthrow everything and consummate the ruin of the country." Arizcorreta replied that he was only trying to avoid a rebellion in which the properties of the hacendados would be the first casualties. The hacendados published another pamphlet repeating their charges and defending the property rights of landowners against charges made in *El Monitor Republicano* that private property in Mexico was based on the right of conquest by the Spanish. The pamphlet also praised the social peace of colonial Mexico, an argument that would become a banner of the conservative party, and claimed that the Indians' poverty stemmed from their racial inferiority.[45]

The landowners' fear may have been linked to the revival of electoral politics under the newly reinstated federalist constitution. In April 1850 *El Monitor Republicano* published an excerpt from the Toluca paper *El Porvenir* attacking an article from another Toluca paper, *Temis y Deucalion*. Copies of the latter two papers apparently no longer exist. *El Porvenir* decried the *Temis y Deucalion* article, written by the radical Ignacio Ramírez, because

> under the pretext of exciting the Indians to work for the triumph of a po-
> litical party in the next elections for the state legislature, it is really di-
> rected at promoting frightful caste war, because it supposes the Indians
> subjugated, states that they have lost the empire of America, and encour-
> ages them to recover it. . . . Such statements are none other than seditious,
> because they suggest that in the country there exist two races, one domi-
> nator and the other dominated, which is absolutely false.[46]

It remains difficult to ascertain whether class divisions surfaced in local electoral politics in the state of Mexico after the reestablish-ment of universal male suffrage made peasants again eligible to vote, but clearly such divisions were feared.

The Michoacán incident took place several years later. Melchor Ocampo was a liberal hacendado who served several times in the 1840s and 1850s as governor of Michoacán, in which capacity he was an active promoter of guerrilla war against the North Americans. Ocampo became increasingly concerned by disparities of wealth in the countryside and in 1851 argued for the abolition of debt peonage and the regulation of the clerical fees for which hacienda workers incurred debt. For these positions Ocampo was accused of atheism and socialism, although he professed Catholicism and was an hacen-dado himself. His criticism of the power exercised by some hacen-dados over their workers was portrayed as an attack on property it-self. Although parochial fees had been regulated since at least the eighteenth century, Ocampo's insistence that the state government had the right to set them was contested fiercely. Parochial fees were eventually negotiated between the diocese and the state congress; nevertheless, no less an authority than Lucas Alamán attributed to this dispute the Jalisco movement that brought back Santa Anna. Ac-cording to Alamán, Ocampo had precipitated the rebellion "with the impious principles that he spread in matters of faith, with the re-forms he attempted in parochial fee schedules and with the alarming measures that he announced against land owners, with which he raised up the clergy and property owners of that State."[47] The anxiety aroused in Mexico's landowners by even mild reform efforts cannot be exaggerated.

This anxiety was heightened by events in Europe, where the great revolutionary wave was made more threatening by the way in which various movements questioned property rights.[48] What is difficult for the modern researcher to grasp is how serious the threat seemed to be. Ultimately, most liberals who wanted to improve income distribution in Mexico were only comfortable with distributing land held by corporate bodies or sponsoring colonization schemes. Nevertheless, specific proposals to those ends were prefaced by statements lamenting the poor distribution of property in Mexico, which, they claimed, held back the country's progress. For instance, the moderate liberal José María Lafragua, in the 1847 *Memoria* of the Ministry of the Interior, stated,

> The most decisive cause of our ills has been the extraordinary disproportion with which territorial property has been distributed, which, making fortunes unequal, makes the poor class victim of the opulent, not only in financial matters but also in social matters, because it subjects the political conduct of a multitude of citizens to the caprices of a landowner, perhaps imbecilic, and they are forced to obey not the inspirations of their hearts, but instead the precepts of the persons upon whom they depend.

Lafragua's argument preceded a proposal for colonization, not land reform, but that must have been small comfort to the wealthy landowners accused of victimizing the poor.[49] Liberals also often used the same arguments to justify breaking up village lands and giving them to peasants as individual property owners.[50] In the 1846–56 period attempts to mediate between landowners and villages, colonization proposals, attacks on corporate property, campaigns against tiendas de raya, proposals to lower parochial fees, efforts to force hacendados to rent unused lands to peasants, and verbal attacks on landowners who had defrauded villages of property were all intertwined and were all carried out in a highly politicized atmosphere in which it was expedient for many federalists and liberal intellectuals to criticize the greed and ignorance of landowners.[51]

The threat seemed dire indeed, and it explains a great deal of the rhetoric about "law and order" that Richard Sinkin, Paul Vanderwood, and Salvador Rueda Smithers have noted for the period.[52] The perceived threat motivated both the formation of the conservative party and the effort to increase state power under Santa Anna. But the fall of Santa Anna added a new factor to the witches' brew of paranoia, namely, the radical, popular federalism of the South, which resurrected the specter of the alliances between peasants and provincial political elites that had threatened the Mexico City–based dominant class during both the War of Independence and the late 1820s. This tradition, with its radical anti-Spanish rhetoric, explicit identification of the Mexico City–based dominant class with Spanish colonialism, and program of wide suffrage, low taxes, and the dispersion of political power, had been further tainted by the efforts of Alvarez on behalf of peasants in the 1840s.

Social Liberals in the Constitutional Congress

When elections for a new constitutional congress were convoked in the autumn of 1855, the Mexico City–based dominant class, its allies in the provinces, and landowners in general felt that they were under attack and that their enemies were firmly seated in power.[53] In retrospect, the radical coalition and the threat it seemed to represent was fraught with fractures of both interest and ideology, though its disintegration was not by any means a foregone conclusion.[54] The Constitutional Congress of 1856–57 must be considered from the perspective not only of its well-known results but also of the possibilities it seemed to contain at the time. Understanding these possibilities requires the examination of both the composition of the Congress and the various laws and constitutional provisions discussed there regarding peasants.

The potential for radical change was most clearly represented within the Congress by a group of delegates usually called "social liberals," the most prominent of whom was Ponciano Arriaga, author of a famous bid for land reform presented to the Congress. Arriaga's proposal is often mentioned by historians as a precursor to Mexico's twentieth century agrarian reform. Generally, however, both Arriaga and his proposal have been seen as isolated within a liberal movement concerned more with upholding the right to private property than with changing class relations in the countryside. Emphasizing this view, Sinkin notes that property rights were not a divisive issue in the Congress, but this interpretation is oversimplified.[55] A review of Arriaga's background and thought is instructive.

Ponciano Arriaga was a radical lawyer from San Luís Potosí. Like many of the younger liberals, he began to achieve prominence in public life in the late 1840s. In his native state he proposed a law establishing a public attorney to represent the poor. In 1849 he was among the congressmen who aided a group from Mexico City's Indian population trying to recover a property from the government-appointed administrator of their resources. Arriaga served as minister of justice under Arista, and his profile increased exponentially with his support for the Revolution of Ayutla. When the Constitutional Congress was elected, Arraiga was the most popular choice among the delegates: he was chosen to represent eight constituencies, the states of Guerrero, Mexico, Michoacán, Jalisco, Puebla, and Zacatecas as well as his native San Luís Potosí and the Federal District. His closest competitors in popularity, Valentín Gómez Farías and Melchor Ocampo, were chosen by only three constituencies each. Arriaga was also Alvarez's first minister of the interior, arguably the most important post in the cabinet. Furthermore, the delegates of the Congress elected him president of that body and also placed him on the committee that wrote the first draft of the constitution. It is impossible to argue that Arriaga was isolated within the liberal party. He was very much a liberal, and when he criticized the distribution of property, he did so within a liberal framework, as is evidenced by his November 1855 letter to Manuel Doblado in which he explained that

> the people continue, as always, miserable and ignorant; in all industries foreigners enjoy advantages and privileges that are noxious to Mexicans; territorial property is monopolized by a few great sirs who have established on their farms a sort of feudal system; taxes weigh on objects of basic subsistence and on all the products of the country; there are no ways of communication; the elements of the Republic's social life are not developed and we Mexicans watch as governments take and leave power without improving our hopes at all.[56]

Arriaga's criticism of the distribution of property was not alien to his liberalism: it was embedded within it.

Arriaga was not alone in the Congress. Several colleagues shared at least some of his ideas, and one who became especially prominent in later years was Ignacio Ramírez. Ramírez had studied at the Colegio de San Gregorio, a school originally established by the Jesuits to educate Indian nobles, while it was headmastered by Juan Rodríguez Puebla, a radical federalist and fervent *indigenista* who in the 1830s was an ally of Juan Alvarez and intellectual opponent of José María Luís Mora. Ramírez participated in a Mexico City conspiracy to supply intelligence to the Ayutla rebels. He shared with the radical federalists of the late 1820s the view that the War of Independence had been a struggle between the people of Mexico and the colonial nobility, upper clergy, landowners, and rich merchants. He also shared their belief that the municipality should be the principal foundation of Mexico's political life and saw in Indian peasant villages an aptitude for local self-government that could be harnessed to bring social and economic development. Ramírez served in later liberal cabinets in which was known for applying the Reform laws with zeal, but he also defended villages affected by the Ley Lerdo and was accused of inciting the peasants to rebellion.[57]

Two other social liberals were even more closely tied to Alvarez. Isidro Olvera had served in the state legislature of Mexico before the conservative reaction, promoting guerrilla war against the North Americans and serving as a liaison between Alvarez and Mariano Riva Palacio immediately after Santa Anna's overthrow. One of the first secretaries of the Constitutional Congress and its last president, Olvera was a delegate for the state of Mexico, a substitute for Jalisco and the Federal District, and, along with Rafael Jaquez, a representative of Guerrero. Jaquez was a young lawyer with a reputation for helping peasants with land disputes who had helped organize the Revolution of Ayutla in the Cuernavaca area.[58]

These men were by no means isolated in the Congress among either Mexican liberals or even their Latin American contemporaries. In addition to those mentioned, Mariano Arizcorreta, Melchor Ocampo, and others considered dangerous to private property were chosen to serve in the Congress. Young intellectuals simultaneously advocated land reform and criticized "feudal" property owners in Argentina and Chile. Jacqueline Covo has noted how the fluidity of the political situation in late 1855 encouraged the formation of various political "clubs" or pressure groups, including an "Indian club" to defend the interests of the "Indian race."[59]

The delegates interested in reforms to improve the lot of Mexico's rural poor were not unified. For instance, Arizcorreta, also a member of the Congress, was a moderate even though he had attacked hacendados in the state of Mexico in 1849. Most of the others were considered *puros*, or radicals. More important, many puros and moderates were decidedly unfriendly toward Mexico's peasantry. Among these was Benito Juárez, governor of Oaxaca and the most famous Mexican liberal of his generation, who, born into a family of Indian peasants, rejected his roots at an early age. As governor Juárez had once sent troops to repress the rebellious peasants of Juchitán and had vilified them in his annual reports.[60] José María Lafragua, the liberal with the most administrative experience and a close friend of Comonfort, considered Mexico's rural masses ignorant fanatics who sought to return to pre-Conquest savagery.[61] Melchor Ocampo was rumored to consider Alvarez and the southern popular federalists barbarians.[62] Mariano Riva Palacio was an ally of Juan Alvarez in national politics but as an hacendado and governor of the state of Mexico showed little sympathy for peasants in their disputes with hacendados.[63] *El Monitor Republicano*, a liberal standardbearer in the late 1840s, routinely carried articles attacking communal landholding as "communism," disparaging Indians as racially inferior, and advocating purely military solutions to peasant unrest.[64] Nevertheless, the leaders of the Congress included the men most feared by Mexico's property holders, and although several—among them Arizcorreta and Ocampo—did not attack private property on the congressional floor, others did. These proposals, often viewed by historians as odd precursors to later agrarian reform efforts, sparked considerable debate in the press even when they were not debated on the floor of the Congress itself. Proposals for agrarian reform began to surface in the press in October 1855, even before the Congress met, and were quickly answered by landowners who argued for colonization rather than land reform. The debate began to heat up in the spring of 1856, when some liberals began to set the stage for possible restrictions on property rights by arguing in the press that property was subject to government efforts to promote public welfare.[65]

In this polarized context several members of the Constitutional Congress criticized the distribution of property in rural Mexico. The first was José María Castillo Velasco, representative from the Federal District. On June 16, 1856, immediately after the introduction of the draft constitution proposed by the constitutional committee, Castillo Velasco suggested a series of amendments linking the longtime federalist ideal of the free municipality as the basic cell of the nation with concern over the distribution of land in rural Mexico. He included an argument for democracy *within* municipalities, a particular concern of peasants in the South, and condemned hacendados for usurping village lands. Arguing that the true root of the incessant threat of caste war was the misery in which Indian villages lived, Castillo Velasco doubted the viability of a modern liberal state where most citizens lived in economic misery. He insisted on the merit of Indians in war and peace. According to Castillo Velasco, the solution to the Republic's problems lay in a land reform that would benefit not only the Indians but also the middle class the delegates themselves hailed from. He proposed the following constitutional amendments:

> 1. Every municipality in agreement with its electoral college may decree the measures and works that it believes convenient to the municipality and impose and collect the taxes it believes necessary for the works it approves, as long as they do not harm another municipality or the state.
> 2. Every village of the Republic should have sufficient lands for the common use of its residents. The states of the federation will buy them, mortgaging public revenues to do so if necessary.

3. Every jobless citizen has the right to acquire enough land to provide his subsistence, for which he will pay, until he is able to redeem the capital, an annuity that will not exceed 3 percent of the land's value. To this end the states will use the vacant lands in their territory and the cofradía lands, buying, if necessary, from private individuals, and recognizing the value of the cofradía lands and those of private individuals on public revenues, which will pay their yield until their capital is redeemed.[66]

This land reform would compensate landowners with bonds backed by government revenues. Furthermore, municipalities would share with their electoral colleges the power to tax their residents, a key provision for municipal autonomy. This proposal seems to consciously emulate or perhaps unconsciously resemble the practice of the former repúblicas de indios, in which major decisions were ratified by both elected municipal officers and the body of electors, or pasados.

Only a few days later, on June 23, Ponciano Arriaga proposed his famous "Voto particular sobre el derecho de propiedad." Arriaga began by noting that many prominent observers of Mexico's ills considered the poor distribution of landed property one of its most important problems. According to Arriaga, the people could be "neither free nor republican" under society's "absurd economic system" despite hundreds of laws and constitutions informed by beautiful theories. Of the Congress Arriaga asked, "Wouldn't it be more logical and frank to deny our four million poor all participation in public affairs, all opportunity for public office, all active and passive vote in elections, declare them objects and not persons, and found a system of government in which the aristocracy of money, or at the most talent, serves as the base of the institutions?" He pointed out that while the delegates could argue about the division of powers forever, real sovereignty would continue to belong to Mexico's property owners unless something was done about it. Although many hacendados were honorable and charitable, he said, the majority were tyrants, especially those of the Morelos region, the Huasteca, the lowlands of Río Verde in San Luís Potosí, and the Valley of Mexico. Arriaga also noted the prevalence of lawsuits brought by Indian villages against hacendados who usurped their lands. To the oft-proposed remedy of foreign colonization, Arriaga offered the alternative of Mexican colonization, that is, populating Mexican lands with Mexicans given the same tax breaks and other advantages that were to be offered to foreign colonists. He proposed not "to destroy property . . . but on the contrary to generalize it."

Arriaga suggested several constitutional amendments, including one that obliged those who possessed more than fifteen square leagues to put their land under cultivation within two years or forfeit it to the federal government. Another would allow the government to confiscate property to give to villages that lacked land but would indemnify the owners. Those rural inhabitants who did not own at least 50 pesos worth of land would be exempt from all taxes, including parochial fees, and hacendados would not be allowed to pay their workers in anything except cash.[67]

The radicals continued their assault on July 7. First, Joaquín García Granados expressed a desire to include in the constitution "municipal power, which is the true power of the people." Then Ignacio Ramírez took the podium and delivered an impassioned speech in which he called workers, both rural and urban, "slaves of capital" and proposed that profits be distributed between workers and capitalists in order to convert workers from slaves into citizens. He appealed for a constitution "founded in the privilege of the needy, of the ignorant, of the weak, so that this way we better our race and so that the public power be none other than the organized welfare."[68] On July 10 José J. González editorialized in *El Monitor Republicano* that the nation's land was common property and the current owners only enjoyed usufruct, or use rights. Meanwhile, Florencio María del Castillo criticized the abuses of landowners in Guanajuato, in the very heart of the area where the Mexico City–based dominant class maintained much of its agricultural investment.[69]

On July 10 both conservative and liberal landowners, including the prominent liberal politician Mariano Riva Palacio, issued a pamphlet that argued against the projects of Castillo Velasco and Arriaga and also Article 17 of the draft constitution, which stated that the freedom to exercise any industry, commerce, or job could not be impeded by anyone, even those who acted as property owners. The landowners felt that this latter article might be used to protect squatters who used land without permission. Much of the pamphlet consists of a philosophical defense of property rights as both universally recognized and the foundation of individual liberty. The authors pointed out that Article 17 in particular threatened not only hacendados but urban landlords as well, because they, too, would be exposed to the unauthorized use of their property. They also attacked the proposals on economic grounds, using the classic liberal doctrine that stated that only firm property rights would encourage investment in improvements. Individual interests responding to market pressures, they said, tended to set the proper size for rural properties, making it profitable to subdivide estates that were too large and combine those that were too small. The pamphleteers pointed out that economies of scale in agriculture allowed investment, and applauded the previous efforts of various state legislatures to divide village lands. Quoting the biblical verse that "the poor will always be with us," they argued that the Congress should not try to eliminate poverty because wealth had always been and would always be divided unequally, and poverty was no more unnatural than the unequal division of any other human attribute. They proposed that poverty be alleviated by indoctrinating the poor in proper work habits, because in Mexico labor was scarce and no one starved who truly wanted to work. The landowners finished by suggesting that the spectacle of a government land reform would reduce the rabble's respect for property rights and lead to more disasters like that of the Yucatán.[70] This pamphlet was seconded by another signed by owners of property in Michoacán, Guanajuato, Guerrero, and Puebla, which additionally attacked the radical proposals as socialist in inspiration and which included an explicit defense of the landowners' treatment of their peons.[71]

In Congress debate shifted to the acrimonious issue of freedom of religion, which, as Richard Sinkin has noted, was linked to questions of what he calls "law and order." Several delegates who attacked religious freedom did so on the grounds that the Catholic Church helped unify Mexico and preserve order. They insinuated that religious tolerance would lead to disorder. For instance, on August 1 José María Lafragua suggested that if the government allowed freedom of religion, Indians would think that their pre-Hispanic religion had been returned to them and thus they could seek the return of their pre-Hispanic wealth. According to him, this idea was not absurd because the nation had been threatened for years by caste war.[72] On August 4 José Antonio Gamboa replied that even in the Yucatán rebellious Indians had shown no desire to abandon Catholicism, insisted that Indians rebelled to end economic oppression, and warned that the government could avert caste war only by taking steps to alleviate that oppression.[73]

On July 27 *El Monitor Republicano* reproduced an article by Zacarías Oñate asserting that the right to property, although natural, was limited because man lives in society.[74] On August 7 Isidro Olvera, delegate from Guerrero, proposed an organic law of property rights, arguing that it was enough "to compare what the villages own today with what they had after the Conquest, according to tradition, to conclude that there has occurred a truly scandalous usurpation." Referring to the landowners' July 10 pamphlet, Olvera doubted the "political innocence with which the petitioners present themselves and the class they belong to, because besides the fact that among the signatures are those of some who constantly opposed and still oppose democracy and liberty, impartial history already wrote in its book that the well-to-do classes of the Republic, always misunderstanding their true interests, have blocked every material and moral advance." Olvera's law would prevent landowners with more than ten square leagues of farmland or twenty of pasture from acquiring more, tax those who held more than ten leagues on Mexico's Central Plateau, force holders of water rights to allow villages at least enough for drinking, force the owners of woods to allow villages that had no other source of firewood to gather enough for cooking, and establish grand juries to review all land disputes and determine the legitimacy of titles.[75]

On August 8 the delegates began to discuss Article 17 of the proposed constitution, which stated that the "freedom to exercise any type of useful and honest industry cannot be restricted by law, authority or private individuals acting as property owners." Mariano Arizcorreta argued that the article as written seemed to protect squatters. Ponciano Arriaga retorted that the phrase "useful and honest" eliminated that possibility. Debate continued until Ignacio Vallarta launched a furious attack on the abuses of hacendados who kept their lands uncultivated and paid their workers in scrip. Although Vallarta was arguing against the article, he inadvertently converted it into a symbol of the liberals' opposition to debt peonage and company stores.[76] The debate over property rights and the right to work raged furiously in both the press and the Congress until the article was returned to committee, then continued sporadically from August through November. The defense of property rights was also one of the banners raised by armed reactionary movements that autumn.[77]

Morelos and the Limits of Popular Federalism

Perhaps the best example of the complexities of the relationship between Mexico's peasantry and the various factions within Mexico's emerging liberal political elite is provided by the conflict that arose over the area that now constitutes the state of Morelos. Florencia Mallon has analyzed this conflict recently in an excellent article, and for that reason it will be only briefly discussed here.[78] The way in which this conflict was played out illustrates both the strength of the model for Mexican society and politics advanced by Juan Alvarez and his allies, peasant and nonpeasant, and the reasons why that popular federalist model never became dominant within Mexican liberalism or the Mexican state. Alvarez was able to put together a fragile coalition that included both those ideologically committed to the program and those who were willing to support it on various issues and at specific moments to pay political debts or discomfort enemies. This coalition was eventually split by varying responses to the burgeoning conservative reaction of 1856–57.

Mallon has artfully outlined the various economic, social, and political developments that led to the 1856 crisis in Morelos. Between the 1780s and the second decade of the twentieth century, this area experienced escalating cycles of conflict between peasant villages and rancheros squeezed by population growth on the one hand and several waves of ambitious Mexico City–based entrepreneurs on the other. Both sides sought to take advantage of the area's warm climate and proximity to Mexico City, the peasants and rancheros by producing winter food crops and the hacendados by producing sugar and sugar-based products. These groups clashed over access to land and water, tenancy, and the wages hacendados paid rural laborers drawn from the villages and ranchos. These cycles of conflict eventually led to the formation of Mexico's most famous peasant movement, *zapatismo*, in the early twentieth century.[79]

After the War of Independence the sugar estates had deteriorated for want of capital. In the 1840s a new group of entrepreneurs purchased some of the estates and began to revitalize them, investing in repairs, evicting tenants, and reviving their claims to lands disputed with villagers. Several related features of this group contributed to the political escalation that followed. Many belonged to the Mexico City–based dominant class with investments in government finances, the new textile factories, and land that had formed the backbone of centralism. Some were members of the colonial dominant class who had retained their haciendas but let their investments lie dormant in the tumultuous years immediately after independence. Several were Spanish citizens who employed their compatriots as managers and foremen. Perhaps more important, all became heavily identified with the resurgent conservatism of the late 1840s and early 1850s led by Lucás Alamán, representative of the Duke of Monteleone, the heir of Cortés who owned haciendas in Morelos.[80] Monteleone's haciendas were the remnants of the Marquesado del Valle, one of Mexico's few truly feudal political entities. The Marquesado had been ceded to Cortés in reward for the Conquest and still served as the legal basis for many of the original land titles of both villages and haciendas in the region. In addition, the conservatives openly discussed the idea of reconstituting Mexico as a monarchy led by a representative of one of Europe's royal families, probably the Spanish Bourbons. Their cultural and political agenda rested on the revival of what they saw as the positive aspects of Spanish colonialism. The combination of all of the above-mentioned attributes of the sugar entrepreneurs was incendiary.

Throughout the 1840s the conflict over resources and wages heated up in Morelos. The landowners evicted tenants and squatters, disputed boundaries with villages and ranchos, refurbished machinery, and tried to restrict the expenditure of scarce cash on labor by both holding down wages and reviving tiendas de raya, company stores that allowed landowners to pay workers in scrip redeemable only in the haciendas' own stores. But this rigorous program struggled after the 1846 restoration of federalism because peasants now had political options that had been denied to them earlier: they could oppose the haciendas by competing for the control of municipal governments and playing on government fears of caste war,[81] and they could form alliances with other actors in the economic and political arenas, the most powerful of whom was Juan Alvarez.

Alvarez seems to have first witnessed the increasing social polarization of Morelos in early 1845 when he passed through while bringing peasant troops to central Mexico to support the new Herrera government. His reputation had preceded him: he had already begun to champion the interests of Guerrero's peasantry in the press and in his correspondence, both private and official, and word of the peasant movements in Guerrero had undoubtedly reached the peasants of Morelos. In April 1845 Alvarez sent a letter to the villages of Morelos stating that he had been commissioned to bring peace to the area as he had in Guerrero. He advised the villagers to be patient while the government considered their complaints against the tiendas de raya, and to ignore attempts to mobilize the villages "with the brilliant prospect of federalism" because those seeking peasant support would only use them. This letter prompted the prefect of the area to ask his superiors whether Alvarez's pacification commission extended to Morelos. They responded negatively. When queried by authorities in Mexico City about rumors that a Morelos village had sought the aid of the successful Indian rebels of Chilapa, Alvarez denied knowledge of such an appeal; when asked about reports that committees of Morelos peasants had sought his aid, he admitted receiving written complaints against some Morelos hacendados but denied that committees had visited. From this point on the hacendados of the area continually complained about the pernicious influence of Alvarez.[82]

This influence, such as it was, seems to have grown during the war with the United States. Alvarez organized guerrillas in the region during the latter stages of the war but seems to have had little control over their actions beyond that provided by his own prestige. These guerrillas and National Guard troops were formed around prominent village leaders and rancheros, and although they often skirmished with U.S. troops they also used some of their newfound power against hacendados. Alvarez tried to check this dynamic, arguing that peasant attempts to press claims on the haciendas in the midst of the war were hurting national unity. The peasants reluctantly complied. Despite Alvarez's efforts, from 1848 to 1854 tensions remained high and rumors flew about real or imagined land invasions and strikes. In some instances, National Guard units formed during the U.S. invasion refused to repress peasants who had invaded hacienda lands.[83]

When the Revolution of Ayutla began in 1854 its organizers found fertile ground in Morelos. By the end of the year many Morelos towns and villages had been visited by armed bands of local men claiming allegiance to Alvarez and the revolution. Mallon has remarked on the diverse social origins of this group of village peasants, hacienda laborers, small merchants, and artisans all unified, as she points out, by "their criticism of the local dominant class, Spanish and Mexican." Alvarez sent men like Faustino Villalva, one of the most famous leaders of the 1840s peasant movements in Guerrero, to raise guerrillas in Morelos, but the groups were actually led by local inhabitants.[84] As noted above, the propaganda used to promote the Revolution of Ayutla included criticism of the revival of Spanish imperial symbols by Santa Anna and the threat that he might turn Mexico into a monarchy or return it to Spanish rule. These elements resonated with the social position of Spaniards in Morelos and their open support for conservatism. The resulting situation was highly explosive, and not surprisingly in February 1855 several Spaniards were killed in rebel raids. In revenge, a party of Spanish hacendados and their employees attacked a rebel group, killing five and capturing three more who were later executed. When the municipality of Cuernavaca accepted the Plan of Ayutla in August, the town residents rioted and stoned the houses of several Spanish hacendados. The town council quieted the mob but the Spanish vice-consul sent an alarming report to his superior in Mexico City.[85]

In this highly charged context Alvarez and his supporters attempted to add the district that now forms Morelos to the state of Guerrero in 1856. Clearly, Alvarez sought to increase his own power: Morelos was the richest fiscal zone of the state of Mexico.[86] However, it is equally clear that he saw the addition of the area to Guerrero as one way to acquire the power to grant peasant demands. Alvarez was aided by many others in this project, not least of all by several delegates to the Constitutional Congress whose influence was strong enough to have the provision reported favorably out of committee. In the end the proposal lost, but it sparked some of the most interesting debates of the Congress.

On November 26, 1856, the committee in charge of territorial issues proposed several changes in the political organization of Mexico. One was the addition of Morelos to Guerrero, which was justified by the various petitions presented by area villages, the need to aid Guerrero because of the economic damage Santa Anna's armies had inflicted there, the desire for a road to Acapulco, and the fact that communication was easier between Morelos and the capital of Guerrero than between Morelos and Toluca.[87] On November 27 Prisciliano Díaz González presented a minority report claiming that the state of Mexico needed the revenue generated by Morelos and doubting that the petitions presented by the villages represented the will of the majority of their inhabitants. Díaz González concluded by suggesting that the move was opposed by the "landowners and other citizens of the districts."[88] On December 15 the addition of Morelos to Guerrero was debated on the floor. Four deputies, Darío Reyes, Ignacio Peña y Barragan, Valentín Gómez Tagle, and Prisciliano Díaz González, spoke against the article; only two, Isidro Olvera and Rafael Jaquez, defended it. Noticeably absent from both camps were the most prominent orators of the Congress, men like Arriaga, Francisco Zarco, Ocampo, and Lafragua. Defending the resolution, Jaquez emphasized the fiscal benefits for impoverished Guerrero and the need to respect the will of the inhabitants, and Olvera concentrated on the contribution the South had made to the fight against Santa Anna and the need to control the abuses of the landowners. The idea's opponents stressed the fiscal value of the area to Mexico and suggested that the people of the area did not want to be added to Guerrero. The measure, defeated 48–33, garnered the votes of such famous liberals as Zarco, Santos Degollado, Francisco Díaz Barriaga, José Antonio Gamboa, Benito Gómez Farías, Ignacio Ramírez, and Ignacio Vallarta as well as those who had spoken in its defense. Other famous liberals like Castillo Velasco, Ocampo, and Arriaga were not present.

This result clearly was not a foregone conclusion. The vote was close, although Zarco noted that the delegation from the state of Mexico had pushed the question to a vote, implying that it knew it had lined up enough support to prevail. The next day Congress considered Díaz González's proposal to preserve the limits of the state of Mexico in their present form, and although Zarco stated that the territorial committee had been so convinced that Morelos would be added to Guerrero that it had not fully considered other modifications of Mexico's boundaries, the article preserving Mexico's boundaries was approved 43–37.[89]

According to Richard Sinkin, these two votes were among the most divisive of the entire Constitutional Congress. Sinkin suggests that the fundamental issue in this and other conflictive votes was "law and order, or a fear of anarchy," a fear that he attributes to threats of rebellion voiced by those opposed to the addition of Morelos to Guerrero.[90] This interpretation does not account for the fact that most of the debate was about the abuses of the landowners; nor does it jive with the evidence, set forth in the previous chapter, that Alvarez had already used Guerrero's 1849 statehood to satisfy many of the demands voiced by peasants. All of this suggests that the conflictive votes on boundaries had a class dimension. Furthermore, it was Rafael Jaquez who reputedly threatened violence against the landowners after the vote went against his position.[91] These threats were not in vain, as will be seen.

Two days later, a group of peasants and rancheros killed several Spanish citizens on the haciendas of San Vicente, Chiconcuac, and Dolores. This episode, analyzed in Florencia Mallon's article, sparked a major international incident because of the assailants' perceived ties to Juan Alvarez. The Spanish government accused Alvarez of ordering the murders, and the military and civil authorities of the area and their superiors in Mexico City chastised Alvarez for protecting José Abascal and Juan Barreto, two men accused of leading the attacks. The debate surrounding this incident illustrates the complex impasse at which Alvarez and his allies had arrived in their drive to advance their inclusive model of Mexican state formation.

Clearly, the Spanish were killed as part of the ongoing struggle between the peasants and rancheros of the area on one side and the Mexico City–based hacendados on the other. The participants in this local struggle also occupied positions in national politics: the peasants had increasingly aligned themselves with a group of social liberals and federalists whose moral leader was Alvarez; the hacendados had in turn identified themselves with the conservatives represented first by Santa Anna's project and later by the reaction that began in 1856. The struggle between these factions was contemporaneous with the murders themselves,[92] which means that the Spanish and conservatives were correct in calling the murders a political act,[93] but not necessarily correct in asserting that Alvarez ordered the murders, or that the two men he protected took part in them. The truth is a little more complex.

Abascal and Barreto were among many local peasant and ranchero leaders who had cooperated with Alvarez in the past, including during the Revolution of Ayutla. Sometimes this political and military cooperation was formalized by calling these men and their followers National Guardsmen, but it is clear from other incidents in the late 1840s and early 1850s that Alvarez did not really control these men. Their cooperation was based on the prestige Alvarez enjoyed as leader of the political and social current to which they belonged.[94] They could and did act without his knowledge or orders, and even against his wishes, as was demonstrated several times during the war with the United States. Nevertheless, even when they did so Alvarez felt constrained to protect them as well as he could because he needed to preserve his ties with the communities and groups these men represented. For example, when some former anti-U.S. guerrillas were imprisoned in the early 1850s during the continuing conflict with the landowners, Alvarez intervened with his friend Mariano Riva Palacio, governor of the state of Mexico. Riva Palacio was by no means sympathetic to rebellious peasants. Knowing that Riva Palacio would not release the men, Alvarez played on Riva Palacio's liberal sensibilities by requesting a prompt trial—no small request, as the monopoly the landowners enjoyed over local power had often facilitated the jailing of peasants for indefinite periods without trial.[95] In sum, Alvarez's protection was not synonymous with approval of the actions of his rebel allies. Alvarez's importance in Morelos was primarily that of a symbol: to the peasants he seems to have represented the possibility of alliance with the liberal, federalist project, whereas to the landowners he was both the quintessential "outside agitator" and an example of what horrors occurred when elites attempted to expand their political base to include the rabble.

In the specific case of the 1856 murders, Alvarez was not convinced that Abascal and Barreto had taken part. He was also conscious of the continuing conflict between hacendados and peasants in which the murders had taken place and was certain that many Spanish hacendados had given material and moral support to the reactionary rebels his forces were in the area to combat. Alvarez needed to protect the two men to maintain his own prestige and political contacts among the peasantry of Morelos. He probably still had hopes of adding the area to Guerrero and, more important, was conscious of the burgeoning conservative reaction. He was convinced that both the social project he was promoting and the liberals in general could not triumph without regional alliances with the peasantry, and events would prove him correct.

Juan Alvarez thus found himself in direct confrontation with his erstwhile liberal allies in late 1856 and early 1857. Benito Haro, the moderate liberal political commander of Morelos, demanded that Alvarez turn in Abascal and Barreto, and Ignacio Comonfort backed Haro to the hilt. Alvarez insisted that the two men were with his troops at the time the crimes were committed and therefore innocent. He complained that Haro was treating his troops as the enemy despite the continued presence of conservative forces in the area, and accused the liberal government of scapegoating his two allies on the basis of rumors spread by the conservative landowners. Ironically, Haro himself had been a military protégé of Alvarez's during the first part of his career, and Alvarez saw his current position as a betrayal. Alvarez could not turn the men over to the government without damaging his political credibility among the Morelos peasantry, but he lacked the national political power to force the government to back off. In the end he solved the problem by arresting the men and then letting them escape in February 1857. Abascal was killed by government pursuers in Morelos a few days later. Barreto was never captured by the liberals but was killed a year later by the conservatives.[96]

The affair led Alvarez to defend his reputation in his famous *Manifiesto del ciudadano Juan Alvarez a los pueblos cultos de Europa y América*. In this lengthy pamphlet Alvarez first explained his late-1856 presence in Morelos pursuing bands of reactionary rebels. He then pointed out that the information the Spanish *hacendados* claimed to have implicating him could only have been acquired if they themselves had either previous knowledge of the crimes or current knowledge of the identity and whereabouts of the criminals, either of which would place Alvarez's accusers themselves in violation of the laws. Alvarez next argued that he and his troops, including Abascal and Barreto, were simply too far away on the day in question to have participated in the murders. He insisted that Abascal and Barreto were innocent and had been singled out because they had "defended liberty; they had tried to overthrow that species of feudalism established by Bermijillo [owner of the properties in question and also Spanish vice-consul] and other Spaniards in the haciendas of Cuautla and Cuernavaca."[97] Alvarez noted that the fact that the assailants had shouted "Viva Alvarez" did not indicate that he was guilty of their crimes. He criticized Haro's orders to turn over Abascal and Barreto but also defended Haro from charges that he had not done everything possible to prevent the attack and find the perpetrators. Only after this series of arguments made in his own defense did Alvarez inject his most famous attack on the hacendados of Morelos, accusing them of usurping peasant lands with the collusion of the judicial system and supporting the conservatives with men, arms, and horses.[98]

The debate over the possible addition of Morelos to Guerrero and the confrontation over Abascal and Barreto demonstrate the impasse reached in 1855–57. Alvarez and the popular federalists of the South had elaborated a state project based on the inclusion of Mexico's rural poor in the post-independence political system. They believed that the rural poor could and should be citizens of the new state. This program rested on municipal autonomy and the similarities between municipalities and traditional Indian village governments. Peasants could be incorporated into the political order by granting their basic demands for responsible local government guaranteed by universal male suffrage, low taxes, and protection from the predations of the rich, particularly but not exclusively the Mexico City–based dominant class associated with centralism, conservatism, monarchism, and Spanish domination. The popular federalist project also included a conscious defense of the worth of the peasantry as the bulwark of the new order and base for Mexico's material wealth and progress. It differed from the liberalism that historians now associate with the triumph of La Reforma in both its federalism and its view of the rural poor. Alvarez and his allies had been able to institutionalize their vision in Guerrero by breaking away from the elite-dominated state governments of Mexico and Puebla in the late 1840s. They had defended their vision in the Revolution of Ayutla and in doing so carried it close to national power. They were unable, however, to institutionalize it at the national level and were forced to ally themselves with more moderate groups just to survive. This survival rested on a series of ad hoc compromises designed to hold the liberal coalition together through such expedients as adding Morelos to Guerrero to reward its liberal peasantry. Unfortunately, the landowners were powerful enough to prevent this transfer, and the conflict there continued.

The Revolution of Ayutla began the ten-year period of institutional change, shifting alliances, and civil war that later became known as La Reforma. Historians generally see La Reforma as crucial to the formation of the Mexican political system but paradoxically often describe the rebellion that opened the period as lacking in ideological content and its participants as marginal to the far-reaching changes that followed. This view parallels more general interpretations of Mexican politics that have discounted any influence the vast majority of Mexico's population might have had both in the political struggles of the nineteenth century and the impact these struggles had on the Mexican state.

Rejecting these views, I have argued that the Ayutla movement that began La Reforma put forward a cohesive political project for Mexico, a project that I have described as popular federalism. This project had been elaborated during the political conflicts of the previous decades and had developed a particularly wide following among distinct social groups in Guerrero, including much of the area's peasantry. In 1854 these groups revolted against the conservative centralist project of Santa Anna and his allies, a project that replaced elected officials with appointed ones throughout the political system, eliminated the local government institutions through which peasants sought to control their lives, raised the specter of Spanish monarchism, and increased taxes on Mexico's poor. The political elite and peasants of Guerrero put forth their own vision of what the Mexican political system should be, a vision that included universal male suffrage, state and municipal autonomy, low taxes, and a generally wide diffusion of government power among local groups. This popular federalist vision facilitated the political alliance between elites and peasants underlying the guerrilla struggle that precipitated the downfall of the conservative government.

After the revolution this popular federalist project and the more intellectual social liberalism combined to pose what was widely perceived as a potent threat to the Mexican social order. This threat was eventually turned back when the conservative reaction it provoked forced its allies to moderate their policies. Popular federalism became only one strain within the eventually triumphant liberalism associated with La Reforma, but it was a strain that changed the nature of Mexican liberalism and hence that of the liberal authoritarian state model still dominant in Mexico. Substantial portions of Mexico's peasantry had refused to be excluded from the polity and in doing so had changed Mexican history.

Conclusion

We the pueblos have become disillusioned that the government that rules us is that of Fernando VII, and knowing that he squandered the treasures of our American soil, we refuse to recognize all except the four gospels that worthy Hidalgo, Allende, Morelos, Galeana, and Guerrero, the first heroes of the patria, preached to us. We know that the first of these gospels is religion. Second, that all foreigners be expelled. Third, that the government be reformed. Fourth, a general prize to our república for the blood sacrifice that was made in achieving our beloved independence. We understand that our liberty lies in law, and not as is said in libertinism. For the promises made in 1810 and the sufferings that we have seen until now, they make us wait. We do not want our prize to be in coins, but instead the lands that we declare until now, and also that all classes of taxes that oppress our república be moderated. The sovereignty of the pueblos asks that republican law rule, not whims.

—The Plan with which the pueblos claim their rights,
 Xonacatlán, Guerrero, October 8, 1843

We are the product of 500 years of struggle: first against slavery, then during the War of Independence against Spain led by insurgents, then to avoid being absorbed by North American imperialism, then to promulgate our constitution and expel the French empire from our soil, and later the dictatorship of Porfirio Díaz denied us the just application of the Reform laws and the people rebelled and leaders like Villa and Zapata emerged, poor men just like us.

—General command of the Zapatista Army of National
 Liberation, Chiapas, December 1993

Guerrero's peasants were actively involved in the formation of Mexico's state. The changing nature of their participation suggests some important insights about both state formation and peasant political activity. Yet there is more of interest here than the simple fact of peasant participation. Uncovering the presence of subaltern groups in historical processes is an important and worthwhile task, but ultimately a more rigorous test of the significance of lower-class struggles and aspirations is whether they helped shape the world we live in today. This test is one that Guerrero's peasants, both Indian and non-Indian, clearly pass. Mexican politics would be very different today if the peasant actions recounted in this book had not taken place.

Several features of Guerrero's history in the first half of the nineteenth century are critical to understanding both Mexican political history in general and the political history of Mexico's working classes in particular. Elite politics exercised a powerful influence on the nature and timing of peasant resistance. Often this influence was inadvertent; Napoleon, for example, had no idea that his attempt to dispossess the Bourbon dynasty in Spain would touch off massive and widespread peasant resistance in New Spain. Certainly that resistance was driven by grievances that were much more immediate to the lives of New Spain's rural people than Napoleon's action, but the cooperation of the very diverse groups that fought together would have been impossible without the stunning events of 1808. Even in the relatively small geographical area on which this book focuses, the insurgency united mulatto sharecroppers, Indian village peasants, parish priests, muleteers, and landowners. The groups and their grievances were too diverse to make an alliance imaginable until the removal of the royal person reshuffled the deck of political symbols and actors.

Elite and popular politics became even more intertwined in subsequent decades. Elite attempts to build a new national state inevitably held great significance for the popular classes and often deliberately sought to change the lives of poor Mexicans. Mexican policymakers in the 1820s, for instance, decided not to protect Mexico's textile industry and thus alienated both urban artisans and coastal sharecroppers. Legislators who strove to implant local self-government as a school for the new citizenry raised expectations that affected rural politics for decades. Even when politicians did not deliberately seek to change life for Mexico's poor they often did so inadvertently; the creation of new sets of rules for Mexican politics inevitably altered the environment in which all social groups pursued claims and resolved conflicts. Land disputes, for instance, were adjudicated under new laws and before judges who were often driven by novel political and social considerations.

The conflictive construction of Mexico's national state affected subaltern politics in another way that ultimately may have had more impact on the changing nature of peasant resistance. Though few in number, the relatively wealthy and literate Mexicans whose names fill the pages of national and regional political histories were actually very diverse and clashed, often violently, on crucial issues of political economy as well as membership in the new polity. Elite disagreement vastly increased the space within which disaffected lower-class groups could maneuver, and cross-class alliances became an effective tool for both popular and elite groups.

These cross-class alliances were also the means through which peasant resistance exerted pressure on elite politics. Peasants made alliances—some temporary and fragile, others long-lasting—with people from different backgrounds and often at least partially determined outcomes in elite conflicts. These alliances changed the character of Mexican independence during the insurgency, brought Vicente Guerrero and the yorkinos to power in the late 1820s, and ultimately prevented the consolidation of a centralist, exclusionary state in the 1840s and 1850s. In other words, it is not only impossible to explain peasant politics without understanding elite politics, it is impossible to explain Mexican elite politics without taking into account the political activity of Mexico's poor.

Mexico attained its independence in a period of rapid change in state structures throughout the Americas and Europe. Most postcolonial states and many other post-Enlightenment states claimed to represent sharp breaks with the "Old Regimes" that had preceded them. Yet the new national states did not entirely rely on contemporary revolutions in political theory for their legitimacy and effective operation; as a practical matter they found it impossible to ignore the customs, traditions, and beliefs that underlay the old order. The new states claimed to be destroying previous structures and beliefs but were instead transforming them. This is not to deny that change took place, but even the most dramatic innovations were actually interpreted through their association with preexisting features of political life and experience.

Mexico's cultural and political elites wrote the laws but their practical interpretation was not simple or unilateral. Mexico was a very large and diverse place, and local social and political practices varied greatly. Each region presented its own set of problems and often its own vocabulary, and local officials needed to translate legal terms into that idiom while taking into account an extremely politicized context. These officials were highly conscious of the long, bloody, and destructive civil war they had just survived. Subaltern groups were aware of the possibilities for alliances with other sectors of the population. Peasants in particular were also the heirs of a long tradition of legal action to defend perceived rights. The combination of legal and illegal tactics available tended to soften the potentially harsh impact of innovations.

What in the end is striking about all of these issues is how much they intersect. In southern Mexico in the first half of the nineteenth century state projects changed the lives of peasants and peasant political action altered the process of state formation. Cross-class alliances involving peasants were crucial players in Mexican politics during the insurgency and in the late 1820s, the 1840s, and the 1850s. Even if we focus only on constitutions and laws we cannot disregard the masses camped on the doorsteps of legislators' minds. Each major burst of constitutional innovation took place in the shadow of recent rural violence. The state and federal constitutions of the mid-1820s took form after the devastation of the independence war, the centralist reaction of the mid-1830s was shaped by the ominous popular effervescence of the late 1820s, and the Constitution of 1857 was written after the widespread rebellions of the 1840s. Elite and popular politics were intertwined. It is impossible to write one history without the other.

Ultimately, no particular social group achieved national dominance in early-nineteenth-century Mexico. The image of early-nineteenth-century Mexico as a kind of estate owner's utopia, so prominent in many early studies of the Mexican Revolution, is clearly wrong. However, it would be equally mistaken to suggest that all peasants were as successful as those in Guerrero, or even that all successful peasant groups followed the same strategies. Moreover, success in retaining land and autonomy was often more due to the lack of competitors than it was to adroit politicking. In the generally weak economy of the early and even mid-nineteenth century, landowners tended to neither aggressively expand nor actively defend their holdings.[1]

Many of Guerrero's peasants achieved their goals through alliances with federalists and later liberals. Faced with a rapidly changing post-1808 state, they generally sought inclusion in the new polity to allow them to defend their interests. The success of this strategy depended on nearby allies as well as a relatively weak set of enemies, and in hindsight it is clear that the local enemies of Guerrero's peasants were unusually anemic. Coastal sharecroppers from 1810 into the 1820s, for instance, opposed provincial Spanish merchants who were almost universally unpopular both locally and in the rest of Mexico. Although these merchants often had business connections to the wealthiest people in New Spain, none of the latter were willing to risk their lives and fortunes on the behalf of the former. Peasants who opposed tax increases in the 1840s faced governments that were too impoverished to forcibly collect the taxes, especially in such remote areas, and in the same decade the Indian peasants of Chilapa faced a local elite that was unable to fully mobilize wealthier national allies on its behalf. Centralist allies active in the national government were more than willing to exploit the Chilapa situation in the press but unprepared to take serious risks to support a few socially unimportant provincial landowners. The local landowners, like the coastal Spanish merchants before them, were not essential to the political coalitions in which they took part.

Peasants were much less successful in places like Chalco and Morelos because their opponents were wealthier and more prominent in national politics. Also, because of their geographic proximity to Mexico City and Toluca, the capital of the state of Mexico, these peasants were more likely to encounter large numbers of relatively well supplied troops. For these reasons peasants on the Central Plateau found it much more difficult both to find allies and to defeat repression.[2] In the Yucatán Indian peasants who had pursued their goals through alliances with disaffected local elites suddenly found themselves isolated when the wealthy whites closed ranks. Yet in the raging civil war that followed, the Maya rebels never became completely resigned to fighting their war single-handedly, and they searched for potential allies among the succession of foreigners they encountered throughout the ensuing century.[3]

Other peasants either explicitly resisted or altogether ignored efforts to include them in the new national state. The most famous example of explicit resistance is that of the Yaqui, who had never really joined colonial society but, as Evelyn Hu-DeHart points out, had accepted both Jesuit missionaries and employment in Spanish mines on their own terms, which were calculated to preserve Yaqui autonomy and resources. The Yaquis recovered even more autonomy in the eighteenth century with the expulsion of the missionaries, and after independence they saw no particular reason to acknowledge the Mexican state with its demands for taxes and soldiers. Elite struggles over state formation allowed the Yaqui to find temporary allies in defending their autonomy as Sonoran conservatives and centralists were willing to trade Yaqui autonomy for their crucial military support. But the Yaqui had little long-term interest in the formation of the Mexican state.[4]

As the example of the Yaqui suggests, the fragmented nature of elite politics also meant that peasant groups chose different allies depending on regional circumstances.[5] Many peasant groups no doubt considered the risks of active participation in elite civil wars too high, especially where the rewards seemed slim.[6] Rodolfo Pastor stresses this option in his study of the Mixteca Alta, where peasants continued to elect village authorities according to local traditions and, as he puts it, "guarded the most prudent of silences" during elite political struggles.[7] However, peasants could preserve such a neutral stance only if they sought nothing from the state, managed conflicts within their own ranks through local mediation, and avoided confrontations with powerful competitors for local resources. Faced with such competitors peasants were forced into one of two responses: either defy the post-colonial state or search for some interpretation of the new rules that would allow them to defend their autonomy and resources. In the long run the second path has been, and remains, the one most commonly chosen by subaltern groups encountering political change.

The experience of Indian peasants in the late colonial and early national period was in some ways similar to that of their ancestors after the Conquest. The institutional environment changed drastically, and many political practices and discourses peasants had adapted to their needs were no longer looked on with favor by officeholders.[8] Yet both in the early colonial period and after independence Indian peasants rapidly acquired the political knowledge they needed to survive, learning the location of the fissures in the elite which allowed them to acquire allies as well as the repertoires that enabled effective politics. In the sixteenth and seventeenth centuries they played Crown and church officials off against the conquerors and their descendants and became adroit plaintiffs in the Spanish court system, stressing tradition and loyalty to the king even when subversively asserting new claims.[9] In the early nineteenth century Indian peasants mapped and exploited the intricacies of elite factionalism and adapted to their needs both the discourses of post-independence politics and techniques like the use of plans or proclamations to seek out potential allies.[10] In neither case was success guaranteed, but both after the Conquest and after independence many peasant groups preserved and even expanded their resources.[11]

In the introduction and elsewhere this book has pointed out several dichotomies that have impeded our understanding of both peasant politics and state formation. Most works on one or the other stress the gulfs between peasants and elites, the local and the national, and tradition and modernity. The introduction outlined some conceptual tools that can help social scientists bridge those gaps, but it is more important to know how peasants bridged those gaps in practice than it is to know how we might theorize about them. Part of the political experience of Guerrero's peasants is perhaps best summarized as the way in which they devised methods for breaking down those dichotomies. They learned not only how elite politics affected their lives but also how they could form alliances with elite politicians. They discovered ways to effectively present their local concerns to national audiences. They also constructed interpretations of "modern" laws and discourses to defend practices they had earlier defended as "tradition." These purportedly backward rural people displayed remarkable flexibility, subtlety, and astuteness.

The particular vision of the post-independence state pioneered by Juan Alvarez and the peasants of Guerrero left a powerful and lasting legacy. Guerrero was a key site for the elaboration of popular federalism and its successor, popular liberalism.[12] This vision's direct influence in other regions of Mexico helped doom both the French Intervention and the conservative government during the War of the Reform and, perhaps more important, left an imprint on popular political culture in several key Mexican regions. The promise of popular liberalism would surface repeatedly in Mexican history, permeating radical intellectual circles and radiating out from there to working-class as well as rural political groups in hitherto untouched regions.

Juan Alvarez did not single-handedly fashion Guerrero's popular federalism, but he was popular federalism's most eloquent spokesman and most fervent missionary. In addition to his efforts to spread this vision to Morelos, in the 1850s Alvarez sent arms, ammunition, and encouragement to Indian peasants in the Sierra de Puebla, helping to support what became one of the strongest popular liberal movements,[13] and he later provided a young Porfirio Díaz with arms and advice at one of the low points of Díaz's career as a popular liberal hero.[14]

Popular federalism and popular liberalism were not synonymous. As it developed in Guerrero popular federalism was characterized by inclusive definitions of citizenship, an emphasis on local autonomy, and opposition to the wealthy few who were accused of both exploiting Mexico's impoverished majority and conniving to subvert Mexico's independence. During the bloody guerrilla struggles of the late 1850s and 1860s popular liberalism replaced and absorbed popular federalism, adding new elements to federalism's already proven repertoire. Many popular liberal movements seem to have been nourished by interpretations of the Constitution of 1857, including equality before the law, the abolition of compulsory personal service and the draft, and even freedom of commerce.[15] These new traits varied significantly from one region to another. For example, anticlericalism became an important feature of popular liberalism in the Sierra de Puebla but remained muted in Guerrero and Morelos.[16] The Constitution of 1857 took on an almost mythic character in Morelos even as peasants continued to champion the Virgin of Guadalupe.[17]

The persistence of popular liberalism owed a great deal more to its effectiveness on the periphery than it did to any widespread embrace by urban liberal intellectuals and politicians at the center. Historians often rightly emphasize the suspicion and disdain with which many prominent liberals viewed Mexico's dark-skinned rural populace. Moreover, many liberals not only denied that Indian peasants were ready for citizenship but doubted their own ability to carry out reforms or even hold Mexico together without seriously reducing local and even state autonomy. Benito Juárez, Sebastián Lerdo, and later to an even greater degree Porfirio Díaz were de facto centralists,[18] yet Mexican liberalism probably would not have survived in the 1850s and 1860s without the support of Indian peasants who associated liberalism with a fierce defense of local autonomy. Juárez and his collaborators were too politically astute to refuse this aid. At the very least the success of Alvarez in the 1840s and 1850s weakened liberal fears that Mexico's rural population was an undifferentiated dark mass ready to devour the country in a bloody caste war; after Ayutla the rural population appeared both more differentiated and more amenable to political recruitment.

During the decades after Ayutla the centralism of liberal administrations and their deliberate rejection of Indian peasant Mexico forced popular liberalism and with it the legacy of popular federalism into an oppositional if not exactly underground existence. Popular liberalism persisted in two sites during the Porfiriato: the circles of radical urban intellectuals and to a lesser extent the Mexican working class, in which it provided an important set of ideals; and certain rural areas, where it was associated with heroic resistance to the French as well as the defense of local rights. There it was often tied to the leaders who had led that resistance and brokered the tenuous compromises on which popular rights continued to rest. Ironically, even Díaz was able to preserve some of this luster in the Sierra Juárez of his home state of Oaxaca.[19]

This popular liberalism provided a significant element of Díaz's support in the Revolution of Tuxtepec that brought him to power[20] and was a key element of working-class ideology in the Porfiriato. Workers idealized the Reform and the Constitution of 1857, attracted to both the liberals' egalitarian discourse and their armed opposition to foreign exploiters.[21] Popular liberalism surfaced repeatedly during the Mexican Revolution and can be seen in both the radical Partido

Liberal Mexicano and the Sonoran Jacobins. The PLM was founded to make real the promises of La Reforma, and though some of its members eventually embraced anarchism, even this shift was a logical extension of radical liberalism. The Sonorans were products of lay schools that exulted La Reforma.[22] Rural federalist liberalism surfaced in many of the popular movements Alan Knight characterizes as *serrano*, which emphasized local rights and resistance to taxation and in some cases explicitly championed the liberal icons of the nineteenth century.[23] Popular liberalism also exerted a significant influence on both agrarian movements like zapatismo and the intellectual architects of agrarian reform.[24]

After the Mexican Revolution popular liberalism once again was pushed into the background. Post-revolutionary governments were in fact more centralist in taste than their Porfirian predecessor. In some sense the 1920s and 1930s repeated the dynamic of the Porfiriato, in which a victorious political elite that had drawn some of its support from the defense of local autonomy at the periphery undermined that autonomy once it held power in the center. Radical popular liberalism was gradually marginalized, though politicians paid it a great deal of lip service. Even so, the movements of the nineteenth century bestowed on Mexico's subsequent leaders a practical legacy: they realized that in Mexico even an authoritarian state had to be inclusive. It had to give regional elites real power, bargain effectively with popular groups, and provide for political mobility if not social equity.

Mexican opposition groups still champion many of the features of popular liberalism, and local autonomy remains a vital standard for Mexican opposition groups. Demands for municipal autonomy and effective suffrage still surface today in the discourse of both peasants who pursue their struggles within the ruling Partido Revolucionario Institucional and those that turn to other groups on both the Right and the Left.[25] Local government continues to be a crucial issue in rural Mexico and municipal palaces a focal point of conflict, as can be seen in the frequent occupations of municipal palaces after disputed elections. In December 1993 one of the first proclamations of the Zapatista Army of National Liberation in Chiapas not only argued for the "just application of the Reform laws" but ordered rebel commanders to permit "the people in the liberated area the right to freely and democratically elect their own administrative authorities."[26]

Popular liberalism remains an ideology of opposition in Mexico. Its persistence throughout more than 100 years of violent struggle and gradual betrayal suggests its unusual effectiveness in expressing the aspirations of Mexico's working classes. What popular liberalism has provided above all is an ideology capable of defending the rights of the poor to land, decent wages, just taxes, and local democracy within the framework of liberal republicanism that Mexico's political elites have used to justify their power. Popular liberalism is often nurtured and spread by the very means that the Mexican state uses to promote its official ideology—primary school textbooks, civic ceremonies, street names and the like—making this vision an unusually insidious enemy of the powerful. Popular liberalism's argument for social and political equity is a haunting challenge to take seriously the ideals of post-Enlightenment liberal nation-states.

Reference Matter

Notes

Introduction

1. B. Anderson, p. 15.
2. See de Tocqueville, esp. pp. 68, 77–78, 137; Tilly, "Reflections" and "War-Making"; Breuilly, pp. 44–45. See also Poggi; Therborn, "Travail," p. 97.
3. For just a few examples, see de Carvalho; Oszlak, "Historical Formation" and *La formación*; Sinkin, *Mexican Reform*; González, ed., *La formación*.
4. Corrigan and Sayer, pp. 2–5.
5. Breuilly, pp. 44–45.
6. Corrigan and Sayer, esp. pp. 2–5; Alonso, pp. 223–24; Breuilly, pp. 45, 50–52; Gailey and Patterson, p. 8; Sahlins; Smith, *Theories*, pp. 170–71, and "State-Making," pp. 243–44, 258.
7. The quotation is from Moore, p. 480. See also Skocpol, p. 193. John Coatsworth, applying some of Moore's ideas to Mexico, is more ambivalent on this point. Coatsworth, "Los orígenes," pp. 210–17 and 221–23.
8. Skocpol, p. 193. See also E. Weber, esp. p. 242.
9. Tilly, "Reflections," pp. 22–24, 61, "War-Making," p. 183, and *Coercion*, pp. 99–103.
10. Tilly, "War-Making," p. 183.
11. Corrigan and Sayer, esp. p. 8.
12. Bright and Harding, p. 5; Gailey, p. 36.
13. Wolf, *Peasant Wars*, p. 295.
14. A few examples published since the 1980s include Arrom; Costeloe, *Central Republic*; González Navarro, *Anatomía*; Green; Ortiz Escamilla; Rodríguez O., "From Royal Subject"; Sims, *Expulsion*; Soto; Stevens; Vázquez, "La crisis"; and Vázquez Mantecón.

15. See Meyer Cosío; Tenenbaum, *Politics*; Potash; Thomson, "Protectionism" and *Puebla*; D. Walker.

16. See Brading, *Los orígenes*, pp. 110, 114; Bushnell and Macauley, pp. 47, 52; Safford, pp. 78–79, 101; D. Walker, p. 162. For Peru in the same period, see Gootenberg, *Between Silver*, p. 154.

17. Brading, *Los orígenes*, pp. 109–13; Bushnell and Macauley, pp. 62, 69–70; Hale, pp. 18, 303–6; Hamnett, "El federalismo," p. 310; Tenenbaum, *Politics*, pp. 42, 89; Vázquez, "El ejército," pp. 320–22, and "Iglesia," p. 212.

18. Annino and Filippi, p. 424; Brading, *Los orígenes*, pp. 101, 109, 130–37.

19. Andrews, pp. 128–29; Bushnell and Macauley, p. 35; Costeloe, *Primera República*, p. 438.

20. Annino, pp. 7–8; Guerra, 2: 325, 331.

21. Mejía Fernández, p. 75; Meyer, *Problemas*, pp. 30–31; Reina, "Las luchas," p. 22. This is largely the thesis proposed by Powell in "Los liberales" and "Priests."

22. Examples are myriad. One of the most prominent is Tutino, *From Insurrection*.

23. For examples see Migdahl, p. 21; E. Weber, pp. 242–43; Wolf, *Peasant Wars*, pp. xi, 295; Van Young, "Moving Towards Revolt," pp. 203–4. For critiques of these ideas see Guha, p. 46; Ileto, p. 7; Stern, "New Approaches," pp. 9–14; Taylor, "Between Global Process," p. 153.

24. Taylor, *Drinking*, pp. 113–52; Florescano, *Memoria*, p. 181; Katz, "Rural Uprisings," p. 80, and "Rural Rebellions," pp. 531–32.

25. Coatsworth, "Patterns," p. 55; Katz, "Rural Rebellions," pp. 531–53; Reina, "Las luchas," pp. 15–16, and "Historia," p. 41.

26. Tilly, "Social Movements," pp. 307–9.

27. For some examples see Borah, p. 412; Carmagnani, *El regreso*, pp. 231–36; Chavez Orosco, p. 46; Farriss, *Maya Society*, pp. 355–66, 375–88; Lira González, *Comunidades*, pp. 202, 207, 229, 292; von Mentz, pp. 57, 65, 77, 144; Pastor, *Campesinos*, pp. 420–22, 447–48, 513–14; Tutino, "Peasants," pp. 237–38.

28. For Mexico see Coatsworth, "Los orígenes," esp. pp. 210–17, 221–23, and "Patterns," pp. 59–61; de la Garza, pp. 44–46, 51; Katz, "Introduction," p. 16; Meyer, "Reflexiones"; Nugent, p. 1; Semo, "Las revoluciones," pp. 279–98, and "Las clases," pp. 59–73. For the Andes see Stern, "Introduction to Part III," pp. 214–17; and C. Walker, "El estudio," pp. 190–91.

29. Examples for Mexico include Mallon, "Peasants and State Formation" and *Peasant and Nation*; Thomson, "Popular Aspects," "Movilización," and "Bulwarks." For the Andes see Mallon, "Nationalist and Antistate Coalitions"; Platt, "Andean Experience" and "Estado tributario." Gootenberg has examined these connections in the earlier period for Peru but only in the urban setting. See Gootenberg, "Social Origins."

30. For a longer and different set of relevant dichotomies see Thomson, "Popular Aspects," p. 288.

31. This point has been made by many historians. See, e.g., von Mentz,

pp. 145–46; Gootenberg, "Beleaguered Liberals," p. 84, and *Between Silver,* pp. 76, 87, 134.

32. These discussions are generally traced to Gramsci, esp. pp. 12–13.

33. Genovese, p. 608.

34. The quotation is from Scott, p. 336, n. 69.

35. For selective reconstruction see Thompson, "Moral Economy," pp. 79, 98. For differential meanings see Corrigan and Sayer, pp. 6, 197.

36. Scott, pp. 41–43.

37. Scott, pp. 333–40.

38. Examples include Brading, *Los orígenes,* pp. 15–16; Flores Galindo, "In Search," pp. 194–95; Florescano, *Memoria,* pp. 299, 306; Gruzinski, *Man-Gods,* p. 154.

39. See, e.g., Ileto's excellent analysis of the Filipino independence movement. Ileto, esp. pp. 2–9, 13, 23, 85–102, 139–44, 215–25, 230–31, 257, 318. The process is central to Gould's analysis of Nicaraguan agrarian struggles. In particular see his general comments on pp. 6–7. See also Platt, "Andean Experience," pp. 286, 314–15; Ranger, p. 227; Salomon, pp. 162–63.

40. Some examples from recent studies of Andean cases include A. Guerrero, pp. 321, 325; Hünefeldt, p. 389; Moscoso, p. 482.

41. Baker, "Introduction," xxiii; Furet, p. 23.

42. On this point see Baker, "Introduction," xii; Thompson, *Making,* p. 343. For Spain and Spanish America see Chevalier, "La emancipación," pp. 153–56; Lafaye, pp. 118, 123, 302; Villoro, pp. 48–50, 99–109.

43. See Gould, pp. 133–81; Thompson, *Making,* pp. 551–52, 760–61.

44. For an extreme example see Bonilla, p. 224. Bonilla is actually voicing an assumption that runs through much of the literature on nations and nationalism by scholars from several different interpretative traditions. See, e.g., E. Weber or B. Anderson, p. 74.

45. The quotation is from Breuilly, p. 30. This point of view is implicit in the definition of nations as "imagined communities" in B. Anderson, p. 15. Those still unconvinced might recall the U.S. Army's first television recruiting commercials of the post–Gulf War "New World Order." In these epics young men and women rode tanks in the deserts of the Middle East while a rock singer repeatedly sang the phrase "My Home Town."

46. De Tocqueville, p. 51. See Mallon, "Nationalist and Antistate Coalitions," pp. 240, 266, for some examples of how these connections worked in an Andean case.

47. In this light Bushnell insightfully makes the connection between electoral norms and the legitimation of the nation-state; however, he leaves aside the eminently local nature of elections (especially indirect ones) and electoral practices. See D. Bushnell, esp. p. 616.

Chapter 1

1. Carmagnani, "Los olvidos," p. 90; Coatsworth, "Obstacles," p. 94; Pietschmann, "Estado," p. 428; Guardino and Walker, pp. 14–17.

2. Salvucci, p. 40; Stein, pp. 21–27; Kicza, pp. 93–94.

3. Tutino, "Creole Mexico," pp. 17–19, 29, 96, 98; Kicza, pp. 16–25, 32–33, 51–53; Liehr, 1: 62–63; Stein, pp. 21–27; Spalding, "Introduction," p. xv.

4. *Cofradías* or "confraternities" were associations set up to organize and finance religious celebrations and ceremonies. For the ties of the dominant class to cofradías, see Kicza, p. 59; Lavrin; Mérida, p. 227.

5. Villoro, pp. 16–17; Kicza, pp. 16–17, 51–53, 147; Spalding, "Colonial Indian," pp. 63–64. The four most important works on the class as a whole include Brading, *Miners,* esp. pp. 95–128; Ladd; Tutino, "Creole Mexico"; and Kicza.

6. Stein.

7. Cervantes Bello, p. 58; Tutino, *From Insurrection,* p. 108. For a comparison to Peru see Flores Galindo, *Aristocracia,* pp. 15–92.

8. Kicza, pp. 96–99, 241; Salvucci, p. 10; Thomson, "Cotton Textile Industry," pp. 248–53, 261, 277–88; Tutino, *From Insurrection,* p. 134; Van Young, "Sectores," pp. 108–9, 112; Hamnett, "Las élites," 294. Tutino calls this class the "provincial elite"; Hamnett refers to it as the provincial or professional bourgeoisie. See Tutino, *From Insurrection,* p. 100; Hamnett, *Roots,* p. 19.

9. Tutino, *From Insurrection,* pp. 105–6; Hamill, pp. 2–3.

10. Most recently, Cardenas, p. 4, minimizes market participation. The evidence against this position seems overwhelming. For generalizations see Pietschmann, "Agricultura," p. 73; Salvucci, p. 20; Spalding, "La red," p. 115; Tutino, "Creole Mexico," p. 287; Liehr, 1: 28. For an Andean comparison see Larson, *Colonialism,* pp. 202–9. For various areas of Guerrero see Cervantes-Delgado, p. 47; Morin, pp. 37–38; and the excellent Dehouve, "El pueblo," pp. 86–102. For peasants marketing grain see Van Young, *Hacienda,* pp. 86–88; and Carmagnani, *El regreso,* pp. 144–48.

11. Basic descriptions abound in the literature. See Carmagnani, *El regreso,* pp. 163–68; Hamnett, *Roots,* pp. 11, 78; von Mentz, pp. 97, 115, 127; Morin, pp. 165, 176, 185; Pastor, "El repartimiento," pp. 206, 215–16, "Estructura," p. 426, and *Campesinos,* pp. 153, 155, 290–91; Pietschmann, "Agricultura," p. 77; Sánchez, *El suroeste,* pp. 95–96; Thomson, "Cotton Textile Industry," pp. 179–82.

12. For the repartimiento in Guerrero see AGN, Civil, vol. 510, exp. 1, fols. 26–26v; vol. 991, exp. 4, fols. 6–7v, 28; Dehouve, "El pueblo," pp. 87–101; AGN, Tributos, vol. 34, exp. 7, fols. 59v–60; AGN, Consulado, vol. 33, exp. 4, fols. 60–61v; Kicza, p. 95. For a case involving maize see AGN, Indios, vol. 164, fol. 203.

13. For general observations see Hamnett, "Las élites," p. 280; Kicza, pp. 82–85, 90; von Mentz, p. 115; Pastor, *Campesinos,* p. 315. For ledgers and other documents demonstrating how this system permeated economic space in Guerrero see AGN, Civil, vol. 502-2, exp. 1, fols. 3–11v; vol. 703, exp. 7; vol. 979, exp. 5, fols. 83v–112v; AGN, Consulado, vol. 14, exp. 6; vol. 33, exp. 1, fols. 1–2v, 74–74v; vol. 33, exp. 3, fols. 19v–33v, 56–56v; vol. 33, exp. 4, fols. 60–61v; AGN, Judicial, vol. 37, exp. 3, fols. 54–56v; AGN, Vínculos, vol. 74, exp. 10, fols. 7–11v.

14. Population data on the area is available in AGN, Padrones, vol. 16, fols. 164, 212; vol. 17, fol. 182; AGN, Tributos, vol. 54, exp. 21, fol. 296; and Ortega, *La imprenta*, pp. 1–2. For the textile industry see AGN, Ex-indiferente de Alcabalas, Chilapa, caja. 4, exp. 15; Dehouve, "El pueblo," 98; Guevara Ramírez, pp. 34–35.

15. One of the largest haciendas in the area, San Sebastián Buenavista, was sold for 20,000 pesos in 1781 (AGN, Ex-indiferente de Alcabalas, Chilapa, caja. 2, exp. 2). This amount is extremely small compared to those common in other parts of New Spain, where haciendas were worth two to ten times as much. For the vast literature on Mexican haciendas see Van Young, "Mexican Rural History."

16. AGN, Ex-indiferente de Alcabalas, Chilapa, caja. 2, exps. 1, 2, 11; caja. 3, exps. 2, 11, 12; caja. 4, exp. 1; caja. 5, exp. 8; AGN, Civil, vol. 502-2, exp. 1, fol. 11v; AGN, Vínculos, vol. 74, exp. 10, fols. 5–7; vol. 75, exp. 6, fols. 35v–38v; ASRA, Mun. Quechultenango, S. Juan Colotlipa 23: 1206; AGN, Padrones, vol. 16, fol. 108; vol. 17, fol. 1.

17. "Tierras de repartimiento" were the community lands held by individual peasant families in usufruct and farmed independently. "Bienes de comunidad" were lands owned by the village whose proceeds were used for communal expenses. Often these lands were rented out although sometimes they were farmed by the village.

18. As we will see, it is often difficult to distinguish cofradías (see n. 4) from bienes de comunidad. For cofradías in this area, see AGN, Indios, vol. 78, exp. 9, fols. 189–202v; vol. 76, exp. 2.

19. AGN, Historia, vol. 578b, fols. 66f–80v. For the occupational structures of the two areas see AGN, Padrones, vol. 16, fols. 107–221; for the 1791 census, AGN, Padrones, vol. 18. Note that this census did not include Indians.

20. AGN, Historia, vol. 122, exp. 2, fols. 38–44v; vol. 122, exp. 5, fol. 165; AGN, Industria y Comercio, vol. 2, exp. 8, fol. 162; AGN, Historia, vol. 498, exp. 7, fol. 9; Aguirre Anaya and Carabarin Gracia, p. 131; AGN, Real Hacienda, Administración General de Alcabalas, caja. 56, exp. 5; caja. 40, exp. 2; AGN, Ex-indiferente de Alcabalas, Chilapa, caja. 4, exp. 6; caja. 4, exp. 15; AGN, Historia, vol. 578b, fols. 66f–80v; AGN, Vínculos, vol. 74, exp. 10, fols. 7–11. This is an unusual detailed account of several trading trips. This kind of putting-out system was common in textile production in New Spain. See Liehr, 1: 36; Morin, pp. 298–99; Pastor, "Estructura," p. 456; Salvucci, pp. 10–14, 28–30; Thomson, "Cotton Textile Industry," pp. 179–82.

21. AGN, Civil, vol. 502-2, exp. 1, fols. 3–3v; AGN, Archivo Histórico de Hacienda, vol. 432, exp. 4.

22. AGN, Historia, vol. 74, fol. 413.

23. "De razón" was a colonial term that included Spanish, Creoles, and mestizos. Dehouve, "El pueblo," p. 94; AGN, Ex-indiferente de Alcabalas, Tlapa, caja. 4, exp. 11; AGN, Padrones, vol. 21, fols. 1–2, 94; AGN, Tributos, vol. 34, exp. 7.

24. Dehouve has recently published a brilliant study of the area's economy in the late colonial period to which the preceding paragraph owes much. Dehouve, "El pueblo," esp. pp. 89–101.

228 *Notes to Pages 22–25*

25. Dehouve, "El pueblo," p. 99; AGN, Ex-indiferente de Alcabalas, Tlapa, caja. 4, exp. 11. Among the artisans' products were a wide variety of cotton textiles. Pavía Guzmán, *Tlappan*, pp. 15–17; Dehouve, "El pueblo," pp. 97–98. See also Dehouve, "Las separaciones," pp. 379–80; Commons de la Rosa, p. 64; AGN, Tierras, vol. 1368, exp. 3, fol. 18.

26. AGN, Archivo Histórico de Hacienda, vol. 672, exp. 3; AGN, Intendencias, vol. 59 (1787); AGN, Tierras, vol. 2433, exp. 6, fols. 3–5; AGN, Indios, vol. 84, exp. 17, fols. 357–76; AGN, Criminal, vol. 5, exp. 2; AGN, Indios, vol. 80, exp. 2, fols. 30–81; AGN, Indios, vol. 78, exp. 4, fols. 86v–96v; ANEG, caja. 36, exps. 356, 357. See AGN, Civil, vol. 979, exp. 5, fols. 83v–112v, for a store inventory from the area.

27. AGN, Tierras, vol. 2828, exp. 3, fol. 2; AGN, Tabacos, vol. 410, exp. 8, fols. 101–101v; AGN, Historia, vol. 122, exp.2, fol. 101; Salvucci, p. 29; Morin, pp. 24, 66–67, 120–21, 148. It should be noted that the only Indian villages that remained, Tecpan and Atoyac, also primarily produced cotton. AGN, Indios, vol. 69, exp. 359, fols. 273v–274; vol. 79, exp. 11, fols. 239–40.

28. AGN, Archivo Histórico de Hacienda, vol. 2166, exp. 4; AGN, Civil, vol. 502-2, exp. 1, fols. 3–3v; AGN, Consulado, vol. 195, exp. 2, fol. 65; AGN, Real Hacienda, Administración General de Alcabalas, caja. 25; caja. 40, exp. 2; AGN, Ex-indiferente de Alcabalas, Acapulco, caja. 4, exps. 3, 8, caja. 16, exp. 7; caja. 19, exp. 7; caja. 21, exp. 2; Morin, pp. 172–77; AGN, Tierras, vol. 2830, exp. 34, fol. 7v; AGN, Vínculos, vol. 74, exp. 10, fols. 7–11v. Until the Bourbon reforms the area was actually part of the Alcaldía Mayor of León. AGN, Alcaldes Mayores, vol. 8, fols. 82–86. For trade with the Bajío see Morin, pp. 123, 168, 172–74, 181.

29. AGN, Bienes Nacionales, vol. 403, exp. 8; AGN, Padrones, vol. 16, fols. 220–430; AGN, Intendencias, vol. 3, fol. 105; AGN, Archivo Histórico de Hacienda, vol. 404, exp. 17; AGN, Civil, vol. 241, exp. 12, fols. 338–39; vol. 1533, exp. 11, fols. 3–4; AGN, Indios, vol. 76, exp. 5; AGN, Tributos, vol. 25, exp. 15, fol. 308; Salcedo Guerrero, pp. 10–11.

30. AGN, Archivo Histórico de Hacienda, vol. 130, exp. 21, vol. 633, exp. 39; AGN, Padrones, vol. 16, fol. 215; AGN, Ex-indiferente de Alcabalas, Acapulco, caja. 2, exp. 1; caja. 14, exp. 4; caja. 15, exp. 4; caja. 16, exp. 3; Salcedo Guerrero, p. 16; Kicza, pp. 66–68, 71; AGN, Real Hacienda, Administración General de Alcabalas, caja. 113; AGN, Civil, vol. 1610, exp. 9; Cervantes-Delgado, "Viajeros," p. 59; Dehouve, "El pueblo," p. 98.

31. Aguirre Beltrán, p. 57; Dehouve, "El pueblo," p. 98; AGN, Alcaldes Mayores, vol. 12, fol. 364; AGN, Historia, vol. 74, fol. 414; AGN, Indios, vol. 60, exp. 55, fol. 86v; AGN, Padrones, vol. 18, fols. 221, 305; AGN, Tributos, vol. 34, exp. 7, fol. 160, vol. 54, exp. 14, fols. 194–99. For a succinct general description see AGN, Historia, vol. 578b, fols. 85–93v.

32. AGN, Alhóndigas, vol. 8, exp. 10; exp. 11; vol. 10, exp. 3, fols. 228–43; AGN, Civil, vol. 472, fols. 98–103; AGN, Consulado, vol. 33, exp. 1, fols. 1–2v, 20–27; exp. 4, fols. 60–61.

33. Baker, "Introduction," p. xii.

34. MacLachlan, pp. 21–28; McAlister, pp. 349–70; Spalding, "¿Quienes son los indios?" p. 151; García Argañarás, p. 31.

35. Anna, "Spain," p. 256; MacLachlan, p. 17; Morse, p. 141.

36. Von Mentz, pp. 88, 95–96; Carmagnani, *El regreso*, p. 13.

37. Borah, pp. 223–26, 237, 304–8, 410; Stern, *Peru's Indian Peoples*, pp. 114–37.

38. Katz, "Rural Uprisings," pp. 77–79, 83–92.

39. For various cases in Guerrero see AGN, Bienes Nacionales, vol. 873, exp. 161; AGN, Civil, vol. 214, exp. 3, fols. 1–15; AGN, Historia, vol. 501, exp. 5, fols. 1–2. Note that the need to morally supervise and collect taxes from Indians was the primary motivator behind the creation of villages through *reducción* and *congregación* in the early colonial period.

40. Pastor, *Campesinos*, p. 210. AGN, Archivo Histórico de Hacienda, vol. 403, exp. 3.

41. AGN, Indios, vol. 70, exp. 147, fol. 168.

42. See Van Young, "Millenium," p. 391, for an example of a republic filling this function.

43. Gibson, p. 36; Dehouve, "Las separaciones," pp. 380–83. For a few examples see AGN, Indios, vol. 70, exp. 225, fol. 249; vol. 70, exp. 238, fols. 263–64; vol. 71, exp. 75, fols. 101v–103.

44. Gibson, p. 44; AGN, Indios, vol. 60, exp. 102, fols. 147–49; vol. 71, exp. 13, fols. 14–15.

45. AGN, Indios, vol. 70, exp. 147, fol. 168.

46. AGN, Indios, vol. 71, exp. 13, fols. 14–15; AGN, Criminal, vol. 5, exp. 8, fols. 236–39.

47. Santos Carrera and Alvarez Hernández, *Historia*, p. 17. See AGN, Tierras, vol. 1099, exp. 1, for a case between two villages that remained unresolved after 25 years of litigation.

48. For the varied disputes over elections in Guerrero, see AGN, Indios, vol. 60, exp. 187; vol. 64, exp. 203, fols. 337–38; vol. 64, exp. 212, fols. 349–52; vol. 65, exp. 168, fols. 79–79v; vol. 66, exp. 11, fols. 17–18v; vol. 71, exp. 57, fols. 76–76v; vol. 71, exp. 173, fols. 232–33v; vol. 100, exp. 38. For some tips on handling factionalism in villages, see Flon's views in AGN, Indios, vol. 70, exp. 147, fol. 168.

49. See Van Young, "Conflict," pp. 55–79; Dehouve, "Las separaciones," pp. 379–404; Thomson, "Agrarian Conflict"; Ducey, "From Village Riot"; Taylor, "Conflict"; Buve, pp. 5–6. For evidence from Guerrero see the list of 1825 tax payments in AGN, Ayuntamientos, vol. 236. Taxpayers were assessed one day's income per trimester. Individuals' incomes were apparently either self-declared or assessed by local officials. In many Indian villages the amounts paid varied greatly. In the isolated, probably monolingual Nahua village of Oapan, for instance, 225 villagers paid 1.5 reales, 27 paid 2 reales, and 14 paid more than 2 reales.

50. Chavez Orosco, pp. 13–14; Miranda and Zavala, pp. 105, 146–49; von Mentz, pp. 94–95; Carmagnani, "Local Governments," pp. 107–8, 117–19, and *El regreso*, pp. 185–95, 203.

51. AGN, Criminal, vol. 320, exp. 2, fols. 22–47v; AGN, Criminal, vol. 320, exp. 5, fols. 159–300; AGN, Criminal, vol. 320, exp. 6, fols. 309–341v; AGN, Criminal, vol. 321, exp. 1, fols. 11–149v; AGN, Criminal, vol. 321, exp. 2,

fols. 199–243; AGN, Criminal, vol. 326, exp. 4, fols. 59–181v; AGN, Criminal, vol. 356, fols. 214–228v; AGN, Criminal, vol. 705, exp. 18, fols. 166–205v; AGN, Civil, vol. 1661.

52. AGN, Criminal, vol. 326, exp. 11, fols. 201; AGN, Criminal, vol. 320, exp. 5, fols. 177–79.

53. O'Phelan, pp. 175–287, gives a convincing argument about how a different set of Bourbon fiscal policies led to Tupac Amaru in late-eighteenth-century Peru.

54. AGN, Alcaldes Mayores, vol. 4, fol. 36; AGN, Tributos, vol. 24, exp. 7, fols. 64–145; AGN, Tributos, vol. 34, exp. 1, fols. 1–12; AGN, Tributos, vol. 34, exp. 2, fols. 48–56; AGN, Tributos, vol. 34, exp. 7, fols. 163–73; Aguirre Beltrán, p. 61.

55. Marichal, pp. 904–5. For donations and loans by the peasants of Guerrero see AGN, Archivo Histórico de Hacienda, vol. 396, exp. 3; AGN, Ex-indiferente de Alcabalas, Tlapa, caja. 4, exp. 12; exp. 13; Calderón Quijano, pp. 63, 67; Miranda and Zavala, p. 157; Tortella Casares, pp. 353–54.

56. AGN, Archivo Histórico de Hacienda, vol. 404, exp. 17; vol. 405, exp. 6; vol. 405, exp. 7.

57. AGN, Bienes Nacionales, vol. 585, exp. 5; AGN, Clero Regular y Secular, vol. 164, exp. 14, fols. 470v–471v; ANEG, caja. 36, exps. 356, 357; Brading, "Tridentine Catholicism," pp. 12–13; Carmagnani, *El regreso,* pp. 133, 141; Chance and Taylor, pp. 8–9; Dehouve, "El pueblo," pp. 95, 99; Pietschmann, "Agricultura," p. 74.

58. AGN, Clero Regular y Secular, vol. 75, fols. 485–86; vol. 120, exp. 11, fols. 358–61; AGN, Criminal, vol. 705, exp. 18, fols. 166, 185, 190v, 204v–205v; AGN, Criminal, vol. 3216, exp. 4, fols. 59–59v; AGN, Historia, vol. 437, exp. 14, fols. 1–13; Dehouve, "El pueblo," p. 95; Farriss, *Crown,* p. 93; Brading, "Tridentine Catholicism," pp. 11–13; Taylor, "Banditry," p. 235.

59. Carmagnani, *El regreso,* pp. 124–25, 133; Florescano, *Memoria,* pp. 243–44; Vega, p. 914; AGN, Archivo Histórico de Hacienda, vol. 404, exp. 6; vol. 404, exp. 7; vol. 404, exp. 9; vol. 404, exp. 16; vol. 405; AGN, Indios, vol. 73, exp. 8, fols. 135–216v; AGN, Tierras, vol. 1385, exp. 3.

60. An example is the Indians of San Miguel Totolapán, who in 1795 asserted that "Our ancestors provided the funds and we have conserved them. . . . We Indians are those who have done this: we Indians are those who have husbanded and increased the funds: we Indians those who have always cared for them and there is no reason that we the owners be deprived of the funds." AGN, Indios, vol. 69, exp. 399, fols. 310v.

61. AGN, Historia, vol. 437, exp. 14, fol. 1; AGN, Indios, vol. 69, exp. 399, fol. 311. Note that priests sometimes expressed similar skepticism about the management of Indian officials. AGN, Bienes Nacionales, vol. 535, exp. 2.

62. AGN, Indios, vol. 69, exp. 399, fols. 311–311v.

63. AGN, Civil, vol. 246, exp. 7, fols. 306–309; AGN, Clero Regular y Secular, vol. 72, exp. 16, fols. 297–303; AGN, Indios, vol. 69, exp. 399, fol. 311; vol. 71, exp. 196, fols. 289–291; Chance and Taylor, pp. 10, 13; Gruzinski, "La 'segunda aculteración,'" pp. 175–82.

64. For the often conflictive relations between villagers and their tenants see AGN, Consulado, vol. 38, exp. 9, fols. 5–25; AGN, Indios, vol. 67, exp. 295, fols. 327–28; AGN, Tierras, vol. 1393, exp. 1, fols. 20–20v; ANEG caja. 36, exp. 356; Dehouve, "El pueblo," p. 94; Sánchez, El suroeste, pp. 4, 54, 56; and Santos Carrera and Alvarez Hernández, Las luchas, pp. 28–45.

65. The documents do not provide good data on the economic relationship between rich peasants and poor peasants. For this reason some of the motivations described above are based on insights derived from a number of excellent works on the contemporary peasantry in both Mexico and other parts of the world, including de la Peña; Popkin; Schryer; Scott; and Warman, We Come to Object.

66. AGN, Criminal, vol. 181, exp. 8, fols. 121–24; vol. 582, exp. 2, fol. 300; vol. 705, exp. 18, fol. 166.

67. AGN, Indios, vol. 71, exp. 185, fols. 262–265v.

68. ANEG, caja. 26, exp. 356; caja, 36, exp. 356; AGN, Tierras, vol. 1393, exp. 1, fols. 20–20v; vol. 1376, exp. 2, fols. 5v–12v. It seems possible that he was lending royal accounts out for interest or even investing the money in his own commercial operations. AGN, Archivo Histórico de Hacienda, vol. 396, exp. 3.

69. AGN, Tierras, vol. 1390, exp. 2, fols. 23v, 26–28, 30.

70. AGN, Indios, vol. 71, exp. 189, fols. 270–71; exp. 201, fol. 307; AGN, Tierras, vol. 1393, exp. 1, fols. 26v, 52–52v.

71. AGN, Tierras, vol. 1390, exp. 2, fols. 20–20v; AGN, Criminal, vol. 326, fols. 221–29. Quote is from fol. 225.

72. AGN, Tierras, vol. 1390, exp. 2, fols. 8–19v.

73. AGN, Tierras, vol. 1390, exp. 2, fols. 21–25.

74. Van Young, "Millenium."

75. AGN, Tierras, vol. 1390, exp. 2, fol. 23v.

76. AGN, Indios, vol. 71, exp. 201, fols. 300–310; AGN, Tierras, vol. 1390, exp. 2, fols. 31–40. See also Chapter 2.

77. On the rise in the number of land disputes see Santos Carrera and Alvarez Hernández, Historia, p. 71. The statistical result was compiled from an unpublished index of disputes in AGN, Tierras, graciously provided by Jonathan Amith, an anthropologist working on colonial land tenure in the area.

78. AGN, Tierras, vol. 1287, exp. 6; vol. 1406, exp. 11, fols. 1–4.

79. For examples of all of the above, see AGN, Indios, vol. 71, exp. 158, fols. 214v–215v; AGN, Tierras, vol. 1264, exp. 5, fols. 1–8; vol. 1406, exp. 3, fols. 12–12v; AGN, Tributos, vol. 53, exp. 17, fols. 253–55.

80. Petates were reed mats. They were used to carry many products on muleback.

81. Dehouve, "El pueblo," p. 97; AGN, Alcaldes Mayores, vol. 11, fols. 358v–362v; AGN, Archivo Histórico de Hacienda, vol. 447, exp. 14; AGN, Civil, vol. 93, exp. 14, fols. 443–90; AGN, Civil, vol. 189, exp. 2, fols. 1–18; AGN, Civil, vol. 1501, exp. 17, fol. 40; AGN, Clero Regular y Secular, vol. 59, exp. 3, fols. 40–190; AGN, Clero Regular y Secular, vol. 195, exp. 12, fols.

211–212; AGN, Consulado, vol. 60, fols. 1–44; AGN, Indios, vol. 66, exp. 164, fols. 202–205v; AGN, Indios, vol. 71, exp. 119, fols. 163v–164; AGN, Intendencias, vol. 62; AGN, Judicial, vol. 35, exp. 1, fols. 3–6; AGN, Tierras, vol. 2830, exp. 34, fols. 7v–18v; AGN, Tributos, vol. 34, exp. 2, fols. 35–56; AGN, Tributos, vol. 34, exp. 7, fol. 166.

82. Hamnett, *Roots*, p. 78; Timmons, *Morelos*, p. 29; and Chance, pp. 200–201.

83. Pastor, *Campesinos*, pp. 157–58.

84. Kicza, pp. 94, 95; Pastor, "El repartimiento," p. 233; Pastor, *Campesinos*, p. 285; Stein, pp. 4–17; MacLachlan, pp. 116–18.

85. For some thoughts on this see Morin, pp. 201–2; Pastor, *Campesinos*, pp. 102, 192, 195; Spalding, "Introduction," p. viii.

86. AGN, Alcaldes Mayores, vol. 11, 358v–362v; AGN, Archivo Histórica de Hacienda, vol. 447, exp. 14; AGN, Civil, vol. 93, exp. 14, fols. 443–90; vol. 189, exp. 2, fols. 1–18; vol. 1501, exp. 17, fol. 40; AGN, Clero Regular y Secular, vol. 59, exp. 3, fols. 40–190; AGN, Clero Regular y Secular, vol. 195, exp. 12, fols. 211–12; AGN, Consulado, vol. 60, fols. 1–44; AGN, Indios, vol. 66, exp. 164, fols. 202–205v; vol. 71, exp. 119, fols. 163v–164; AGN, Intendencias, vol. 62; AGN, Judicial, vol. 35, exp. 1, fols. 3–6; AGN, Padrones, 17, fols. 289–290v; AGN, Tierras, vol. 2830, exp. 34, fols. 7v–18v; AGN, Tributos, vol. 34, exp. 2, fols. 35–56; exp. 7, fol. 166; Pastor, *Campesinos*, pp. 275, 280; Pietschmann, "Agricultura," p. 80.

87. AGN, Historia, vol. 498, exp. 7, fols. 1–24. It is by no means clear that the subdelegado in this case extracted a profit, for the only documents available are his own reports. If he did, however, he had improved on the old repartimiento by financing production with capital legally borrowed from the community's own funds!

88. AGN, Tierras, vol. 2830, exp. 34, fol. 7v; AGN, Tributos, vol. 34, exp. 2, fol. 36; AGN, Indios, vol. 66, exp. 164, fol. 203v.

89. AGN, Indios, vol. 66, exp. 164, fol. 203; AGN, Indios, vol. 71, fols. 163v–164.

90. Carmagnani, *El regreso*, pp. 171–74; Chance and Taylor, p. 16.

91. The use of village elites as intermediaries and the connection to election disputes has been noted by scholars for other areas. See Chance, pp. 200–201; Larson, "Caciques," p. 207; Pastor, "El repartimiento," p. 214; Pastor, *Campesinos*, p. 156.

92. Thompson's comments on pre-industrial England also apply here. Thompson, "Moral Economy," pp. 134–35.

93. Morin, pp. 201–2.

94. For economic conditions on the coast see AGN, Ex-indiferente de Alcabalas, Acapulco, caja. 4, exp. 8; caja. 16, exp. 7; caja. 19, exp. 7; caja. 21, exp. 2; AGN, Real Hacienda, Administración General de Alcabalas, caja. 25; Morin, pp. 172–77; AGN, Tierras, vol. 2830, exp. 34, fol. 7v. For the determinants of conditions in the volatile textile market see Thomson, *Puebla*, pp. 35, 42.

95. This formulation owes much to conversations with Ducey and his essay "Peasant Participation."

96. Salvucci, p. 133; Santos Carrera and Alvarez Hernández, *Las luchas*, p. 12; Morin, pp. 137, 201–2; Genovese, p. 178.

97. AGN, Indios, vol. 58, exp. 220, fol. 340v; AGN, Indios, vol. 71, exp. 158, fols. 214v–215v; Santos Carrera and Alvarez Hernández, *Historia*, 67.

98. This dynamic is similar to that discussed in Genovese's work on slaves.

99. For an example see the case of Ajuchitlán discussed above, esp. AGN, Criminal, vol. 320, exp. 5, fol. 279; AGN, Criminal, vol. 321, exp. 1, fol. 22; AGN, Criminal, vol. 326, exp. 4, fols. 84–85v; AGN, Criminal, vol. 356, fol. 214.

Chapter 2

1. "Outsiders" here include practically anyone not an Indian peasant. Included are rural priests, rancheros, muleteers, small merchants, hacendados, military leaders, and a wide variety of other rural people.

2. Archer, "Banditry," pp. 61, 68, 71; Hamnett, "Economic and Social Dimension," pp. 13–14, and *Roots*, pp. 74–75; Tutino, *From Insurrection*, pp. 42–46; Van Young, "Age of Paradox," p. 64, "Islands," pp. 131, 135, "Moving Towards Revolt," pp. 181, 185, and "Quetzalcóatl," esp. p. 11. See Archer's review of the literature, "¡Viva Nuestra Señora."

3. Taylor, "Banditry," pp. 234–36; Gruzinski, "La 'segunda aculteración.'" For economic demands see Katz, "Introduction," pp. 7–8; O'Phelan, pp. 175–222, 273–87; Lynch, pp. 11–12; Marichal; Vega. Farriss argues for a loss of peasant political autonomy and access to cofradías and cajas de comunidad in the Yucatán; see *Maya Society*, pp. 355–66. Carmagnani minimizes the impact of the Bourbon reforms on peasantry of Oaxaca; see *El regreso*, p. 234. The effect of the Bourbon reforms on the prospects for Creoles was first suggested as a cause of the revolt by Alamán. See Lynch, pp. 17–19. For the effect of the reforms on clerical privilege and possibly peasant religion see Farriss, *Crown*; Brading, "Tridentine Catholicism," pp. 7–13; Taylor, "Between Global Process," pp. 151–62.

4. Tutino, *From Insurrection*, pp. 41–126; Wolf, "Mexican Bajío," pp. 177–99; Florescano, *Orígen*, p. 87; Van Young, *Hacienda*, pp. 224, 269, and "Moving Towards Revolt," pp. 189–95; Taylor, "Banditry"; Martin, "Haciendas" and *Rural Society*, pp. 99–113. The preceding review of the literature on both the Bourbon reforms and agrarian changes owes much to Ducey, "Peasant Participation."

5. Hamnett, *Revolución*, pp. 96–397, and " Economic and Social Dimension," p. 11; Tutino, *From Insurrection*, pp. 140–45; Van Young, "Moving Towards Revolt," pp. 197–99; Taylor, "Banditry"; Pastor, *Campesinos*, p. 498.

6. For a relatively recent case see Santos Carrera and Alvarez Hernández, *Historia*, pp. 168, 173.

7. For the document see Hernández y Dávalos, 1: 879–80. For the debate surrounding it see Teja Zambre, pp. 499–505; Timmons, "José María Morelos," pp. 183–95. See also Mejía Fernández, pp. 50–57.

8. Van Young, "Moving Towards Revolt," pp. 183–84, 197–99, "Islands," and "Age of Paradox," p. 83.

9. Archer, "¡Viva Nuestra Señora," p. 149.

10. Taylor, *Drinking*, pp. 134–38.

11. Rodríguez O., "From Royal Subject," p. 38.

12. Villoro, pp. 54–55.

13. Lafaye, p. 118; Rodríguez O., "From Royal Subject," 29.

14. For examples see Martin, *Rural Society*, pp. 190–92; Liehr, 2: 143.

15. AGN, Historia, vol. 46, exp. 32, fols. 476–77, exp. 33, fols. 488–500; AGN, Historia, vol. 50, exp. 21, fols. 363–65; AGN, Historia, vol. 432, exp. 3, fols. 41–81.

16. See Taylor, "Banditry," p. 219, for comparison with another region.

17. Archer, "Banditry," p. 80. For examples in Guerrero see AGN, Operaciones de Guerra, vol. 76, fols. 140–42; vol. 79, fols. 122v, 156–57, 274–278v, 294–95; vol. 82, fols. 311–311v; vol. 86, fol. 212; vol. 201, fol. 192; vol. 466; vol. 976, exp. 37, fols. 124–25; Castillo Ledón, 3: 96.

18. AGN, Operaciones de Guerra, vol. 201, fols. 179–180; vol. 466. For detailed accounts of the shifting allegiances of individuals see AGN, Operaciones de Guerra, vol. 89, fols. 109–110v; AGN, Infidencias, vol. 48, exp. 2, fol. 53.

19. Altamirano, *Morelos en Zacatula*, p. 112; Aguirre Colorado, García, and Rodríguez, pp. 12–14; AGN, Infidencias, vol. 5, exp. 2, fols. 59–61; Herrejón Peredo, *Morelos: Documentos*, p. 100; Hernández y Dávalos, 5: 29.

20. AGN, Operaciones de Guerra, vol. 829, exp. 4, fols. 54–57; exp. 5, fols. 60–61; Herrejón Peredo, *Morelos: Documentos*, pp. 91–95.

21. Aguirre Colorado, García, and Rodríguez, p. 102; Altamirano, *Morelos en Tixtla*, pp. 203, 206, and *Morelos en el Veladero*, pp. 6–77; AGN, Historia, vol. 104, exp. 33, fol. 143; vol. 409, fols. 239–258v; AGN, Operaciones de Guerra, vol. 9, fols. 96, 178v; Díaz y Díaz, *Caudillos*, p. 100; Gomezjara, p. 61; Hernández y Dávalos, 4: 284–86.

22. AGN, Operaciones de Guerra, vol. 71, exp. 32, fols. 229–229v; vol. 72, exp. 4, fol. 14v; Hernández y Dávalos, 5: 26.

23. For some early examples see AGN, Infidencias, vol. 5, exp. 2, fol. 63; vol. 55, exp. 24, fols. 227–227v.

24. Vargas Martínez, p. 23; Aguirre Colorado, García, and Rodríguez, p. 73; AGN, Infidencias, vol. 131, exp. 3, fols. 12–13; exp. 34, fols. 185–186v; Hernández y Dávalos, 2: 245–46; AGN, Operaciones de Guerra, vol. 829, exp. 7, fols. 63–65; AGN, Intendencias, vol. 73.

25. Altamirano, *Morelos en Tixtla*, p. 186; Altamirano, *Morelos en el Veladero*, pp. 171, 173; Aguirre Colorado, García, and Rodríguez, pp. 32, 51; AGN, Inquisición, vol. 1452, fols. 309–310v; Ortega, ed., *Colección*, 17: 75, 120.

26. AGN, Operaciones de Guerra, vol. 829, exp. 7, fols. 63–65; BN, Fondo Alvarez, carpeta 1, documento 102; AGN, Operaciones de Guerra, vol. 829, exp. 32, fol. 155; vol. 917, exp. 4, fols. 13–14. This is a loose translation of "muy sobre sí."

27. Aguirre Colorado, García, and Rodríguez, pp. 81–82; AGN, Operaciones de Guerra, vol. 976, exp. 1, fol. 7; BN, Fondo Alvarez, carpeta 1, documentos 22, 100, 105; carpeta 2, documentos 112, 114.

28. Avilés, pp. 13–14; Castillo Ledón, 3: 91, 92; AGN, Operaciones de Guerra, vol. 976, exp. 2, fol. 20; AGN, Infidencias, vol. 24, exp. 9, fols. 228–230; AGN, Historia, vol. 103, exp. 8, fol. 29; exp. 9, fols. 37–38; exp. 26, fols. 104–5, 110; exp. 27, fol. 109; vol. 105, exp. 30, fols. 107, 109; exp. 41, fols. 146–47; exp. 70, fol. 251.

29. AGN, Historia, vol. 105, exp. 21, fols. 84–85.

30. AGN, Archivo Histórico de Hacienda, vol. 1982, exp. 4; Herrejón Peredo, *Morelos: Documentos*, pp. 156, 163–64; AGN, Operaciones de Guerra, vol. 976, exp. 5, fol. 30v; exp. 15, fol. 70v.

31. AGN, Operaciones de Guerra, vol. 70, exp. 15, fols. 46–46v; vol. 976, exp. 19, fols. 83–88; exp. 25, fols. 102–3.

32. AGN, Operaciones de Guerra, vol. 70. exp. 22, fols. 68–71v; exp. 23, fols. 76–77; vol. 976, exp. 29, fols. 11–114.

33. Archer, "Banditry," p. 68; Guevara Ramírez, p. 40; Chavez Guerrero, *Vicente Guerrero*, p. 26; M. Ochoa Campos, *Breve historia*, pp. 92–93; BN, Fondo Alvarez, carpeta 2, documento 115; Aguirre Colorado, García, and Rodríguez, p. 73; AGN, Operaciones de Guerra, vol. 829, exp. 30, fol. 153; vol. 935, exp. 260, fol. 506; AGN, Historia, vol. 103, exp. 25, fols. 100–101; vol. 104, exp. 4, fols. 6–8, exp. 5, fols. 9–11; AGN, Infidencias, vol. 131, exp. 3, fols. 12–13, 116–17; exp. 34, fols. 185–186v, exp. 47, fol. 246v; Herrejón Peredo, *Morelos: Documentos*, p. 187; Vargas Martínez, p. 39; AGN, Criminal, vol. 174, exp. 12, fols. 403–407v.

34. This was also true in two villages to the south, Zumpango del Río and Chilpancingo. AGN, Operaciones de Guerra, vol. 919, fols. 6, 48–54, 94, 103–106v, 116–116v, 160–61.

35. AGN, Infidencias, vol. 131, exp. 19, fol. 80; vol. 143, exps. 32, 48, 101; AGN, Criminal, vol. 5, exp. 4, fols. 35–36; AGN, Operaciones de Guerra, vol. 15, exp. 3, fols. 40–51; vol. 471; Hernández y Dávalos, 5: 884–85.

36. Hernández y Dávalos, 5: 878–79, 884–85, 887; AGN, Operaciones de Guerra, vol. 15, exp. 3, fols. 40–51; AGN, Infidencias, vol. 24, exp. 9, fol. 224; vol. 131, exp. 19, fols. 82–83; fols. 116–17; vol. 143, exps. 32, 46, 49, 101. The reference to previous disobedience is from AGN, Operaciones de Guerra, vol. 470.

37. AGN, Operaciones de Guerra, vol. 70, exp. 39, fols. 49–50; AGN, Operaciones de Guerra, vol. 976, exp. 1, fols. 1–6; exp. 2, fol. 15v; exp. 5, fol. 37v; exp. 37, fols. 124–25; exp. 38, fols. 126–29; exp. 42, fols. 140–44; AGN, Historia, vol. 105, exp. 5, fols. 6–11; exp. 61, fols. 228–30; Hernández y Dávalos, 5: 252–56; J. Ocampo, p. 52.

38. AGN, Tributos, vol. 34, exp. 1, fols. 1–12; exp. 7, fols. 160–67.

39. AGN, Tributos, vol. 54, exp. 14, fols. 194–99.

40. Unlike subdelegados elsewhere, Paris rarely shows up in an unfavorable light in the documents about the area. For an example of a dispute that he arbitrated see AGN, Civil, vol. 454, exp. 1, fol. 33v. Interestingly enough,

in contrast to most assessments royal offícals made of the loyalty of their jurisdictions, Paris placed far more confidence in his relatively poor mulattos than in the local vecinos de razón. See AGN, Historia, vol. 105, exp. 5, fols. 6–11.

41. Archer, "Banditry," pp. 71–73; Hamnett, *Roots*, pp. 125–49.

42. Chavez Guerrero, *Vicente Guerrero*, p. 26; M. Ochoa Campos, *Breve historia*, pp. 92–93.

43. For Morelos see Timmons, *Morelos*, pp. 14–24, and Herrejón Peredo, *Morelos: Vida*, pp. 28–29, 38. For Guerrero see Avilés, pp. 9–10; Chavez Guerrero, *Vicente Guerrero*, pp. 23–24, 30; Salcedo Guerrero, "Vicente Guerrero's Struggle," pp. 8–9. For Trujano and Carmen see Cordero y T., p. 462; M. Ochoa Campos, *Valerio Trujano*, pp. 6–9; M. Ochoa Campos, *Juan del Carmen*, p. 9.

44. Archer, "Banditry," p. 66; Hamnett, *Roots*, p. 25.

45. Salcedo Guerrero, "Vicente Guerrero's Struggle," pp. 6, 12; Sánchez, "Mulas," pp. 41–42, 45; Morin, p. 160; AGN, Padrones, vol. 16, fols. 107–221; vol. 18.

46. Archer, "Banditry" p. 66; Green, pp. 163–64; Lemoine, "Vicente Guerrero," p. 9; M. Ochoa Campos, *Valerio Trujano*, p. 6; Pastor, *Campesinos*, p. 321; Sprague, pp. 1–2.

47. Gomezjara, pp. 61–62; Morin, p. 177; Pastor, "El repartimiento," pp. 215–16. In discussing muleteer support for the Tupac Amaru movement in Peru O'Phelan points to the burden of increased alcabala payments and restrictive regulations to ensure its payment. See O'Phelan, pp. 273–87.

48. For a few examples see Altamirano, *Morelos en el Veladero*, pp. 176–77; Cordero y T., p. 449.

49. Brading, "El clero," pp. 13–19; Farriss, *Crown*, pp. 18, 119.

50. Timmons, *Morelos*, pp. 12, 23–24, 31–33; Herrejón Peredo, *Morelos: Vida*, p. 151. Villoro, p. 122, offers an interesting view on how the split between the high and low clergies may have affected future church/state relations in Mexico.

51. Farriss, *Crown*, pp. 95, 99, 238–45, Taylor, "Between Global Process," pp. 151–52; Taylor, "Banditry," pp. 236, 245.

52. Herrejón Peredo, ed., *Los procesos*, pp. 395–96.

53. Farriss, *Crown*, p. 199.

54. See, for instance, AGN, Operaciones de Guerra, vol. 15, exp. 4, fols. 55v–70v.

55. AGN, Operaciones de Guerra, vol. 9, fols. 199–200; vol. 15, exp. 3, fols. 40–51; AGN, Infidencias, vol. 54, exp. 3, fols. 122v–132v.

56. AGN, Operaciones de Guerra, vol. 194, exp. 21, fol. 36; Bravo, *Manifiesto*, pp. 5–6; BN, Fondo Alvarez, carpeta 1, documento 105; carpeta 2, documentos 112, 114.

57. AGN, Criminal, vol. 173, exp. 11, fol. 246; vol. 583, exp. 1, fol. 32; AGN, Tierras, vol. 2827, exp. 10, fols. 15v–16; vol. 2828, exp. 3, fol. 4; Chavez Guerrero, *Vicente Guerrero*, p. 30; M. Ochoa Campos, *Valerio Trujano*, p. 8; Pavía Guzmán, *Provincias*, p. 31.

58. Hermengildo could not read or write and married a mestiza. Timmons, *Morelos*, pp. 54–55; Vargas Martínez, pp. 10, 13–14; H. Ochoa Campos, p. 18.

59. See Chapter 1 and AGN, Ex-indiferente de Alcabalas, Acapulco, caja. 4, exp. 8; caja. 16, exp. 7; caja. 19, exp. 7; caja. 21, exp. 2; AGN, Real Hacienda, Administración General de Alcabalas, caja. 25; Morin, pp. 172–74, 177. The evidence seems to confirm the hypothesis presented by Hamnett, *Roots*, pp. 145–46.

60. H. Ochoa Campos, pp. 21–22.

61. H. Ochoa Campos, pp. 16–20; Gomezjara, p. 61.

62. Thompson, *Customs*, p. 53.

63. Van Young, "Quetzalcóatl," pp. 110–11.

64. On the centrality of the king to legitimacy see Van Young, "Quetzalcóatl," pp. 113–14; García Argañarás, p. 31; Mirafuentes Galvan. For village rebellions in general see Taylor, *Drinking*, pp. 113–51.

65. Guerra, 1: 44; Rodríguez O., "From Royal Subject," p. 26; Stoetzer, pp. 192–94. For Suarez see Hamilton, pp. 37, 41; MacLachlan, pp. 10–12.

66. Chavez Orozco, p. 35; Rodríguez O., "From Royal Subject," p. 8; Lemoine, *Morelos: Su vida*, p. 191.

67. Herrejón Peredo, "Hidalgo: La justificación," pp. 162–80; Herrejón Peredo, *Hidalgo: Razones*, pp. 34–36; Lemoine, *Morelos: Su vida*, p. 264.

68. The quotation is from Van Young, "Quetzalcóatl," p. 121.

69. Rodríguez O., "From Royal Subject," p. 30; MacLachlan, p. 132; Rodríguez O., "La independencia," p. 590.

70. AGN, Historia, vol. 432, exp. 3, fol. 41.

71. The quotation is from Florescano, *Memoria*, p. 187. Brading makes an almost identical statement in Brading, *Los orígenes*, p. 15.

72. Lemoine, *Morelos: Su vida*, pp. 185–86; Herrejón Peredo, *Morelos: Vida*, pp. 49, 74; Timmons, *Morelos*, p. 63; AGN, Operaciones de Guerra, vol. 83, fols. 295–96; vol. 467; AGN, Infidencias, vol. 133, fols. 86–87; Santos Carrera and Alvarez Hernández, *Historia*, p. 185.

73. Flores Galindo, "In Search," p. 200.

74. Florescano, *Memoria*, p. 291; AGN, Infidencias, vol. 24, exp. 3, fol. 120v; vol. 131, exp. 1, fols. 5–6; Taylor, "Virgin," p. 24. Castro Gutiérrez notes that the failed rebels of the Mariano scare in Nayarit in 1801 also planned to portray the Virgin of Guadalupe on a banner. See Castro Gutiérrez, "La rebelión," p. 5.

75. Taylor, "Virgin," esp. pp. 19, 23–24. See also Lafaye, pp. 280–81; Florescano, *Memoria*, p. 294; Brading, *Los orígenes*, pp. 15–16, 42, and "Tridentine Catholicism," pp. 1–3.

76. Taylor, "Virgin," p. 23; AGN, Operaciones de Guerra, vol. 829, exp. 7, fols. 63–65.

77. Taylor, "Virgin," 20–21.

78. AGN, Infidencias, vol. 131, exp. 11, fols. 59v–60; vol. 55, exp. 24, fols. 227–227v.

79. AGN, Infidencias, vol. 131, exp. 11, fol. 58. Even literate correspondents

of Morelos displayed considerable enthusiasm for the idea of "Cutting off European heads." AGN, Operaciones de Guerra, vol. 15, exp. 4, fol. 55v.

80. For opposing views see Hamnett, *Roots*, p. 13; Rodríguez O., "Introduction," p. 7. For royalist fears see AGN, Infidencias, vol. 131, exp. 29, fols. 167–69.

81. For Godoy as a Francophile see Hamill, p. 2. For the first wave of official anti-French propaganda see Herr, pp. 304–12, 335. For the second wave see Hamill, 14–15; Tanck de Estrada, p. 227; Herrejón Peredo, *Morelos: Vida*, pp. 231–32. For its echo in insurgent discourse see Santos Carrera and Alvarez Hernández, *Historia*, p. 199; AGN, Operaciones de Guerra, vol. 77, fol. 296; vol. 933, exp. 27, fol. 33.

82. For an opposing view see Van Young, "Quetzalcóatl," pp. 120–21. Note that Morelos's forces sometimes propagated the idea that Fernando VII himself was in New Spain leading the resistance. Lemoine, *Morelos: Su vida*, p. 169. For some of the myriad expressions of the idea that the Europeans were planning to turn New Spain over to Napoleon see AGN, Infidencias, vol. 60, exp. 4, fols. 181, 184; AGN, Operaciones de Guerra, vol. 15, exp. 4, fol. 61; vol. 917, exp. 5, fols. 15–16; vol. 939, fols. 210, 685; Rodríguez O., "From Royal Subject," pp. 23–24, 31; Villoro, p. 102; Lemoine, *Morelos: Su vida*, p. 191; Archer, "Banditry," p. 60.

83. Herrejón Peredo, *Los procesos*, p. 189.

84. AGN, Historia, vol. 50, exp. 21, fols. 363–65.

85. Villoro, p. 136; AGN, Infidencias, vol. 60, exp. 4, fol. 181v.

86. Villoro, pp. 74–75. Lemoine, *Morelos: Su vida*, p. 192; Herrejón Peredo, *Los procesos*, pp. 95–396.

87. Szeminski, pp. 168, 171–74.

88. Villoro, pp. 74–75.

89. See Cohn, pp. 79–80, on this point.

90. For the determinants of price see Thomson, "Protectionism," pp. 129–30.

91. This has been noted elsewhere in New Spain, too. See Hamnett, *Roots*, pp. 26–27, 32–33; Lafaye, p. 118; Taylor, "Banditry," p. 217.

92. AGN, Infidencias, vol. 144, exp. 29, fol. 31; AGN, Operaciones de Guerra, vol. 939, fol. 684.

93. AGN, Infidencias, vol. 55, exp. 24, fols. 227–227v; vol. 133, fol. 3; AGN, Operaciones de Guerra, vol. 72, exp. 23, fols. 157–58; vol. 917, fol. 28; vol. 919, exp. 1, fol. 3; vol. 919, exp. 23, fol. 32.

94. Aguirre Colorado, García, and Rodríguez, pp. 15, 86; Bustamante, *Cuadro*, 2: 20–22; Herrejón Peredo, *Morelos: Documentos*, pp. 120–22, 151. On the identification of the enemy in eighteenth-century Andean revolts see Spalding, "¿Quienes son los indios?" p. 191; Szeminski.

95. Herrejón Peredo, *Morelos: Vida*, pp. 58–60; MacLachlan, p. 91; AGN, Infidencias, vol. 144, exp. 29, fol. 31; AGN, Operaciones de Guerra, vol. 939, fols. 684–685v.

96. Lemoine, *Morelos: Su vida*, pp. 162, 265–66; AGN, Infidencias, vol.

144, fols. 4, 60; AGN, Operaciones de Guerra, vol. 919, exp. 24, fols. 33–34; Hamnett, *Roots*, p. 149; Pastor, "Estructura," pp. 427–28.

97. Lemoine, *Morelos: Su vida*, pp. 175–76, 164–65, 265; Santos Carrera and Alvarez Hernández, *Historia*, pp. 178–79; AGN, Operaciones de Guerra, vol. 924, exp. 53, fol. 80.

98. Lemoine, *Morelos: Su vida*, pp. 264–65; AGN, Operaciones de Guerra, vol. 829, exp. 5, fol. 61; vol. 914, exp. 22, fols. 29–30; AGN, Historia, vol. 105, exp. 21, fol. 84; Archivo Parroquial de Chilapa (microfilm MXE-3-432 roll 1, located in the AGN); AGN, Tributos, vol. 62, exp. 2, fol. 117; Lemoine, *Morelos: Su vida*, pp. 566–72; Castillo Ledón, 1: 143; Timmons, *Morelos*, p. 108. The taxes collected by the insurgents varied considerably over time and area. See AGN, Infidencias, vol. 133, fol. 2.

99. Lemoine, *Morelos: Su vida*, pp. 162, 264; AGN, Infidencias, vol. 144, exp. 5.

100. Hernández y Dávalos, 5: 108; Lemoine, *Morelos: Su vida*, pp. 162, 265, 384–85; Timmons, *Morelos*, p. 105.

101. AGN, Operaciones de Guerra, vol. 935, exp. 242, fols. 476–476v.

102. AGN, Operaciones de Guerra, vol. 919, exp. 74, fols. 129–129v. In another case Morelos's intervention was asked for but his decision is not in surviving documents.

103. Hernández y Dávalos, 3: 450; Herrejón Peredo, *Los procesos*, p. 261; AGN, Infidencias, vol. 914, exp. 18, fol. 22; AGN, Operaciones de Guerra, vol. 917, exp. 13, fol. 37; exp. 164, fol. 285; vol. 918, exp. 40, fols. 54–55; exp. 47, fols. 64–65.

104. This is an old argument about eighteenth-century enlightened monarchies. See de Tocqueville, p. 68; McAlister, p. 369; Morse, p. 142.

105. MacLachlan, pp. 76, 85–86, 101, 128.

106. The argument for France is from Baker, "Enlightenment," p. 284; Furet, pp. 15, 173–74, 179–80, 185. Evidence for Spain and its New World that seems to indicate similar developments can be seen in Herr, pp. 73, 154–63, 183–200, 262–63, 282, 349, 355–57; MacLachlan, pp. 81–82; Hamill, pp. 6–8, 69, 72, 82.

107. For Hidalgo see Herrejón Peredo, *Hidalgo: Razones*, pp. 35–36. Morelos, however, was so accused. See Herrejón Peredo, *Los procesos*, pp. 293–383, esp. pp. 334–35.

108. Lemoine traces this transition ably in *Morelos y la Revolución*, pp. 259–310. There on pp. 260–65 and in "Morelos y la generación," pp. 33–37, Lemoine argues that the insurgents' invocations of Fernando VII were disingenuous. However, this assertion does not detract from the importance of the transformation of the manner in which they legitimated their actions with their followers.

109. For donations in Guerrero see AGN, Archivo Histórico de Hacienda, vol. 396, exp. 3; AGN, Ex-indiferente de Alcabalas, Tlapa, caja. 4, exp. 12; exp. 13. For an example of an appeal read by Morelos see Herrejón Peredo, *Morelos: Vida*, pp. 231–32.

110. Herrejón Peredo, *Morelos: Vida,* pp. 52–56. For an interesting interpretation of the Spanish transition see Guerra, 1: 189–90.

111. Villoro, pp. 99–109; the quotation is from p. 108. See also Herr, p. 347.

112. AGN, Operaciones de Guerra, vol. 74, exp. 44, fol. 137; vol. 917, exp. 150, fols. 261–62; vol. 919, fols. 31–34v, 55; vol. 935, exp. 242, fols. 476–476v. For a comparison to Peru in the same period see Guardino, p. 112.

113. AGN, Infidencias, vol. 133, fols. 108–108v, 119, 127, 210; AGN, Operaciones de Guerra, vol. 74, exp. 121, fol. 386; vol. 917, exp. 152, fols. 265–265v; vol. 918, exp. 25, fols. 38–38v; vol. 933, exp. 107, fols. 137–41; Ortega, ed., *Colección,* 17: 160; Lemoine, *Morelos: Su vida,* pp. 412–17. Villages resisted attempts by insurgent officials to depose or impose their officials as fiercely as they had the efforts of colonial officials. AGN, Operaciones de Guerra, vol. 91, exp. 68, fols. 119–120v.

114. The constitution is found in Bustamante, *Cuadro,* 3: 157–89. For instance, electors for the 1813 Congress of Chilpancingo were chosen by the "pastors, military commanders, republics, and principal residents" in Tecpan, whereas in Cutzmala they were chosen by "owners and renters of *haciendas* or *ranchos,* military chiefs, and other upright persons." AGN, Infidencias, vol. 144, exp. 14, fol. 16; AGN, Operaciones de Guerra, vol. 943, exp. 74, fol. 84. See also Guedea, "Las elecciones," pp. 309–10.

115. AGN, Operaciones de Guerra, vol. 917, exp. 142, fols. 248–49; exp. 158, fols. 276–77; vol. 918, exp. 48, fols. 66–67; exp. 45, fols. 61–62; vol. 919, exp. 68, fols. 119–120v.

116. Herrejón Peredo, *Morelos: Documentos,* p. 174; Lemoine, *Morelos: Su vida,* pp. 531–32; AGN, Infidencias, vol. 144, exp. 21, fol. 23.

117. AGN, Operaciones de Guerra, vol. 914, exp. 19, fols. 23–23v; vol. 943, exp. 75, fol. 87; exp. 132, fol. 190; exp. 141, fol. 203. For disputes within villages see AGN, Operaciones de Guerra, vol. 914, exp. 12, fols. 13–13v; vol. 919, fols. 6, 48–54, 68–84v, 94, 103–106v, 116–116v, 160–61, 164. For disputes between priests and peasants see AGN, Infidencias, vol. 133, fol. 163; AGN, Operaciones de Guerra, vol. 919, fols. 23–25, 56–67v, 85–88v, 92.

118. AGN, Operaciones de Guerra, vol. 918, exp. 48, fols. 66–67; vol. 919, exp. 8, fols. 9–10; Lemoine, *Morelos: Su vida,* pp. 328–29, 403–5.

119. AGN, Infidencias, vol. 144, exp. 16, fol. 18; Lemoine, *Morelos: Su vida,* pp. 331–35.

120. Hamnett, *Roots,* pp. 150–77; Salcedo Guerrero, "Vicente Guerrero's Struggle," p. 35.

121. Archer, "La Causa," pp. 102–5; Archer, "¡Viva Nuestra Señora," p. 147. See also Salcedo Guerrero, "Vicente Guerrero's Struggle," p. 80; Lemoine, "Vicente Guerrero," pp. 9–10.

122. Timmons, *Morelos,* p. 133.

123. The recommendation to abandon the area is found in AGN, Operaciones de Guerra, vol. 74, exp. 127, fols. 410v–411v. Armijo's report is in AGN, Operaciones de Guerra, vol. 74, exp. 156, fols. 529v–533v. Salcedo Guerrero, "Vicente Guerrero's Struggle," pp. 29–81, and Sprague, pp. 23–26,

provide military histories of the guerrilla struggle. For various assessments of the support given to the insurgents see AGN, Operaciones de Guerra, vol. 73, fols. 37v, 103; vol. 70, exp. 22, fols. 68–71v; exp. 23, fols. 76–77; vol. 74, exp. 126, fol. 401v; exp. 127, fols. 410v–411v; exp. 164, fols. 568–69; exp. 156, fols. 529–533v; vol. 305, exp. 31, fols. 65–65v; Ramírez Fentanes, *Vicente Guerrero*, pp. 78–79.

124. AGN, Operaciones de Guerra, vol. 73, fol. 204. For other comments on the obstinate oppostion of the *costeños* to the royal government see AGN, Operaciones de Guerra, vol. 72, fols. 216–28; vol. 73, fols. 242–242v; vol. 75, fols. 20–23.

125. The April 1819 estimate is from AGN, Operaciones de Guerra, vol. 86, fols. 347–50. For the coastal war see AGN, Operaciones de Guerra, vol. 73, fols. 6–7; vol. 77, fols. 106v, 276–77; vol. 78, fols. 62–62v; vol. 86, fols. 84–84v, 370–71; vol. 466; vol. 939, fols. 271, 275–76, 574v; vol. 924, exp. 12, fol. 14; AGN, Infidencias, vol. 144, exp. 89, fol. 205; exp. 92, fol. 212; Avilés, p. 36; Chavez Guerrero, *Vicente Guerrero*, p. 83.

126. AGN, Operaciones de Guerra, vol. 73, fols. 195–97; vol. 74, fols. 1–3, 189v, 479; vol. 75, exp. 119, fol. 373; vol. 81, fols. 438–44; vol. 466, vol. 467; vol. 468, fols. 107, 172; vol. 469, fols. 2v, 12v; vol. 470; vol. 915, fols. 205–6.

127. AGN, Operaciones de Guerra, vol. 80, fols. 56–57; vol. 81, fols. 448–49.

128. Ramírez Fentanes, *Vicente Guerrero*, p. 123; Salcedo Guerrero, "Vicente Guerrero's Struggle," pp. 119, 137–40; Avilés, pp. 37–38; AGN, Operaciones de Guerra, vol. 80, fols. 298–307, 313v, 317v; vol. 82, fols. 74, 276–94; vol. 83, fols. 166v, 194–95, 280.

129. See, for instance, his June 2, 1815, report to the viceroy in AGN, Operaciones de Guerra, vol. 74, fols. 562–562v.

130. For the general outlines of royalist stategy and tactics see Hamnett, "Royalist Counter-Insurgency"; and Archer, "La Causa."

131. AGN, Operaciones de Guerra, vol. 74, fols. 568–569v.

132. AGN, Operaciones de Guerra, vol. 73, fols. 42v, 103, 213–213v, 335; vol. 74, fol. 189v.

133. AGN, Operaciones de Guerra, vol. 73, fol. 317.

134. AGN, Historia, vol. 103, exp. 46, fols. 184–86; AGN, Operaciones de Guerra, vol. 71 exp. 17, fols. 85–86; exp. 22, fol. 102; vol. 78, fol. 227v.

135. For examples see Ramírez Fentanes, *Vicente Guerrero*, pp. 58, 95, 100; AGN, Operaciones de Guerra, vol. 86, fols. 84–84v.

136. AGN, Operaciones de Guerra, vol. 80, fols. 56–57; vol. 81, fols. 438–44; AGN, Operaciones de Guerra, vol. 82, fols. 276–94. See also Archer, "¡Viva Nuestra Señora," pp. 158–59.

137. AGN, Operaciones de Guerra, vol. 82, fols. 311–311v. See also Archer, "¡Viva Nuestra Señora," p. 165. For an insurgent counteroffer see Salcedo Guerrero, "Vicente Guerrero's Struggle," p. 119.

138. AGN, Operaciones de Guerra, vol. 71, exp. 11, fols. 51–51v; exp. 32, fols. 229–229v; vol. 81, fols. 448–49; vol. 82, fols. 361–62; vol. 467. Archer notes this phenomenon but suggests that it represented a type of land re-

form. My suspicion is that the fiscal and political dimensions were more important. See Archer, " Young Antonio López," p. 6; Archer, "¡Viva Nuestra Señora," p. 149.

139. Archivo Parroquial de Chilapa (microfilm MXE-3-432 roll 1, located in the AGN); AGN, Operaciones de Guerra, vol. 77, fol. 92v.

140. AGN, Archivo Histórico de Hacienda, vol. 219, exp. 10; vol. 266, exp. 22; vol. 266, exp. 33; vol. 441, exps. 1, 15, 19; AGN, Civil, vol. 559, fol. 372; AGN, Ex-indiferente de Alcabalas, Tetela, caja. 4, exp. 6; AGN, Indios, vol. 77, exp. 14, fol. 288; AGN, Intendencias, vol. 60.

141. AGN, Operaciones de Guerra, vol. 71, exp. 39, fols. 250–250v; vol. 81, fol. 136; vol. 83, fols. 194–95.

142. For some works that support this interpretation see Brading, *Los orígenes*, p. 83; Farriss, *Crown*, pp. 246–51; San Juan Victoria, p. 93, and the others cited below.

143. Brading, *Los orígenes*, p. 97; Flores Caballero, p. 57.

144. Villoro, p. 191.

145. Flores Caballero, p. 58.

146. Alamán, *Historia*, 4: 666–68, 5: 331–33.

147. Rodríguez O., "From Royal Subject," p. 39. See also Archer, "Banditry," p. 59; Pastor, "Estructura," p. 429. For an interesting comparison with contemporary England see Thompson, *Making*, pp. 605, 625, 682.

148. AGN, Operaciones de Guerra, vol. 71, exp. 39, fols. 250–250v.

149. Jiménez Codinach, p. 44; Samponaro, pp. 11–12.

150. Hamnett, *Revolución*, p. 307.

151. AGN, Operaciones de Guerra, vol. 777. This oft-repeated counterinsurgency ratio shows up in Higham, p. 219, among other places.

152. Hamnett, *Revolución*, p. 297; Lemoine, "1821," p. 29.

153. Rodríguez O., "La independencia," p. 581.

154. AGN, Operaciones de Guerra, vol. 83, fols. 270, 277–78; vol. 777; vol. 941, fols. 81–82.

155. *Los insurgentes; Proclama de un americano*; Bustamante, *Memoria*, pp. 3–13; AGN, Operaciones de Guerra, vol. 83, fol. 289; vol. 941, fols. 81–82.

156. Chevalier, "La emancipación," p. 157. Apparently, when the same constitution was in force in 1812–14 very few were set up outside important urban areas, possibly because of the more tenuous military position of the viceregal government then. Cunniff, pp. 70–80.

157. AGN, Ayuntamientos, vol. 120, exp. 2; ACDEM, Expedientes, 1821, libro 4, exp. 7, fols. 1–2; AGN, Gobernación, caja. 13, exp. 1; Archivo Parroquial de Chilapa (microfilm MXE-3-432, roll 1, located in the AGN).

158. Archer, "La Causa," pp. 106–8.

159. *El indio constitucional a todos los americanos*, pp. 6–8; *El indio y la india*.

160. Chavez Guerrero, *Vicente Guerrero*, p. 87; Hamnett, *Revolución*, pp. 308–10.

161. Chavez Guerrero, *Vicente Guerrero*, pp. 103–4; Sprague, pp. 41–42; Salcedo Guerrero, "Vicente Guerrero's Struggle," pp. 164–67.

162. Vicente Guerrero to Iturbide, January 20, 1821, in *Cartas de los se-ñores generales*, pp. 3–6. This was Article 22 of the Constitution, found in Padilla Serra, ed., p. 12. See also *Instrucción que para facilitar*, Article 4, on citizenship.

163. Iturbide to Guerrero, January 10, 1821, in *Cartas de los señores generales*, pp. 1–3.

164. Guerrero to Iturbide, January 20, 1821, in *Cartas de los señores generales*, pp. 3–6.

165. Lemoine, "Vicente Guerrero," p. 13. For more on the negotiations see Jiménez Codinach, pp. 46–48; Sprague, p. 41.

166. The Plan of Iguala can be found in Bustamante, *Cuadro*, 5: 115–18. See also Jiménez Codinach, pp. 46–47; *Advertencia*, p. 1.

167. AGN, Civil, vol. 69, exp. 5, fols. 45–52; AGN, Operaciones de Guerra, vol. 70, exp. 61, fols. 251–52; vol. 89, fol. 485; Alessio Robles, ed., p. 13; Sprague, p. 47.

168. AGN, Operaciones de Guerra, vol. 70, exp. 63, fols. 261–62; AGN, Operaciones de Guerra, vol. 89, fols. 467–69; Archer, "La Causa," pp. 107–8.

169. See Skocpol, pp. 178, 181, 209. Spalding notes that the Spanish colonial system did not rely on the state's military capacity to maintain order. See Spalding, "Introducción," p. 21.

170. Topik, p. 333. See also Rodríguez O., "La independencia," p. 581.

Chapter 3

1. The term "old solidarities" is used here is to refer to the myriad interlocking forms of organization, identity, and power that characterized the early modern world. Among the most important were corporate villages, religious orders, guilds, and tribes.

2. Corrigan and Sayer, pp. 5–6.

3. This is the corollary of Tilly's observation that resistance to state formation forced authorities to concede institutions and rights. See Tilly, "War-Making," p. 183. Similar processes are also at work in class relations. For an excellent case analysis, see Genovese.

4. Lira González, *Comunidades*, esp. pp. 202, 207, 229, 292; Pastor, *Campesinos*, esp. pp. 447–48.

5. Sánchez Agesta, p. 33. Quote from Sánchez Agesta, p. 64. This tradition had also formed one of the cornerstones of the ideology of the insurgency.

6. González, *Estudios*, pp. 11–13, 31–36.

7. Lira González, *Comunidades*, pp. 182–83, 206, 298. For an interesting case in Guerrero involving the free market, that linchpin of the new world order, see ACDEM, Expedientes, 1842, libro 121, exp. 258. Note that colonial law itself was more a codification of precedent than rationally ordered code. See Santos Carrera and Alvarez Hernández, *Las luchas*, p. 21.

8. Note that when order was finally achieved in the 1880s it was accomplished through the first means, sealing off disgruntled peasants from potential allies.

9. Alamán, *Esposición*, p. 3; *Desengaño*.

10. *El amigo;* Bustamante, *El indio,* pp. 34, 39; *Consuelo,* pp. 3–7; *Conversación;* Palafox y Mendoza, pp. 1–7; *La malinche,* pp. 1–6; *Parabien a los indios; Segunda parte.*

11. AHEM, Epoca Independiente, vol. 34, exp. 9, fol. 2; Brading, *Los orígenes,* p. 131; Green, pp. 126, 127, 175; Harrell, pp. 224, 303; *Memoria,* State of Mexico, Relaciones, 1828, pp. 6, 19; *Memoria,* State of Mexico, Relaciones, 1829, pp. 6, 14, 20–21; Bustamante, *El indio,* pp. 52–54; *Dictamen de la Comisión Primera de Hacienda sobre que el Gobierno,* pp. 3–6, 8.

12. Benson, *La diputación,* esp. p. 21. See also Rodríguez O., "La Constitución."

13. Benson, "Introduction," pp. 7–8; Berry, p. 23; Cunniff, pp. 70–80; Guedea, "Las primeras elecciones"; Lira González, *Comunidades,* p. 56; Rodríguez O., "From Royal Subject," p. 38.

14. De la Torre Villar, p. 66; Berry, p. 28; Flores Caballero, pp. 52–55. The Consulado de México, vehicle of the colonial dominant class, had opposed the Cortes' extension of suffrage to Indians and mestizos. See Anna, "Spain," pp. 259–61.

15. Jiménez Codinach, pp. 46–47.

16. The constitution is reproduced in Padilla Sierra, pp. 9–58. The provisions referring to local government are found in articles 309–23, pp. 49–51. Note that these provisions actually differ from Pastor's observation that the head town of each needed to have 1,000 inhabitants. See Pastor, *Campesinos,* pp. 420–21.

17. Cunniff, pp. 82–83; Chevalier, "La emancipación," p. 157. For the 1820–21 period in Guerrero see AGN, Ayuntamientos, vol. 120, exp. 2; ACDEM, Expedientes, 1821, libro 4, exp. 7 fols. 1–2; AGN, Gobernación, caja. 13, exp. 1; Archivo Parroquial de Chilapa (microfilm MXE-3-432 roll 1, located in the AGN). For later see AGN, Ayuntamientos, vol. 7, fols. 85–87; Alanis Boyzo, "Instalación," p. 25.

18. Lira González, *Comunidades,* pp. 202, 206; Pastor, *Campesinos,* p. 420. For a discussion of the debates surrounding the writing of some of the early legislation, see Hale, pp. 89–95, 233.

19. Von Mentz, p. 139. For a contemporary view of the change in local adminstration brought about by the new municipalities, see *Oyen y callen,* pp. 5–6.

20. Note Guerra, 1: 259, on this point. See also Vázquez, "El federalismo," p. 15.

21. Lira González, *Comunidades;* Pastor, *Campesinos,* pp. 421–22. Guerra, 1: 261, 277, also notes this phenomenon.

22. Lira González, *Comunidades,* pp. 57–62, 205, 255.

23. ACDEM, Expedientes, 1820, libro 3, exp. 125; AGN, Ayuntamientos, vol. 7, fols. 85–87; AHEM, Epoca Colonial, vol. 11, exp. 6, fols. 5–6; exp. 10, fols. 5–6; vol. 13, exp. 1, fols. 5–6; exp. 2, fols. 5–6; exp. 7, fols. 5–6; exp. 15, fols. 4–5; vol. 29, exp. 11, fols. 5–6.

24. AGN, Gobernación, legajo 72, exp. 9; AHEM, Epoca Independiente, vol. 117, exp. 17, fol. 2; vol. 173, exp. 1, fols. 80–81; *Planes,* 2: 91, 94, 223, 429;

El Patriota, January 9, 1828. The quotation is from AHEM, Epoca Independiente, vol. 164, exp. 2, fol. 27v.

25. For an example see AHEM, Epoca Colonial, vol. 66, exp. 15, fol. 1.

26. On municipal functions see AHEM, Epoca Independiente, vol. 72, exp. 38, fols. 2–6; AHEM, Epoca Independiente, vol. 146, exp. 5, fols. 1–2; *Ley dictada por el Congreso Constituyente*, pp. 16–21; von Mentz, p. 66.

27. For examples of how this worked see AGN, Archivo de Guerra, vol. 99, fol. 82v; AGN, Gobernación, legajo 1946, exp. 1, fol. 538; AHEM, Epoca Independiente, vol. 92, exp. 6, fols. 2–3; vol. 170, exp. 4, fols. 5, 20.

28. ACDEM, Expedientes, 1822, libro 8, exp. 59; AGN, Gobernación, 1a829(7)5; von Mentz, pp. 141–42; Pastor, *Campesinos*, pp. 427–28.

29. M. Weber, p. 78.

30. Green, p. 186; Dublán and Lozano, 2: 684–87; AHEM, Epoca Colonial, vol. 11, exp. 5.

31. Samponaro, pp. 2–3, 194–98; Santoni, pp. 276–80; Sims, *Descolonización*, p. 16; Montes de Oca; *Reglamento*, p. 4. For examples of laws with varying degrees of internal democracy in the forces see *Ley orgánica para la milicia cívica*, pp. 14–17; *Reglamento*, p. 13; Zarco, *Crónica*, pp. 905–913; Dublán and Lozano, 2: 716–19, 5: 20–22.

32. For regulations on service see *Memoria*, State of Mexico, Relaciones, 1826, p. 59; *Ley orgánica para la milicia cívica*, pp. 3–7; *Reglamento*, pp. 5–6; Dublán and Lozano, 5: 414–21. For militia unit strengths in the area see *Memoria*, State of Mexico, Relaciones, 1826, addendum 2, table 2; 1827, addendum 2, table 2; 1828, table 7; *Memoria*, State of Puebla, Relaciones, 1826, sección milicia, cuadro 1; *Memoria*, Federal Government, Guerra, 1822, pp. 28–29; *Memoria*, State of Mexico, Relaciones, 1848, cuadro 12. For an example of the use of militias to legitimate political movements in Guerrero see *Planes*, 2: 395; for their similar importance in nineteenth-century Venezuela see Gilmore, pp. 26, 49–52, 103–20.

33. For instance, it is clear from a myriad of administrative records that a single official based in Acapulco replaced the subdelegados of Tecpan, Chilapa, and Tixtla as well as the Capitán of Acapulco. Strangely, in this particular case the new administrative boundaries faithfully replicated the pre-Bourbon order.

34. Pastor, *Campesinos*, pp. 446–47; Sánchez, *El suroeste*, pp. 41, 53–56.

35. For examples of citizenship provisions see *Constitución política del Estado de Puebla*, pp. 6–9; *Constitución política del Estado de México*, p. 4; *Constitución política del Estado de Michoacán*, p. 9. Hamnett's thesis is from Hamnett, *Revolución*, p. 47. For the 1812 regulations see Berry, pp. 18–19; for 1820, *Instrucción que para facilitar*; for 1823, Lemoine, ed., *Insurgencia*, p. 360. For an example of a delayed literacy qualification see *Constitución política del Estado de Chiapas*, p. 12. For the wording on the unemployed see Green, p. 193.

36. Hobsbawm, p. 267; Corrigan and Sayer, p. 17; Therborn, "Rule," p. 11.

37. For municipalities see ACDEM, Expedientes, 1841, libro 107, exp. 20; 1843, libro 129, exp. 284, fols. 9–10; AHEM, Epoca Independiente, vol. 151;

exp. 9; AHEM, Hacienda, vol. 13, exp. 27; University of Texas, Nettie Lee Benson Collection, Riva Palacio Papers (microfilm located in the AGN; hereafter Riva Palacio Papers) roll 76, document 143; AGN Gobernación, caja. 149, exp. 12; *Ley dictada por el Congreso Constituyente*, pp. 29–31. For repúblicas in the colonial period see AGN, Archivo Histórico de Hacienda, vol. 386, exp. 6; vol. 405; AGN, Indios, vol. 76, exp. 2, fols. 21–33v.

38. AGN, Gobernación, caja. 149, exp. 12; ACDEM, Expedientes, 1838, libro 88, exp. 27, fol. 5; 1838, libro 88, exp. 55, fol. 2v; 1840, libro 102, exp. 163, fol. 1; 1840, libro 106, exp. 388, cuad. 2, fols. 15–18; 1840, libro 106, exp. 388, cuad. 4, fol. 26. By 1845 at least some municipalities no longer spent public funds on religious functions; see ACDEM, Expedientes, 1845, libro 144, exp. 319, fols. 2–11. Note that this change occurred under a centralist government. Others continued to do so; see ACDEM, Expedientes, 1846, libro 156, exp. 283, fol. 1. Sometimes municipal officers collected separate special funds for religious expenses; see AHEM, Epoca Independiente, vol. 151, exp. 9, fol. 9.

39. AHEM, Epoca Independiente, vol. 127, exp. 17, fol. 1; Brading, *Los orígenes*, p. 94; Green, p. 179; Argandar; *Instrucción que para facilitar*, articles 1–3; *Proyecto*, p. 4.

40. Note the interesting statement from a non-Indian municipality that "the three national holidays are Holy Thursday, Corpus Cristi, and Our Lady of Guadalupe." ACDEM, Expedientes, 1842, libro 121, exp. 231, fol. 3. See also ACDEM, Expedientes, 1846, libro 156, exp. 300, fol. 2; AGN, Archivo Histórico de Hacienda, vol. 1871, exp. 7.

41. The phrase "imagined community" is from B. Anderson.

42. Tilly, "War-Making," pp. 175–83.

43. Dehouve, "El pueblo," pp. 93–94; Stein, p. 18.

44. One real was an eighth of one peso. *Memoria*, State of Mexico, Relaciones, 1826, p. 44; *Memoria*, State of Michoacán, Relaciones, 1829, table 8; 1830, table 7; *Memoria*, State of Puebla, Relaciones, 1826, pp. 31–32; *Colección de los decretos y órdenes más importantes*, p. 138. For lists of taxpayers and what they paid see AGN, Ayuntamientos, vol. 242; AGN, Gobernación, caja. 149, exp. 12.

45. *Memoria*, State of Mexico, Relaciones, 1828, p. 42; ACDEM, Expedientes, 1840, libro 100, exp. 91, fol. 2; *Memoria*, State of Puebla, Relaciones, 1826, table 3; *Colección de los decretos y órdenes más importantes*, pp. 6–9, 72.

46. AHEM, Hacienda, vol. 19, exp. 15, fols. 1–2; Colín, 2: 69; *Colección de decretos y órdenes de los Congresos*, p. 483; *Ley dictada por el Congreso Constituyente*, p. 31.

47. ACDEM, Expedientes, 1824, libro 15, exp. 3, fols. 1–2; AGN, Archivo Histórico de Hacienda, vol. 1946, exp. 8.

48. For example see AGN, Archivo Histórico de Hacienda, vol. 404, exp. 17; vol. 405, exp. 7.

49. *Memoria*, State of Puebla, Relaciones, 1826, pp. 31–32.

50. For examples see AGN, Ayuntamientos, vol. 236; AGN Gobernacion, caja. 149, exp. 12.

51. Pastor, *Campesinos*, p. 428.

52. Guerra, 1: 261.

53. AGN, Operaciones de Guerra, vol. 89, fol. 224; Lemoine, ed., *Insurgencia*, p. 299.

54. Platt, "Andean Experience," p. 286.

55. Corrigan and Sayer, p. 5; the quotation is from p. 6.

56. Guerra, 2: 329.

57. Much of the evidence for this assertion will be discussed below. An example outside of Guerrero has been discussed by Lechuga Barrios, pp. 17–19.

58. An example is the association of annual elections with religious services. *Proyecto*, p. 4. For comparison see Carmagnani, *El regreso*, p. 203.

59. AHEM, Epoca Colonial, vol. 41, exp. 13, fol. 1; ACDEM, Expedientes, 1823, libro 11, exp. 25. We do not know nearly enough about electoral practices in colonial *repúblicas*. Carmagnani has found that in some Oaxacan villages only about one in six tributaries were electors. They achieved this right either by birth into principal families or by serving in minor offices. See Carmagnani, "Local Governments," pp. 117–19; Carmagnani, *El regreso*, pp. 192–95.

60. Alanis Boyzo, "Instalación," p. 26; *Constitución política del Estado de Puebla*, pp. 11–15; ACDEM, Expedientes, 1824, libro 15, exp. 37, fols. 1–2; exp. 49. The last document describes a municipal election in San Juan Chontalcuatlán in northern Guerrero, an example of how local practices still varied. Here, although only secondary electors voted in the election of municipal officers, as the laws provided, all residents attended the election, a practice not provided for in law.

61. Green, p. 175; Lemoine, ed., *Insurgencia*, pp. 361–65; *Ley sobre la reforma*, p. 9; *Ley que arregla*, p. 37; *Ley dictada por el Congreso Constituyente*, pp. 8–13. Complete records for primary elections in Guerrero in which fraud is not alleged are difficult to find because such records remained in poorly preserved municipal archives. Where fraud was alleged, evidence of elections is more common because relevant documentation was sent to the state or federal level to pursue claims. See AHEM, Epoca Independiente, vol. 137, exp. 4, fol. 4. Warren analyzes the better-preserved evidence of elections in Mexico City in "Will."

62. For this region the most important set of such private correspondence is that of Mariano Riva Palacio, an important politician whose correspondence exists in the Nettie Lee Benson Collection at the University of Texas. For attempts to influence primary-level elections, see Riva Palacio Papers, roll 77, document 797; roll 78, documents 1237, 1239, 1258, 1269; roll 79, documents 1968, 1971, 1985; roll 82 documents 3608, 3686. For elections described as contested see Riva Palacio Papers, roll 80, document 2577; roll 85, document 5537. Most of these documents refer to various elections of the 1840s because Riva Palacio's career dates from that period, but there is no reason to believe that earlier elections were substantially different.

63. For examples see Riva Palacio Papers, roll 78, document 1266; roll 79, document 1967; roll 81, document 3141; roll 83, document 4644.

64. AHEM, Epoca Independiente, vol. 155, exp. 9, fol. 2v; *Oyen y callen*, pp. 7, 9.

65. *Planes*, 2: 91, 94; AGN, Tierras, vol. 3362, exp. 2.

66. AGNDF, notary 532, November 20, 1829.

67. Chiapas surprisingly continued with a large number of municipalities, whereas Michoacán reduced its number of them. See *Constitución política del Estado de Chiapas*, p. 37; *Constitución política del Estado de Michoacán*, p. 49. The size of colonial repúblicas varied greatly. See Carmagnani, "Local Governments," p. 111.

68. In the state of Mexico as a whole they tended downward. See Alanis Boyzo, "Instalación," p. 27. For actual numbers of municipalities see the tables in the back of *Memoria*, State of Mexico, Relaciones, 1826, 1827, 1828, and 1834.

69. *Ley que arregla*, pp. 28–29; *Ley dictada por el Congreso Constituyente*, p. 4; *Memoria*, State of Mexico, Relaciones, 1826, pp. 12–13; *Constitución política del Estado de México*, pp. 29–30.

70. AHEM, Epoca Independiente, vol. 155, exp. 9; AHEM, Epoca Colonial, vol. 11, exp. 6, fols. 5–6; exp. 10, fols. 5–6; vol. 13, exp. 1, fols. 5–6; exp. 2, fols. 5–6; exp. 7, fols. 5–6; exp. 15, fols. 4–5; vol. 29, exp. 11, fols. 5–6.

71. The quotation is from *Ley que arregla*, pp. 31–32. See also *Ley dictada por el Congreso Constituyente*, pp. 5–6; *Constitución política del Estado de México*, pp. 29–30. For salaried officials see *Constitución política del Estado de México*, pp. 27, 29; *Constitución política del Estado de Michoacán*, pp. 18, 32, 47–48; *Ley que arregla*, pp. 8, 25.

72. AGN, Gobernación, caja. 121, exp. 2.

73. This pattern could crop up surprisingly close to the centers of power. Lira González describes such a situation in the Federal District itself in *Comunidades*, pp. 57–62, 205.

74. See, for instance, BN, Fondo Alvarez, caja. 1, document 45.

75. Guerra, 1: 261, 277; Pastor, *Campesinos*, pp. 421–22.

76. For this kind of conflict in Peru see Mallon, "Nationalist and Antistate Coalitions," p. 240. For Cocula see AGN, Ayuntamientos, vol. 242. For Mochitlán see López Miramontes, ed.

77. AHEM, Epoca Independiente, vol. 155, exp. 10, fol. 4; *Memoria*, State of Mexico, Relaciones, 1826, table 1.

78. This withdrawal of settlements from municipalites was done by decree, as in the moving of Tesca from the municipality of Tecpan to that of Acapulco in 1833. AGN, Gobernación, caja. 161, exp. 14.

79. See AHEM, Epoca Independiente, vol. 155, exp. 10, fols. 2–7, for such a case in which the village of Atliaca in 1831 sought to leave the municipality of Apango and join that of Tixtla. See the 1828 request of Asacualoya to leave the municipality of Chilapa in AHEM, Epoca Independiente, vol. 49, exp. 31. For a request to move the municipal seat see AHEM, Epoca Independiente, vol. 155, exp. 12, fols. 2–4.

80. For general complaints see *Abusos*, pp. 1–3; *Oyen y callen*, p. 7. For specific complaints in Guerrero see *El Patrota*, March 12, 1828, and AGN, Gobernación, legajo 8, exp. 15, fol. 8–13.

81. AGN, Gobernación, caja. 113, exp. 6, fol. 355.

82. ACDEM, Expedientes, 1824, exp. 53.

83. AHEM, Epoca Independiente, vol. 38, exp. 19; vol. 149, exp. 14.

84. Guerra, 1: 47.

85. Ortiz Escamilla, pp. 242–44, notes some of these dimensions of federalism.

86. See the "Representación que el ilustre Ayuntamiento de Teloloapan dirige al Exmo. Sr. Presidente de la República Mexicana, pidiendo el sistema Federal," in AHEM, Epoca Independiente, vol. 178, exp. 7, fol. 39.

87. AHEM, Epoca Independiente, vol. 146, exp. 12, fol. 2; AHEM, Control Público, vol. 24, exp. 44, fol. 2.

88. AHEM, Epoca Independiente, vol. 155, exp. 9, fols. 1–2v; *Memoria,* State of Puebla, Relaciones, 1826, pp. 5, 8–10; *Memoria,* State of Mexico, Relaciones, 1835, pp. 32–34; *Ley que arregla,* pp. 28–29; *Oyen y callen,* pp. 3–10.

89. Sordo Cedeño and Vázquez have uncovered significant evidence of this connection. See Sordo Cedeño, pp. 95, 225; Vázquez, "El federalismo," pp. 39–40.

90. See AGN, Historia, vol. 283, fols. 112, 148, 360–360v for the centralist area and fol. 338 for the federalist area. Surprisingly, the town council of Zitlala in the centralist area declared its neutrality on the question. See fols. 400–400v.

91. *Decreto para el arreglo interior,* pp. 10, 22; Chevalier, "La emancipación," p. 157.

92. *Memoria,* State of Puebla, Relaciones, 1849, p. 10; *Memoria,* Federal Government, Relaciones, 1847, p. 167; *Memoria,* State of Mexico, Relaciones, 1849, anexo 5; *Colección de decretos y órdenes de los Congresos Constituyentes,* p. 525; *Ley sobre los lugares,* p. 1.

93. The provision is in Tena Ramírez, ed., p. 207. See also the electoral law of November 1836 in García Orozco, p. 58.

94. Tena Ramírez, ed., p. 409; AHEM, Epoca Independiente, vol. 25, exp. 3, fol. 42; Santoni, p. 282; *Colección de decretos y órdenes de los Congresos Constituyentes,* p. 583; *Ley sobre elecciones,* p. 5.

95. Income data is of course difficult to come by, as it was for the various parish committees and officers charged with determining voter eligibility. Similar committees in Guerrero assessing tax liability usually estimated a typical peasant's income at 2 reales per day, which would be 78 pesos per year on the basis of a six-day week. AGN, Ayuntamientos, vol. 242; AGN Gobernación, caja. 149, exp. 12.

96. For the complicated rules see García Orozco, pp. 2–105. For the list see *Lista alfabética.* A similar list is not available for Puebla, so that the 17 voters were not all those allowed to vote in the future state of Guerrero. Also, notably, 288 of the 890 voters correspond to those who resided in Mexico City or areas now inside the Federal District.

97. *Leyes,* p. 13.

98. *Decreto para el arreglo interior,* p. 22.

99. Dublán and Lozano, 4: 11–21, 142–44, 147–50, 474.

100. Piquero.

101. Piquero, pp. 3–4, 164.

102. Piquero, pp. 142–43.

103. Piquero, pp. 162–64, 172. The quotations are from pp. 162–63.

104. On colonial tribute see Dehouve, "El pueblo," pp. 93–94; Stein, p. 18.

105. ACDEM, Expedientes, 1840, libro 100, exp. 91, fol. 2. By 1840 the entire justification for the older personal tax revolved around its use for local education. ACDEM, Expedientes, 1841, libro 112, exp. 424, fols. 2–3. The national government assigned the capitación to the departments in the mid-1840s, after it had proven quite difficult to collect. AHEM, Epoca Independiente, vol. 25, exp. 34, fol. 1; *Ley sobre capitación*, p. 1.

106. *Decreto para el arreglo interior*, p. 29; Pastor, *Campesinos*, pp. 431–33.

107. ACDEM, Expedientes, 1841, libro 113, exp. 444, fols. 2–3.

108. ACDEM, Expedientes, 1841, libro 113, exp. 444, fols. 2–3; 1842, libro 118, exp. 73. In the latter case a justice was dismissed not for jailing two men who refused to participate in "community labor" but instead for insulting them and jailing them while he was drunk.

109. AHEM, Control Público, vol. 18, exp. 58, fol. 57v.

110. ACDEM, Expedientes, 1840, libro 104, exp. 272, fols. 2–2v.

111. AHEM, Epoca Independiente, vol. 157, exp. 6, fol. 1. For the peasant offensive in the early nineteenth century see Coatsworth, "Patterns," p. 55.

112. Lira González, *Comunidades*, p. 75; Pastor, *Campesinos*, pp. 424, 427, 429.

113. *Ley dictada por el Congreso Constituyente*, pp. 29–31. The Spanish text reads, "Las tierras que en común han poseido los pueblos con los demás derechos y acciones que les pertenecen." See also Hale, pp. 233–38.

114. *Memoria*, State of Mexico, Relaciones, 1835, pp. 37–38.

115. AHEM, Hacienda, vol. 3, exp. 21, fol. 2. The Spanish text is "los terrenos realengos o valdíos que ecsisten en el territorio de sus municipalidades."

116. *Memoria*, State of Mexico, Relaciones, 1835, pp. 38–39.

117. For Mexico see Hale, p. 238. For Puebla see *Memoria*, State of Puebla, Relaciones, 1849, pp. 31–32; González Navarro, *Anatomía*, p. 142.

118. AHEM, Epoca Independiente, vol. 139, exp. 3, fols. 1–3.

119. AHEM, Epoca Independiente, vol. 139, exp. 3, fols. 4–7.

120. AHEM, Epoca Independiente, vol. 139, exp. 3, fols. 8–14.

121. AHEM, Epoca Independiente, vol. 139, exp. 3, fols. 17–20.

122. AHEM, Epoca Independiente, vol. 139, exp. 3, fol. 21.

123. *Memoria*, State of Puebla, Relaciones, 1826, p. 10.

124. *Memoria*, State of Mexico, Relaciones, 1835, p. 37.

125. ACDEM, Expedientes, 1840, libro 99, exp. 2, fols. 30v–31.

126. ACDEM, Expedientes, 1840, libro 106, exp. 388, cuad. 6, fol. 10.

127. ACDEM, Expedientes, 1840, libro 106, exp. 388, cuad. 5, fol. 11v.

128. ACDEM, Expedientes, 1840, libro 99, exp. 1, fol. 15.

129. ACDEM, Expedientes, 1840, libro 106, exp. 388, cuad. 3, fol. 19.

130. ACDEM, Expedientes, 1840, libro 102, exp. 142; ACDEM, Expedientes, 1845, libro 144, exp. 319, fol. 2.

131. ACDEM, Expedientes, 1840, libro 106, exp. 388, cuad. 4, fol. 11v.

132. AGN, Archivo Histórico de Hacienda, 405, exp. 5, is a lengthy report on this quest for information in one part of Guerrero in the early 1800s.

133. *Colección de los decretos y órdenes más importantes*, 216; AGNDF, notary 532, November 20, 1829.

134. Pastor, *Campesinos*, p. 442; *Memoria*, State of Mexico, Relaciones, 1835, proyecto de ley 9; ACDEM, Expedientes, 1841, libro 108, exp. 103, fols. 1–2; M. Ochoa Campos, *La reforma*, pp. 280–81; AGNDF, notary 417, February 22, 1840; AGNDF, notary 417, April 7, 1840; AGNDF, notary 417, May 2, 1840.

135. ACDEM, Expedientes, 1838, libro 94, exp. 170, fol. 1; ACDEM, Expedientes, 1840, libro 101, exp. 101, fols. 1–3.

136. Among these were José María Luís Mora and later Lorenzo Zavala. See Hale, pp. 99, 127. Peasant definitions of federalism were sometimes ignored by politicans in other ways, too. After the restoration of federalism in 1846 some states continued to tax peasants at the same rate the centralists had. See *Ley de Hacienda*, pp. 1–2; *Memoria*, State of Puebla, Relaciones, 1849, p. 74; *Reformas*, pp. 11–12.

Chapter 4

1. Costeloe, *La primera república*, pp. 438–39. A more recent example is Donald Stevens's impressive application of quantitative analysis of political divisions to data describing a set of men who were either presidents or cabinet ministers. Stevens, pp. 49–106.

2. In particular see Rodríguez O., "La Constitución."

3. For the social bases of the struggle see Mallon, "Peasants and State Formation"; Mallon, *Peasant and Nation*; Thomson, "Movilización" and "Bulwarks." For the ideological conflict see Hale; Noriega.

4. Two recent examples are Thomson, *Puebla*, p. 206, and, more systematically, Stevens, pp. 29–45. Vázquez is an important exception; see "La crisis," p. 557. Charles Hale notes that liberalism and conservatism became well-formed alternatives after the war with the United States but nevertheless searches for their roots in the writings of Mora as early as the 1820s. See Hale.

5. For examples of this agreement see de la Garza, p. 51; Flores Caballero, pp. 66, 71, 81, 84; San Juan Victoria, p. 93.

6. Vázquez, "Iglesia," pp. 224–29; Staples, "Clerics."

7. AGN, Archivo Histórico de Hacienda, vol. 1871, exp. 5; AGN, Gobernación, caja. 32, exp. 6; Flores Caballero, p. 66; Harrell, p. 14.

8. AGN, Aduanas, vol. 422; *Memoria*, Federal Government, Guerra, 1823, p. 39.

9. Pastor, *Campesinos*, pp. 455, 467–68.

10. Flores Caballero, p. 71. For other evidence of public healing see Argan-

dar; Flores Caballero, p. 62; Guerrero, *El General Guerrero* and *Manifiesto patriótico.*

11. On the problems facing Iturbide see Flores Caballero, p. 62; Tenenbaum, "Banqueros," pp. 17–20; and esp. Anna, *Mexican Empire*, pp. 25–26 and 237–39. For the movement against him in Guerrero see AGN, Gobernación, caja. 43, exp. 10; AGN, Gobernación, caja. 45, exp. 5; AGN, Gobernación, caja. 48, exp. 11; Ramírez Fentanes, ed., *Coleccion*, p. 16; Guerrero, *El ciudadano Guerrero* and *Vicente Guerrero a José María Lobato*; and esp. AGN Gobernación, caja. 55, exp. 12.

12. For interpretations of Mexico's economic woes see Cardenas, pp. 12–13; Coatsworth, "Obstacles," pp. 92–94; Chowning, "Contours," pp. 119–22; Thomson, "Protectionism," p. 131; Van Young, "A modo," p. 22; D. Walker, pp. 21–22.

13. AGN, Aduanas, vols. 366, 406, 428; AHEM, Epoca Independiente, vol. 173, exp. 1, fol. 56; BN, Fondo Alvarez, carpeta 2, documento 121; Irecheta Cenecorta, "El cobro"; *Memoria*, State of Mexico, Relaciones, 1826, table 12; 1828, table 19; 1829, table 10; 1831, table 8; *Memoria*, Federal Government, Hacienda, 1823, tables, 5, 6; 1826, table 4; 1830, table 7; 1835, table 4; 1837, table 3; 1846, table 2; *Cuenta general; Balanza general del comercio marítimo por los puertos de la República Mexicana en el año de 1825*, pp. 1–5; *Balanza general del comercio marítimo por los puertos de la República Mexicana en el año de 1826*, p. 1; *Balanza general del comercio marítimo por los puertos de la República Mexicana en el año de 1827*, pp. 1–5; *Balanza general del comercio marítimo por los puertos de la República Mexicana en el año de 1828.*

14. ACDEM, Expedientes, 1840, libro 106, exp. 388, cuad. 4, fol. 20; AGN, Gobernación, 1a829(4)14; *Memoria*, State of Mexico, Relaciones, 1828, p. 10; Toro, pp. 416–17.

15. AGN, Archivo Histórico de Hacienda, vol. 110; AGN, Ayuntamientos, vol. 30, fols. 301–2; AGN, Gobernación, caja. 376, exp. 13, fols. 3–4; Hernández Rodríguez, pp. 135–36; *Memoria*, Federal Government, Hacienda, 1850, table 2; 1851, table 2; Old Nick, pp. 770–71; Toro, pp. 415–18; Records of the U.S. Department of State, microfilm, M143, vol. 1, rolls 1 and 2; Vicuña Mackenna, pp. 43, 45, 49.

16. AGN, Administración General de Alcabalas, caja. 56; ACDEM, Expedientes, 1834, libro 78, exp. 176; AGN, Aduanas, vol. 428; AHEM, Epoca Independiente, vol. 164, exp. 2, fol. 31; BN, Fondo Alvarez, caja. 1, documento 35; *Memoria*, State of Puebla, Relaciones, 1826, pp. 25–26; Potash, pp. 13–17; Sánchez, *El suroeste*, p. 61.

17. The protectionist political economy will be discussed below. For its economic effect in Guerrero see ACDEM, Expedientes, 1840, libro 102, exp. 142, fols. 32, 72, 114v; ACDEM, Expedientes, 1840, libro 103, exp. 230; ACDEM, Expedientes, 1849, libro 178, exp. 271, fol. 1; AGN, Gobernación, legajo 106, exp. 2, fol. 7; AGNDF, Notary 169, December 20, 1837; AGNDF, notary 169, June 7, 1838; AGNDF, notary 426, December 11, 1828; AGNDF, notary 426, August 21, 1840; AGNDF, notary 719, January 2, 1839; Estrada, "Derrotero," p. 429; J. García, pp. 440–42; González Navarro, *Anatomía,*

p. 133; Keremitis, pp. 25, 29; *Memoria*, Federal Government, Agricultura e Industria, 1843, p. 17, table 4; 1844, table 4; 1845, p. 50; *Memoria*, State of Mexico, Relaciones, 1834, p. 12; 1835, p. 17; 1849, p. 16; *Memoria*, State of Puebla, Relaciones, 1849, p. 67; Riva Palacio Papers, roll 79, document 1907; Romero, p. 246; *Reflecsiones sobre la prohibición*, p. 6.

18. Hamnett, *Revolución*, p. 85.

19. ACDEM, Expedientes, 1826, libro 27, fols. 1–8; 1840, libro 99, exp. 2, fol. 27; AGN, Gobernación, caja. 379, exp. 4; *Memoria*, State of Mexico, Relaciones, 1828, 12, table 2; 1834, p. 12; 1849, p. 18, anexo 2; *Memoria*, Federal Government, Relaciones, 1847, table 3.

20. Flores Caballero, pp. 84–87; Harrell, pp. 64–66; Sims, *Descolonización*, pp. 10–13, 22–25, 121, and *Expulsion*, p. 18.

21. Rodríguez O., "Introduction," p. 7; Sims, *Descolonización*, p. 13.

22. Flores Caballero. For expressions of this fear see Gallardo, p. 2; Bringas Colín, pp. 18–20.

23. Sims, *Descolonización*, p. 12, and *Expulsion*, p. 9.

24. Harrell, pp. 19, 29–33; Sims, *Descolonización*, pp. 14–15, and *Expulsion*, pp. 11–12; AGN, Gobernación, caja. 54, exp. 1.

25. Flores Caballero, p. 84; Sampanaro, pp. 89–90.

26. Flores Caballero, pp. 90, 94–98, 101–2, 105–7, 126–28; Harrell, pp. 180, 183, 234, 297–300; Sims, *Descolonización*, pp. 27–30, 61; AHEM, Epoca Independiente, vol. 16, exp. 1, fol. 3.

27. AGN, Gobernación, legajo 66, exp. 11, fols. 5–43; *Memoria*, State of Mexico, Relaciones, 1828, p. 3; 1829, p. 16; *Los pueblos*.

28. AGN, Gobernación, legajo 66, exp. 11, fol. 16.

29. ACDEM, Expedientes, 1827, libro 33; AGN, Gobernación, legajo 8, exp. 15. That competitor was an Englishman, Juan Ashley, who was struggling to set up a cotton gin on the coast. The municipal council of Tecpan in 1825 refused to rent Ashley enough land for his establishment, so Ashley called on the help of higher authorities, who prevailed on the municipality.

30. Gallardo; *Memoria*, State of Mexico, Relaciones, 1828, p. 3.

31. Montes de Oca.

32. C. Bushnell, pp. 51–62; Díaz y Díaz, *Caudillos*, pp. 30–31, 102; Gomezjara, p. 58; Heredia Alvarez, *Conmemoración*, pp. 2–6; Muñoz y Pérez, pp. 3–7; Pérez Hernández, 1: 345.

33. See *Los Pueblos*.

34. AGN, Expulsión de Españoles, vol. 15, exp. 2, fol. 388; AGN, Expulsión de Españoles, vol. 19, exp. 1, fol. 7.

35. Sims, *Descolonización*, pp. 102–4.

36. AHEM, Epoca Independiente, vol. 94, exp. 7, fol. 10; vol. 96, exp. 4, fols. 2–7; vol. 97, exp. 3, fols. 2–3; AGN, Expulsión de Españoles, vol. 47, exp. 4, fols. 124, 142, 171.

37. These issues are discussed in Chapters 1 and 2.

38. This problem is discussed in Chapter 3. Rentals clearly continued; see ANEG, caja. 36, exp. 359. Sánchez, *El suroeste*, pp. 41, 54–56, found similar rentals in the area of Michoacán just across the state border.

39. AHEM, Epoca Independiente, vol. 170, exp. 4, fol. 28.

40. AHEM, Epoca Independiente, vol. 17, exp. 3; vol. 171, exp. 3, fols. 24–46v; AGN, Gobernación, 1a829(6)19. Incidentally, some of the renters actually were Spanish. See AGN, Expulsión de Españoles, vol. 17, exp. 2, fol. 8; AGN, Operaciones de Guerra, vol. 75, fol. 381.

41. AHEM, Epoca Independiente, vol. 176, exp. 9, fols. 2–3; AHEM, Epoca Independiente, vol. 176, exp. 11, fols. 2–3; AHEM, Epoca Independiente, vol. 183, exp. 1, fol. 130.

42. AHEM, Control Público, vol. 24, exp. 44, fol. 4; AHEM, Epoca Independiente, vol. 172, exp. 10, fols. 22–28, 50–58, 63; Estrada, "Derrotero," p. 430; *Noticias históricas*, pp. 34–35; Ortega, ed., *Colección*, 1: 200v, 5: 154–55, 168; Romero, p. 247.

43. Vázquez, "Dos décadas," p. 9; Tenenbaum, *Politics*, pp. 1–35.

44. Harrell, pp. 76–77; San Juan Victoria, pp. 94–97.

45. Vazquez, "Dos décadas," p. 9; Tenenbaum, *Politics*, pp. 1–35.

46. Potash, pp. 21–22.

47. Costeloe, *La primera república*, tends to rely on this in his explanations; see pp. 440–41.

48. San Juan Victoria, pp. 100–101.

49. Sims, *Descolonización*, p. 16, and *Expulsion*, p. 12.

50. Green, p. 192.

51. Brading, *Los orígenes*, 130. Compare the observation of Parcero, p. 32, that these were the groups who inhabited the "outskirts" with the generalization for Latin America as a whole made by Safford, p. 101.

52. Alpuche e Ynfante, p. 5; Alamán, *Documentos diversos*, 3: 41. For additional yorkino descriptions of their opponents see *Oigan todos los congresos* and *Los antiguos patriotas*.

53. Brading, *Los orígenes*, p. 130; Harrell, pp. 106–8, 223–27.

54. Perhaps the best-written and most explicit elaboration of these ideas is that of *Oigan todos los congresos*.

55. Harrell, pp. 223–27.

56. Brading, *Los orígenes*, pp. 130–31; Hale, p. 102; Harrell, pp. 250–251; Lepkowski, p. 102; *Los antiguos patriotas*; BN, Fondo Alvarez, caja. 1, documentos 4, 11; *Malditos sean los gachupines*; *Oigan todos los congresos*.

57. Brading, *Los orígenes*, pp. 130–31; Arrom, pp. 258–60; Thomson, *Puebla*, p. 207.

58. Harrell, pp. 249–50.

59. *Oigan todos los congresos*; Green, p. 175.

60. Alanis Boyzo, "La conspiración," pp. 4–5; Gaxiola, p. xiv; Sims, *Descolonización*, p. 18; Flores Caballero, p. 90.

61. AGN, Gobernación, caja. 110, exp. 2; Sims, *Descolonización*, p. 16; *Memoria*, State of Mexico, Relaciones, 1828, p. 33.

62. AHEM, Epoca Independiente, vol. 34, exp. 9; *Memoria*, State of Mexico, Relaciones, 1829, pp. 6, 14, 20–21; Green, p. 126; Reyes Heroles, 3: 556–60.

63. Hale, pp. 122–33; Reyes Heroles, 3: 560–63; *Dictamen de la Comisión Primera de Hacienda*, pp. 3–6; Alamán, *Esposición*, pp. 4, 9.

64. Brading, *Los orígenes*, p. 131.

65. Green, p. 126.

66. Costeloe, *La primera república*, pp. 137–66.

67. Sims, *Descolonización*, p. 39; Parrish, p. 195; *El Patriota*, January 9, 1828.

68. Harrell, p. 205.

69. Flores Caballero, p. 118; Harrell, p. 198.

70. AGNDF, notary 164, July 27, 1837; *Colección de documentos*, pp. 272–77; Riva Palacio Papers, roll 76, document 217; Green, pp. 163–64; Harrell, pp. 78–79.

71. Harrell, p. 239, 248; Sims, *Descolonización*, p. 40.

72. *Los antiguos patriotas*; *El cuando del Señor General Don Vicente Guerrero*; *Oigan todos los congresos*.

73. Sprague, pp. 74–78.

74. Costeloe, *La primera república*, p. 167.

75. Costeloe, *La primera república*, pp. 178–79.

76. Sprague, p. 144. Note that Guerrero was not yet a state.

77. Costeloe, *La primera república*, pp. 193–95.

78. Costeloe, *La primera república*, pp. 203–16; Green, pp. 159–62.

79. AGN, Gobernación, legajo 1946, exp. 1, fols. 527, 538, 543–44, 599–600; Díaz y Díaz, *Caudillos*, p. 79.

80. AGN, Gobernación, legajo 72, exp. 14; legajo 1946, exp. 1, fols. 523, 604–5.

81. AGN, Gobernación, caja. 110, exp. 2; legajo 72, exps. 46, 55; AHEM, Epoca Independiente, vol. 97, exp. 25, fol. 2; "Cartas," 21: 197.

82. BN, Fondo Alvarez, carpeta 1, documento 5; Muñoz y Pérez, p. 11.

83. AGN, Gobernación, legajo 1946, exp. 2, fol. 323.

84. BN, Fondo Alvarez, carpeta 1, documento 5. Foreshadowing the events of the 1840s and 1850s, bandits attacked haciendas owned and administrated by Spanish nationals in the Cuernavaca region; see Sims, *Descolonización*, p. 82. During the War of the South a year later the hacendados of Cuautla, Cuernavaca, and the Llanos of Apam asked permission to form a self-defense force. AGN, Gobernación, caja. 133, exp. 11.

85. AGN, Gobernación, caja. 110, exp. 2.

86. AGN, Gobernación, legajo 1946, exp. 2, fol. 325v; Ramírez Fentanes, ed., *Colección*, p. 37; González Navarro, "Guerrero," pp. 40–41.

87. AGN, Gobernación, caja. 110, exp. 2; legajo 1946, exp. 1, fols. 546–549v.

88. Arrom, pp. 258–60; Flores Caballero, p. 120; Harrell, pp. 277–78; Sims, *Descolonización*, pp. 76–82, and *Expulsion*, pp. 50–51.

89. AGN, Gobernación, caja. 113, exp. 6, fol. 475; *Oigan todos los congresos*.

90. Ramírez Fentanes, ed., *Colección*, p. 33; Harrell, pp. 250–51.

91. "Cartas," 21: 217. AGN, Gobernación, caja. 113, fol. 269; caja. 110, exp. 2.

92. "Cartas," 21: 217; AGN, Gobernación, caja. 113, exp. 6, fol. 32.

93. Green, p. 164.

94. Harrell, pp. 285–91; Potash, pp. 36–37; Sims, *Descolonización,* pp. 43, 51.

95. Green, p. 164; Ramírez Fentanes, *Vicente Guerrero,* p. 11. Di Tella argues for fundamental similarities between nineteenth-century popular politics and twentieth-century populism; see pp. 30–32.

96. AGN, Gobernación, caja. 116, exp. 16.

97. Hale, p. 230; Green, p. 126, is mistaken on this point, although he is correct in noting Zavala's argument for land reform as governor of the state of Mexico.

98. Harrell, p. 315.

99. Harrell, pp. 296–97.

100. Guerrero, *Manifiesto del ciudadano,* pp. 16–17.

101. Arrom, pp. 258–60; Brading, *Los orígenes,* p. 130; Harrell, pp. 293–96; Potash, pp. 28, 31, 36–38; Salvucci, p. 164.

102. *Dictamen de la Comisión Primera de Hacienda de la Cámara.*

103. Harrell, pp. 318–19; Guerrero, *Manifiesto del ciudadano,* p. 10; *El Dean.*

104. Guerrero, *Manifiesto del ciudadano,* pp. 8–9.

105. Harrell, pp. 282–84.

106. Costeloe, *La primera república,* pp. 223–26; Green, pp. 166–68; D. Walker, p. 3.

107. Harrell, pp. 329–30.

108. Harrell, pp. 334–35, 359–60.

109. Harrell, p. 355.

110. Ramírez Fentanes, ed., *Colección,* p. 60.

111. AGN, Gobernación, 1a830(1)1; Sprague, p. 95; Green, p. 194; Ramírez Fentanes, ed., *Colección,* pp. 114–15; Gaxiola, p. xvi.

112. Chowning explores the rise and fall of cross-class alliances in Michoacán in "Mysterious Career."

113. Alamán, *Documentos diversos,* 3: 45.

114. AHEM, Epoca Independiente, vol. 180, exp. 2, fol. 32v.

115. *Memoria,* Federal Government, Relaciones, 1831, p. 10.

116. *Memoria,* Federal Government, Guerra, 1831, p. 13.

117. Muzquiz, pp. 2–3.

118. AHEM, Control Público, vol. 18, exp. 28, fols. 2–6; vol. 24, exp. 44, fol. 4.

119. AHEM, Epoca Independiente, vol. 180, exp. 2, fols. 26–30, 181, 198, 219, 224, 294; Ramírez Fentanes, ed., *Colección,* pp. 84, 97, 103–4, 133.

120. AHEM, Epoca Independiente, vol. 180, exp. 2, fols. 2, 13, 19, 22–24.

121. Díaz y Díaz, *Caudillos,* p. 120; AHEM, Epoca Independiente, vol. 180, exp. 2, fol. 2; Ramírez Fentanes, ed., *Colección,* pp. 130, 146, 211; *Memoria,* Federal Government, Guerra, 1831, p. 13; Muñoz y Pérez, pp. 18–19; Ortega, ed., *Colección,* 5: 220, 363–64; AGN, Archivo de Guerra, vol. 290, fol. 221. Díaz y Díaz is incorrect in stating that the word "aristocrat" in this context refered to local hacendados—it had been in wide use before then as a code for the Mexico City–based dominant class. See Díaz y Díaz, *Caudillos,* p. 120, and the discussion of yorkino political discourse above.

122. Ramírez Fentanes, ed., *Colección*, pp. 86, 228–30.

123. Harrell, pp. 336–37.

124. Ramírez Fentanes, ed., *Colección*, pp. 84, 90, 103–4; *Aurora de la Libertad*, October 23, 1830; *Noticias estraordinarias*.

125. Ramírez Fentanes, ed., *Colección*, p. 228.

126. AHEM, Epoca Independiente, vol. 146, exp. 3, fols. 1–2; vol. 165, exp. 28, fol. 2.

127. AGN, Gobernación, 1a829(6)15; the quotation is from 1a829(7)1.

128. *Memoria*, Federal Government, Guerra, 1831, p. 13; Chavez Guerrero, *Vicente Guerrero*, p. 216; Ramírez Fentanes, ed., *Colección*, p. 82; Díaz y Díaz, *Caudillos*, p. 106; González Navarro, "La venganza," p. 679, and "Guerrero," p. 43; Green, pp. 206, 231; von Mentz, p. 91; Ortega, ed., *Colección*, 5: 61–62.

129. For Chilapa-Tixtla see AGN, Gobernación, vol. 76, caja. 1, exp. 3; AHEM, Epoca Independiente, vol. 180, exp. 2, fol. 2; Ortega, ed., *Colección*, 5: 363–64; Bermudez, p. 38. For the Tierra Caliente see AHEM, Epoca Independiente, vol. 17, exp. 3; vol. 171, exp. 3, fols. 24–46v; AGN, Gobernación, 1a829(6)19; Ramírez Fentanes, ed., *Colección*, p. 97. Incidentally, some of the renters actually were Spanish. See AGN, Expulsión de Españoles, vol. 17, exp. 2, fol. 8; AGN, Operaciones de Guerra, vol. 75, fol. 381.

130. C. Bushnell, pp. 77–79; Díaz y Díaz, *Caudillos*, p. 108; Muñoz y Pérez, pp. 15–18.

131. Ramírez Fentanes, ed., *Colección*, pp. 162–64; Muñoz y Pérez, pp. 20–21.

132. Harrell, pp. 381–84; C. Bushnell, pp. 82–85; Ortega, *Bravo*, p. 14.

133. Ramírez Fentanes, ed., *Colección*, p. 193; AGN, Archivo de Guerra, vol. 290, fols. 270–270v; AGN, Gobernación, vol. 143, exp. 2; AHEM, Epoca Independiente, vol. 176, exp. 14, fols. 32–33v, 57–59, 62, 67–70, 74; *Memoria*, Federal Government, Relaciones, 1832, p. 5. On Codallos see Chowning, "Mysterious Career."

134. Vázquez, "Iglesia," p. 214.

135. Green, p. 191; Harrell, pp. 361–63.

136. *Culebrina*; El Payo del Rosario.

137. Warren, "Will."

138. Costeloe, *La primera república*, pp. 327–65; Rodríguez O., "Origins," pp. 145–62; Vázquez, "Los pronunciamientos," pp. 163–86.

139. For an example see Thomson, "Protectionism," p. 133.

140. Hale, p. 18.

141. The history of this issue is treated in Staples, *La Iglesia*, pp. 35–58. For this period in particular see Staples, *La Iglesia*, pp. 69–73; Vázquez, "Iglesia," pp. 217–20.

142. San Juan Victoria, pp. 109–10; Hamnett, "Partidos," p. 578.

143. Hale, p. 149; Vázquez, "La crisis," p. 558; Sordo Cedeño, p. 28.

144. Vázquez, "Iglesia," pp. 219–20, and "Un viejo tema," 624.

145. Costeloe, *Central Republic*, pp. 33–34. See also *Apelación*; *La plebe*; *Reflecsiones sobre las leyes*, pp. 4–5; *Si asesinan a Santa Anna*.

146. C. Bushnell, pp. 51–62; Díaz y Díaz, *Caudillos*, pp. 30–31, 102; Go-

mezjara, p. 58; Heredia Alvarez, *Conmemoración*, pp. 2–6; Muñoz y Pérez, pp. 3–7; Pérez Hernández, 1: 345.

147. C. Bushnell, p. 111; Pérez Hernández, 1: 347; Toro, p. 422. An early-twentieth-century survey measured the area of La Providencia as being 17,863 hectares. It is found in the Colección Mario Anzaldua, a private collection in Chilpancingo, Guerrero.

148. Muñoz y Pérez, p. 9. See Pérez Hernández, 1: 354, for a description of his archive in the 1850s when Pérez Hernández was his personal secretary. Sra. Blanca Heredia, widow of Alvarez's great-grandson, provided the information on the archive's loss.

149. AHEM, Epoca Independiente, vol. 164, exp. 2, fols. 1, 5; Dominguez, pp. 26–27; Guevara Ramírez, p. 63; Díaz y Díaz, *Caudillos*, p. 112; Ortega, ed., *Colección*, 15: 22–39; AGN, Gobernación, 1a831(1)13.

150. AHEM, Epoca Independiente, vol. 164, exp. 2, fols. 26–51.

151. *Noticias estraordinarias.*

152. AHEM, Epoca Independiente, vol. 164, exp. 2, fols. 35–36, 54, 58, 62; BN, Fondo Alvarez, carpeta 1, documento 93; Díaz y Díaz, *Caudillos*, pp. 115–19; Dominguez, p. 27; *Registro Oficial*, September 4, 1832; September 8, 1832; October 18, 1832; *Planes*, 2: 164.

153. AHEM Epoca Independiente, vol. 38, exp. 19; vol. 149, exp. 14; C. Bushnell, pp. 101–2; *Planes*, 2: 196; Dominguez, pp. 27–28; Muñoz y Pérez, pp. 30–31; Ortega, ed., *Colección*, 14: 4, 15: 42, 67–68, 108–9; *La Lima del Vulcano*, April 2, 1834; *La Oposición*, December 2, 1834.

154. Dominguez, pp. 29–30; AHEM, Epoca Independiente, vol. 164, exp. 9, fols. 2, 11–12; exp. 11, fols. 2–3; vol. 173, exp. 1, fols. 2, 11–11v, 17, 27–28, 48, 51–54v, 80–81; C. Bushnell, pp. 105–10; Díaz y Díaz, *Caudillos*, pp. 129–32; *Documentos relativos a la sublevación*, pp. 3–4.

155. All of this legislation is described in Chapter 3. See also Vázquez, "La crisis," p. 58.

156. Vázquez, "Iglesia," pp. 205–29; "La crisis," pp. 558–60, 562. Sordo Cedeño, p. 109, points out that neither the church nor the military pushed centralism in the Congress.

157. Tenenbaum, *Politics*, p. 42.

158. On this point see Chowning, "Mysterious Career"; Vázquez, "Un viejo tema," p. 624.

159. AGN, Gobernación, legajo 106, exp. 2, fol. 7; Potash, pp. 39–83; Thomson, *Puebla*, pp. 217–79.

160. Potash, pp. 126–30; Thomson, "Protectionism," pp. 132–35, and *Puebla*, p. xxiv; Vázquez, "La crisis," p. 563.

161. Potash, pp. 48–65, 91–92.

162. The "agiotistas" were a group of rich speculators who loaned Mexico's early post-independence governments funds at high rates of interest. For their investments in factories see Tenenbaum, *Politics*, pp. 70–72; Meyer Cosío, p. 115; Potash, pp. 152–53.

163. Thomson, "Protectionism," pp. 134–35; D. Walker, pp. 154–55.

164. For the debate on raw cotton imports, see AGN, Archivo Histórico de

Hacienda, vol. 117, fols. 355–56; ACDEM, Expedientes, 1840, libro 103, exp. 230, fols. 1–6; AGN, Gobernación, caja. 259, exp. 1; caja. 282, exp. 1; *Memoria,* Federal Government, Agricultura e Industria, 1843, pp. 15, 23; 1845, pp. 40–51; Potash, pp. 134–35, 141–42; Thomson, "Protectionism," p. 140; D. Walker, pp. 156–57; Bravo and Alvarez, p. 30. The issue surfaced again after the war with the United States. See *Alza; Colección de artículos.* For the traffic in licenses, see Potash, p. 142; Tenenbaum, *Politics,* pp. 71–72; Thomson, "Protectionism," p. 136; D. Walker, p. 158.

165. Thomson, "Protectionism," p. 133, and *Puebla,* pp. 247–62.

166. Taylor, *Drinking,* pp. 113–51.

167. *Reflecsiones sobre la prohibición,* p. 6; AGN, Gobernación, legajo 8, exp. 15, fols. 8–13; AGNDF, notary 169, December 20, 1837; June 7, 1838; notary 426, December 11, 1828; notary 719, January 2, 1839; AHEM, Epoca Independiente, vol. 97, exp. 20, fols. 5–7.

168. AHEM, Epoca Independiente, vol. 173, exp. 6, fol. 2.

169. AHEM, Epoca Independiente, vol. 173, exp. 6, fols. 2, 11, 22, 30–37v; 45; AHEM, Epoca Independiente, vol. 178, exp. 6, fols. 1–2; *Memoria,* State of Mexico, Relaciones, 1835, pp. 44–45.

170. AGN, Archivo de Guerra, vol. 12, fols. 477–78; AHEM, Control Público, vol. 32, exp. 3, fols. 2–3; Ortega, ed., *Colección,* 1: 63; AHEM, Epoca Independiente, vol. 173, exp. 10, fols. 2–9v.

171. AGN, Archivo de Guerra, vol. 12, fol. 505v.

172. AGN, Archivo de Guerra, vol. 12, fols. 401–502; the quotation is from fol. 477.

173. AGN, Archivo de Guerra, vol. 12, fols. 401–502; AHEM, Epoca Independiente, vol. 146, exp. 13, fol. 1.

174. Others who have described parts or all of this coalition include Brading, *Los orígenes,* pp. 130–31; Flores Caballero, pp. 66, 71, 81; Safford, p. 94; San Juan Victoria, pp. 118–20; Vázquez, "Iglesia," pp. 212–13.

175. See Brading, *Los orígenes,* p. 140; Flores Caballero, p. 84; San Juan Victoria, pp. 118–20.

176. Florencia Mallon, personal communication.

Chapter 5

1. Potash, pp. 133–44.

2. For Guzmán see Olveda, pp. 154–65; C. Bushnell, pp. 112–14, 127; University of Texas, Nettie Lee Benson Collection, Gómez Farías Papers (microfilm located in the AGN; hereafter Gómez Farías Papers), roll 118, documents 532, 558; University of Texas, Nettie Lee Benson Collection, Hernández y Dávalos Papers (microfilm located in the AGN; hereafter Hernández y Dávalos Papers), roll 75, HD23.4984; Ortiz Escamilla, pp. 253, 280–81; Sánchez, *El suroeste,* pp. 101–6. For the protectionist issue in Guerrero see Dominguez, pp. 37–38, and AGN, Gobernación, legajo 106, exp. 54. For support of the Plan of Tacubaya see AHEM, Epoca Independiente, vol. 167, exp. 7, fols. 1–3; C. Bushnell, pp. 118, 137; Díaz y Díaz, *Caudillos,* pp. 156–62, 168.

3. For alignments in Guerrero see Díaz y Díaz, _Caudillos_, pp. 95–96, 111–12; Gomezjara, pp. 71–72; Santos Carrera and Alvarez Hernández, _Historia_, pp. 194–95; Alanis Boyzo, "La conspiración," p. 11. For Alvarez's allies in the Montaña and the Tierra Caliente see ACDEM, Expedientes, 1841, libro 113, exp. 441, fols. 3–4; AGN, Archivo de Guerra, vol. 74, fols. 334–463; AHEM, Epoca Independiente, vol. 164, exp. 9, fols. 2–12; vol. 173, exp. 1, fols. 11–11v; vol. 178, exp. 7, fols. 18–33.

4. Díaz y Díaz, _Caudillos_, pp. 162–63; Dominguez, pp. 35–38; Heredia Alvarez, _Conmemoración_, p. 35; Riva Palacio Papers, roll 78, documents 1183, 1190, 1194; Bravo and Alvarez.

5. For colonial disputes see AGN, Indios, vol. 64, exp. 10; vol. 71, exp. 4; vol. 76, exp. 10; AGN, Civil, vol. 639, exp. 2; AGN, Tierras, vol. 1156, exp. 1; vol. 1313, exp. 2; vol. 1313, exp. 5; vol. 1363, exp. 10; vol. 1368, exp. 4; vol. 1514, exp. 6. For their continuation past independence see AGN, Tierras, vol. 2747, exp. 5, fols. 1–34; AGNDF, notary 417, December 30, 1829; AHEM, Epoca Independiente, vol. 154, exp. 1, fols. 2–5.

6. Fernández de Recas, pp. 51–65; Santos Carrera and Alvarez Hernández, _Historia_, pp. 93–97; AGN, Vínculos, vol. 74, exp. 10, esp. fols. 3v, 41v, 45v; vol. 75, exp. 6, fols. 35v–40v; AGN, Indios, vol. 64, exp. 10, fols. 22–24.

7. Herrera's family was one of several in the area descended from former colonial administrators. See AGN, Archivo Histórico de Hacienda, vol. 466, exp. 10; AGN, Historia, vol. 283, exp. 148. For the sale see AGNDF, notary 169, September 6, 1838; notary 332, December 13, 1838; notary 464, October 17, 1839.

8. ACDEM, Expedientes, 1840, libro 104, exp. 272, fols. 2–6. Herrera's claim is exactly that made by members of the Indian nobility of the Oaxacan Mixteca 130 years previously. This claim had not been upheld by colonial courts at all. See Pastor, _Campesinos_, pp. 169–78; Carmagnani, _El regreso_, pp. 89–95.

9. On these laws and their application in this case see ACDEM, Expedientes, 1838, libro 94, exp. 170, fol. 1; 1840, libro 101, exp. 101; libro 103, exp. 225, fol. 2; 1841, libro 113, exp. 443, fols. 5–7; AGNDF, notary 417, February 22, 1840; April 7, 1840; May 2, 1840; M. Ochoa Campos, _La reforma_, pp. 280–81; Pastor, _Campesinos_, p. 442; _Ley dictada por el Congreso Constituyente_, pp. 29–31; _Memoria_, State of Mexico, Relaciones, 1835, pp. 38–39.

10. _Decreto para el arreglo interior_, p. 22; Tena Ramírez, ed., p. 207; García Orozco, p. 58. Peasant incomes were typically estimated by contemporaries to be equivalent to 78 pesos per year. See AGN, Ayuntamientos, vol. 242; AGN, Gobernación, caja. 149, exp. 12.

11. Dublán and Lozano, 4: 11–12, 147–50.

12. The government never collected the amount it had expected. See AGN, Gobernación, caja. 285, exp. 2, fols. 24–26v; _Memoria_, State of Oaxaca, Relaciones, 1848, document 6; _Memoria_, Federal Government, Hacienda, 1845, pt. 2; 1846, p. 75; _Memoria_, State of Mexico, Hacienda, 1849, addenda 21, 23; Alarcon, pp. 5–8; Piquero.

13. ACDEM, Expedientes, 1838, libro 94, exp. 170; 1840, libro 101, exp. 101;

libro 103, exp. 225; 1841, libro 113, exp. 437; AGNDF, notary 417, February 22, 1840; April 7, 1840; May 2, 1840.

14. ACDEM, Expedientes, 1840, libro 104, exp. 272.

15. This pamphlet, which includes all the communications among the various actors, constitutes Alvarez, *El General: Juan Alvarez a sus conciudadanos*, and is the source for the events chronicled above.

16. Alvarez, *Manifiesto que dirige a la nación*, reproduced in Muñoz y Pérez, pp. 283–85; Bustamante, *Apuntes*, pp. 58–59; Díaz y Díaz, *Caudillos*, p. 172; Guevara Ramírez, p. 66; Reina, ed., *Las rebeliones*, p. 86; Riva Palacio Papers, roll 78, documents 1267, 1272.

17. AHEM, Epoca Independiente, vol. 56, exp. 17, fols. 50, 101; Hernández y Dávalos Papers, roll 75, HD 23.4957; Díaz y Díaz, *Caudillos*, pp. 172–73; Bustamante, *Apuntes*, p. 59; Reina, ed., *Las rebeliones*, p. 86; Riva Palacio Papers, roll 78, documents 1289, 1297; Ortega, ed., *Colección*, 7: 284–85; Alvarez, *Manifiesto que dirige a la nación*, in Muñoz y Pérez, pp. 286–87.

18. Ortega, ed., *Colección*, 7: 273–75; Riva Palacio Papers, roll 78, documents 1300, 1306, 1313, 1328; Alvarez, *Manifiesto que dirige a la nación*, in Muñoz y Pérez, pp. 287–88.

19. AGN, Gobernación, caja. 263, exp. 2; caja. 269, exp. 10.

20. Ortega, ed., *Colección*, 7: 294, 313–14, 325, 330–32, 356–58, 377; AGN, Gobernación, caja. 269, exp. 12, fols. 10–11, 15, 23, 32–35; Guevara Ramírez, p. 67; AHEM, Epoca Independiente, vol. 145, exp. 6, fols. 4–26; vol. 165, exp. 1, fol. 1; *Memoria*, Federal Government, Guerra, 1844, 56–59; *Memoria*, Federal Government, Relaciones, 1844, p. 54.

21. Parrish, pp. 265–66; Reina, ed., *Las rebeliones*, pp. 93–94; Ortega, ed., *Colección*, 7: 346, 374; ACDEM, Expedientes, 1843, libro 129, exp. 295, fols. 1–3; AGN, Gobernación, caja. 269, exp. 12, fols. 25–30, 113, 118; BN, Fondo Alvarez, carpeta 1, documents 66, 72, 87; carpeta 2, document 125. The agreement is reproduced in Reina, ed., *Las rebeliones*, pp. 103–4.

22. ACDEM, Expedientes, 1844, libro 133, exp. 140, fol. 1; libro 135, exp. 331, fol. 2; 1845, libro 146, exp. 428; AGN, Archivo de Guerra, vol. 174, fols. 73–74v, 83–88v; AGN, Gobernación, caja. 285, exp. 2 fols. 3–4, 12v, 14, 15, 19v, 29–29v, 32–32v, 37, 43–44v, 47–47v, 54, 60–60v, 71–71v, 78; BN, Fondo Alvarez, carpeta 1, document 90; Ortega, ed., *Colección*, 7: 393–94, 398, 468–70; Reina, ed., *Las rebeliones*, p. 109; *Memoria*, Federal Government, Guerra, 1845, pp. 6–9; Alvarez, *Manifiesto que dirige a la nación*, in Muñoz y Pérez, p. 351.

23. Reina, ed., *Las rebeliones*, pp. 109, 115–16; Riva Palacio Papers, roll 78, document 1534; Guevara Ramírez, pp. 67–68. For national events see Vázquez, "La crisis," pp. 561, 568–69.

24. ACDEM, Expedientes, 1845, libro 138, exp. 77; AGN, Gobernación, caja. 285, exp. 2, fols. 76–82, 86, 88–91, 95–97v; caja. 295, exp. 13, fol. 1v; legajo 208(1), exp. 1(4), fols. 21–30; exp. 1(7), fols. 85–88; AHEM, Control Público, vol. 19, exp. 13, fol. 1; BN, Fondo Alvarez, carpeta 1, document 3; C. Bushnell, pp. 143–46; Riva Palacio Papers, roll 78, documents 1583, 1606; roll 79, documents 1620, 1784; Ortega, ed., *Colección*, 7: 13–17.

25. C. Bushnell, pp. 149–50; Gómez Farías Papers, roll 119, documents 1158, 1249; Riva Palacio Papers, roll 79, documents 1679, 1685, 1783, 1784, 1817.

26. AGN, Gobernación, caja. 295, exp. 3, fol. 103; caja. 292, exp. 6, fol. 1; caja. 323, exp. 3; legajo 208(1), exp. 4, fols. 485, 493, 511, 514, 516, 520–21, 524, 529v, 535, 676; Ortega, ed., *Colección*, 7: 484, 8: 95–98, 108–12; C. Bushnell, pp. 151–53; Riva Palacio Papers, roll 79, documents 1866, 1910; *Diario Oficial*, May 14, 1846.

27. Soto, pp. 49–52, 60, 66–68, 77–78, 104, 118; Vázquez, "La crisis," pp. 563, 569–70; Hamnett, "Partidos," pp. 583–84; AHEM, Epoca Independiente, vol. 174, exp. 11, fols. 2–5v; BN, Fondo Alvarez, carpeta 1, document 7; Díaz y Díaz, *Caudillos*, p. 189.

28. *Diario Oficial*, May 6, 1846.

29. *Diario Oficial*, May 4, 1846; May 5, 1846; May 6, 1846; May 10, 1846; AGN, Gobernación, legajo 208(1), exp. 4, fols. 559, 565, 574–77, 588–91, 595, 602–3, 606, 611; caja. 323, exp. 3; caja. 324, exp. 4; exp. 5, fols. 46–51v, 70–70v, 151–151v; Ortega, ed., *Colección*, 8: 354–55; Soto, pp. 126, 128.

30. Díaz y Díaz, *Caudillos*, pp. 189–94; AHEM, Epoca Independiente, vol. 169, exp. 11, fols. 38, 40–43v; Soto, p. 193; *Diario Oficial*, May 9, 1846; May 11, 1846; May 12, 1846; May 17, 1846; June 13, 1846; June 30, 1846; AGN, Gobernación, caja. 323, exp. 3; caja. 324, exp. 4; exp. 5; Ortega, ed., *Colección*, 8: 208–15, 239–43.

31. Ortega, ed., *Colección*, 9: 136–37; AHEM, Epoca Independiente, vol. 174, exp. 16, fols. 2–3.

32. AGN, Archivo de Guerra, vol. 356, fols. 1–157; AGN, Gobernación, caja. 324, exp. 2; C. Bushnell, pp. 182–83; Riva Palacio Papers, roll 80, document 2677; Ortega, ed., *Colección*, 9: 398, 400–1.

33. Reina, ed., *Las rebeliones*, pp. 117–18; AGN, Gobernación, caja. 367, exp. 22; *El Siglo XIX*, March 27, 1849; April 6, 1849; Riva Palacio Papers, roll 81, documents 3262, 3282, 3367; Ortega, ed., *Colección*, 9: 21–24.

34. Some examples are found in AGN, Gobernación, caja. 269, exp. 12, fol. 10; caja. 285, exp. 2, fol. 78; caja. 324, exp. 5, fols. 151–151v; Ortega, ed., *Colección*, 7: 313–14, 393.

35. *Diario Oficial*, May 6, 1846; AGN, Archivo de Guerra, vol. 174, fols. 73–74v, 83–88v; AGN, Archivo de Guerra, vol. 356, fols. 46, 146–46v; AGN, Gobernación, caja. 285, exp. 2, fol. 15.

36. AGN, Gobernación, caja. 285, exp. 2, fols. 43, 47, 60, 78, 86, 88, 95–97v. For the rational choice literature see Olson, pp. 2, 133–34; Popkin, pp. 255–57.

37. Reina, ed., *Las rebeliones*, pp. 83–120, esp. 107; Hart, pp. 249–52.

38. See Chapter 3.

39. Some these documents are found in ACDEM, Expedientes, 1842, libro 123, exp. 356, fols. 1–1v; 1844, libro 135, exp. 331, fol. 2; 1845, libro 140, exp. 185, fols. 1–2; libro 142, exp. 241, fol. 1; libro 146, exp. 428; caja. 263, exp. 2; caja. 269, exp. 12, fol. 10; caja. 271, exp. 1; caja. 281, exp. 3; caja.

285, exp. 2, fols. 3–8v, 9–11v, 12v, 15, 24–26v, 32–35, 37, 66, 71; caja. 295, exp. 13, fol. 1v; caja. 300, exp. 7; caja. 323, exp. 3; legajo 208(1), exp 1(4); AHEM, Epoca Independiente, vol. 188, exp. 17; AHEM, Hacienda, vol. 16, exp. 37, fol. 2; BN, Fondo Alvarez, carpeta 1, document 90; *Memoria*, State of Michoacán, Relaciones, 1846, p. 11; *Memoria*, State of Michoacán, Relaciones, 1848, document 21; *Memoria*, Federal Government, Relaciones, 1845, 84–85; 1847, pp. 44–45; Ortega, ed., *Colección*, 1: 327, 7: 294, 313–14, 325, 356–58, 377, 382, 393, 9: 398, 400–1; Riva Palacio Papers, roll 79, document 1620. Some secondary sources also refer to taxation; see Díaz y Díaz, *Caudillos*, pp. 181, 225; González Navarro, *Anatomía*, pp. 180–81; Guevara Ramírez, pp. 66–8; Reina, ed., *Las rebeliones*, pp. 107–8, 117. For the tobacco monopoly see Ortega, ed., *Colección*, 7: 356–58. For head taxes as an issue in nineteenth-century Peru see Mallon, "Nationalist and Antistate Coalitions," p. 255.

40. AGN, Gobernación, caja. 285, exp. 2, fols. 3–4.

41. Village schools were common but enrollments were not high. See ACDEM, Expedientes, 1840, libro 102, exp. 142, fols. 3–6, 25; libro 104, exp. 279, fol.6; libro 106, exp. 288, fol. 7; 1841, libro 115, exp. 600, fol. 1; 1844, libro 132, exp. 124, fol. 3; AGN, Gobernación, vol. 285, exp. 2, fol. 95.

42. These issues have been prominent in social science since the revival of interest in the work of Gramsci. Perhaps the most influential work today is that of Scott. Van Young discusses these problems with specific reference to Latin American peasantries in "To See Someone Not Seeing."

43. For 1842 see Hernández y Dávalos Papers, roll 75, HD 23.4957; Ortega, ed., *Colección*, 7: 261, 272. For the 1845 description see AGN, Gobernación, caja. 285, exp. 2, fols. 95–97.

44. ACDEM, Expedientes, 1840, libro 104 exp. 272, fol. 2.

45. Ortega, ed., *Colección*, 7: 374.

46. AGN, Gobernación, caja. 323, exp. 3.

47. ACDEM, Expedientes, 1845, libro 139, exp. 138; Ortega, ed., *Colección*, 7: 376, 485–88.

48. Guerra, 1: 261; Pastor, *Campesinos*, p. 428. A relatively early example is the proclamation of September 1844 in Ortega, ed., *Colección*, 7: 393–94. Prominent later examples include the 1846 calls of Alvarez and others for rebellion against Paredes in AGN, Gobernación, caja. 324, exp. 5, fols. 46–51, 70–70v, and *Diario Oficial*, May 12, 1846. Alvarez seems never to have even feigned acceptance of the centralist restriction of citizenship. See *El Siglo XIX*, October 13, 1841. An example of the elite disdain for peasant citizenship is found in *Documentos relativos a las sesiones*, p. 6.

49. The phrase is from a document captured by government troops and published in the *Diario Oficial*, May 6, 1846.

50. Ortega, ed., *Colección*, 7: 356.

51. ACDEM, Expedientes, 1845, libro 142, exp. 241, fol. 2.

52. AGN, Gobernación, caja. 285, exp. 2, fol. 95; ACDEM, Expedientes, 1845, libro 142, exp. 241, fol. 3; 1846, libro 148, exp. 4, fol. 1; AGN, Gobernación,

caja. 323, exp. 3; Ortega, ed., *Colección*, 2: 137. This emphasis on local government is worth comparing with the description of zapatista political ideology provided in Warman, "Political Project," esp. p. 327.

53. ACDEM, Expedientes, 1845, libro 142, exp. 241, fol. 2; Ortega, ed., *Colección*, 7: 332; AGN, Archivo de Guerra, vol. 174, fol. 88; ASRA, Chilapa, Poblado de Lamatzintla, Dotacion Ejido, 23: 10228.

54. Ortega, ed., *Colección*, 7: 208–15; *Diario Oficial*, May 5, 1846; May 9, 1846; May 12, 1846; AGN, Gobernación, caja. 324, exp. 5; AHEM, Epoca Independiente, vol. 169, exp. 11, fols. 38, 40–43v, 109.

55. *Memoria*, Federal Government, Relaciones, 1847, p. 36; AGN, Gobernación, caja. 323, exp. 3; legajo 208(1), exp. 3(29) fols. 435–36; AHEM, Epoca Independiente, vol. 169, exp. 11, fol. 110.

56. On the failure of centralism see Costeloe, *Central Republic*, esp. pp. 299–301. See Ortega, ed., *Colección*, 7: 330, 389.

57. *Diario Oficial*, May 4, 1846; May 5, 1846; May 6, 1846; May 10, 1846; AGN Gobernación, legajo 208(1), exp. 4. fol. 559; caja. 324, exp. 5, fols. 46–51, 70–70v; AHEM, Epoca Independiente, vol. 169, exp. 11, fol. 38, 40–43v.

58. Tenenbaum, *Politics*.

59. AGN, Archivo Histórico de Hacienda, vol. 498, exps. 45, 48; Reina, ed., *Las rebeliones*, 117; González Navarro, *Anatomía*, 29; *Diario Oficial*, May 6, 1846; Riva Palacio Papers, roll 84, document 4899.

60. Reed, pp. 32–34; Joseph, pp. 173–78.

61. Díaz y Díaz, *Caudillos*. For some of the studies of twentieth-century caciques see Ankerson; Fowler Salamini; Falcón; Schryer. For Alvarez recommending the appointment and replacement of officials see AGN, Gobernación, legajo 200, exps. 84, 86, 94; legajo 208(1), exp. 4, fols. 624–624v; BN, Fondo Alvarez, carpeta 1, document 18; Ortega, ed., *Colección*, 7: 120–22, 367; Riva Palacio Papers, roll 81, document 3378. For interventions on behalf of prisoners see BN, Fondo Alvarez, carpeta 1, document 9; Riva Palacio Papers, roll 84, document 5164. For disputes between peasants see Riva Palacio Papers, roll 82, document 3585. For tiendas de raya see Ortega, ed., *Colección*, 8: 1. For taxes see Díaz y Díaz, *Caudillos*, p. 181; AGN, Gobernación, legajo 200, exp. 4. For Alvarez as a mediator see AHEM, Epoca Independiente, vol. 174, exp. 16, fols. 2–3; AHEM, Epoca Independiente, vol. 187, exp. 7, fol. 13; AHEM, Control Público, vol. 19, exp. 13, fol. 1; BN, Fondo Alvarez, carpeta 1, document 3; Riva Palacio Papers, roll 78, documents 1289, 1297, 1399; roll 79, document 1783; roll 80, document 2677; roll 84, document 4819. Others also acted as mediators. See the file of José María Pavon in Archivo del Condumex, Reforma-Intervención-Imperio, 1–7, 58.

62. Ortega, ed., *Colección*, 7: 346; Reina, ed., *Las rebeliones*, p. 86; Riva Palacio Papers, roll 78, documents 1155, 1226, 1240; roll 82, documents 3995, 4025.

63. *El Siglo XIX*, October 13, 1841.

64. BN, Fondo Alvarez, carpeta 1, document 18.

65. BN, Fondo Alvarez, carpeta 1, documents 9, 18; Ortega, ed., *Colección*,

7: 330, 389, 8: 208–15; *Diario Oficial,* May 6, 1846; May 12, 1846; *El Siglo XIX,* October 13, 1841; ACDEM, Expedientes, 1843, libro 129, exp. 295, fols. 1–3; AGN, Gobernación, caja. 323, exp. 3; caja. 324, exp. 5; legajo 208(1), exp. 3(29), fols. 435–36; AHEM, Epoca Independiente, vol. 169, exp. 11, fols. 38, 40–43v, 109, 110; ASRA Chilapa, Poblado de Lamatzintla, Dotacion Ejido, 23: 10228.

66. For letters to official superiors see Díaz y Díaz, *Caudillos,* pp. 183–184; Riva Palacio Papers, roll 79, document 1655; Ortega, ed., *Colección,* 8: 186–89. For the public debate see, in order, Alvarez, *El General Juan Alvarez a sus conciudadanos; El Monitor Constitucional,* March 5, 1845, in Ortega, ed., *Colección,* 2: 136–46; Alvarez, *Manifiesto que dirige a la nación;* Riva Palacio Papers, roll 79, document 1624, 1668; *No hay peor sordo;* Bustamante, *El nuevo Bernal Díaz del Castillo.* For private correspondence see Riva Palacio Papers, roll 78, documents 1151, 1284, 1333.

67. For some of the correspondence between Alvarez and Gómez Farías see Gómez Farías Papers, roll 119, documents 1249, 1310; roll 121, documents 1678, 2549.

68. AGNDF, notary 169, February 25, 1839; notary 529, December 4, 1837; notary 539, December 6, 1839; notary 739, May 2, 1838; C. Bushnell, p. 187; Giron, pp. 98, 105–106; Ortega, *Bravo,* p. 29; Riva Palacio Papers, roll 78, documents 1151, 1284, 1333; roll 85, document 5611.

69. AGNDF, notary 170, May 5, 1837; Pérez Hernández, 1: 351; González Navarro, *Anatomía,* pp. 161, 224; Johnson, p. 40; AGNDF, notary 715, April 25, 1836.

70. Lira González, *Comunidades,* p. 83; Mora, *Obras,* pp. 37, 152–53; Riva Palacio Papers, roll 79, document 1945.

71. Meyer, *Problemas,* p. 21; Reina, ed., *Las rebeliones,* pp. 27, 117–18; Stern, "Introduction to Part III," p. 215; Joseph, p. 178; *El Monitor Constitucional,* March 5, 1845, in Ortega, ed., *Colección,* 2: 136–46; *No hay peor sordo;* Brading, *Los orígenes,* p. 128; González Navarro, *Anatomía,* p. 33; C. Bushnell, p. 138.

72. Sierra, pp. 237–38; Hale, p. 36; Vázquez, "Los primeros tropiezos," p. 767. Bushnell and Macauley, p. 78, do not even mention it.

73. AGN, Gobernación, caja. 328, exp. 14; Soto, p. 193. Costeloe, *Central Republic,* p. 292.

74. C. Bushnell, pp. 152, 160–65, 168; Gómez Farías Papers, roll 118, document 558; roll 119, document 1310; roll 121, document 2549; Riva Palacio Papers, roll 79, document 1702.

75. AHEM, Control Público, vol. 13, exp. 32, fols. 2–4; Díaz y Díaz, *Caudillos,* p. 205; Heredia Alvarez, *Conmemoración,* p. 21; Muñoz y Pérez, p. 43; Ortega, ed., *Colección,* 8: 5. The song is found in Vicuña Mackenna, pp. 53–55; notably, it also associates the U.S. invasion with the economic hardship caused by imported manufactured goods.

76. Heredia Alvarez, *Conmemoración,* p. 18; AGN, Gobernación, caja. 333, exp. 3; caja. 337, exp. 1; Arreola Cortés, pp. 33–34; Irecheta Cenecorta, "Guerrillas," pp. 22–26; M. Ocampo, 2: 256–59; Roa Barcena, pp. 248–64.

77. Ortega, ed., *Colección*, 7: 62, 17: 354–55; C. Bushnell, p. 171; Muñoz y Pérez, p. 47; AGN, Gobernación, caja. 328, exp. 14, fols. 1–7.
78. AGN, Gobernación, legajo 225, exp. 15, fols. 245–74; Díaz y Díaz, *Caudillos*, 219–21; Dominguez, p. 53; Irecheta Cenecorta, "Guerrillas," p. 27; Ortega, ed., *Colección*, 9: 21–24, 136; Riva Palacio Papers, roll 80, document 2475; *El Monitor Republicano*, November 16, 1847.
79. Bravo and Alvarez.
80. AGN, Gobernación, caja. 365, exps. 8, 12, 15; *Memoria*, Federal Government, Guerra, 1850, pp. 8, 10; *Memoria*, Federal Government, Relaciones, 1847, pp. 44–45.
81. Cardenas Barraza, esp. pp. 94–96; ACDEM, Expedientes, 1847, libro 165, exp. 400, fol. 1; 1849, libro 174, exp. 60, fol. 1; libro 175, exp. 157, fol. 4; AHEM, Epoca Independiente, vol. 91, fol. 2; vol. 106, exp. 67, fol. 4; vol. 148, exp. 6; Riva Palacio Papers, roll 80, document 2870; roll 81, document 3159; Díaz y Díaz, *Caudillo*, p. 24; Dominguez, pp. 51–52, 54–56, 64; AGN, Gobernación, caja. 367, exp. 24; *Memoria*, Federal Government, Relaciones, 1849, pp. 7, 15.
82. *Documentos relativos a las sesiones*, pp. 2–76; *Memoria*, State of Puebla, Relaciones, 1849, pp. 23, 28, seccion hacienda, anexos 1, 18; *El Siglo XIX*, March 16, 1849; Hernández Rodríguez, pp. 24–25.
83. Dominguez, pp. 62–63, 66–67; ACDEM, Expedientes, 1849, libro 178, exp. 261, fol. 1; *El Siglo XIX*, March 21, 1849.
84. ACEG, Actas, vol. 3, fol. 258; AGEG, Archivo Histórico, caja. 1, exp. 9; ACEG, Decretos, vol. 1, fols. 144, 145, 205, 208; AHEM, Epoca Independiente, vol. 10, exp.45, fol. 7; *Reformas*, pp. 11–12; *Ley orgánica provisional*, p. 41.
85. ACEG, Decretos, vol. 1, 143, 146, 148–49, 184–85, 192, 195; González Dávila, p. 311; AGN, Archivo Hístorico de Hacienda, vol. 1817; Figueroa de Contín, pp. 150–51; *Ley orgánica provisional*, pp. 4, 27; *Constitución política del Estado libre*, 21. Alvarez's remarkable argument is from an 1841 letter found in BN, Fondo Alvarez, carpeta 1, document 18. For a partial list of municipalities ten years after the founding of the new state see *El Eco de la Reforma*, January 12, 1861.
86. Green, p. 193; *Constitución política del Estado de Puebla*, pp. 6–9; *Constitución política del Estado de México*, p. 4; *Instrucción que para facilitar*; Disposiciones, p. 22; Brading, *Los orígenes*, p. 103.
87. García Orozco, pp. 207, 409; Santoni, p. 282; *Ley sobre elecciones*, p. 5.
88. ACEG, Decretos, vol. 1, 131; *Ley orgánica provisional*, p. 28; *Constitución política del Estado libre*, p 3; Riva Palacio Papers, roll 85, document 5464.
89. *Documentos relativos a las sesiones*, pp. 6, 22–24, 42.
90. ACEG, Actas, vol. 1, 357–64; vol. 2, 6–9, 39–41; von Mentz, pp. 130–34.
91. Thompson makes some suggestions of the importance this might hold to the subjects involved; see *Making*, pp. 759–60.
92. ACEG, Actas, vol. 2, 3; *Constitución política del Estado libre*, p. 5. For colonial rebellions see Chapter 1 and Taylor, *Drinking*, pp. 113–51.

93. AGN, Gobernación, caja. 383, exp. 8; González Navarro, *Anatomía*, p. 167; *Memoria*, Federal Government, Guerra 1851, p. 5.

94. AGN, Gobernación, caja. 426, exp. 7; Díaz y Díaz, *Caudillos*, pp. 254–57; Riva Palacio Papers roll 84, documents 4872, 4899; roll 85, document 5491.

95. ACDEM, Expedientes, 1846, libro 155, exp. 248, fol. 1; AGN, Bienes Nacionalizados, vol. 211, exp. 101/21. For the 1884 agreements see ASRA, Quechultenango, Poblado de Nanzintla, Bienes Comunales, 276.1/35; Poblados de Nanzintla and Jocutla, Bienes Comunales, 276.1/35.

Chapter 6

1. Coatsworth, "Los orígenes," p. 213; Sinkin, *Mexican Reform*, p. 171; Tenenbaum, *Politics*, pp. 136–37; Mallon, "Peasants and State Formation"; Thomson, "Movilización" and "Bulwarks"; Garner.

2. Bazant, "Mexico," 3: 452. See Sinkin, *Mexican Reform*, pp. 34–35, 96; Sierra, p. 261.

3. González Navarro, *Anatomía*, pp. 288–367.

4. Hale, pp. 14–41.

5. The letter is reproduced in Arrangoiz, pp. 421–22, and Muñoz y Pérez, pp. 169–72.

6. Guerra, 1: 147.

7. On states see Vázquez Mantecón, pp. 45–48. On towns see AGN, Ayuntamientos, vol. 30, fol. 4; AHEM, Epoca Independiente, vol. 11, exp. 29, fol. 2; Dublán and Lozano, 6: 407; Vázquez Mantecón, p. 111. For the capitación see AGN, Gobernación, 3a837-47-54, (1)1; Vázquez Mantecón, pp. 139, 167, 253. For other taxes see Vázquez Mantecón, pp. 140, 142, and *Colección de disposiciones*, pp. 1, 2, 14, 22.

8. For the church see Vázquez Mantecón, pp. 234, 235, 239, 243. On corporate membership and rights see the election instructions in AGN, Gobernación, 2a854, (2)2. For book burning see Covo, "La idea," p. 71. On peasants and communities see Lira González, *Comunidades*, pp. 186, 213, 224; AGN, Gobernación, legajo 257, exp. 2; legajo 1607, exp. 1; Vázquez Mantecón, pp. 75–76, 115, 149–50.

9. For ceremonies and the Order of Guadalupe see Vázquez Mantecón, pp. 8, 50, 112, 274, 275. The Independence Day discourses were published as Medina y Lavalle and Espinosa.

10. For Guerrero's death see McGowan, p. 54; AGN, Gobernación, caja. 161, exp. 14. For Alamán, U.S. troops, and peasants see Mallon, "Peasants and State Formation," p. 16; González Navarro, *Anatomía*, p. 24, and "Guerrero," p. 43; Lira González, *Comunidades*, p. 212

11. The quote is from Alvarez, *A todos sus compatriotas*. See also the proclamation printed in Muñoz y Pérez, pp. 64–65. On the general character of opposition to Santa Anna see Vázquez Mantecón, p. 293.

12. Hernández Rodríguez, pp. 10–12, 21, 101–4, 106–9; Heredia Alvarez, *Anécdotas*, p. 119; Bazant, *Antonio Haro y Tamariz*, pp. 26–27; Muñoz y Pérez, pp. 53–54; AGNDF, notary 242, May 19, 1839; AGNDF, notary 286, Janu-

ary 17, 1839; Riva Palacio Papers, roll 78, document 1583; AGN, Gobernación, legajo 200, exp. 84; Aguirre Beltrán, p. 49; Chevalier, "Conservadores," p. 146; Díaz y Díaz, *Caudillos*, p. 260; Wilson, p. 139. Hernández Rodríguez is by far the best biography of Comonfort and also reprints many valuable documents.

13. C. Bushnell, p. 216; Díaz y Díaz, *Caudillos*, p. 261; Muñoz y Pérez, p. 68; AGN, Archivo de Guerra, vol. 53, fols. 32–33.

14. Díaz y Díaz, *Caudillos*, pp. 258–59; Muñoz y Pérez, p. 53.

15. For Moreno see Díaz y Díaz, *Caudillos*, pp. 258–60. For Guzmán see Olveda; Ortiz Escamilla; C. Bushnell, p. 218; Díaz y Díaz, *Caudillos*, p. 266; Portilla, p. 115.

16. Muñoz y Pérez, pp. 57, 95; Olveda, p. 191; Portilla, p. 51.

17. C. Bushnell, pp. 216–26; Carranco Cardoso, p. 21; Chavez Guerrero, p. 77; Díaz y Díaz, *Caudillos*, p. 266; Dublán and Lozano, 7: 94; Johnson, pp. 47, 50–52, 55; Ortega, ed., *Colección*, 2: 279–82, 11: 86–87, 109, 118, 139, 163, 281, 12: 66, 97–98, 13: 9–10, 27, 109, 174–75; Portilla, pp. 107, 121–23; Vázquez Mantecón, p. 287.

18. AGN, Gobernación, caja. 370, exp. 16; caja. 426, exp. 5, fol. 1; AHEM, Epoca Independiente, vol. 115, exp. 3, fol. 1; Díaz y Díaz, *Caudillos*, pp. 240–42, 250–51, 253; González Navarro, *Anatomía*, p. 350; Muñoz y Pérez, pp. 59–60.

19. C. Bushnell, pp. 209–11; Díaz y Díaz, *Caudillos*, p. 256; Portilla, p. 36.

20. Díaz y Díaz, *Caudillos*, pp. 254–58; Muñoz y Pérez, p. 53; Portilla, pp. 37–45.

21. C. Bushnell, pp. 212–13; Díaz y Díaz, *Caudillos*, pp. 257–58; Records of the U.S. Department of State, M143, microfilm, vol. 2, roll 1; Vázquez Mantecón, p. 281; Portilla, pp. 39–41.

22. Sierra, p. 261; Bazant, "Mexico," p. 452; Díaz y Díaz, *Caudillos*, p. 258; Sinkin, *Mexican Reform*, p. 96. See also C. Bushnell, pp. 215–16.

23. The Plan of Ayutla both in its original form and as modified in Acapulco on March 11, 1854, is found in Portilla, pp. xv–xxvii. See Vázquez Mantecón, p. 293.

24. For examples see the proclamations of Comonfort and Moreno in Portilla, pp. xxvii–xxviii, xxxiii–xxxiv, xxxcii–xl. The stationery printed for official revolutionary documents is found in AGN, Archivo de Guerra, vol. 191, fol. 164.

25. Alvarez's proclamations in Portilla, pp. xxix–xxxiii; broadsheet found in Archivo del Condumex, Reforma-Intervención-Imperio, 1–7, 14.

26. Alvarez, *A todos sus compatriotas*.

27. Alvarez, *Expediente*, p. 4.

28. Proclamation of Alvarez in Muñoz y Pérez, pp. 64–65.

29. Letter in Muñoz y Pérez, pp. 59–60.

30. See in particular the support for freedom of religion in Alvarez, *A todos sus compatriotas*, and the anticlericalism expressed by Alvarez's secretary, José María Pérez Hernández, in *Expediente*, p. 4.

31. See Johnson, esp. pp. 45, 49–50, and 80; C. Bushnell, pp. 218–19; Muñoz y Pérez, pp. 73, 77, 89; L. Díaz, ed., 1: 114; and Portilla, pp. 69–70, 108, 137–38. The quotation is from Wilson, p. 138.

32. AGN, Gobernación, 2a854, (2)2; AGN, Gobernación, legajo 1607, exp. 3; AHEM, Epoca Independiente, vol. 169, exp. 17, fol. 3; C. Bushnell, p. 231; Díaz y Díaz, *Caudillos*, pp. 267, 272, 275; Johnson, pp. 75–76; Muñoz y Pérez, pp. 85–86, 91; Vázquez Mantecón, p. 169; Portilla, pp. 88–89, xxxix–xl.

33. Díaz y Díaz, *Caudillos*, pp. 262–63, 274–75; Johnson, pp. 71–72; McGowan, pp. 39, 41; Vázquez Mantecón, pp. 54–55.

34. Díaz y Díaz, *Caudillos*, p. 266; Mallon, "Peasants and State Formation," p. 20; Gómez Farías Papers, roll 123, documents 3659, 3665.

35. Vázquez Mantecón, pp. 57, 216–17; Portilla, pp. 67–68.

36. AGN, Gobernación, 2a854(2)2; legajo 1040, exps. 1, 2, 3, 4; C. Bushnell, p. 231; Vázquez Mantecón, pp. 54–56.

37. Most of the above chronology is from the document summaries in *Guía del Archivo Histórico Militar*. See also Muñoz y Pérez, p. 92; Vázquez Mantecón, p. 291; Portilla, pp. 108–9, 113–41.

38. Díaz y Díaz, *Caudillos*, p. 287; L. Díaz, ed., 1: 220, 228; González Navarro, "La venganza," pp. 688–89; Heredia Alvarez, *Anécdotas*, pp.105–6; McGowan, p. 7; Muñoz y Pérez, pp. 110–11; Vanderwood, p. 33.

39. Thomson, "Bulwarks," p. 36.

40. Mallon, "Peasants and State Formation," pp. 20–21; Portilla, pp. 250–51; C. Bushnell, pp. 240–41; Hernández Rodríguez, p. 43; Díaz y Díaz, *Caudillos*, pp. 279–87.

41. G. García, *Los gobiernos*, p. 156; Heredia Alvarez, *Conmemoración*, pp. 57–58; Hernández Rodríguez, pp. 147–51; Vanderwood, p. 39; Portilla, p. 65; Muñoz y Pérez, p. 127; Heredia Alvarez, *Anécdotas*, pp. 106–7.

42. Perhaps the most recent work to emphasize the Congress is Sinkin, *Mexican Reform*, esp. pp. 55–73. See also Sinkin, "Mexican Consitutional Congress," p. 1.

43. Hale, pp. 14–41.

44. On the caste war see Reed; González Navarro, *Raza*; Joseph, pp. 173–78; Montalvo Ortega. On the Sierra Gorda see Reina, "Sierra Gorda."

45. For the 1848–49 events see Mallon, "Peasants and State Formation," p. 16; Sindico, pp. 315–17. The three pamphlets cited are *Comunicación*; Arizcorreta; *Respuesta de algunos propietarios*. The dispute is outlined in González Navarro, *Anatomía*, pp. 161–67. On the "siege mentality" developed by landholders of the time see Tutino, "Agrarian Social Change," p. 112. Administrative officals did not by any means always support landowners in conflicts. See Irecheta Cenecorta, "Andrés Quintana Roo," p. 12, for a case in the northern part of the state of Mexico.

46. *El Monitor Republicano*, April 16, 1850. The article refers to *El Porvenir* (Toluca), April 11, 1850, and an unspecified issue of *Temis y Deucalion*. See also Rueda Smithers, pp. 42–45, and the prologue in Maciel, ed., *Ignacio Ramírez*, 1: xlv–xlvii.

47. The quote is from Alamán's letter to Santa Anna in Arrangoiz, p. 421. For a complete account of the incident see González Navarro, *Anatomía*, pp. 34, 99–102 and Arreola Cortés, pp. 25–28, 37; M. Ocampo, *Obras*, 1: 21.

48. See *Memoria*, Federal Government, Relaciones, 1849, pp. 5, 41.

49. *Memoria*, Federal Government, Relaciones, 1847, p. 40.

50. For an example see *El Monitor Republicano*, April 19, 1850.

51. Hale, p. 229; *El Monitor Republicano*, May 5, 1849; July 15, 1849.

52. Sinkin, *Mexican Reform*, pp. 62–64; Vanderwood, pp. 39–60; Rueda Smithers.

53. Ruiz Castañeda, p. 43.

54. Reyes Heroles, 3: 586.

55. Sinkin, *Mexican Reform*, pp. 68–69, 170.

56. The quote is from G. García, ed., *Los gobiernos*, p. 30. The only biography of Arriaga is Ramírez Arriaga. For Arriaga in San Luís see Ramírez Arriaga, pp. 179–222. For Arriaga and the parcialities see Lira González, *Comunidades*, p. 171. For his positions in the cabinet and Congress see C. Bushnell, p. 241; L. Díaz, ed., 1: 4; Hernández Rodríguez, p. 43; Muñoz y Pérez, p. 214; Ruiz Castañeda, p. 125; Zarco, *Historia*, p. 344.

57. Brading, "Liberal Patriotism," pp. 30–36; Vázquez Mantecón, p. 283; González y González, p. 486; Maciel, "Ideología," pp. 126–27; Reyes Heroles, 3: 656–60. Ramírez was also selected as a representative of Guerrero in the 1861 National Congress; *El Eco de la Reforma*, March 30, 1861. On the crucial issue of local self-government see his 1846 essay "Intereses de las localidades," in Maciel, ed., *Ignacio Ramírez*, 1: 210–12.

58. For Olvera see Zarco, *Crónica*, 2; L. Díaz, ed., 1: 446; González Navarro, *Anatomía*, p. 10; ACDEM, Expedientes, 1848, libro 172, exp. 234; Covo, "La idea," p. 76; Riva Palacio Papers, roll 85, document 5788. For Jaquez see Riva Palacio Papers, roll 84, document 4670; roll 85, documents 5322, 5725, 5732. For a full list of delegates elected from various localities see Muñoz y Pérez, pp. 213–19.

59. On Argentina and Chile see Halperín Donghi, pp. 108–9; Zeitlin, pp. 67–69. For the clubs see Covo, "Los clubs," pp. 441–442; L. Díaz, ed., 1: 232.

60. Tutino, "Rebelión," pp. 88–101; Sinkin, *Mexican Reform*, p. 40; *Memoria*, State of Oaxaca, Relaciones, 1850.

61. Sinkin, *Mexican Reform*, p. 129.

62. L. Díaz, ed., 1: 207.

63. Tutino, "Agrarian Social Change," esp. pp. 122–23.

64. For examples see *El Monitor Republicano*, July 1, 1849; April 19, 1850. *El Siglo XIX* was no better; see March 26, 1849.

65. Ruiz Castañeda, pp. 52, 112–15; Ramírez Arriaga, pp. 364–65; Reyes Heroles, 3: 608–12.

66. Castillo Velasco's argument and amendments are in Zarco, *Historia*, pp. 362–65. See also Reyes Heroles, 3: 590–92.

67. Arriaga's proposition is found in Zarco, *Historia*, pp. 387–404. The quotations are from pages 387, 389, and 402.

68. Zarco, *Historia*, pp. 467–70.

69. Ramírez Arriaga, pp. 365, 367–68; Ruiz Castañeda, p. 116.

70. *Representación*. For more on the alarm caused by Arriaga's proposal see L. Díaz, ed., 1: 291.

71. *Representaciones*. The inclusion of Guerrero does not necessarily indicate that any landowners resident in the state were involved. A perusal of the names of those who signed it in Morelia suggests that the inclusion of Guerrero was due to the signature of a representative of the Leiva brothers who owned land near Chilapa.

72. Sinkin, *Mexican Reform*, pp. 62–63; Zarco, *Historia*, p. 630.

73. Zarco, *Historia*, p. 662. Note that Gamboa proceeded to suggest that the best antidote to caste war was European immigration, which religious tolerance would facilitate.

74. Ramírez Arriaga, p. 366.

75. Zarco, *Historia*, pp. 690–97; Reyes Heroles, 3: 597–99.

76. Zarco, *Crónica*, pp. 457–58; Ruiz Castañeda, pp. 107–12.

77. For Congress, see Zarco, *Historia*, pp. 710–11, 903. For the press see *Crónica de la Semana*, August 10, 1856; Ruiz Castañeda, pp. 117–21. For property rights in reactionary proclamations to justify armed rebellion against the liberals, see Archivo del Condumex, Reforma-Intervención-Imperio, 1–7, 77.

78. Mallon, "Peasants and State Formation."

79. For the cycle of the late colonial period see Martin, "Haciendas," pp. 407–27; and Martin, *Rural Society*, esp. pp. 99–113. Zapatismo and the economic and social conditions that led to it have inspired dozens of studies, but the best remains Womack.

80. González Navarro, "La venganza," p. 686; Green, p. 127; Old Nick, 1: 775; Vicuña Mackenna, pp. 59–60; and above all Mallon, "Peasants and State Formation," pp. 10–15.

81. For company stores in Morelos see AGN, Gobernación, caja. 367, exp. 19; González Navarro, *Anatomía*, p. 155. For struggles over municipalities see von Mentz, pp. 145–47. For fears of caste war and their effect on politics see the clash between Mariano Arizcorreta and the hacendados described above.

82. On the cane field incident see AGN, Gobernación, caja. 304, exp. 14; Alvarez's letter to the Morelos peasantry is found in Biblioteca Nacional, Fondo Alvarez, carpeta 1, document 13; and Ortega, ed., *Colección*, 8: 1. For the rest of the events detailed see AGN, Gobernación, legajo 208(1), exp. 1(2), fol. 106, exp. 2(24), fol. 255. For complaints against Alvarez see von Mentz, p. 62.

83. See Mallon, "Peasants and State Formation," pp. 14–18; Reina, ed., *Las rebeliones*, pp. 157–67; AGN, Gobernación, caja. 367, exp. 19; legajo 208(1), exp. 4, fols. 582–85; Díaz y Díaz, *Caudillos*, 223; Riva Palacio Papers, roll 84, document 5164; González Navarro, *Anatomía*, p. 433.

84. The quote is from Mallon, "Peasants and State Formation," p. 20. See also Ortega, ed., *Colección*, 11: 64.

85. AHEM, Epoca Independiente, vol. 96, exp. 13; *El Siglo XIX*, March 2, 1855; Mallon, "Peasants and State Formation," p. 33.

86. Von Mentz, p. 59.

87. Zarco, *Historia*, pp. 1060–65.

88. Zarco, *Historia*, pp. 1073–77; the quotation is from p. 1077.

89. The debates and votes of the two days are found in Zarco, *Historia*, pp. 1120–25, and *Actas*, pp. 536–41, which includes the roll calls. See also Zarco, *Crónica*, p. 876; Díaz y Díaz, *Caudillos*, p. 297; Riva Palacio Papers, roll 86, document 6046. On previous dates in reference to other issues, Ramírez and Olvera had argued for the addition of Morelos to Guerrero, whereas Arriaga had argued against it on the grounds that it would not affect the condition of the rural poor in other states. See Zarco, *Historia*, pp. 455, 457, 470.

90. Sinkin, *Mexican Reform*, pp. 62–63; the quotation is from p. 62.

91. C. Bushnell, pp. 257–58.

92. See *Guía de los documentos*, p. 73; Haro, p. 4.

93. The best discussion of the incident is found in Mallon, "Peasants and State Formation." Some printed primary sources of interest include Alvarez, *Manifiesto del ciudadano*; Haro; Casasola; *Defensa*; Aguilar y Medina.

94. According to Alvarez, Abascal and Barreto with 40 men had volunteered to help pursue the local reactionaries Alvarez sought. See Alvarez, *Manifiesto del ciudadano*, in Muñoz y Pérez, p. 457.

95. Riva Palacio Papers, roll 84, document 5164. For Riva Palacio and the peasantry, see Tutino, "Agrarian Social Change," esp. pp. 122–23.

96. For the deaths of the two accused, see Díaz y Díaz, *Caudillos*, p. 298. For Comonfort's position, see his letter to Joaquín Moreno in Hernández Rodríguez, p. 155. For Haro's earlier relations with Alvarez, see Gómez Farías Papers, roll 117, document 135; Riva Palacio Papers, roll 80, document 2729; Haro, pp. 11–12. Even Haro admitted that the evidence linking Abascal and Barreto to the murders was hearsay. See Haro, pp. 36–37, 41–42.

97. Alvarez, *Manifiesto del ciudadano*, in Muñoz y Pérez, pp. 440–58; the quotation is from p. 458.

98. Alvarez, *Manifiesto del ciudadano*, in Muñoz y Pérez, pp. 458–66.

Conclusion

1. Tutino, *From Insurrection*, pp. 228–41; Coatsworth, "Patterns," p. 55.

2. Mallon, "Peasants and State Formation"; for Chalco, see Tutino, "Agrarian Social Change."

3. Reed, pp. 53–59; Joseph, pp. 177–79; Sullivan.

4. Hu-DeHart, pp. 18–93.

5. Hu-DeHart, pp. 56–93; Ducey, "From Village Riot"; Meyer, *Esperando a Lozada*; Reina, "Sierra Gorda," pp. 282–87.

6. For the case of Cusco see C. Walker, "Peasants."

7. Pastor, *Campesinos*, pp. 426–27.

8. Farriss, *Maya Society*, pp. 355–66; Carmagnani, *El regreso*, pp. 231–36.

9. Stern, *Peru's Indian Peoples*, pp. 114–37.

10. For other Mexican examples see Meyer, *Esperando a Lozada;* Ducey, "From Village Riot."

11. Indian peasants were not the only subalterns who learned new ways to pursue their interests after independence. The urban poor did so actively in Mexico and other parts of Latin America. See Warren, "Vagrants"; Meisel; Chambers.

12. The only other important site that seems to have been uninfluenced by Guerrero was the Huasteca. See Ducey, "From Village Riot," esp. chs. 4, 6.

13. Thomson, *Patriarch*, ch. 3; Mallon, "Peasants and State Formation."

14. Escudero, p. 93.

15. Thomson, "Popular Aspects," pp. 271–73.

16. Thomson, "Bulwarks," pp. 62–67.

17. Womack, p. 71; Knight, 1: 311.

18. Perry, p. 344.

19. Pérez García, 1: 203, 2: 89–91, 102–4.

20. Katz, "Liberal Republic," 65–66. See also the text of the Plan of Tuxtepec in González Navarro, Ross, and de la Torre Villar, eds. 1: 364–67.

21. R. Anderson, p. 323; M. Díaz, pp. 498–99; Knight, 1: 137–38.

22. Cockcroft, pp. 9, 31, 61; Gómez Quiñones, p. 16; Aguilar Camín, pp. 153–54.

23. Knight, 1: 121–22; Garner.

24. Womack, pp. 71, 399; Warman, "Political Project," pp. 322, 327; Shadle, pp. 1–2.

25. An example from the 1980s is that of Juchitán. See Rubin.

26. Declaration of the Zapatista Army of National Liberation, January 1994, translated and posted on the Internet by Jessica Zoe Varish.

Bibliography

Primary Sources

ARCHIVES

Chilpancingo

Archivo de la Cámara de Diputados del Estado de Guerrero
Archivo de Notarias del Estado de Guerrero
Archivo del Gobierno del Estado de Guerrero
Colección Mario Anzaldua

Mexico City

Archivo de la Secretaría de Reforma Agraria
Archivo del Condumex
Archivo General de la Nación

Administración General de Alcabalas	Fomento
Aduanas	Gobernación
Alcaldes Mayores	Historia
Alhóndigas	Indios
Archivo de Guerra	Industria y Comercio
Archivo Histórico de Hacienda	Infidencias
Ayuntamientos	Inquisición
Bienes Nacionales	Intendencias
Bienes Nacionalizados	Judicial
Civil	Operaciones de Guerra
Clero Regular y Secular	Padrones
Consulado	Real Hacienda
Criminal	Tabacos
Ex-indiferente de Alcabalas	Tierras
Expulsión de Españoles	Tributos
	Vínculos

Archivo General de Notarias del Distrito Federal
Biblioteca Nacional
   Fondo Alvarez   Fondo Lafraugua
Hermeroteca Nacional

Toluca

Archivo de la Cámara de Diputados del Estado de México
Archivo Histórico del Estado de México

MICROFILMS

Archivo Parroquial de Chilapa
University of Texas Nettie Lee Benson Collection
   Gómez Farías Papers   Riva Palacio Papers
   Hernández y Dávalos Papers

U.S. State Department M143

MEMORIAS

Federal Government

Agricultura e Industria 1843, 1845, 1846
Guerra 1822, 1823, 1831, 1844, 1845, 1846, 1849, 1850, 1851, 1857
Hacienda 1823, 1826, 1830, 1835, 1837, 1844, 1845, 1846, 1850, 1851
Relaciones 1823, 1831, 1832, 1844, 1845, 1847, 1849

State of Mexico

Hacienda 1835, 1849
Relaciones 1826, 1827, 1828, 1829, 1831, 1834, 1835, 1849

State of Michoacán

Relaciones 1829, 1830, 1846, 1848

State of Oaxaca

Relaciones 1848, 1850

State of Puebla

Relaciones 1826, 1827, 1830, 1849

NEWSPAPERS

Aurora de la Libertad   *El Monitor Republicano*
Aurora del Sur   *La Oposición*
Crónica de la Semana   *El Patriota*
Diario del Gobierno de la   *El Porvenir*
   República Mexicana   *Registro Oficial*
Diario Oficial   *Restaurador de la Libertad*
El Eco de la Reforma   *El Siglo XIX*
La Lima del Vulcano   *El Universal*

OTHER PUBLICATIONS

Abusos de las elecciones populares. Mexico City: Alejandro Valdes, 1820.
Actas oficiales y minutario de decretos del Congreso Extraordinario Constituyente de 1856–1857. Mexico City: El Colegio de México, 1957.
Advertencia importante sobre las próximas elecciones de los Ayuntamientos. Mexico City: Alejandro Valdes, 1821.
Aguilar y Medina, Luís M. *Defensa leída el 5 de agosto de 1858 en los estrados de la Exma. Tercera Sala de la Suprema Corte de Justicia por . . . abogado defensor de Trinidad Carrillo y Quirina Galvan, acusados en la causa relativa a los robos y homocidios que se verificaron en la Hda. de Chiconcuac, en la noche de 17 de diciembre de 1856, y en la de S. Vicente Zacoalpan, la mañana del 18 del mismo més y año.* Mexico City: Imprenta de Manuel Castro, 1858.
Alamán, Lucás. *Documentos diversos (Inéditos y muy raros).* Mexico City: Editorial Jus, 1945–48.
———. *Esposición que hace a la Cámara de Diputados del Congreso General el apoderado del Duque de Terranova y Monteleone.* Mexico City: Imprenta de José Fernández, 1828.
Alarcon, Juan N. *Manifestación del Prefecto del Distrito de Puebla sobre la conducta que ha observado en la exacción de la contribución personal.* Puebla: Antigua en el Portal de las Flores, 1844.
Alessio Robles, Vito, ed. *La correspondencia de Agustín de Iturbide después de la proclamación del Plan de Iturbide.* Mexico City: n.p., 1945.
Alpuche e Ynfante, José María. *Manifiesto que el Diputado por el Estado de Tabasco hace de su conducta pública en la Cámara en la elección de presidente celebrada en favor de Don V. Guerrero.* New York: C. S. Van Winkle, 1830.
Alvarez, Juan. *A todos sus compatriotas.* Acapulco: Imprenta del Sur, 1854.
———. *Expediente mandado formar por el Sr. Presidente Interino G. D. Juan Alvarez sobre el préstamo que se quiso contratar en la Alta California para fomentar la Revolución de Ayutla.* Mexico City: Ignacio Cumplido, 1856.
———. *El General Juan Alvarez a sus conciudadanos.* Mexico City: Ignacio Cumplido, 1841.
———. *El General Juan Alvarez desmintiendo las calumnias acerca del pretentido protectorado americano.* Mexico City: n.p., 1855.
———. *Manifiesto del ciudadano Juan Alvarez a los pueblos cultos de Europa y América.* Mexico City: Ignacio Cumplido, 1857.
———. *Manifiesto del General Alvarez.* Mexico City: n.p., 1855.
———. *Manifiesto que dirige a la nación.* Mexico City: Ignacio Cumplido, 1845.
Alvarez, Juan, and Isidro Montes de Oca. *Proclama de los Generales Alvarez y Montes de Oca.* N.p., 1834.
Alza de prohibiciones: Artículos publicados en el periódico titulado El Universal. Mexico City: R. Rafael, 1851.

El amigo de los Indios al autor del Primer Indio Constitucional. Mexico City: Ontiveros, 1820.

Los antiguos patriotas a sus conciudadanos. Mexico City: n.p., 1828.

Apelación al sentido común de los mexicanos. N.p., 1833.

Arancel a que deben sujetarse en el estado de Oaxaca para el cobro de derechos u honarios, los jueces, asesores, abogados, escribanos, procuradores y demás personas que intervienen en los juicios. Oaxaca: n.p., 1849.

Argandar, Francisco. *Elogio funebre de los primeros heróes y víctimas de la patria.* Mexico City: Imprenta del Gobierno, 1823.

Arizcorreta, Mariano. *Manifestación que hace al público el ciudadano Lic. Mariano Arizcorreta contra la comunicación dirigida a los propietarios de fincas rústicas del Estado de México.* Mexico City: n.p., 1849.

Balanza general del comercio marítimo por los puertos de la República Mexicana en el año de 1825. Mexico City: Imprenta del Aguila, 1827.

Balanza general del comercio marítimo por los puertos de la República Mexicana en el año de 1826. Mexico City: Imprenta del Aguila, 1828.

Balanza general del comercio marítimo por los puertos de la República Mexicana en el año de 1827. Mexico City: Imprenta del Aguila, 1829.

Balanza general del comercio marítimo por los puertos de la República Mexicana en el año de 1828. Mexico City: Imprenta del Aguila, 1831.

Bermudez, José María. *Verdadera causa de la Revolución del Sur.* Toluca: Imprenta del Gobierno del Estado, 1831.

Biart, Luicen. *Tierra Caliente.* Madrid: Imprenta de Medina y Navarro, n.d.

Bravo, Nicolás. *Manifiesto.* Mexico City: Imprenta de Galvan, 1828.

Bravo, Nicolás, and Juan Alvarez. *Manifiesto de los Excelentísimos Señores Generales D. Nicolás Bravo y D. Juan Alvarez dirigido a los Supremos Poderes de la Nación y los Departamentos sobre que se erija en la parte meridional de Departamento de México uno nuevo con la denominación de Departamento de Acapulco.* Mexico City: Ignacio Cumplido, 1842.

Bustamante, Carlos María de. *Apuntes para la historia del gobierno de General López de Santa Anna.* Mexico City: Imprenta de J. M. Lara, 1845.

———. *Honor y patriotismo del General D. Nicolás Bravo demonstrado en los últimos días del fugaz imperio de Iturbide.* Mexico City: Imprenta de Galvan, 1828.

———. *El indio mexicano o avisos al Rey Fernando Séptimo para la pacificación de la América Septrional.* Mexico City: Instituto Mexicano de Seguro Social, 1981.

———. *Memoria presentada al Exmo. Ayuntamiento Constitucional de México.* Mexico City: Imprenta Constitucional, 1820.

———. *El nuevo Bernal Díaz de Castillo.* Mexico City: Vicente García Torres, 1847.

Caamaño, Marcial. "Breves noticias del Distrito de Morelos [1856]." *Boletín de la Sociedad Mexicana de Geografía y Estadística* 7 (1859): 543–44.

"Cartas al General Vicente Guerrero." *Boletín del Archivo General de la Nación* 21 (1950): 191–234, 415–70; 22 (1951): 89–101, 251–342.

Cartas de los señores generales D. Agustín de Iturbide y D. Vicente Guerrero. Mexico City: Imprenta Imperial, 1821.

Casas, D. Fr. Bartolomé de las. *Crueldades que los españoles cometieron en los indios mexicanos.* Mexico City: Oficina de la Testamentaría de Ontiveros, 1826.

Casasola, José María. *Acusación fiscal que en la Tercera Sala de la Suprema Corte de Justica pronunció el Sr. Ministro fiscal de ella . . . en la causa instruida a varios reos por el asalto, robos y asesinatos cometidos la noche del 17 y la mañana del 18 de diciembre de 1856, en las haciendas de Chiconcuac y S. Vicente.* Mexico City: Imprenta de A. Boix, 1858.

Castillo Ledón, Luís. *Morelos: Documentos inéditos y poco conocidos.* 3 vols. Mexico City: Secretaría de Educación Pública, 1927.

Clamores de la América y recurso a la protección de María Santísma de Guadalupe. Mexico City: Imprenta de Arizpe, 1811.

Clamores de los vendadores de la Plaza del Mercado. Mexico City: Benavente, 1821.

Colección de acuerdos y decretos espedidos por el Primer Congreso Constitucional en sus úlimas sesiones estraordinarias y por el segundo y tercero de los años 1830 y 1831. Puebla: Imprenta del Gobierno, 1832.

Colección de artículos del Siglo XIX sobre alzamiento de prohibiciones. Mexico City: Ignacio Cumplido, 1851.

Colección de decretos y órdenes de los Congresos Constituyentes del Estado Libre y Soberano de México. Toluca: n.p., 1850.

Colección de disposiciones relativas a la renta de alcabalas y derecho de consumo. Mexico City: Imprenta de J. M. Lara, 1853.

Colección de documentos históricos mexicanos. Mexico City: Librería de la Viuda de Ch. Bouret, 1920.

Colección de los decretos y órdenes más importantes que espidió el Primer Congreso Constitucional del Estado de Puebla en los años de 1826, 1827, y 1828. Puebla: Imprenta del Gobierno, 1828.

Colección de los supremos decretos que imponen varias contribuciones directas mandadas restablecer por él de 30 de mayo de 1853. Puebla: Imprenta de José María Macias, 1853.

Colín, Mario. *Guía de documentos impresos del Estado de México.* 4 vols. Mexico City: Biblioteca Enciclopédica del Estado de México, 1976–81.

Comunicación dirigida a los propietarios de fincas rústicas del Estado de México y Acta de la Junta celebrada en 6 de agosto con motivo de la circular de 18 de julio del gobierno de dicho Estado. Mexico City: Ignacio Cumplido, 1849.

Constitución política del Estado de Chiapas. Villahermosa: J. M. Corrales, 1826.

Constitución política del Estado de México. Mexico City: Vicente G. Torres, 1846.

Constitución política del Estado de Michoacán. Morelia: Imprenta de Oñate, 1835.

Constitución política del Estado de Puebla. Puebla: n.p., 1825.

Constitución política del Estado Libre y Soberano de Guerrero. Tixtla: Tip. del Gobierno del Estado, 1851.

Constituciones de la muy ilustre Archicofradía de Ciudadanos de la Santa Veracruz. Mexico City: Imprenta del Aguila, 1828.

Consuelo a los indios y aliento a los ciudadanos. Mexico City: Alejandro Valdes, 1820.

Contestación del Ilmo. Sr. Arzobispo a la tercera comunicación que le dirigió el Exmo. Sr. Ministro de Justica. Mexico City: Andrade y Escalante, 1856.

Conversación entre Cortés y Moctezuma. Mexico City: Ontiveros, 1820.

Cortes de caja y estado general de la Comisaría General de Guerra de la División Comonfort. Mexico City: Andrade y Escalante, 1855.

Costeño de Acapulco, El. (pseud.). *La ejecución de justicia contra el Coronel Mangoy, la causa son los coyotes porque intentó su espulsión.* Mexico City: Imprenta del Coreo, 1827.

El cuando del Señor General Don Vicente Guerrero. Mexico City: Alejandro Valdes, 1828.

Cuenta general de valores y distribución de los rentas del erario federal en el octavo año ecónomico de 1831 a 1832. N.p., n.d.

Cuentas de la Comisaría y Sub-Comisaría del Ejercito Restaurador de la Libertad. Mexico City: Vicente García Torres, 1856.

Culebrina bien cargada para la gachupinada. Puebla: Oficina Nacional, 1832.

De la liberalidad del indio. Mexico City: Benavente, 1820.

El Dean y el Cabildo de Esta Iglesia Metropolitana, gobernador del Arzobispado, a sus diocesanos. Queretaro: R. Escandon, 1829.

Décimas a la entrada del Sr. Presidente D. Juan Alvarez. Mexico City: Cristobal Velasco, 1856.

Decreto para el arreglo interior de los Departamentos. Mexico City: Imprenta de Lara, 1837.

Decreto sobre extinción de alcalabas en el Estado de México. Toluca: Manuel Gallo, 1847.

Decretos y acuerdos expedidos por la Terecera Legislatura Constitucional del Estado Libre y Soberano de Puebla. Puebla: Imprenta de José María Macias, 1850.

Defensa de Florentino López, conocido con el nombre del Tío Fino acusado de complicidad moral en los robos y asesinatos que ejecutaron en la noche del 17 y mañana del 18 de diciembre de 1856 en las Haciendas de S. Vicente y Chiconcuac. Mexico City: n.p., 1858.

Delgado de Jesús María, P. Santiago. *Catecismo de urbanidad civil y cristiana.* Mexico City: Alejandro Valdes, 1825.

Desengaño a los indios haciendoles ver lo mucho que deben a los españoles. Mexico City: n.p., n.d.

Díaz, Lilia, ed. *La versión francesa de México.* Mexico City: El Colegio de México, 1963.

Díaz y Díaz, Fernando, ed. *Santa Anna y Juan Alvarez frente a frente.* Mexico City: El Colegio de México, 1972.

Dictamen de la Comisión Primera de Hacienda de la Cámara de Diputados sobre prohibición de géneros toscos de algodón y lana. Mexico City: Imprenta del Aguila, 1829.

Dictamen de la Comisión Primera de Hacienda sobre que el Gobierno ocupe los bienes conocidos en el Distrito Federal, por el Duque de Monteleone. Mexico City: Las Escalerillas, 1833.

Discurso que en memoria de las glorias de la Patria, pronunció en el Puerto de Acapulco en el aniversario del día 16 de setiembre. Mexico City: Martin Rivera, 1838.

Disposiciones sobre elecciones. Mexico City: n.p., 1851.

Documentos relativos a la sublevación del General Don Juan Alvarez en el Sur del Estado de México y a los últimos sucesos del Estado de Zacatecas. Mexico City: Ignacio Cumplido, 1835.

Documentos relativos a las sesiones habidas en el Congreso del Estado sobre la Agregación del Departamento de Tlapa para formar el nuevo Estado de Guerrero. Puebla: Imprenta de José María Macias, 1849.

Dublán, Manuel, and José María Lozano, eds. *Legislación mexicana.* Mexico City: n.p., 1976.

Espinosa, Rafael. *Oración cívica pronunciada en la plaza de Chilpancingo de los Bravos el 27 de setiembre de 1854.* N.p., n.d.

Estrada, Juan. "Datos estadísticos de la Prefectura del Centro: Su cabecera, Ciudad Guerrero (1852)." *Boletín de la Sociedad Mexicana de Geografía y Estadística* 3 (1852): 71–76.

———. "Derrotero estadístico de los pueblos que componen el Distrito de Acapulco, hecho en ocasión de la visita que hizo el Prefecto en fines de 1836." *Boletín de la Sociedad Mexicana de Geografía y Estadística* 7 (1859): 429–38.

Exposición que la Junta Departamental de México hace al Congreso sobre los inconvenientes que obstan a la imposición de las contribuciones de dos y tres al millar sobre fincas rústicas y urbanas, y derechos de patente y capitación. Mexico City: José Uribe y Alcalde, 1839.

Fleuri, Abad Claude. *Catecismo histórico o compendio de la historia sagrada y de la doctrina cristiana para la instrucción de los niños.* Mexico City: José Uribe y Alcalde, n.d.

Gallardo, Felis Galan. *No lo quisieron sin pelos, ahora lo querrán peludo, con la ley quedaron varios, con Montes de Oca ninguno.* Guadalajara: Urbano Sanroman, n.d.

García, Género, ed. *Los gobiernos de Alvarez y Comonfort según el Archivo del General Doblado.* Mexico City: Librería de la Viuda de Ch. Bouret, 1910.

———. *La Revolución de Ayutla según el Archivo del General Doblado.* Mexico City: Librería de la Viuda de Ch. Bouret, 1910.

García, Juan B. "Apuntes estadísticos del Distrito de Galeana (Tecpan) del estado de Guerrero (1853)." *Boletín de la Sociedad Mexicana de Geografía y Estadística* 7 (1859): 439–47.

García, Ruben, ed. *Dos informes de Fray Pedro Ramírez sobre el asedio de Acapulco*. Mexico City: Museo Nacional, 1933.

García Orozco, Antonio, ed. *Legislación electoral mexicana: 1812–1977*. Mexico City: Reforma Política, 1978.

González Navarro, Moises, Stanley Ross, and Ernesto de la Torre Villar, eds. *Historia documental de México*. Mexico City: Universidad Nacional Autónoma de México, 1964.

Guerrero, Vicente. *El ciudadano Guerrero a la nación mexicana*. Mexico City: Benavente, 1823.

———. *El General Guerrero a todos los militares de su mando*. Mexico City: Imprenta de Benavides, 1821.

———. *Manifiesto del ciudadano Vicente Guerrero, segundo Presidente de los Estados Unidos Mexicanos, a sus compatriotas*. Mexico City: Imprenta del Aguila, 1829.

———. *Manifiesto patriótico que hizo siendo comandante general de la primera división del Ejercito de Tres Garantías*. Mexico City: Ontiveros, 1821.

———. *Vicente Guerrero a José María Lobato*. Mexico City: Benavente, 1823.

Haro, Benito. *Memoria justificada de la conducta que observó en la Comandancia Principal del Distrito de Cuernavaca, con ocasión de los sucesos acaecidos en la Hacienda de S. Vicente en el més de diciembre del año anterior*. Mexico City: Vicente Segura, 1857.

Hernández y Dávalos, Juan. *Colección de documentos para la historia de la Guerra de Independencia de México de 1808–1821*. 6 vols. Mexico City: n.p., 1882.

Herrejón Peredo, Carlos. *Hidalgo: Razones de la insurgencia y biografía documental*. Mexico City: Secretaría de Educación Pública, 1986.

———, ed. *Morelos: Documentos inéditos de vida revolucionaria*. Zamora: El Colegio de Michoacán, 1987.

———, ed. *Morelos: Vida preinsurgente y lecturas*. Zamora: El Colegio de Michoacán, 1984.

———, ed. *Los procesos de Morelos*. Zamora: El Colegio de Michoacán, 1985.

Himno nacional al Exmo. Sr. Presidente D. Juan Alvarez. Mexico City: Cristobal Velasco, 1856.

El indio constitucional. Mexico City: Alejandro Valdes, 1820.

El indio constitucional a todos los Americanos, segundo papel. Mexico City: n.p., 1820.

El indio y la india del pueblo de Actopan. Mexico City: José María Betancourt, 1820.

La indita liberal siguiendo a Pedraza y a Santa Anna. Mexico City: Alejandro Valdes, 1833.

Instrucción para los Ayuntamientos Constitucionales, Juntas Provinciales, y Gefes Políticos. Mexico City: Oficina del Gobierno, 1820.

Instrucción que para facilitar las elecciones parroquiales y de partido . . . Mexico City: n.p., 1820.

Los insurgentes rendidos a la Constitución. Mexico City: Imprenta de Valdes, 1820.
Jefes del ejercito mexicano en 1847. Mexico City: Sociedad Mexicana de Geografía y Estadística, 1914.
Labarrieta, Antonio. *Informe sobre la conducta que observó Iturbide siendo comandante general del Bajio.* Mexico City: Juan Bautista Arizpe, 1821.
Lemoine, Ernesto, ed. *Insurgencia y república federal 1808–1824.* Mexico City: Banco Internacional, 1986.
———, ed. *Manuscrito Cárdenas: Documentos del Congreso de Chilpancingo hallados entre los papeles del caudillo José Ma. Morelos, sorprendido por los realistas en la acción de Tlacotepec el 24 de febrero de 1814.* Mexico City: Instituto Mexicano de Seguro Social, 1980.
Ley de Hacienda del Estado de Puebla 1848. N.p., 1848.
Ley dictada por el Congreso Constituyente del Estado de México para la organización de los cuerpos municipales del mismo Estado. Mexico City: Imprenta Cargo de Rivera, 1825.
Ley orgánica para la milicia cívica del Estado de Puebla. Puebla: Imprenta del Gobierno, 1829.
Ley orgánica provisonal para el arreglo interior del Estado de Guerrero. Mexico City: Ignacio Cumplido, 1850.
Ley que arregla el gobierno económico-político del estado Libre y Soberano de Puebla. Puebla: Oficina del Gobierno, 1827.
Ley sobre capitación, Oaxaca. N.p., 1845.
Ley sobre elecciones de Ayuntamiento en el Departamento de México. Mexico City: Vicente García Torres, 1845.
Ley sobre la reforma del sistema de elecciones para ayuntamientos. Puebla: Imprenta del Gobierno, 1831.
Ley sobre los lugares donde deben establecer municipalidades. Mexico City: Vicente García Torres, 1845.
Leyes a las que ha debido arreglarse la elección de los Supremos Poderes Ejecutivo y Legislativo de la Unión. Mexico City: M. Payno, 1848.
Lista alfabética de los individuos que tienen derecho de votar por clase de propiedad raiz rústica y urbana e industria agrícola. Mexico City: Vicente García Torres, 1846.
Lista de los señores que voluntariamente han concurrido con las cantidades que se expresan para el vestuario de las tropas de la División del Señor Guerrero. Mexico City: Imprenta de Zuñiga y Ontiveros, 1821.
López Miramontes, Alvaro, ed. *Tumultos y sublevaciones en Mochitlán, Guerrero.* Chilpancingo: Universidad Autónoma de Guerrero, 1976.
Maciel, David, ed. *Ignacio Ramírez, El Nigromante: Obras Completas.* 4 vols. Mexico City: Centro de Investigación Científica Ing. Jorge L. Tamayo, 1984.
Malditos sean los gachupines que vinieron a este suelo y tanto daño han causado. Mexico City: Alejandro Valdes, 1826.
La malinche de la Constitución. Mexico City: Alejandro Valdes, 1820.
Martínez de Lejarza, Juan José. *Análisis estadístico de la Provincia de Michoacán en 1822.* Mexico City: Imprenta del Supremo Gobierno, 1824.

Medina y Lavalle, Ten. Cor. Francisco G. *Discurso que en el solemne aniversario de la independencia pronunció en el pueblo de Ixcateopan del Estado de Guerrero el 16 de setiembre de 1851.* Orizaba: J. M. Naredo, 1851.

Montes de Oca, Isidoro. *Proclama del Sr. Brigadier Don Isidoro Montes de Oca, Comandante General del Rumbo de Acapulco.* México Imprenta de Doña Herculana del Villar, 1822.

Mora, José María Luís. *Obras sueltas.* Mexico City: Porrua, 1963.

Muñoz, Celso. "Apuntes estadísticos del Distrito de Tasco del Estado de Guerrero (1853)." *Boletín de la Sociedad Mexicana de Geografía y Estadística* 7 (1859): 456–58.

Muzquiz, Melchor. *El Gobernador del Estado a los propietarios y demás habitantes del mismo.* Toluca: Imprenta del Gobierno, 1830.

Navarrete (Diputado). *Discurso a favor de los indios.* Mexico City: Alejandro Valdes, 1821.

No hay peor sordo que el que no quiere oir: Dase idea de lo ocurrido en la Cámara de Diputados en la sesión secreta de 15 de noviembre de 1845 sobre la guerra que hacen los indios del Departamento del Sur de México. Mexico City: Imprenta de Lara, 1845.

Noticias estraordinarias del campo sobre México, y proclamas de los ciudadanos Alvarez y Montes de Oca. Puebla: Oficina Nacional, 1832.

Nuevas Capitanías Generales de Provincia establecidas en el territorio del Imperio Mexicano. Mexico City: Joaquin y Bernardo Miramon, 1821.

Ocampo, Melchor. *Obras completas.* Mexico City: Ediciones El Caballito, 1978.

Oigan todos los congresos el voto de la república, o sea: La expresión de la voluntad general con respecto a los patriotas, en quienes deben recaer los altos empleos de Presidente y Vice-presidente. Mexico City: Ontiveros, 1828.

Old Nick (pseud.). "Un paseo a México, 1859 y 1860." *Boletín de la Sociedad Mexicana de Geografía y Estadística* 1 (1869): 766–89.

Ortega, Miguel, ed. *Colección de documentos y apuntes para la historia del Edo. de Guerrero.* Mexico City: n.p., 1948.

Otero, Mariano. *Ensayo sobre el verdadero estado de la cuestión social y política que se agita en la República Mexicana.* Mexico City: Instituto Nacional de la Juventud, 1964.

Oyen y callan; pero a su tiempo hablan: Representación dirigida a la Soberana Junta Provisional Gubernativa por los jueces de letras foráneos, sobre los vicios de los ayuntamientos, y nulidad de sus elecciones. Mexico City: Ontiveros, 1821.

Pacheco, Nicolás. *Demonstración compendiosa y evidente de los muchos y graves males que acarrea la insurreción para el uso y utilidad de los indios y otras gente semejante.* Mexico City: Ontiveros, 1812.

Padilla Serra, Antonio, ed. *Constituciones y leyes fundamentales de España (1808–1947).* Granada: Universidad de Granada, 1954.

Palafox y Mendoza, Juan de. *De la naturaleza del indio.* Mexico City: Benavente, 1820.

Parabien a los indios. Mexico City: Joaquin y Bernardo de Miramon, 1820.
Parabien a los señores comerciantes. Mexico City: Ontiveros, 1821.
Payo del Rosario, El. (pseud.). *O se van los gachupines o nos cortan el pescuezo.* Mexico City: Las Escalerillas, 1831.
Pérez Hernández, José María. *Diccionario geográfico, estadístico, histórico y biográfico, de industria y comercio de la República Mexicana.* Mexico City: Imprenta del Cinco de Mayo, 1874.
Piquero, Ygnacio. *Breve instrucción sobre las contribuciones directas establecidas en la nación desde el año de 1836.* Mexico City: Vicente García Torres, 1845.
Plana mayor general del ejercito. Mexico City: Imprenta de la Calle de Medinas, 1849.
Planes en al nación mexicana. Mexico City: Cámara de Diputados, 1987.
La plebe poblana a la plebe mexicana. Mexico City: Ignacio Cumplido, 1833.
Portilla, Anselmo de la. *Historia de la revolución de México contra la dictadura del General Santa Anna, 1853–5.* Mexico City: Vicente García Torres, 1856.
Proclama de un americano a los insurgentes y demás habitantes de Nueva España. Mexico City: Alejandro Valdes, 1820.
Proclama de un cura indio del Obispado de Valladolid, a todos los padres curas y vicarios indios, y a nuestros hijos los caziques, gobernadores y demás indios de esta América. Mexico City: n.p., 1811.
Proclama del Sr. Brigadier Don Isidoro Montes de Oca, Comandante General del Rumbo de Acapulco. Mexico City: Imprenta de Doña Herculana del Villar, 1822.
La protección de N. Guadalupana y la unión constante de estos habitantes, harán inexpugnable a esta Monarquía, digna posesión de nuestro amado Fernando VII. Mexico City: n.p., n.d.
Proyecto de nuevo reglamento para las elecciones de los representantes del Pueblo en las primeras Cortes. Mexico City: Benavente, 1821.
Los pueblos toman las armas: La ley de espulsión esperan. Puebla: Imprenta del Patriota, 1827.
Que mueran los gachupines y la patria será libre. Puebla: Moreno Hermanos, 1827.
Ramírez Fentanes, Luís, ed. *Colección de los documentos más importantes relativos al C. General de División Vicente Guerrero que existen en el Archivo Histórico Militar.* Mexico City: Comisión de Historia Militar, 1955.
Reflecsiones sobre la prohibición de hilazas y mantas estrangeras de algodón. Mexico City: Ignacio Cumplido, 1835.
Reflecsiones sobre las leyes de espulsión de españoles. Mexico City: Las Escalerillas, 1833.
Reflexiones sobre los males que va a esperimentar la Nación a consecuencia del decreto de 10 del corriente que dispone cese el cobro de alcabalas el més de diciembre próximo. Mexico City: Imprenta de la Sociedad Literaria, 1846.

Reformas a la Ley de Hacienda. Puebla: n.p., 1849.

Reglamento para organizar, armar y disciplinar la Guardía Nacional en los Estados, Distrito y Territorios de la Federación. Mexico City: Vicente García Torres, 1846.

Reina, Leticia, ed. *Las rebeliones de campesinos en México (1819–1906).* Mexico City: Siglo XXI, 1980.

Representación que hacen al Congreso Constituyente varios dueños de propiedades territoriales contra algunos artículos de los proyectos de leyes fundamentales que se discuten actualmente. Mexico City: Ignacio Cumplido, 1856.

Representaciones que hacen al Congreso Constituyente varios dueños de fincas rústicas y urbanas en Michoacán, Guanajuato, Guerrero, y Puebla. Mexico City: n.p., 1856.

Respuesta de algunos propietarios de fincas rústicas a la manifestación del Señor Lic. Mariano Arizcorreta. Mexico City: n.p., 1849.

Respuesta de los proprietarios de Cuernavaca y Morelos al manifiesto de don Juan Alvarez. Mexico City: n.p., 1857.

Ripalda, Padre. *Libro primero de doctrina para las escuelas municipales del Departamento de Jalisco.* Mexico City: Imprenta de Galvan, 1839.

Roa Barcena, José María. *Recuerdos de la invasión norteamericana (1846–1848).* Xalapa: Universidad Veracruzana, 1986.

Romero, José Guadalupe. *Noticias para formar la historia y la estadística del Obispado de Michoacán.* Mexico City: Vicente García Torres, 1862.

Segunda parte del Indio Constitucional. Mexico City: Alejandro Valdes, 1820.

Si asesinan a Santa Anna no quedará un gachupín. Mexico City: Las Escalerillas, 1833.

Suarez, Francisco. "Apuntes estadísticos del Distrito de Teloloapan del Estado de Guerrero (1853)." *Boletín de la Sociedad Mexicana de Geografía y Estadística* 7 (1859): 448–55.

Sustos a los regatones. Mexico City: Alejandro Valdes, 1820.

Tamariz, Mariano. *Esposición que hace a la Cámara de Diputados del Congreso General el apoderado del Duque de Terranova y Monteleone.* Mexico City: Miguel González, 1833.

Tena Ramírez, Felipe, ed. *Leyes fundamentales de México 1808–1957.* Mexico City: Porrua, 1957.

Toro, M. M. "Noticia estadística del Distrito de Tabares, perteneciente al Estado de Guerrero." *Boletín de la Sociedad Mexicana de Geografía y Estadística* 7 (1859): 407–28.

Urbino, Thelésfor José de. *Gachupines: ¿Qué mas dicha? Mexicanos ¿Quereis mas?* Mexico City: Imprenta del Finado Ontiveros, 1825.

Vicuña Mackenna, Benjamín. *Páginas de mi diario durante tres años de viaje 1853–1854–1855.* Santiago: Universidad de Chile, 1936.

Wilson, Robert. *Mexico: Its Peasants and Priests; or, Adventures and Historical Researches in Mexico and Its Silver Mines.* New York: Harper and Brothers, 1856.

Zarco, Francisco. *Crónica del Congreso Extraordinario Constituyente (1856–1857)*. Mexico City: El Colegio de México, 1957.
———. *Historia del Congreso Extraordinario Constituyente (1856–7)*. Mexico City: El Colegio de México, 1956.

SECONDARY SOURCES

Aguilar Camín, Hector. "Los jefes sonorenses de la Revolución Mexicana." In David Brading, ed., *Caudillos y campesinos en la Revolución Mexicana*, pp. 125–60. Mexico City: Fondo de Cultura Económica, 1985.

Aguirre Anaya, Carmen, and Alberto Carabín Gracia. "Formas artesanales y fabriles de los textiles de algodón en la ciudad de Puebla, siglos XVIII y XIX." In *Puebla de la Colonia a la Revolución: Estudios de historia regional*, pp. 125–54. Puebla: Universidad Autónoma de Puebla, 1987.

Aguirre Beltrán, Gonzalo. *Cuijla*. Mexico City: Secretaría de Educación Pública, 1985.

Aguirre Colorado, Rafael, Ruben García, and Pelagio A. Rodríguez. *Campañas de Morelos sobre Acapulco 1810–13*. Mexico City: Comisión de Historia Militar, 1933.

Alamán, Lucás. *Historia de Méjico*. Mexico City: Editorial Jus, 1942.

Alanis Boyzo, Rodolfo. "La conspiración de Montaño: Un intento de implantar el centralismo en México." *Boletín del Archivo General del Estado de México* 4 (1980): 3–15.

———. "Instalación del primer ayuntamiento en el municipio de Capulhuac." *Boletín del Archivo General del Estado de México* 6 (1980): 25–29.

Alonso, Ana María. "U.S. Military Intervention, Revolutionary Mobilization, and Popular Ideology in the Chihuahuan Sierra, 1916–1917." In Daniel Nugent, ed., *Rural Revolt in Mexico and U.S. Intervention*, pp. 199–228. San Diego: Center for U.S.-Mexican Studies, 1988.

Altamirano, Ignacio. *Morelos en el Veladero*. Mexico City: Imprenta de Vicente Agueros, 1910.

———. *Morelos en Tixtla*. Mexico City: Imprenta de Vicente Agueros, 1910.

———. *Morelos en Zacatula*. Mexico City: Imprenta de Vicente Agueros, 1910.

Anderson, Benedict. *Imagined Communities: Reflections on the Origins and Spread of Nationalism*. London: Verso, 1983.

Anderson, Rodney. *Outcasts in Their Own Land: Mexican Industrial Workers, 1906–1911*. DeKalb: Northern Illinois University Press, 1976.

Andrews, George Reid. "Spanish American Independence: A Structural Analysis." *Latin American Perspectives* 12 (1985): 105–32.

Ankerson, Dudley. *Agrarian Warlord: Saturnino Cedillo and the Mexican Revolution in San Luís Potosí*. DeKalb: Northern Illinois University Press, 1984.

Anna, Timothy E. *The Mexican Empire of Iturbide*. Lincoln: University of Nebraska Press, 1990.

———. "Spain and the Breakdown of the Imperial Ethos: The Problem of Equality." *Hispanic American Historical Review* 62 (1982): 254–72.

Annino, Antonio. "El pacto y la norma: Los orígenes de la legalidad oligárquica en México." *Historias* 5 (1984): 3–31.

Annino, Antonio, and Alberto Filippi. "Las formas de poder: Proyecto político y efectividad." In Antonio Annino et al., eds., *America Latina: Dallo Stato Coloniale allo Stato Nazione*, 2: 417–26. Milan: Franco Angeli, 1987.

Archer, Christon. *The Army in Bourbon Mexico, 1760–1810.* Albuquerque: University of New Mexico Press, 1977.

———. "Banditry and Revolution in New Spain, 1790–1821." *Bibliotheca Americana* 1 (1982): 59–88.

———. "La Causa Buena: The Counterinsurgency Army of New Spain and the Ten Years War." In Jaime E. Rodríguez O., ed., *The Independence of Mexico and the Origins of the New Nation*, pp. 85–108. Los Angeles: University of California at Los Angeles Latin American Center, 1989.

———. "The Royalist Army in New Spain: Civil-Military Relations, 1810–1821." *Journal of Latin American Studies* 13 (1981): 57–82.

———. "¡Viva Nuestra Señora de Guadalupe! Recent Interpretations of Mexico's Independence Period." *Mexican Studies / Estudios Mexicanos* 7 (1991): 143–65.

———. "The Young Antonio López de Santa Anna: Veracruz Counterinsurgent and Incipient Caudillo." In William H. Beezeley and Judith Ewel, eds., *The Human Condition in Latin America: The Nineteenth Century*, pp. 3–16. Wilmington, Del.: Scholarly Resources, 1989.

Arrangoiz, Francisco Paula de. *México desde 1808 hasta 1867.* Mexico City: Porrua, 1968.

Arreola Cortés, Raul. *Melchor Ocampo: Paladín de la Revolución Liberal.* Mexico City: Secretaría de Educación Pública, 1968.

Arrom, Silvia M. "Popular Politics in Mexico City: The Parian Riot, 1828." *Hispanic American Historical Review* 68 (1988): 245–68.

Avilés, René. *Vicente Guerrero, el insurgente ciudadano.* Mexico City: Sociedad Amigos del Libro Mexicano, 1957.

Baker, Keith Michael. "Enlightenment and Revolution in France: Old Problems, Renewed Approaches." *Journal of Modern History* 53 (1981): 281–303.

———. "Introduction." In Keith Michael Baker, ed., *The Political Culture of the Old Regime*, pp. xi–xxiv. Vol. 1 of *The French Revolution and the Creation of Modern Political Culture.* New York: Pergamon, 1987.

Bastian, Jean-Pierre. "Jacobinismo y ruptura revolucionaria durante el Porfiriato." *Mexican Studies / Estudios Mexicanos* 7 (1991): 29–46.

Bazant, Jan. *Antonio Haro y Tamariz y sus aventuras políticas, 1811–1869.* Mexico City: El Colegio de México, 1985.

———. "Mexico from Independence to 1867." In Leslie Bethell, ed., *From Independence to c. 1870*, pp. 423–70. Vol. 3 of *The Cambridge History of Latin America.* New York: Cambridge University Press, 1985.

Benson, Nettie Lee. *La diputación provincial y el federalismo mexicano.* Mexico City: El Colegio de México, 1955.

―――. "Introduction." In Nettie Lee Benson, ed., *Mexico and the Spanish Cortes, 1810–1822,* pp. 3–9. Austin: University of Texas Press, 1966.

Berry, Charles. "The Election of Mexican Deputies to the Spanish Cortes, 1810–1822." In Nettie Lee Benson, ed., *Mexico and the Spanish Cortes, 1810–1822,* pp. 10–42. Austin: University of Texas Press, 1966.

Bonilla, Heraclio. "The Indian Peasantry and 'Peru' during the War with Chile." In Steve J. Stern, ed., *Resistance, Rebellion and Consciousness in the Andean Peasant World, Eighteenth to Twentieth Centuries,* pp. 219–31. Madison: University of Wisconsin Press, 1987.

Borah, Woodrow. *Justice by Insurance: The General Indian Court of Colonial Mexico and the Legal Aides of the Half Real.* Berkeley: University of California Press, 1983.

Brading, David. "El clero mexicano y el movimiento insurgente de 1810." *Relaciones* 2 (1981): 5–26.

―――. "Historia patria y democracia en México." *Historias* 15 (1986): 64–70.

―――. "Liberal Patriotism and the Mexican Reform." *Journal of Latin American Studies* 20 (1988): 27–48.

―――. *Miners and Merchants in Bourbon Mexico, 1763–1810.* Cambridge: Cambridge University Press, 1971.

―――. *Los orígenes del nacionalismo mexicano.* Mexico City: Era, 1988.

―――. "Tridentine Catholicism and Enlightened Despotism in Bourbon Mexico." *Journal of Latin American Studies* 15 (1983): 1–22.

Breuilly, John. *Nationalism and the State.* Chicago: University of Chicago Press, 1985.

Bright, Charles, and Susan Harding. "Processes of Statemaking and Popular Protest: An Introduction." In Charles Bright and Susan Harding, eds., *Statemaking and Social Movements: Essays in History and Theory,* pp. 1–15. Ann Arbor: University of Michigan Press, 1984.

Bringas Colín, Martha Idalia. "Cuatro pasquines de sentimiento anti-español." *Boletín del Archivo General del Estado de México* 1 (1979): 17–20.

Bushnell, Clyde Gilbert. *La carrera política y militar de Juan Álvarez.* Mexico City: Gobierno del Estado de Guerrero, 1988.

Bushnell, David. "La evolución del principio representativo, de liberal a democrático, en Latinoamerica independiente." In Antonio Annino et al., eds., *America Latina: Dallo Stato Coloniale allo Stato Nazione,* 2: 613–31. Milan: Franco Angeli, 1987.

Bushnell, David, and Neill Macauley. *The Emergence of Latin America in the Nineteenth Century.* New York: Oxford University Press, 1988.

Bustamante, Carlos María de. *Cuadro histórico de la revolución mexicana de 1810.* Mexico City: Instituto Nacional de Estudios Históricos de la Revolución Mexicana, 1985.

Buve, Raymond. "Political Patronage and Politics at the Village Level in Central Mexico: Continuity and Change in Patterns from the Late Colonial Period to the End of the French Intervention (1867)." *Bulletin of Latin American Research* 11 (1992): 1–28.

Calderón Quijano, José Antonio. *El Banco de San Carlos y las comunidades de indios de Nueva España.* Seville: Banco de España, 1963.

Cardenas, Enrique. "Algunas cuestiones sobre la depresión mexicana del XIX." *HISLA: Revista Latinoamericana de Ciencias Sociales* 3 (1984): 3–22.

Cardenas Barraza, Irma. "El Estado de México y la erección de Guerrero." *Cuadernos de Historia* 2 (1980): 73–104.

Carmagnani, Marcello. "Finanzas y Estado en México, 1820–1880." *Ibero Americanisches Archiv* 9 (1983): 277–317.

———. "Local Governments and Ethnic Government in Oaxaca." In Karen Spalding, ed., *Essays in the Political, Economic and Social History of Latin America,* pp. 107–24. Newark: University of Delaware, 1982.

———. "Los olvidos de Clio." *Historias* 6 (1984): 85–98.

———. "La política en el estado oligárguiquico latinoamericano." *Historias* 1 (1982): 5–14.

———. *El regreso de los dioses: La reconstitución de la identidad étnica en Oaxaca, siglos xvii y xviii.* Mexico City: Fondo de Cultura Económica, 1988.

Carranco Cardoso, Leopoldo. *Acciones militares en el Estado de Guerrero.* Mexico City: Sociedad Mexicana de Geografía y Estadística, 1963.

Carvalho, José Murilo de. "Political Elites and State Building: The Case of Nineteenth Century Brazil." *Comparative Studies in Society and History* 24 (1981): 378–99.

Castro Gutiérrez, Felipe. "El indio rebelde de la máscara de oro: La historia y el mito en la ideología plebeya." *Históricas* 21 (1987): 12–20.

———. "La rebelión del indio Mariano (Nayarit 1801)." Instituto de Investigaciones Históricas, Universidad Autónoma Nacional de México, Mexico City, n.d.

Cervantes Bello, Francisco J. "La Iglesia y la crisis del crédito colonial en Puebla (1800–1814)." In Leonor Ludlow and Carlos Marichal, eds., *Banca y poder en México (1800–1925),* pp. 51–74. Mexico City: Grijalbo, 1986.

Cervantes-Delgado, Roberto. "Viajeros y cronistas del Estado de Guerrero." In *Ensayos para la historia del Estado de Guerrero,* pp. 41–92. Chilpancingo: Instituto Guerrerense de la Cultura, 1985.

Chambers, Sarah. "Honor for a New Republic: The Negotiation of Citizenship in Early Republican Arequipa, Peru." Paper presented at the 1994 Annual Meeting of the Conference on Latin American History, San Francisco, January 1994.

Chance, John K. "Capitalismo y desigualdad entre los zapatecos de Oaxaca: Una comparación entre el valle y los pueblos del rincón, época colonial." In María de los Angeles Romero Frizzi, ed., *Lecturas históricas del Estado de Oaxaca, Epoca Colonial,* pp. 193–204. Mexico City: Instituto Nacional de Antropología e Historia, 1986.

Chance, John K., and William B. Taylor. "Cofradías and Cargos: An Historical Perspective on the Mesoamerican Civil-Religious Hierarchy." *American Ethnologist* 12 (1985): 1–26.

Chavez Guerrero, Herminio. *Ignacio Manuel Altamirano*. Chilpancingo: Instituto Guerrerense de la Cultura, 1985.
————. *Valerio Trujano: El insurgente olvidado*. Mexico City: Trillas, 1962.
————. *Vicente Guerrero: El consumador, biografía*. Mexico City: Cultura y Ciencia Política, 1971.
Chavez Orosco, Luís. *Las instituciones democráticas de los indígenas mexicanos en la época colonial*. Mexico City: Insitituto Indigenista Interamericano, 1943.
Chevalier, François. "Conservadores y liberales en México." *Secuencia* 1 (1985): 136–49.
————. "La emancipación y el municipio rural libre en México: De los comuneros al liberalismo." *Cuadernos Americanos* 43 (1983): 153–63.
Chowning, Margaret. "Contours of the Post-1810 Depression in Mexico: A Reappraisal from a Regional Perspective." *Latin American Research Review* 27 (1992): 119–50.
————. "The Mysterious Career of Juan José Codallos: Race, Class, Kinship, and Politics." Presented at "Culture, Power, and Politics in Nineteenth Century Mexico: A Conference in Memory of Nettie Lee Benson," University of Texas at Austin, April 15–16, 1994.
Coatsworth, John. "Comment on 'The United States and the Mexican Peasantry.'" In Daniel Nugent, ed., *Rural Revolt in Mexico and U.S. Intervention*, pp. 61–68. San Diego: Center for U.S.-Mexican Studies, 1988.
————. "The Limits of Colonial Absolutism: The State in Eighteenth Century Mexico." In Karen Spalding, ed., *Essays in the Political, Economic, and Social History of Colonial Latin America*, pp. 25–51. Newark: University of Delaware, 1982.
————. "The Mexican Mining Industry in the Eighteenth Century." In Nils Jacobsen and Hans Jürgen Puhle, eds., *The Economies of Mexico and Peru during the Late Colonial Period*, pp. 26–45. Berlin: Bibliotheca Ibero-Americana, 1986.
————. "Obstacles to Economic Growth in Nineteenth Century Mexico." *American Historical Review* 83 (1978): 8–100.
————. "Los orígenes del autoritarismo moderno en México." *Foro Internacional* 16 (1975): 205–32.
————. "Patterns of Rural Rebellion in Latin America: Mexico in Comparative Perspective." In Friedrich Katz, ed., *Riot, Rebellion and Revolt: Rural Social Conflict in Mexico*, pp. 21–62. Princeton: Princeton University Press, 1988.
Cockcroft, James. *Precursores intelectuales de la Revolución Mexicana*. Mexico City: Siglo XXI, 1981.
Cohn, Norman. *The Pursuit of the Millenium: Revolutionary Millenarians and Mystical Anarchists of the Middle Ages*. New York: Oxford University Press, 1976.
Commons de la Rosa, Aurea. *Geohistoria de las divisiones territoriales del Estado de Puebla (1519–1970)*. Mexico City: Universidad Nacional Autónoma de México, 1971.

Cordero y T., Enrique. *Historia comprendida del Estado de Puebla*. Puebla: Bohemia Poblana, 1965.

Corrigan, Philip, and Derek Sayer. *The Great Arch: English State Formation as Cultural Revolution*. New York: Basil Blackwell, 1985.

Costeloe, Michael. *The Central Republic in Mexico, 1835–1846: Hombres de Bien in the Age of Santa Anna*. New York: Cambridge University Press, 1993.

———. *La primera república federal de México (1824–1835)*. Mexico City: Fondo de Cultura Económica, 1975.

Covo, Jacqueline. "Los clubs en la Revolución de Ayutla." *Historia Mexicana* 26 (1977): 438–55.

———. "La idea de la Revolución Francesa en el Congreso Constituyente de 1856–7." *Historia Mexicana* 38 (1988): 69–78.

Cruz Valdés, H. Reina. "Aproximación al estudio de movimientos populares durante la primera mitad del siglo xix en el Estado de Puebla: La Revolución del Sur." In *Movimientos populares en la historia de México y América Latina*, pp. 185–92. Mexico City: Universidad Nacional Autónoma de México, 1987.

Cunniff, Roger. "Mexican Municipal Electoral Reform, 1810–1822." In Nettie Lee Benson, ed., *Mexico and the Spanish Cortes, 1810–1822*, pp. 59–86. Austin: University of Texas Press, 1966.

Dehouve, Daniele. "El pueblo de indios y el mercado: Tlapa en el siglo XVIII." In Arij Ouweneel and Cristina Torales Pacheco, eds., *Empresarios, indios, y estado: Perfil de la economía mexicana del siglo XVIII*, pp. 86–102. Amsterdam: Centro de Estudios y Documentación Latinoamericanos, 1988.

———. "Las separaciones de pueblos en la región de Tlapa (siglo XVIII)." *Historia Mexicana* 33 (1984): 379–404.

Di Tella, Torcuato. *Latin American Politics: A Theoretical Framework*. Austin: University of Texas Press, 1990.

Díaz, María Elena. "The Satiric Penny Press for Workers in Mexico, 1900–1910: A Case Study in the Politicisation of Popular Culture." *Journal of Latin American Studies* 22 (1990): 496–26.

Díaz y Díaz, Fernando. *Caudillos y caciques: Antonio López de Santa Anna y Juan Alvarez*. Mexico City: El Colegio de México, 1972.

Dominguez, Miguel. *La erección del Estado de Guerrero*. Mexico City: Secretaría de Educación Pública, 1949.

Ducey, Michael. "From Village Riot to Regional Rebellion: Social Protest in the Huasteca, Mexico 1760–1870." Ph.D. diss., University of Chicago, 1992.

———. "Peasant Participation in Mexico's Independence: Some Thoughts on the Recent Literature." Seminar Paper, University of Chicago, March 20, 1986.

Escudero, Ignacio. *Historia militar del General Porfirio Díaz*. Mexico City: Editorial Cosmos, 1975.

Falcón, Romana. *El agrarismo en Veracruz: La etapa radical (1828–1935).* Mexico City: El Colegio de México, 1977.

Farriss, Nancy. *Crown and Clergy in Colonial Mexico, 1579–1821.* London: Athlone Press, 1968.

———. *Maya Society under Colonial Rule: The Collective Enterprise of Survival.* Princeton: Princeton University Press, 1984.

Fernández de Recas, Guillermo. *Mayorazgos en la Nueva España.* Mexico City: Universidad Autónoma Nacional de México, 1965.

Figueroa de Contín, Esperanza. *Atlas geográfico e histórico del Estado de Guerrero.* Chilpancingo: Fondo Nacional Para Actividades Sociales, 1980.

Flores Caballero, Romeo. *Counterrevolution: The Role of the Spaniards in the Independence of Mexico, 1804–1838.* Lincoln: University of Nebraska Press, 1974.

Flores Galindo, Alberto. *Aristocracia y plebe: Lima 1760–1830.* Lima: Mosca Azul Editores, 1984.

———. "In Search of an Inca." In Steve J. Stern, ed., *Resistance, Rebellion and Consciousness in the Andean Peasant World, Eighteenth to Twentieth Centuries,* pp. 193–210. Madison: University of Wisconsin Press, 1987.

———. "Independencia y clase sociales." *Debates en Sociología* 7 (1982): 99–114.

Florescano, Enrique. *Memoria mexicana.* Mexico City: Joaquin Mortiz, 1987.

———. *Orígen y desarrollo de los problemas agrarios de México.* Mexico City: Era, 1976.

Fowler Salamini, Heather. *Agrarian Radicalism in Veracruz, 1920–1938.* Lincoln: University of Nebraska Press, 1978.

Furet, François. *Interpreting the French Revolution.* New York: Cambridge University Press, 1981.

Gailey, Christine. "Culture Wars: Resistance to State Formation." In Christine Gailey and Thomas Patterson, eds., *Power Relations and State Formation,* pp. 35–56. Washington, D.C.: American Anthropological Association, 1987.

Gailey, Christine, and Thomas Patterson. "Power Relations and State Formation." In Christine Gailey and Thomas Patterson, eds., *Power Relations and State Formation,* pp. 1–26. Washington, D.C.: American Anthropological Association, 1987.

Garavaglia, Juan Carlos, and Juan Carlos Grosso. *Las alcabalas novohispanas (1776–1821).* Mexico City: Archivo General de la Nación, 1987.

García Argañarás, Fernando. "Historical Structures, Social Forces, and Mexican Independence." *Latin American Perspectives* 13 (1986): 19–43.

Garner, Paul. "Federalism and Caudillismo in the Mexican Revolution: The Genesis of the Oaxacan Sovereignty Movement (1915–20)." *Journal of Latin American Studies* 27 (1985): 111–33.

Garza, Luís Alberto de la. "Hombres de bien, demagogos y revolución en la Primera República." *Historias* 15 (1986): 42–53.

Gaxiola, Francisco. Gobernantes del Estado de México: Muzquiz-Zavala-Olaguibel. Mexico City: Biblioteca Enciclopédica del Estado de México, 1975.

Genovese, Eugene. Roll, Jordan, Roll: The World the Slaves Made. New York: Vintage Books, 1976.

Gibson, Charles. The Aztecs Under Spanish Rule. Stanford: Stanford University Press, 1964.

Gilmore, Robert. Caudillismo and Militarism in Venzuela, 1810–1910. Athens: Ohio University Press, 1964.

Giron, Nicole. "Ignacio Manuel Altamirano en la vida política del Estado de Guerrero." In Ensayos para la Historia del Estado de Guerrero, pp. 93–106. Chilpancingo: Instituto Guerrerense de la Cultura, 1985.

Gómez Quiñones, Juan. Sembradors: Ricardo Flores Magón y el Partido Liberal Mexicano. Los Angeles: Atzlán Publications, 1973.

Gomezjara, Francisco. Bonapartismo y lucha campesina en la Costa Grande de Guerrero. Mexico City: Ediciones Posada, 1979.

González, María del Refugio. Estudios sobre la Historia del Derecho Civil en México durante el siglo XIX. Mexico City: Universidad Nacional Autónoma de México, 1981.

———, ed. La formación del estado mexicano. Mexico City: Porrua, 1984.

González Dávila, Amado. Geografía del Estado de Guerrero y síntesis histórica. Mexico City: Ediciones Quetzalcoatl, 1959.

González Navarro, Moises. Anatomía del poder político en México, 1848–1853. Mexico City: El Colegio de México, 1983.

———. "Guerrero y la tradición agrarista del Sur." In Memoria de la mesa redonda sobre Vicente Guerrero, pp. 39–45. Mexico City: Instituto Mora, 1982.

———. "Instituciones indígenas del México independiente." In La política indigenista en México: Métodos y resultados, 1: 217–313. Mexico City: Instituto Nacional Indigenista, 1973.

———. Raza y tierra: La guerra de castas y el henequén. Mexico City: El Colegio de México, 1970.

———. "Tipología del liberalismo mexicano." Historia Mexicana 32 (1982): 198–225.

———. "La venganza del Sur." Historia Mexicana 21 (1972): 677–92.

González y González, Luís. "El agrarismo liberal." Historia Mexicana 7 (1958): 469–96.

Gootenberg, Paul. "Beleaguered Liberals: The Failed First Generation of Free Traders in Peru." In Joseph Love and Nils Jacobsen, eds., Guiding the Invisible Hand: Economic Liberalism and the State in Latin American History, pp. 63–97. New York: Praeger, 1988.

———. Between Silver and Guano: Commercial Policy and the State in Postindependence Peru. Princeton: Princeton University Press, 1989.

———. "The Social Origins of Protectionism and Free Trade in Nineteenth-Century Lima." Journal of Latin American Studies 14 (1982): 329–58.

Gould, Jeffrey. To Lead as Equals: Rural Protest and Political Consciousness *in Chinandega, Nicaragua, 1912–1979.* Chapel Hill: University of North Carolina Press, 1990.

Gramsci, Antonio. *Selections from the Prison Notebooks.* New York: International Publishers, 1985.

Green, Stanley C. *The Mexican Republic: The First Decade, 1823–1832.* Pittsburgh: Pittsburgh University Press, 1987.

Gruzinski, Serge. *Man-Gods of the Mexican Highlands: Indian Power and Colonial Society, 1520–1800.* Stanford: Stanford University Press, 1989.

——. "La 'segunda aculteracíon': El estado ilustrado y la religiosidad indígena de la Nueva España (1775–1800)." *Estudios de Historia Novohispana* 8 (1985): 175–201.

Guardino, Peter. "Las guerrillas y la independencia peruana: Un ensayo de interpretación." *Pasado y presente* 2 (1989): 111–17.

Guardino, Peter, and Charles Walker. "The State, Society and Politics in Peru and Mexico in the Late Colonial and Early Republican Periods." *Latin American Perspectives* 19 (1992): 10–43.

Guedea, Virginia. "Las elecciones entre los insurgentes." In Virginia Guedea and Jaime E. Rodríguez O., eds., *Five Centuries of Mexican History / Cinco Siglos de Historia de México,* 1: 303–15. Mexico City: Instituto Mora and University of California at Irvine, 1992.

——. *José María Morelos y Pavon: Cronología.* Mexico City: Universidad Nacional Autónoma de México, 1981.

——. "Las primeras elecciones populares en la ciudad de México: 1812–1813." *Mexican Studies / Estudios Mexicanos* 7 (1991): 1–28.

Guerra, François Xavier. *México: Del Antiguo Régimen a la Revolución.* 2 vols. Mexico City: Fondo de Cultura Económica, 1988.

Guerrero, Andrés. "Curagas y tenientes políticos: La ley de la costumbre y la ley del estado (Otalvo 1830–1875)." *Revista Andina* 2 (1989): 321–66.

Guevara Ramírez, Luís. *Síntesis histórica del Estado de Guerrero.* Mexico City: Gráfica Cerventina, 1959.

Guha, Ranjit. "The Prose of Counter-Insurgency." In Ranjit Guha and Gayatri Chakravorty Spivak, eds., *Selected Subaltern Studies,* pp. 45–86. New York: Oxford University Press, 1988.

Guía de los documentos más importantes sobre el Plan y la Revolución de Ayutla que existen en el Archivo Histórico de Defensa Nacional. Mexico City: Comisión de Historia Militar, 1954.

Guía del Archivo Histórico Militar de México. Mexico City: Dirección del Archivo Militar, 1949.

Hale, Charles. *El liberalismo mexicano en la época de Mora.* Mexico City: Siglo XXI, 1984.

Halperín Donghi, Tulio. "Argentina: Liberalism in a Country Born Liberal." In Joseph Love and Nils Jacobsen, eds., *Guiding the Invisible Hand: Economic Liberalism and the State in Latin American History,* pp. 99–116. New York: Praeger, 1988.

Hamill, Hugh. *The Hidalgo Revolt: Prelude to Mexican Independence.* Gainesville: University of Florida Press, 1966.

Hamilton, Bernice. *Political Thought in Sixteenth Century Spain: A Study of the Political Ideas of Vitoria, Suarez and Molina*. Oxford: Oxford University Press, 1963.

Hamnett, Brian. "The Economic and Social Dimension of the Revolution of Independence in Mexico, 1800–1824." *Ibero-Amerikanisches Archiv* 6 (1980): 1–27.

———. "Las élites y la revolución: El caso mexicano." In *Congreso Bicentenario de Simón Bolívar*, 2: 276–95. Caracas: Academía Nacional de la Historia, 1985.

———. "El federalismo de 1823–1824 en México." In Inge Buisson, Gunter Kahle, Hans-Joachim Konig, and Horst Pietschmann, eds., *Problemas de la formación del estado y de la nación en Hispanoamérica*, pp. 303–17. Bonn: Bohlau Verlag, 1984.

———. "Partidos políticos mexicanos e intervención militar, 1823–1855." In Antonio Annino et al., eds., *America Latina: Dallo Stato Coloniale allo Stato Nazione*, 2: 573–91. Milan: Franco Angeli, 1987.

———. *Política y comercio en el sur de México, 1750–1821*. Mexico City: Instituto Mexicanao de Comercio Exterior, 1976.

———. *Revolución y contrarevolución en México y el Peru (Liberalismo, realeza y separatismo 1800–1824)*. Mexico City: Fondo de Cultura Económica, 1978.

———. *Roots of Insurgency: Mexican Regions, 1750–1824*. New York: Cambridge University Press, 1986.

———. "Royalist Counter-Insurgency and the Continuity of Rebellion, Guanajuato and Michoacán, 1813–1820." *Hispanic American Historical Review* 62 (1982): 1–26.

Harrell, Eugene Wilson. "Vicente Guerrero and the Birth of Modern Mexico, 1821–1831." Ph.D. diss., Tulane University, 1976.

Hart, John. "The 1840's Southwestern Peasants' War." In Friedrich Katz, ed., *Riot, Rebellion and Revolt: Rural Social Conflict in Mexico*, pp. 249–68. Princeton: Princeton University Press, 1988.

Heredia Alvarez, Ricardo. *Anécdotas presidenciales de México*. Mexico City: Editorial Epoca, 1974.

———. *Conmemoración del centenario de la muerte del General Don Juan Alvarez*. Mexico City: Sociedad Mexicana de Geografía y Estadística, 1967.

Hernández Rodríguez, Rosaura. *Ignacio Comonfort: Trayectoria Política, Documentos*. Mexico City: Universidad Nacional Autónoma de México, 1967.

Herr, Richard. *The Eighteenth Century Revolution in Spain*. Princeton: Princeton University Press, 1958.

Herrejón Peredo, Carlos. "Hidalgo: La justificación de la insurgency." *Cuadernos Americanos* 42 (1983): 162–80.

Higham, Robin. *Air Power*. London: MacDonald, 1972.

Historia de la cuestión agraria mexicana: Estado de Guerrero 1867–1940. Mexico City: Universidad Autónoma de Guerrero, 1987.

Hobsbawm, Eric. "Mass-Producing Traditions: Europe, 1870–1914." In Eric Hobsbawm and Terence Ranger, eds., *The Invention of Tradition*, pp. 263–307. New York: Cambridge University Press, 1983.

Hu-DeHart, Evelyn. *Yaqui Resistance and Survival: The Struggle for Land and Autonomy, 1821–1910.* Madison: University of Wisconsin Press, 1984.

Hünefeldt, Christine. "Poder y contribuciones: Puno, 1825–1845." *Revista Andina* 7 (1989): 367–407.

Ibarra, Héctor. *Nicolás Bravo: Historia de una venganza.* Mexico City: Editorial Botas, 1952.

Ileto, Reynaldo Clemena. *Pasyon and Revolution.* Quezon City: Ateneo de Manila University Press, 1979.

Irecheta Cenecorta, María del Pilar. "Andrés Quintana Roo vs. el Pueblo de Almoloya: Un litigio por posesión de aguas." *Boletín del Archivo General del Estado de México* 8 (1981): 8–16.

———. "El cobro del peage en el Camino de Acapulco: Defensa de un estado federado ante el poder central." *Boletín del Archivo General del Estado de México* 2 (1979): 10–14.

———. "Guerrillas durante la invasión norteamericana, 1846–1848." *Boletín del Archivo General del Estado de México* 3 (1979): 22–33.

Jiménez Codinach, Guadalupe. "Introducción al Libro Uno." In *Planes en la Nación Mexicana: Libro Uno 1808–1830*, pp. 27–99. Mexico City: Cámara de Diputados, 1987.

Johnson, Richard A. *The Mexican Revolution of Ayutla, 1854–5.* Rock Island, Ill.: Augustana College Library, 1939.

Joseph, Gilbert M. "The United States, Feuding Elites, and Rural Revolt in Yucatan, 1836–1915." In Daniel Nugent, ed., *Rural Revolt in Mexico and U.S. Intervention*, pp. 167–97. San Diego: Center for U.S.-Mexican Studies, 1988.

Kanter, Deborah. "Indian Education in Late Colonial Mexico: Policy and Practice." Master's thesis, Department of History, University of Virginia, 1987.

Katz, Friedrich. "Introduction: Rural Revolts in Mexico." In Friedrich Katz, ed., *Riot, Rebellion and Revolt: Rural Social Conflict in Mexico*, pp. 3–17. Princeton: Princeton University Press, 1988.

———. "The Liberal Republic and the Porfiriato, 1867–1910." In Leslie Bethell, ed., *Mexico Since Independence*, pp. 49–124. New York: Cambridge University Press, 1991.

———. "Rural Rebellions After 1810." In Friedrich Katz, ed., *Riot, Rebellion and Revolt: Rural Social Conflict in Mexico*, pp. 521–60. Princeton: Princeton University Press, 1988.

———. "Rural Uprisings in Preconquest and Colonial Mexico." In Friedrich Katz, ed., *Riot, Rebellion and Revolt: Rural Social Conflict in Mexico*, pp. 65–94. Princeton: Princeton University Press, 1988.

Keremitis, Dawn. *La industria textil mexicana en el siglo XIX.* Mexico City: Secretaría de Educación Pública, 1973.

Kicza, John. *Colonial Entrepreneurs: Families and Business in Mexico City.* Albuquerque: University of New Mexico Press, 1983.

Knight, Alan. *The Mexican Revolution.* Cambridge: Cambridge University Press, 1986.

Laclau, Ernesto. "Populismo y transformación del imaginario político in América Latina." *Boletín de Estudios Latinoamericanos y del Caribe* 42 (1987): 25–38.

Ladd, Doris. *The Mexican Nobility at Independence, 1780–1826.* Austin: University of Texas Press, 1976.

Lafaye, Jacques. *Quetzalcóatl and Guadalupe: The Formation of Mexican National Consciousness, 1531–1813.* Chicago: University of Chicago Press, 1976.

Larson, Brooke. "Caciques, Class Structure and the Colonial State in Bolivia." *Nova Americana* 2 (1979): 198–235.

———. *Colonialism and Agrarian Transformation in Bolivia.* Princeton: Princeton University Press, 1988.

Larson, Brooke, and Robert Wasserstrom. "Consumo forzoso en Cochabamba y Chiapas durante la época colonial." *Historia Mexicana* 33 (1982): 361–408.

Lavrin, Asunción. "El capital eclesiástico y las elites sociales en Nueva España." *Mexican Studies / Estudios Mexicanos* 1 (1985): 1–28.

Lechuga Barrios, Carmen. "La lucha de los indígenas de Jilotepec por sus derechos en 1824." *Boletín del Archivo General del Estado de México* 8 (1981): 17–24.

Lemoine, Ernesto. "1821: ¿Consumación o contradicción de 1810?" *Secuencia* 1 (1985): 25–35.

———. *Morelos: Su vida revolucionaria a través de sus escritos y otros testimonios de la época.* Mexico City: Universidad Nacional Autónoma de México, 1965.

———. "Morelos y la generación de la independencia." In María del Refugio González, ed., *La formación del estado mexicano,* pp. 33–41. Mexico City: Porrua, 1984.

———. *Morelos y la Revolución de 1810.* Mexico City: Gobierno del Estado de Michoacán, 1984.

———. "Vicente Guerrero, úlima opción de la insurgencia." In *Memoria de la mesa redonda sobre Vicente Guerrero,* pp. 9–13. Mexico City: Instituto Mora, 1982.

Lepkowski, Tadeusz. "Formación de nacionalidades en America Latina (1780–1830): Reflexiones generales y algunos casos específicos." In *Congreso Bicentenario de Simón Bolívar,* 3: 37–57. Caracas: Academía Nacional de la Historia, 1985.

Liehr, Reinhard. *Ayuntamiento y oligarquía en Puebla, 1787–1810.* 2 vols. Mexico City: Secretaría de Educación Pública, 1976.

Lira González, Andrés. *Comunidades indígenas frente a la ciudad de México: Tenochitlán y Tlatelolco, sus pueblos y barrios, 1812–1919.* Zamora: El Colegio de Michoacán, 1983.

———. "Los indígenas y el nacionalismo mexicano." *Relaciones* 5 (1984): 75–94.

Lynch, John. *The Spanish-American Revolutions, 1808–1826.* New York: Norton, 1973.

McAlister, Lyle. "Social Structure and Social Change in New Spain." *Hispanic American Historical Review* 43 (1963): 349–70.

McGowan, Gerald. *Prensa y poder.* Mexico City: El Colegio de México, 1978.

Maciel, David. "Ideología y praxis: Ignacio Ramírez y el Congreso Constituyente, 1856–1857." *Cuadernos Americanos* 221 (1978): 119–29.

MacLachlan, Colin. *Spain's Empire in the New World.* Berkeley: University of California Press, 1988.

Mallon, Florencia. "Nationalist and Antistate Coalitions in the War of the Pacific: Junin and Cajamarca, 1879–1902." In Steve J. Stern, ed., *Resistance, Rebellion and Consciousness in the Andean Peasant World, Eighteenth to Twentieth Centuries*, pp. 232–79. Madison: University of Wisconsin Press, 1987.

———. *Peasant and Nation: The Making of Post-Colonial Mexico and Peru.* Berkeley: University of California Press, 1995.

———. "Peasants and State Formation in Nineteenth Century Mexico: Morelos, 1848–1858." *Political Power and Social Theory* 7 (1988): 1–54.

Marichal, Carlos. "Las guerras imperiales y los préstamos novohispanos, 1781–1804." *Historia Mexicana* 39 (1990): 881–907.

Martin, Cheryl English. "Haciendas and Villages in Late Colonial Morelos." *Hispanic American Historical Review* 62 (1982): 407–27.

———. *Rural Society in Colonial Morelos.* Albuquerque: University of New Mexico Press, 1985.

Meisel, Seth. "War, Women and Citizenship in Cordoba, 1810–1852." Paper presented at the XVIII International Congress of the Latin American Studies Association, Atlanta, March 12, 1994.

Mejía Fernández, Miguel. *Política agraria en México en el siglo XIX.* Mexico City: Siglo XXI, 1979.

Mentz, Brígida von. *Pueblos de indios, mulatos y mestizos, 1770–1870: Los campesinos y las transformaciones proto-industriales en el poniente de Morelos.* Mexico City: Centro de Investigaciones y Estudios Superiores en Antropología Social, 1988.

Mérida, José Luís. "La iglesia y el estado ante la configuración de un nuevo modelo político hispanoamericano." In Inge Buisson, Gunter Kahle, Hans-Joachim Konig, and Horst Pietschmann, eds., *Problemas de la formación del estado y de la nación en Hispanoamérica*, pp. 219–45. Bonn: Bohlau Verlag, 1984.

Meyer, Jean. *Esperando a Lozada.* Guadalajara: El Colegio de Michoacán, 1984.

———. *Problemas campesinos y revueltas agrarias (1821–1910).* Mexico City: Secretaría de Educación Pública, 1973.

———. "Reflexiones sobre movimientos agrarios y historia nacional en México." In Prodyot C. Mukherjee, ed., *Movimientos agrarios y cambio social en Asia y Africa*, pp. 246–47. Mexico City: El Colegio de Michoacán, 1974.

Meyer Cosío, Rosa María. "Empresarios, crédito y especulación (1820–1850)." In Leonor Ludlow and Carlos Marichal, eds., *Banco y poder en México (1800–1925)*, pp. 99–117. Mexico City: Grijalbo, 1986.

Migdahl, Joel S. *Peasants, Politics and Revolution: Pressures Towards Political and Social Change in the Third World*. Princeton: Princeton University Press, 1974.

Mirafuentes Galvan, José Luís. "Legitimidad política y subversión en el noreste de México: Los intentos del indio José Carlos Ruvalcaba de cornoarse José Carlos V, rey de los naturales de la Nueva Vizcaya (Sonora-Sinaloa, 1771)." *Históricas* 26 (1989): 3–22.

Miranda, José, and Silvio Zavala. "Instituciones indígenas en la Colonia." In *La política indigenista en México: Métodos y resultados*, 1: 43–206. Mexico City: Instituto Nacional Indigenista, 1973.

Montalvo Ortega, Enrique. "Revolts and Peasant Mobilizations in Yucatán: Indians, Peons and Peasants from the Caste War to the Revolution." In Friedrich Katz, ed., *Riot, Rebellion and Revolt: Rural Social Conflict in Mexico*, pp. 295–317. Princeton: Princeton University Press, 1988.

Moore, Barrington, Jr. *The Social Origins of Dictatorship and Democracy: Lord and Peasant in the Making of the Modern World*. Boston: Beacon, 1966.

Morin, Claude. *Michoacán en la Nueva España del siglo xviii*. Mexico City: Fondo de Cultura Económica, 1979.

Morse, Richard M. "The Heritage of Latin America." In Louis Hartz, ed., *The Founding of New Societies*, pp. 123–77. New York: Harcourt, 1964.

Moscoso, Martha. "Comunidad, autoridad indígena y poder repúblicano." *Revista Andina* 7(1989): 481–99.

Muñoz y Pérez, Daniel. *El General Don Juan Alvarez*. Mexico City: Academia Literaria, 1959.

Noriega, Alfonso. *El pensamiento conservador y el conservadurismo mexicano*. Mexico City: Universidad Nacional Autónoma de México, 1972.

Noticias históricas sobre los pueblos de Ajuchitlan, Coyuca, Cutzmala, Cohuayutla, Petatlan, Tecpan, Atoyac. Mexico City: Vargas Rea, 1947.

Nugent, Daniel. "Rural Revolt in Mexico, Mexican Nationalism and the State, and Forms of U.S. Intervention." In Daniel Nugent, ed., *Rural Revolt in Mexico and U.S. Intervention*, pp. 1–21. San Diego: Center for U.S.-Mexican Studies, 1988.

Ocampo, Javier. *Las ideas de un día: El pueblo mexicano ante la consumación de su independencia*. Mexico City: El Colegio de México, 1969.

Ochoa Campos, Humberto. *El brazo derecho (Tata Gildo)*. Mexico City: Cuadernos de Lectura Popular, 1967.

Ochoa Campos, Moises. *Breve historia del Estado de Guerrero*. Mexico City: Porrua, 1968.

———. *Juan del Carmen: El brazo derecho de Vicente Guerrero*. N.p., 1972.

———. *La reforma municipal: Historia municipal de México.* Mexico City: Universidad Nacional Autónoma de México, 1955.

———. *Valerio Trujano.* N.p.: Colección Letras Guerrerenses, 1972.

Olson, Mancur. *The Logic of Collective Action.* Cambridge, Mass.: Harvard University Press, 1971.

Olveda, Jaime. *Gordiano Guzmán: Un cacique del siglo XIX.* Mexico City: Secretaría de Educación Pública, 1980.

O'Phelan Godoy, Scarlett. *Un siglo de rebeliones anti-coloniales: Peru y Bolivia, 1700–1783.* Cusco: Centro de las Casas, 1988.

Ortega, Miguel. *Bravo no traicionó a Guerrero.* Mexico City: Editorial Mundial, 1935.

———. *La imprenta y el periodismo en el Sur en el siglo XIX.* Mexico City: Pluma y Lapiz de México, 1943.

Ortega y Medina, Juan. "Impacto del liberalismo europeo." *Secuencia* 1 (1985): 15–24.

Ortiz Escamilla, Juan. "El pronounciamiento federalista de Gordiano Guzmán, 1837–1842." *Historia Mexicana* 38 (1988): 241–82.

Oszlak, Oscar. *La formación del estado argentino.* Buenos Aires: Editorial de Belgrano, 1982.

———. "The Historical Formation of the State in Latin America: Some Theoretical and Methodological Guidelines for Its Study." *Latin American Research Review* 16 (1981): 3–33.

Parcero, María de la Luz. "La acción de Lorenzo de Zavala en le gobierno de Vicente Guerrero." In *Memoria de la mesa redonda sobre Vicente Guerrero,* 31–35. Mexico City: Instituto Mora, 1982.

Parrish, Leonard. "The Life of Nicolas Bravo, Mexican Patriot (1786–1854)." Ph.D. diss., University of Texas at Austin, 1951.

Pastor, Rodolfo. *Campesinos y reformas: La Mixteca, 1700–1856.* Mexico City: El Colegio de México, 1987.

———. "Estructura y vida social en la Mixteca Alta del siglo XVIII." In María de los Angeles Romero Frizzi, ed., *Lecturas históricas de Oaxaca: Epoca Colonial,* pp. 419–75. Mexico City: Instituto Nacional de Antropología e Historia, 1986.

———. "El repartimiento de mercancias y los alcaldes mayores novohispanos: Un sistema de explotación, de sus origenes a la crisis de 1810." In Woodrow Borah, ed., *El gobierno provincial en la Nueva España, 1570–1781,* pp. 201–36. Mexico City: Universidad Nacional Autónoma de México, 1985.

Pavía Guzmán, Edgar. *Provincias guerrerenses en la Costa de la Mar del Sur.* Chilpancingo: n.p., 1985.

———. *Tlappan, una provincia guerrense: Datos y hechos históricos (siglos VI–XVIII).* Chilpancingo: n.p., 1984.

Peña, Guillermo de la. *A Legacy of Promises: Agriculture, Politics and Ritual in the Morelos Highlands of Mexico.* Austin: University of Texas Press, 1981.

Pérez García, Rosendo. *La Sierra Juárez*. Mexico City: Gráfica Cervantes, 1955.

Perry, Laurens Ballard. *Juárez and Díaz: Machine Politics in Mexico*. DeKalb: Northern Illinos University Press, 1978.

Pietschmann, Horst. "Agricultura e industria rural indígena en el México de la segunda mitad del siglo XVIII." In Arij Ouweneel and Cristina Torales Pacheco, eds., *Empresarios, indios, y estado: Perfil de la economía mexicana del siglo XVIII*, pp. 71–85. Amsterdam: Centro de Estudios y Documentación Latinoamericanos, 1988.

———. "Estado colonial y mentalidad social: El ejercicio del poder frente a distintos sistemas de valores, siglo XVIII." In Antonio Annino et al., eds., *America Latina: Dallo Stato Coloniale allo Stato Nazione*, 2: 427–47. Milan: Franco Angeli, 1987.

Platt, Tristan. "The Andean Experience of Bolivian Liberalism, 1825–1900: Roots of Rebellion in Nineteenth Century Chayanta (Potosí)." In Steve J. Stern, ed., *Resistance, Rebellion and Consciousness in the Andean Peasant World, Eighteenth to Twentieth Centuries*, pp. 280–323. Madison: University of Wisconsin Press, 1987.

———. "Estado tributario y librecambio en Potosí durante el siglo XIX: Mercado indígena y lucha de ideologias monetarias." In Antonio Annino et al., eds., *America Latina: Dallo Stato Coloniale allo Stato Nazione*, 1: 98–143. Milan: Franco Angeli, 1987.

Poggi, Gianfranco. *The Development of the Modern State: A Sociological Approach*. Stanford: Stanford University Press, 1978.

Popkin, Samuel. *The Rational Peasant: The Political Economy of Rural Society in Vietnam*. Berkeley: University of California Press, 1979.

Potash, Robert. *Mexican Government and Industrial Development in the Early Republic: The Banco de Avio*. Amherst: University of Massachusetts Press, 1983.

Powell, Thomas. "Los liberales, el campesinado indígena y los problemas agrarios durante la Reforma." *Historia Mexicana* 21 (1972): 653–75.

———. "Priests and Peasants in Central Mexico: Social Conflict during La Reforma." *Hispanic American Historical Review* 57 (1977): 296–313.

Ramírez Arriaga, Manuel. *Ponciano Arriaga el desconocido*. Mexico City: Sociedad Mexicana de Geografía y Estadística, 1965.

Ramírez Fentanes, Luís. *Vicente Guerrero, Presidente de México*. Mexico City: Comisión de Historia Militar, 1958.

Ranger, Terence. "The Invention of Tradition in Colonial Africa." In Eric Hobsbawm and Terence Ranger, eds., *The Invention of Tradition*, pp. 211–62. New York: Cambridge University Press, 1983.

Reed, Nelson. *The Caste War of the Yucatan*. Stanford: Stanford University Press, 1964.

Reina, Leticia. "Historia y antropología de las rebeliones indígenas y campesinas en la colonia y en el siglo XIX: Un recuento." *Historias* 17 (1987): 39–56.

———. "Las luchas campesinas, 1820–1907." In Leticia Reina, ed., *Las lu-*

chas populares en México en el siglo XIX, pp. 13–172. Mexico City: Centro de Investigaciones y Estudios Superiores en Antropología Social, 1983.
———. "The Sierra Gorda Peasant Rebellion, 1847–1850." In Friedrich Katz, ed., *Riot, Rebellion and Revolt: Rural Social Conflict in Mexico*, pp. 269–94. Princeton: Princeton University Press, 1988.
Reyes Heroles, Jesús. *El liberalismo mexicano*. Mexico City: Universidad Nacional Autónoma de México, 1961.
Rodríguez O., Jaime E. "La Constitución de 1824 y la formación del estado mexicano." *Historia Mexicana* 40 (1991): 507–35.
———. "From Royal Subject to Republican Citizen: The Role of the Autonomists in the Independence of Mexico." In Jaime E. Rodríguez O., ed., *The Independence of Mexico and the Origins of the New Nation*, pp. 19–43. Los Angeles: University of California at Los Angeles Latin American Center, 1989.
———. "La independencia de la América Española: Una reinterpretación." *Historia Mexicana* 42 (1993): 571–620.
———. "Introduction." In Jaime E. Rodríguez O., ed., *The Independence of Mexico and the Origins of the New Nation*, pp. 1–15. Los Angeles: University of California at Los Angeles Latin American Center, 1989.
———. "The Origins of the 1832 Rebellion." In Jaime E. Rodríguez O., ed., *Patterns of Contention in Mexican History*, pp. 145–62. Wilmington, Del.: Scholarly Resources, 1992.
Rubin, Jeffrey W. "State Policies, Leftist Oppositions, and Municipal Elections: The Case of the COCEI in Juchitan." In Arturo Alvarado, ed., *Electoral Patterns and Perspectives in Mexico*, pp. 127–60. San Diego: Center for U.S.-Mexican Studies, 1987.
Rueda Smithers, Salvador. *El diablo de Semana Santa: El discurso político y el orden social en la Ciudad de México en 1850*. Mexico City: Instituto Nacional de Antropología e Historia, 1991.
Ruiz Castañeda, María del Carmen. *La prensa periódica en torno a la Constitución de 1857*. Mexico City: Universidad Nacional Autónoma de México, 1959.
Safford, Frank. "The Bases of Political Alignment in Early Republican Spanish America." In Richard Graham and Peter Smith, eds., *New Approaches to Latin American History*, pp. 71–111. Austin: University of Texas Press, 1974.
Sahlins, Peter. "The Nation in the Village: State-building and Communal Struggles in the Catalan Borderland During the Eighteenth and Nineteenth Centuries." *Journal of Modern History* 60 (1988): 234–63.
Salazar Aldame, Jaime. *Movimientos populares durante el Porfiriato en el Estado de Guerrero*. Chilpancingo: Universidad Autónoma de Guerrero, 1983.
———. "Movimientos populares durante el Porfiriato en el Estado de Guerrero (1885–1891)." In Friedrich Katz, ed., *Porfirio Díaz frente al descontento popular regional (1891–1893)*, pp. 97–183. Mexico City: Universidad Iberoamericana, 1986.

————. "Período 1867–1910." In *Historia de la cuestión agraria mexicana: Estado de Guerrero 1867–1940*, pp. 9–79. Mexico City: Universidad Nacional Autónoma de México, 1987.

Salcedo Guerrero, Mario. "Vicente Guerrero's Struggle for Mexican Independence, 1810–1821." Ph.D. diss., University of California at Santa Barbara, 1977.

Salomon, Frank. "Ancestor Cults and Resistance to the State in Arequipa ca. 1748–1754." In Steve J. Stern, ed., *Resistance, Rebellion and Consciousness in the Andean Peasant World, Eighteenth to Twentieth Centuries*, pp. 148–65. Madison: University of Wisconsin Press, 1987.

Salvucci, Richard. *Textiles and Capitalism in Mexico: An Economic History of the Obrajes, 1539–1840*. Princeton: Princeton University Press, 1987.

Samponaro, Frank Nicholas. "The Political Role of the Army in Mexico, 1821–1848." Ph.D. diss., State University of New York at Stony Brook, 1974.

San Juan Victoria, Carlos. "Las utopias oligarquicas conocen sus limites (1821–1834)." In María del Refugio González, ed., *La formación del estado mexicano*, pp. 89–120. Mexico City: Porrua, 1984.

Sánchez, Gerardo. "Mulas, hatajos y arrieros en el Michoacán del siglo XIX." *Relaciones* 5 (1984): 41–53.

————. *El suroeste de Michoacán: Estructura economico-social, 1821–1851*. Morelia: Universidad Michoacana, 1979.

Sánchez Agesta, Luís. *Historia del constitucionalismo español (1808–1836)*. Madrid: Centro de Estudios Constitucionales, 1984.

Santoni, Pedro. "A Fear of the People: The Civic Militia of Mexico in 1845." *Hispanic American Historical Review* 68 (1988): 269–88.

Santos Carrera, Moises, and Jesús Alvarez Hernández. *Historia de la cuestión agraria mexicana, Estado de Guerrero: Épocas prehispanica y colonial*. Chilpancingo: Universidad Autónoma de Guerrero, 1988.

————. *Las luchas campesinas en el siglo XVIII (El caso de S. Francisco Xochipala 1710–1776)*. Chilpancingo: Universidad Autónoma de Guerrero, 1987.

Schryer, Frans. *The Rancheros of Pisaflores: The History of a Peasant Bourgeoisie in Twentieth Century Mexico*. Toronto: University of Toronto Press, 1980.

Scott, James. *Weapons of the Weak: Everyday Forms of Peasant Resistance*. New Haven: Yale University Press, 1985.

Semo, Enrique. "Las clases sociales en la Revolución de la Independencia." In *Movimientos populares en la historia de México y América Latina*, pp. 59–73. Mexico City: Universidad Nacional Autónoma de México, 1987.

————. "Las revoluciones en la historia de México." In Enrique Semo, ed., *Historia mexicana: Economía y lucha de clases*, pp. 279–98. Mexico City: Era, 1985.

Shadle, Stanley. *Andrés Molina Enríques: Mexican Land Reformer of the Revolutionary Era*. Tucson: University of Arizona Press, 1994.

Sierra, Justo. *The Political Evolution of the Mexican People.* Austin: University of Texas Press, 1969.

Sims, Harold. *Descolonización en México: El conflicto entre mexicanos y españoles.* Mexico City: Fondo de Cultura Económica, 1982.

——. *La expulsión de los españoles de México (1821–1828).* Mexico City: Fondo de Cultura Económica, 1974.

——. *The Expulsion of México's Spaniards, 1821–1836.* Pittsburgh: University of Pittsburgh Press, 1990.

Sindico, Domenico. "Los grupos económicos regionales y sus relaciones con el poder político local en México en el siglo XIX: El caso de Morelos." In Antonio Annino et al., eds., *America Latina: Dallo Stato Coloniale allo Stato Nazione,* 1: 311–22. Milan: Franco Angeli, 1987.

Sinkin, Richard. "The Mexican Constitutional Congress, 1856–1857: A Statistical Analysis." *Hispanic American Historical Review* 53 (1973): 1–26.

——. *The Mexican Reform, 1855–1876: A Study in Liberal Nation-building.* Austin: University of Texas Institute of Latin American Studies, 1979.

Skocpol, Theda. "France, Russia, and China: A Structural Analysis of Social Revolution." *Comparative Studies in Society and History* 18 (1976): 175–210.

Smith, Anthony. "State-Making and Nation-Building." In John Hall, ed., *States in History,* pp. 228–63. London: Basil Blackwell, 1986.

——. *Theories of Nationalism.* New York: Holmes and Meier, 1983.

Sordo Cedeño, Reynaldo. *El Congreso en la Primera República Centralista.* Mexico City: El Colegio de México and Instituto Tecnológico Autónomo de México, 1993.

Soto, Miguel. *La conspiración monárquica en México 1845–1846.* Mexico City: EOSA, 1988.

Spalding, Karen. "The Colonial Indian: Past and Future Research Perspectives." *Latin American Research Review* 7 (1972): 47–62.

——. "Introducción." In Karen Spalding, ed., *De indio a campesino,* pp. 19–27. Lima: Instituto de Estudios Peruanas, 1974.

——. "Introduction." In Karen Spalding, ed., *Essays in the Political Economic and Social History of Colonial Latin America,* pp. vii–xx. Newark: University of Delaware, 1982.

——. "¿Quienes son los indios?" In Karen Spalding, ed., *De indio a campesino,* pp. 147–93. Lima: Instituto de Estudios Peruanas, 1974.

——. "La red desintegrante." In Karen Spalding, ed., *De indio a campesino,* pp. 89–123. Lima: Instituto de Estudios Peruanas, 1974.

Sprague, William Forrest. *Vicente Guerrero, Mexican Liberator: A Study in Patriotism.* Chicago: Donnelley and Sons, 1939.

Staples, Anne. "Clerics as Politicians: Church, State, and Political Power in Independent Mexico." In Jaime E. Rodríguez O., ed., *Mexico in the Age of Democratic Revolutions, 1750–1850,* pp. 223–41. Boulder: Lynne Reinner Publishers, 1994.

———. *La iglesia en la Primera República Federal Mexicana (1824–1835)*. Mexico City: El Colegio de México, 1976.

Stein, Stanley. "Bureaucracy and Business in the Spanish Empire, 1759–1804: Failure of a Bourbon Reform in Mexico and Peru." *Hispanic American Historical Review* 61 (1981): 2–28.

Stern, Steve J. "Introduction to Part III." In Steve J. Stern, ed., *Resistance, Rebellion and Consciousness in the Andean Peasant World, Eighteenth to Twentieth Centuries*, pp. 213–18. Madison: University of Wisconsin Press, 1987.

———. "New Approaches to the Study of Peasant Rebellion and Consciousness: Implications of the Andean Experience." In Steve J. Stern, ed., *Resistance, Rebellion and Consciousness in the Andean Peasant World, Eighteenth to Twentieth Centuries*, pp. 3–25. Madison: University of Wisconsin Press, 1987.

———. *Peru's Indian Peoples and the Challenge of Spanish Conquest: Huamanga to 1640*. Madison: University of Wisconsin Press, 1982.

Stevens, Donald. *Origins of Instability in Early Republican Mexico*. Durham: Duke University Press, 1991.

Stoetzer, O. Carlos. *The Scholastic Roots of the Spanish American Revolution*. New York: Fordham University Press, 1979.

Sullivan, Paul. *Unfinished Conversations: Mayas and Foreigners Between Two Wars*. Berkeley: University of California Press, 1989.

Szeminski, Jan. "Why Kill the Spaniard? New Perspectives on Andean Insurrectionary Ideology in the Eighteenth Century." In Steve J. Stern, ed., *Resistance, Rebellion and Consciousness in the Andean Peasant World, Eighteenth to Twentieth Centuries*, pp. 166–92. Madison: University of Wisconsin Press, 1987.

Tanck de Estrada, Dorothy. *La educación ilustrada (1786–1836): Educación primaria en la Ciudad de México*. Mexico City: El Colegio de México, 1977.

Taylor, William B. "Banditry and Insurrection: Rural Unrest in Central Jalisco, 1790–1816." In Friedrich Katz, ed., *Riot, Rebellion and Revolt: Rural Social Conflict in Mexico*, pp. 205–46. Princeton: Princeton University Press, 1988.

———. "Between Global Process and Local Knowledge: An Inquiry into Early Latin American Social History, 1500–1900." In Oliver Zunz, ed., *Reliving the Past: The Worlds of Social History*, pp. 115–90. Chapel Hill: University of North Carolina Press, 1985.

———. "Conflict and Balance in District Politics: Tecali and the Sierra Norte de Puebla in the Eighteenth Century." In Arij Ouweneel and Simon Miller, eds., *The Indian Community of Colonial Mexico*, pp. 270–94. Amsterdam: CEDLA, 1990.

———. *Drinking, Homicide, and Rebellion in Colonial Mexican Villages*. Stanford: Stanford University Press, 1979.

———. "The Virgin of Guadalupe in New Spain: An Inquiry into the Social History of Marian Devotion." *American Ethnologist* 14 (1987): 9–33.

Teja Zambre, Alfonso. "Morelos, hombre de guerra y hombre de paz." *Historia Mexicana* 8 (1959): 499–511.

Tenenbaum, Barbara. "Banqueros sin bancos: El papel de los agiotistas en México (1826–1854)." In Leonor Ludlow and Carlos Marichal, eds., *Banco y poder en México (1800–1925)*, pp. 75–97. Mexico City: Grijalbo, 1986.

———. *The Politics of Penury: Debts and Taxes in Mexico, 1821–1856*. Albuquerque: University of New Mexico Press, 1986.

Therborn, Goran. "The Rule of Capital and the Rise of Democracy." *New Left Review* 103 (1977): 3–41.

———. "The Travail of Latin American Democracy." *New Left Review* 113–14 (1979): 71–109.

Thompson, E. P. *Customs in Common: Studies in Traditional Popular Culture*. New York: New Press, 1993.

———. *The Making of the English Working Class*. New York: Vintage, 1966.

———. "The Moral Economy of the English Crowd in the Eighteenth Century." *Past and Present* 50 (1971): 76–136.

Thomson, Guy. "Agrarian Conflict in the Municipality of Cuetzalán (Sierra de Puebla): The Rise and Fall of 'Pala' Agustín Dieguillo, 1861–1894." *Hispanic American Historical Review* 71 (1991): 205–58.

———. "Bulwarks of Patriotic Liberalism: The National Guard, Philharmonic Corps and Patriotic Juntas in Mexico, 1847–88." *Journal of Latin American Studies* 22 (1990): 31–68.

———. "The Cotton Textile Industry in Puebla During the Eighteenth and Early Nineteenth Centuries." In Nils Jacobsen and Hans Jürgen Puhle, eds., *The Economies of Mexico and Peru During the Late Colonial Period*, pp. 169–202. Berlin: Bibliotheca Ibero-Americana, 1986.

———. "Movilización conservadora, insurrección liberal y rebeliones indígenas, 1854–1876." In Antonio Annino et al., eds., *America Latina: Dallo Stato Coloniale allo Stato Nazione*, 2: 592–614. Milan: Franco Angeli, 1987.

———. *Patriarch of the Sierra: Juan Francisco Lucas and the Mexican State, 1854–1917*. Wilmington, Del.: Scholarly Resources, forthcoming.

———. "Popular Aspects of Liberalism in Mexico, 1848–1888." *Bulletin of Latin American Research* 10 (1991): 265–92.

———. "Protectionism and Industrialization in Mexico, 1821–1854: The Case of Puebla." In Christoper Abel and Colin Lewis, eds., *Latin America, Economic Imperialism and the State: The Political Economy of the External Connection from Independence to the Present*, pp. 125–46. London: Athlone Press, 1985.

———. *Puebla de los Angeles: Industry and Society in a Mexican City, 1700–1850*. Boulder: Westview Press, 1989.

Tilly, Charles. *Coercion, Capital, and European States, A.D. 990–1990*. London: Basil Blackwell, 1990.

———. "Reflections on the History of European State-Making." In Charles Tilly, ed., *The Formation of Nation States in Western Europe*, pp. 3–83. Princeton: Princeton University Press, 1975.

————. "Social Movements and National Politics." In Charles Bright and Susan Harding, eds., *Statemaking and Social Movements: Essays in History and Theory*, pp. 297–317. Ann Arbor: University of Michigan Press, 1984.

————. "War-Making and State Making as Organized Crime." In Peter Evans, Dietrich Rueschmeyer, and Theda Skocpol, eds., *Bringing the State Back In*, pp. 169–91. New York: Cambridge University Press, 1985.

Timmons, Wilbert. "José María Morelos—Agrarian Reformer?" *Hispanic American Historical Review* 45 (1965): 183–95.

————. *Morelos: Sacerdote, soldado, estadista.* Mexico City: Fondo de Cultura Económica, 1983.

Tocqueville, Alexis de. *The Old Regime and the French Revolution.* New York: Doubleday, 1955.

Topik, Steven. "Mexican Independence in Comparative Perspective." In Jaime E. Rodríguez O., ed., *The Independence of Mexico and the Origins of the New Nation*, pp. 331–38. Los Angeles: University of California at Los Angeles Latin American Center, 1989.

Torre Villar, Ernesto de la. "El origen del estado mexicano." In María del Refugio González, ed., *La formación del estado mexicano*, pp. 55–71. Mexico City: Porrua, 1984.

Tortella Casares, Teresa. *Indice de los primitivos acionistas del Banco Nacional de San Carlos.* Madrid: Archivo Histórico del Banco de España, 1986.

Tutino, John. "Agrarian Social Change and Peasant Rebellion in Nineteenth Century Mexico: The Example of Chalco." In Friedrich Katz, ed., *Riot, Rebellion and Revolt: Rural Social Conflict in Mexico*, pp. 95–140. Princeton: Princeton University Press, 1988.

————. "Creole Mexico: Spanish Elites, Haciendas, and Indian Towns, 1750–1810." Ph.D. diss., University of Texas at Austin, 1976.

————. *From Insurrection to Revolution in Mexico: Social Bases of Agrarian Violence, 1750–1940.* Princeton: Princeton University Press, 1986.

————. "Peasants and Politics in Nineteenth Century Mexico." *Latin American Research Review* 22 (1987): 237–44.

————. "Rebelión indígena en Tehuantepec." *Cuadernos políticos* 24 (1980): 88–101.

Van Young, Eric. "A modo de conclusión: El siglo paradójico." In Arij Ouweneel and Cristina Torales Pacheco, eds., *Empresarios, indios, y estado: Perfil de la economía mexicana del siglo XVIII*, pp. 206–31. Amsterdam: Centro de Estudios y Documentación Latinoamericanos, 1988.

————. "The Age of Paradox: Mexican Agriculture at the End of the Colonial Period, 1750–1810." In Nils Jacobsen and Hans Jürgen Puhle, eds., *The Economies of Mexico and Peru During the Late Colonial Period*, pp. 64–90. Berlin: Bibliotheca Ibero-Americana, 1986.

————. "Conflict and Solidarity in Indian Village Life: The Guadalajara Region in the Late Colonial Period." *Hispanic American Historical Review* 64 (1984): 55–79.

————. *Hacienda and Market in Eighteenth Century Mexico: The Rural*

Economy of the Guadalajara Region, 1675–1820. Berkeley: University of California Press, 1981.

———. "Islands in the Storm: Quiet Cities and Violent Countrysides in the Mexican Independence Era." *Past and Present* 118 (1988): 130–55.

———. "Mexican Rural History Since Chevalier: The Historiography of the Colonial Hacienda." *Latin American Research Review* 18 (1983): 5–61.

———. "Millenium on the Northern Marches: The Mad Messiah of Durango and Popular Rebellion in Mexico, 1800–1815." *Comparative Studies in Society and History* 28 (1986): 386–413.

———. "Moving Towards Revolt: Agrarian Origins of the Hidalgo Rebellion in the Guadalajara Region." In Friedrich Katz, ed., *Riot, Rebellion and Revolt: Rural Social Conflict in Mexico*, pp. 176–204. Princeton: Princeton University Press, 1988.

———. "Quetzalcóatl, King Ferdinand, and Ignacio Allende Go to the Seashore; or Messianism and Mystical Kingship in Mexico, 1800–1821." In Jaime E. Rodríguez O., ed., *The Independence of Mexico and the Origins of the New Nation*, pp. 109–27. Los Angeles: University of California at Los Angeles Latin American Center, 1989.

———. "Sectores medios rurales en el México de los Borbones: El interior de Guadalajara en el siglo XVIII." *HISLA: Revista Latinoamericana de Ciencias Sociales* 7 (1986): 99–117.

———. "To See Someone Not Seeing: Historical Studies of Peasants and Politics in Mexico." *Mexican Studies: Estudios Mexicanos* 6 (1990): 133–59.

Vanderwood, Paul. *Disorder and Progress: Bandits, Police and Mexican Development*. Lincoln: University of Nebraska Press, 1981.

Vargas Martínez, Ubaldo. *Hermengildo Galeana*. Mexico City: Secretaría de Educación Pública, 1964.

Vázquez, Josefina. "Los años olvidados." *Mexican Studies / Estudios Mexicanos* 5 (1989): 313–26.

———. "La crisis y los partidos políticos, 1833–1846." In Antonio Annino et al., eds., *America Latina: Dallo Stato Coloniale allo Stato Nazione*, 2: 557–72. Milan: Franco Angeli, 1987.

———. "Dos décadas de desilusiones: En búsqueda de una formula adecuada de gobierno (1832–1851)." In *Planes en la nación mexicana: Libro dos 1831–1834*, pp. 7–40. Mexico City: Cámara de Diputados, 1987.

———. "El ejército: Un dilema del gobierno mexicano (1841–1846)." In Inge Buisson, Gunter Kahle, Hans-Joachim Konig, and Horst Pietschmann, eds., *Problemas de la formación del estado y de la nación en Hispanoamérica*, pp. 319–38. Bonn: Bohlau Verlag, 1984.

———. "El federalismo mexicano, 1823–1847." In Marcello Carmagnani, ed., *Federalismos latinoamericanos México/Brasil/Argentina*. Mexico City: El Colegio de México and Fondo de Cultura Económica, 1993.

———. "Iglesia, ejército y centralismo." *Historia Mexicana* 39 (1989): 205–34.

———. "Los primeros tropiezos." In *Historia general de México*, pp. 735–818. Mexico City: El Colegio de México, 1981.

————. "Los pronunciamientos de 1832: Aspirantismo político e ideología."
    In Jaime E. Rodríguez O., ed., *Patterns of Contention in Mexican History*,
    pp. 163–86. Wilmington, Del.: Scholarly Resources, 1992.
————. "Un viejo tema: El federalismo y centralismo." *Historia Mexicana*
    42 (1993): 621–31.
Vázquez Mantecón, Carmen. *Santa Anna y la encrucijada del Estado: La
    dictadura (1853–1855)*. Mexico City: Fondo de Cultura Económica, 1986.
Vega, Josefa. "Los primeros préstamos de la Guerra de Independencia, 1809–
    1812." *Historia Mexicana* 39 (1990): 909–31.
Villoro, Luís. *El proceso ideológico de la Revolución de Independencia*.
    Mexico City: Universidad Nacional Autónoma de México, 1967.
Walker, Charles. "El estudio del campesinado en las ciencias sociales pe-
    ruanas." *Allpanchis* 33 (1989): 161–205.
————. "Peasants, Caudillos, and the State in Peru: Cusco in the Transition
    from Colony to Republic, 1780–1840." Ph.D. diss., University of Chicago,
    1992.
Walker, David W. *Kinship, Business and Politics: The Martínez del Río
    Family in Mexico, 1824–67*. Austin: University of Texas Press, 1986.
Warman, Arturo. "The Political Project of Zapatismo." In Friedrich Katz, ed.,
    Riot, Rebellion and Revolt: Rural Social Conflict in Mexico, pp. 321–37.
    Princeton: Princeton University Press, 1988.
————. *We Come to Object: Peasants of Morelos and the Mexican State*.
    Baltimore: Johns Hopkins University Press, 1980.
Warren, Richard. "Vagrants and Citizens: Politics and the Poor in Mexico
    City, 1808–1836." Ph.D. diss., University of Chicago, 1994.
————. "The Will of the Nation: Political Participation in Mexico, 1808–
    1836." Paper presented at the XVII International Congress of the Latin
    American Studies Association, Los Angeles, September 1992.
Weber, Eugen. *Peasants into Frenchmen: The Modernization of Rural
    France, 1870–1914*. Stanford: Stanford University Press, 1976.
Weber, Max. "Politics as a Vocation." In H. H. Gerth and C. Wright Mills,
    eds., *Max Weber: Essays in Sociology*, pp. 77–128. New York: Oxford Uni-
    versity Press, 1946.
Wolf, Eric. "The Mexican Bajio in the Eighteenth Century." In *Synoptic
    Studies of Mexican Culture*, pp. 177–99. New Orleans: Tulane Univer-
    sity, 1957.
————. *Peasant Wars of the Twentieth Century*. New York: Harper and
    Row, 1969.
Womack, John, Jr. *Zapata and the Mexican Revolution*. New York: Alfred A.
    Knopf, 1968.
Zeitlin, Maurice. *The Civil Wars in Chile (or The Bourgeois Revolutions
    That Never Were)*. Princeton: Princeton University Press, 1984.

Index

In this index an "f" after a number indicates a separate reference on the next page, and an "ff" indicates separate references on the next two pages. A continuous discussion over two or more pages is indicated by a span of page numbers, e.g., "57–59." *Passim* is used for a cluster of references in close but not consecutive sequence.

Library of Congress Cataloging-in-Publication Data

Guardino, Peter F.
  Peasants, politics, and the formation of Mexico's national state :
Guerrero, 1800–1857 / Peter F. Guardino.
     p.   cm.
Originally presented as the author's thesis (doctoral—University
of Chicago, 1992) under title: Peasants, politics, and state
formation in 19th century Mexico.
  Includes bibliographical references and index.
  ISBN 0-8047-2572-1 (cloth) : ISBN 0-8047-4190-5 (paper)
    1. Peasantry—Mexico—Guerrero (State)—Political activity—
History—19th century.   2. Guerrero (Mexico : State)—History.
3. Guerrero (Mexico : State)—Politics and government.   I. Title.
HD1531.M6G83   1996
322.4'4'097273—dc20
95-38593   CIP

⊗ This book is printed on acid-free, recycled paper.

Original printing 1996

Last figure below indicates year of this printing:
05 04 03 02 01